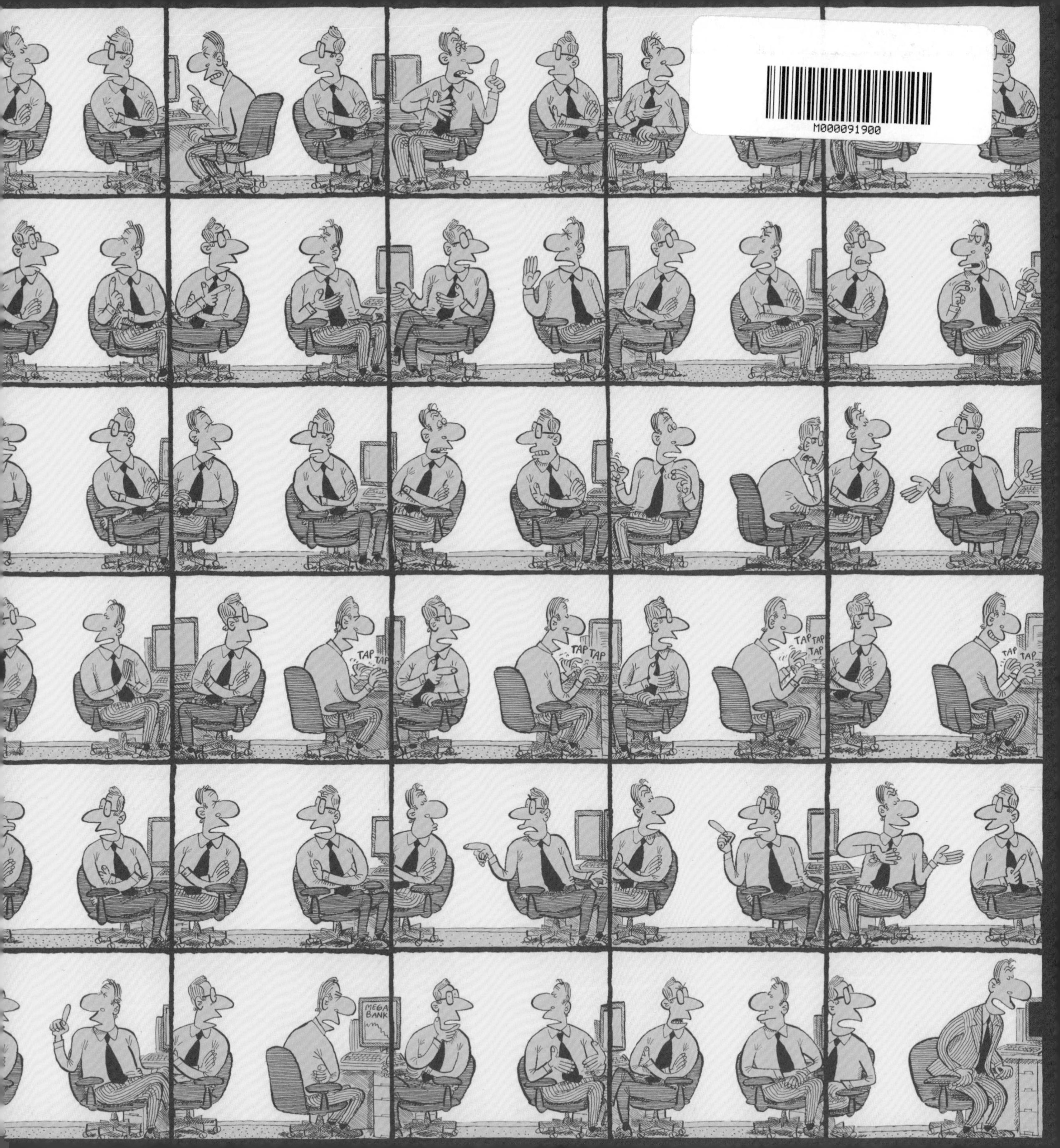
TAP TAP
TAP TAP
TAP TAP TAP
TAP TAP
MEGA BANK

The Best Of
Alex
2018

Charles Peattie & Russell Taylor

Masterley Publishing

The Best Of

Alex

2018

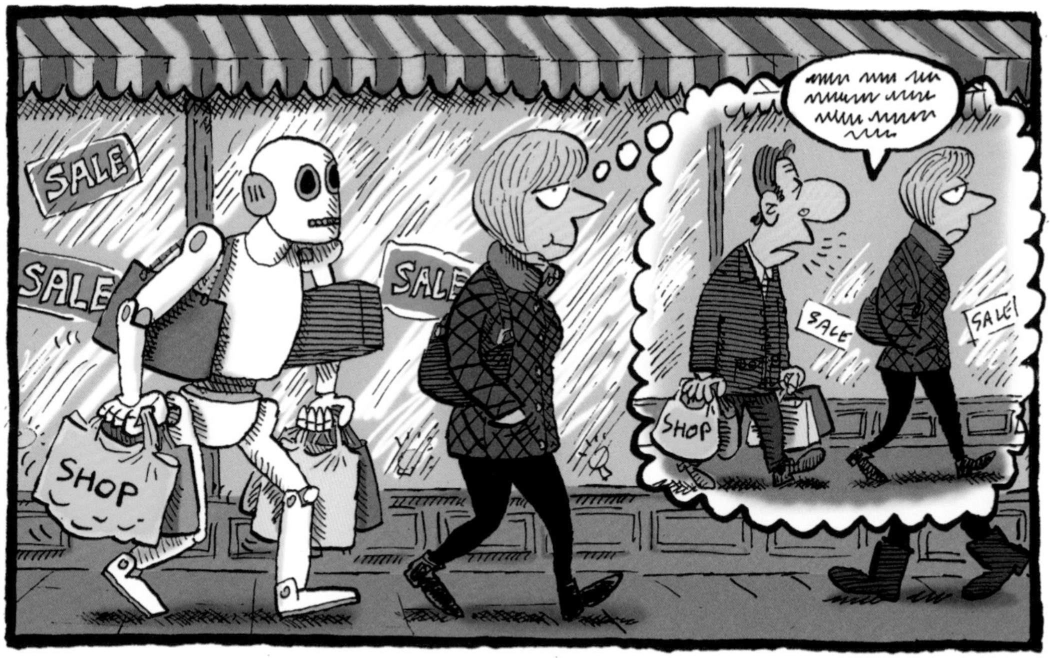
SALE
SALE
SALE
SHOP
SALE
SALE!
SHOP

First Published in 2018 by MASTERLEY PUBLISHING

Layout and Design: Suzette Field

Colouring and Artworking: Sofie Dodgson and Miki Lowe

ISBN: 978-1911610175
Printed in the UK by CPI William Clowes Beccles NR34 7TL

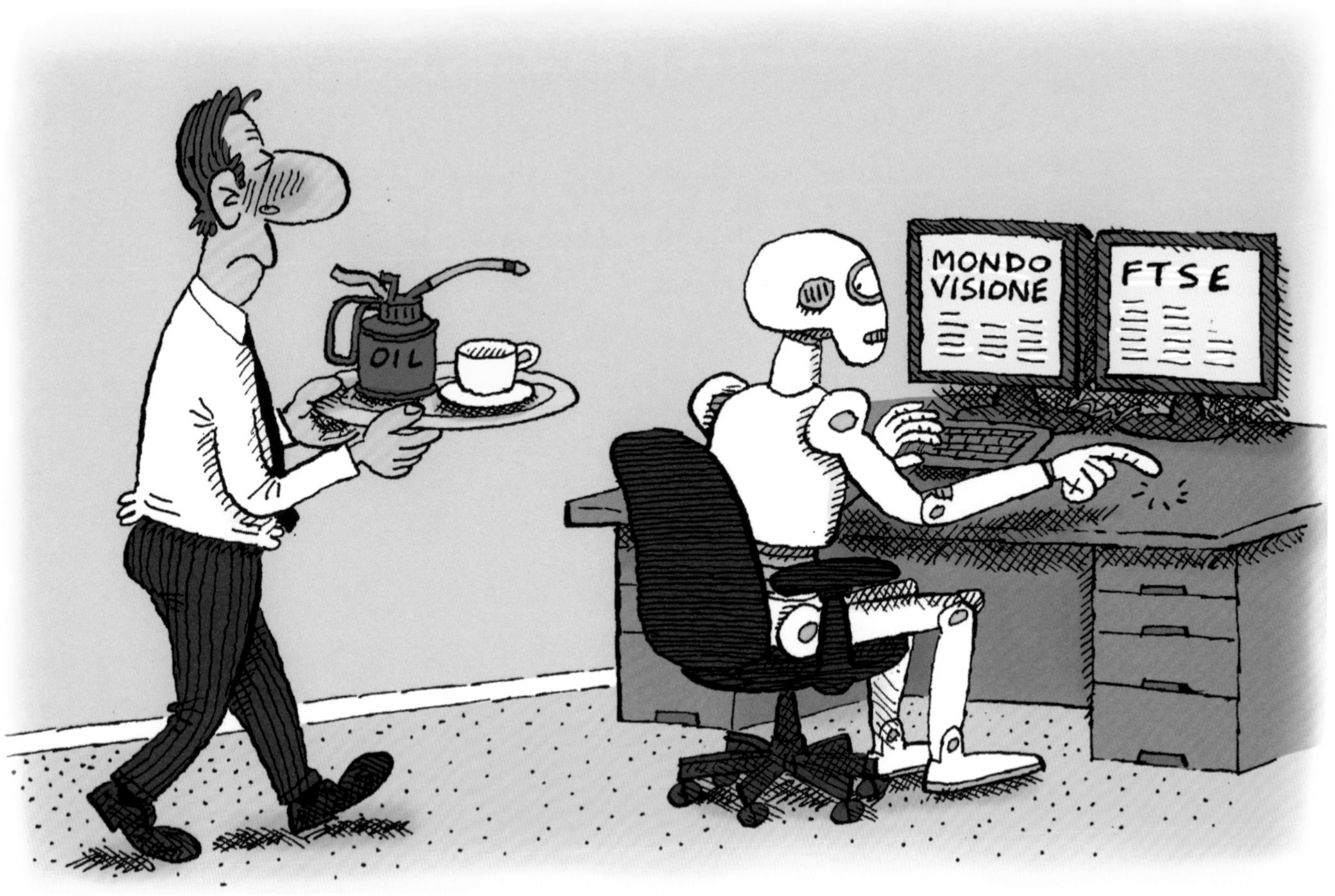
MONDO VISIONE
FTSE
OIL

Our usual gratitude goes to our generous sponsors.

FTSE Russell is a leading global provider of benchmarks, analytics and data solutions with multi-asset capabilities.

Mondo Visione is the leading source of insight and knowledge about the world's exchanges and trading venues. As a conference and event organiser it helps to shape the development of markets.

FOREWORD

Welcome to the latest addition to your bookshelf, which if you're a proper Alex aficionado will already be groaning under the weight of the 28 published cartoon collections that span Alex's impressively long career in the City.

You may be pleased to hear that to ease the burden on your domestic furniture we've recently finished a complete overhaul of the Alex website, which you can find at www.alexcartoon.com. This digital celebration of all things Masterley not only displays the daily strip in full colour, but has an archive containing four decades' worth of Alex cartoons: from his earliest days as a brash, carefree Yuppie in the late 1980s to his current incarnation as corporate sage and scourge of compliance.

For those of you for whom the cartoon sometimes gets lost in the daily deluge of emails that greet you when you log on to your computer each morning, there is the Alex app. It delivers the adventures of your favourite cartoon banker direct to your mobile or tablet in an accessible frame-by-frame format and in full colour. Perfect for reading the morning's cartoon on the train or on the loo, before your phone is confiscated by compliance on the way into your highly-policed workplace. Available from the App Store or Google Play.

Now that all 7,274 (plus a few more by the time you read this) Alex cartoons are online, you can have the strangely oxymoronic experience of using your smartphone or tablet to read about the black and white days when men in pinstripe suits went out for long claret-soaked lunches and showed off about owning brick-sized mobile phones with aerials.

And for the technophobes and nostalgics among you there's always this old-fashioned, reassuring heavy, physical copy of Alex's latest adventures, but you might want to check with a structural engineer first.

Charles Peattie   Russell Taylor

Charles Peattie and Russell Taylor

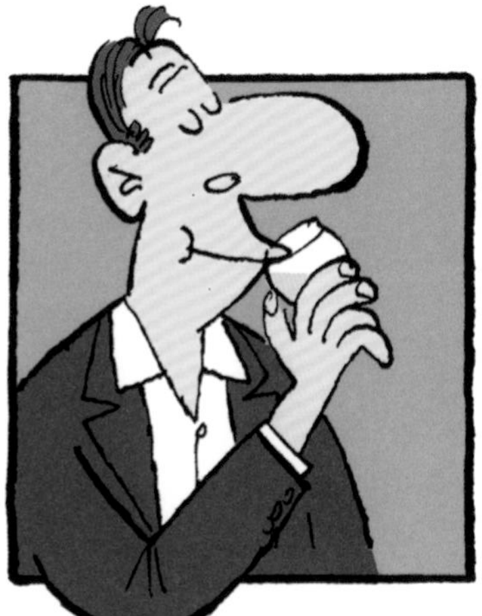

Alex - investment banker

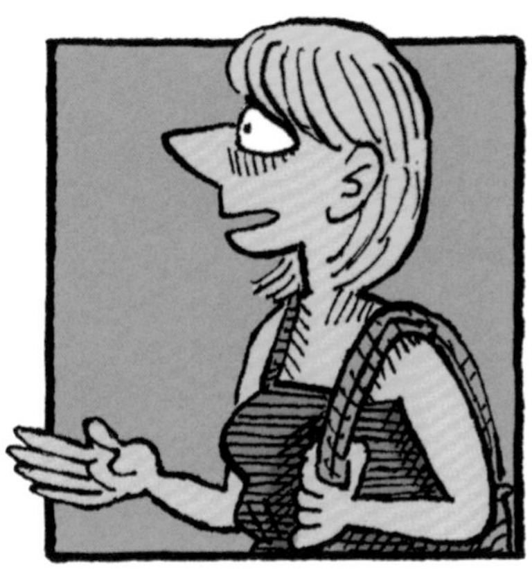

Penny - Alex's wife

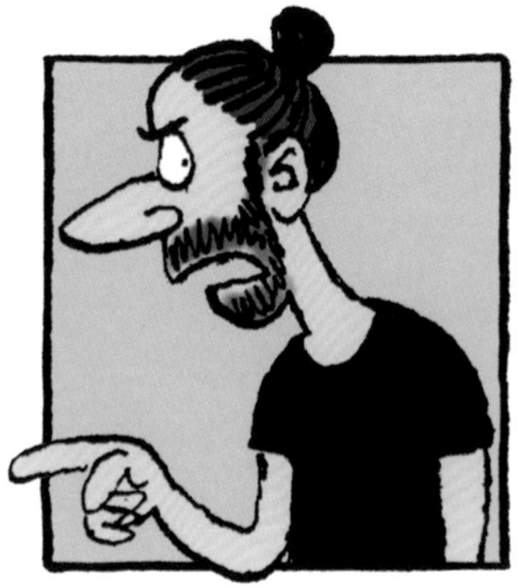

Christopher - their son

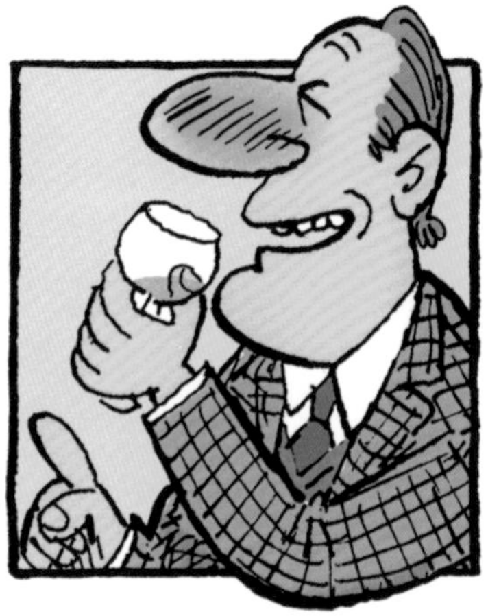

Rupert - senior banker

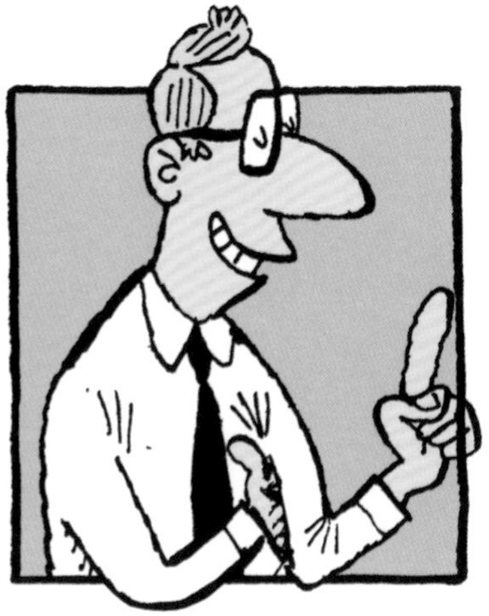

Clive - Alex's colleague

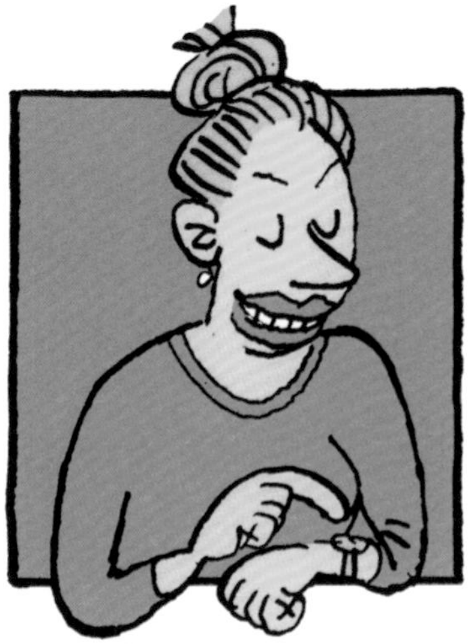

Bridget - Clive's wife

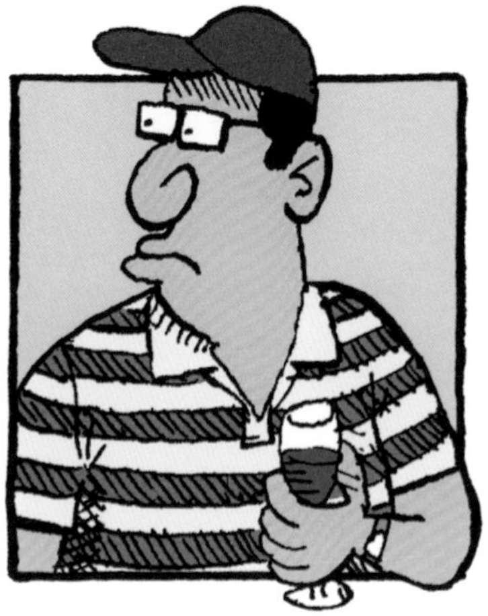

Cyrus - Alex's boss

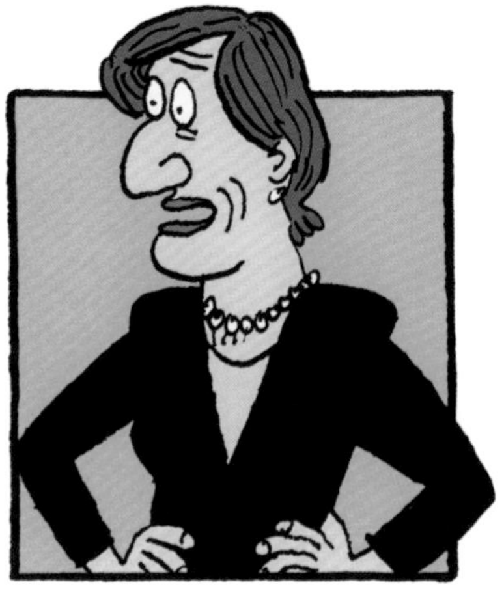

Stephanie - transgender banker

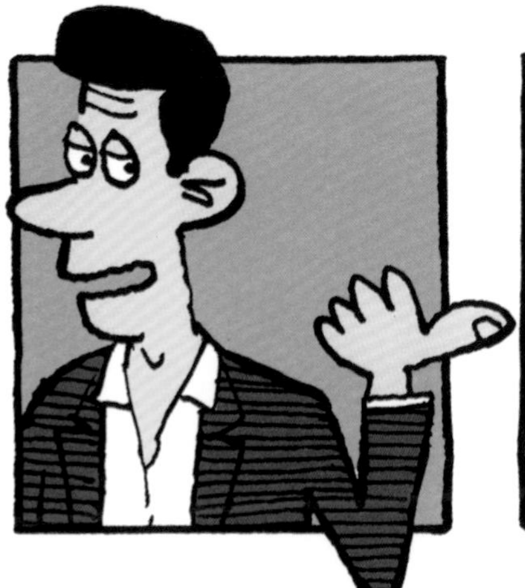

Leo - graduate trainee

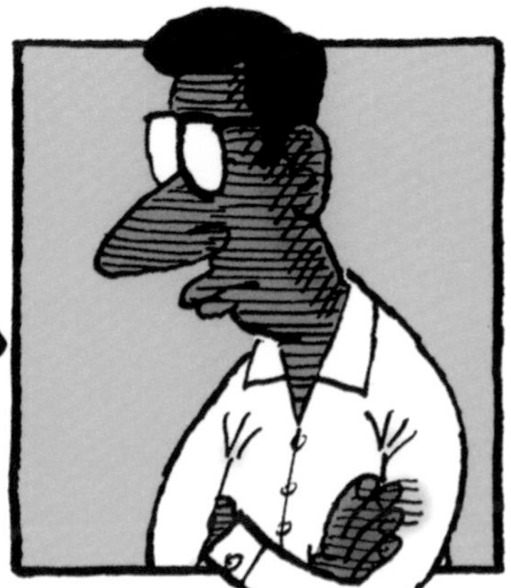

Vijay - compliance officer

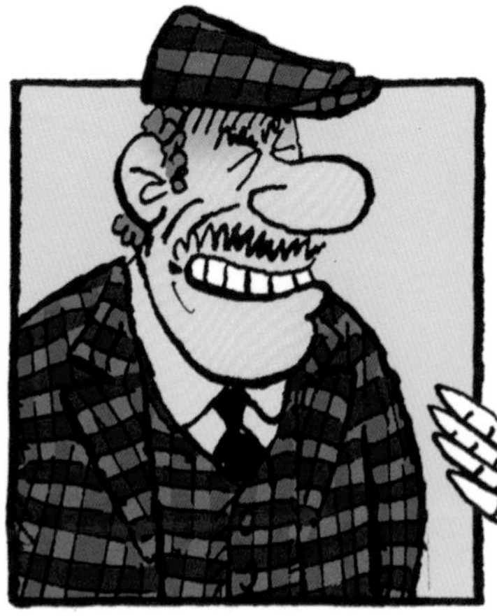

Hardcastle - Alex's client

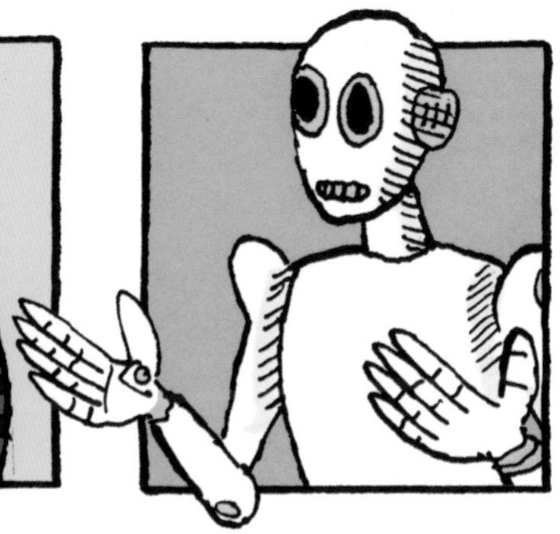

Robot - the future

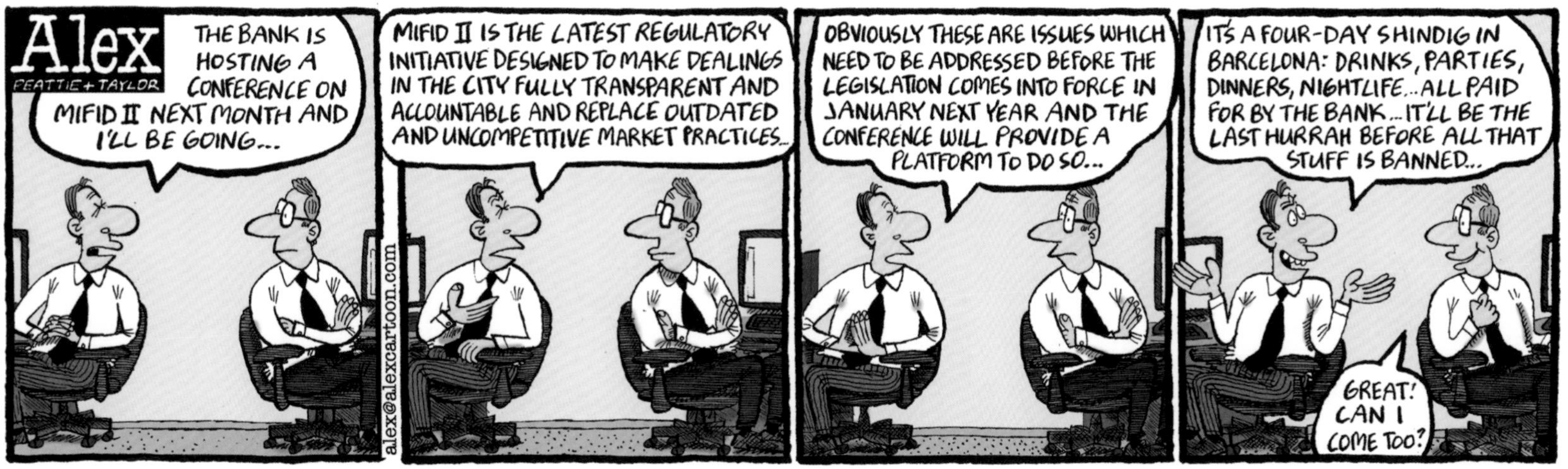
Alex
PEATTIE + TAYLOR
THE BANK IS HOSTING A CONFERENCE ON MIFID II NEXT MONTH AND I'LL BE GOING...
MIFID II IS THE LATEST REGULATORY INITIATIVE DESIGNED TO MAKE DEALINGS IN THE CITY FULLY TRANSPARENT AND ACCOUNTABLE AND REPLACE OUTDATED AND UNCOMPETITIVE MARKET PRACTICES...
alex@alexcartoon.com
OBVIOUSLY THESE ARE ISSUES WHICH NEED TO BE ADDRESSED BEFORE THE LEGISLATION COMES INTO FORCE IN JANUARY NEXT YEAR AND THE CONFERENCE WILL PROVIDE A PLATFORM TO DO SO...
IT'S A FOUR-DAY SHINDIG IN BARCELONA: DRINKS, PARTIES, DINNERS, NIGHTLIFE... ALL PAID FOR BY THE BANK... IT'LL BE THE LAST HURRAH BEFORE ALL THAT STUFF IS BANNED...
GREAT! CAN I COME TOO?

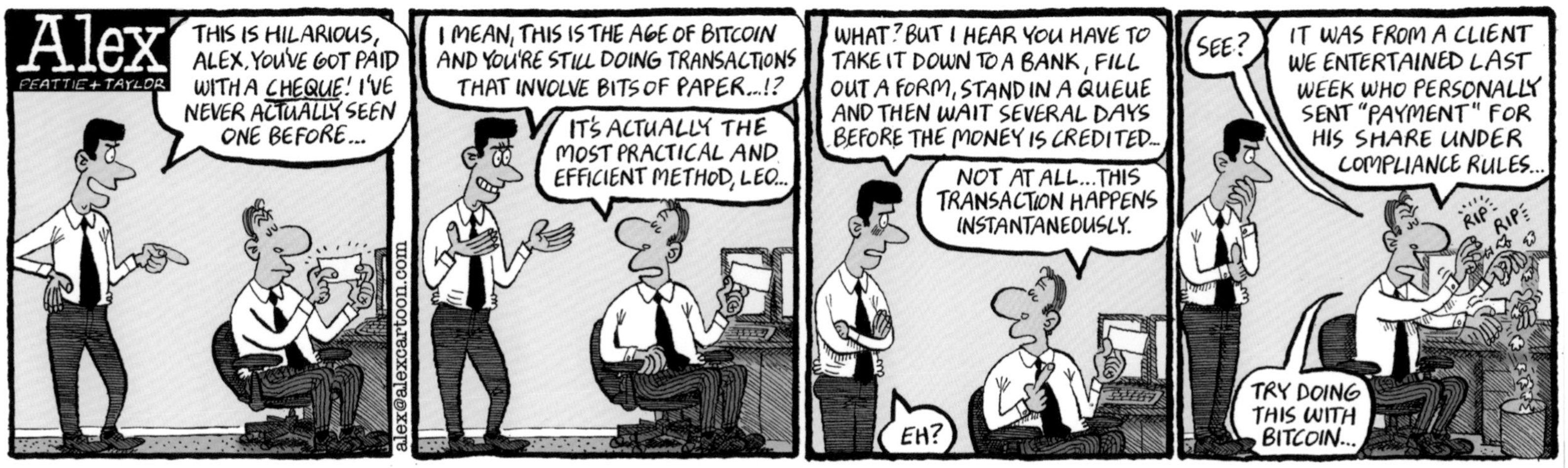
Alex
PEATTIE + TAYLOR
THIS IS HILARIOUS, ALEX. YOU'VE GOT PAID WITH A CHEQUE! I'VE NEVER ACTUALLY SEEN ONE BEFORE...
I MEAN, THIS IS THE AGE OF BITCOIN AND YOU'RE STILL DOING TRANSACTIONS THAT INVOLVE BITS OF PAPER...!?
IT'S ACTUALLY THE MOST PRACTICAL AND EFFICIENT METHOD, LEO...
alex@alexcartoon.com
WHAT? BUT I HEAR YOU HAVE TO TAKE IT DOWN TO A BANK, FILL OUT A FORM, STAND IN A QUEUE AND THEN WAIT SEVERAL DAYS BEFORE THE MONEY IS CREDITED...
NOT AT ALL... THIS TRANSACTION HAPPENS INSTANTANEOUSLY.
EH?
SEE?
IT WAS FROM A CLIENT WE ENTERTAINED LAST WEEK WHO PERSONALLY SENT "PAYMENT" FOR HIS SHARE UNDER COMPLIANCE RULES...
RIP RIP
TRY DOING THIS WITH BITCOIN...

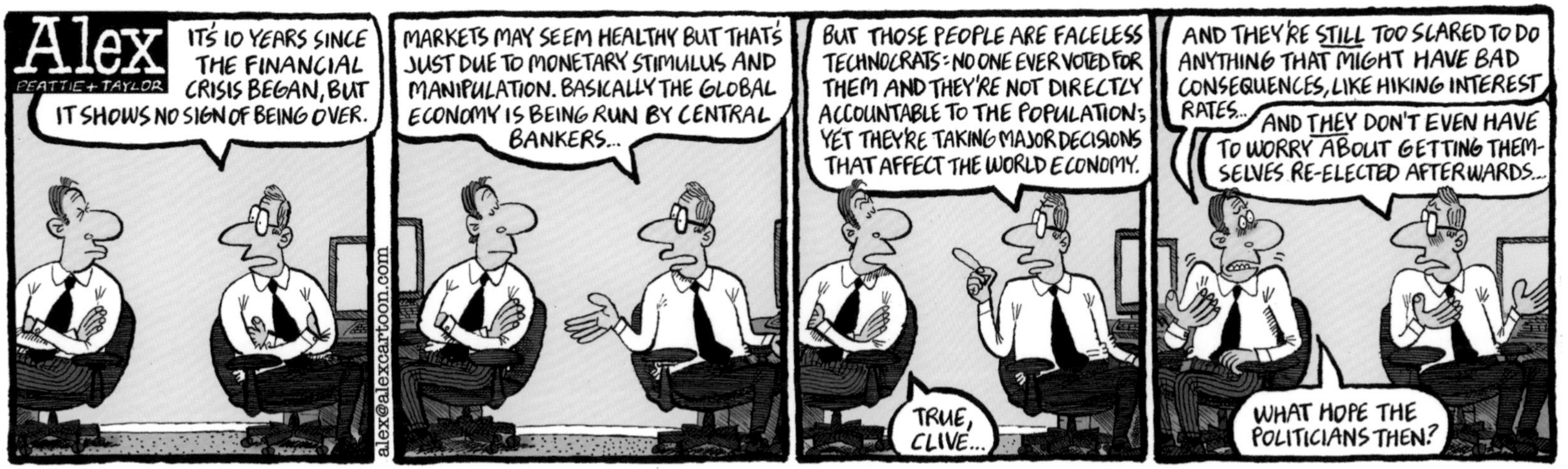
Alex
PEATTIE + TAYLOR
IT'S 10 YEARS SINCE THE FINANCIAL CRISIS BEGAN, BUT IT SHOWS NO SIGN OF BEING OVER.
MARKETS MAY SEEM HEALTHY BUT THAT'S JUST DUE TO MONETARY STIMULUS AND MANIPULATION. BASICALLY THE GLOBAL ECONOMY IS BEING RUN BY CENTRAL BANKERS...
alex@alexcartoon.com
BUT THOSE PEOPLE ARE FACELESS TECHNOCRATS: NO ONE EVER VOTED FOR THEM AND THEY'RE NOT DIRECTLY ACCOUNTABLE TO THE POPULATION; YET THEY'RE TAKING MAJOR DECISIONS THAT AFFECT THE WORLD ECONOMY.
TRUE, CLIVE...
AND THEY'RE STILL TOO SCARED TO DO ANYTHING THAT MIGHT HAVE BAD CONSEQUENCES, LIKE HIKING INTEREST RATES...
AND THEY DON'T EVEN HAVE TO WORRY ABOUT GETTING THEMSELVES RE-ELECTED AFTERWARDS...
WHAT HOPE THE POLITICIANS THEN?

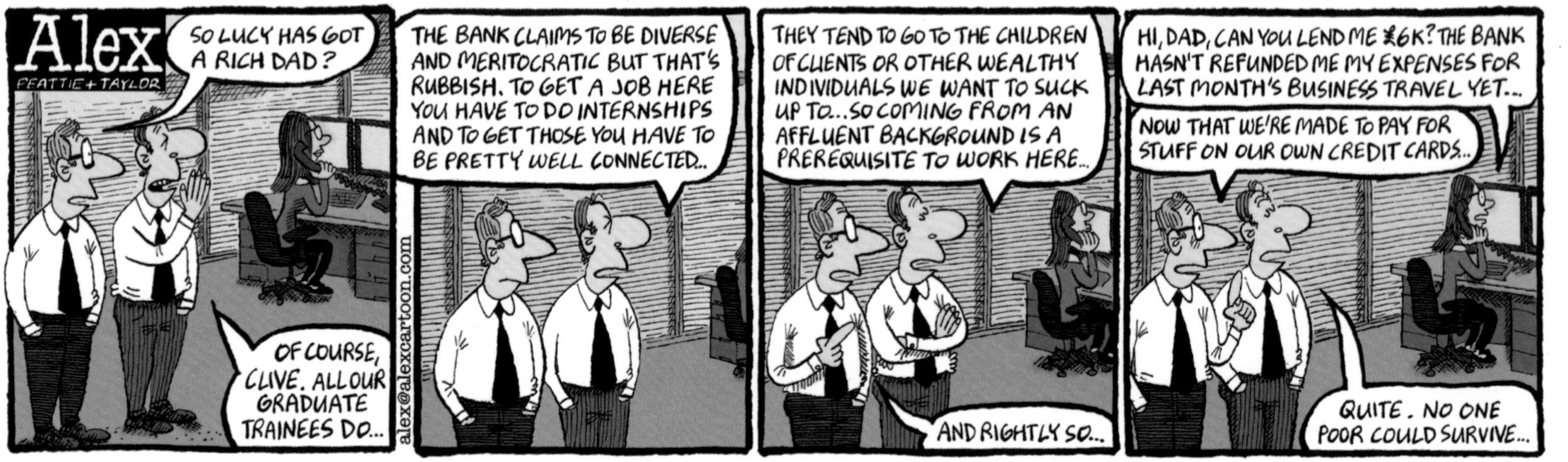
Alex
BEATTIE + TAYLOR
SO LUCY HAS GOT A RICH DAD?
OF COURSE, CLIVE. ALL OUR GRADUATE TRAINEES DO...
alex@alexcartoon.com
THE BANK CLAIMS TO BE DIVERSE AND MERITOCRATIC BUT THAT'S RUBBISH. TO GET A JOB HERE YOU HAVE TO DO INTERNSHIPS AND TO GET THOSE YOU HAVE TO BE PRETTY WELL CONNECTED...
THEY TEND TO GO TO THE CHILDREN OF CLIENTS OR OTHER WEALTHY INDIVIDUALS WE WANT TO SUCK UP TO... SO COMING FROM AN AFFLUENT BACKGROUND IS A PREREQUISITE TO WORK HERE...
AND RIGHTLY SO...
HI, DAD, CAN YOU LEND ME £6K? THE BANK HASN'T REFUNDED ME MY EXPENSES FOR LAST MONTH'S BUSINESS TRAVEL YET...
NOW THAT WE'RE MADE TO PAY FOR STUFF ON OUR OWN CREDIT CARDS...
QUITE. NO ONE POOR COULD SURVIVE...

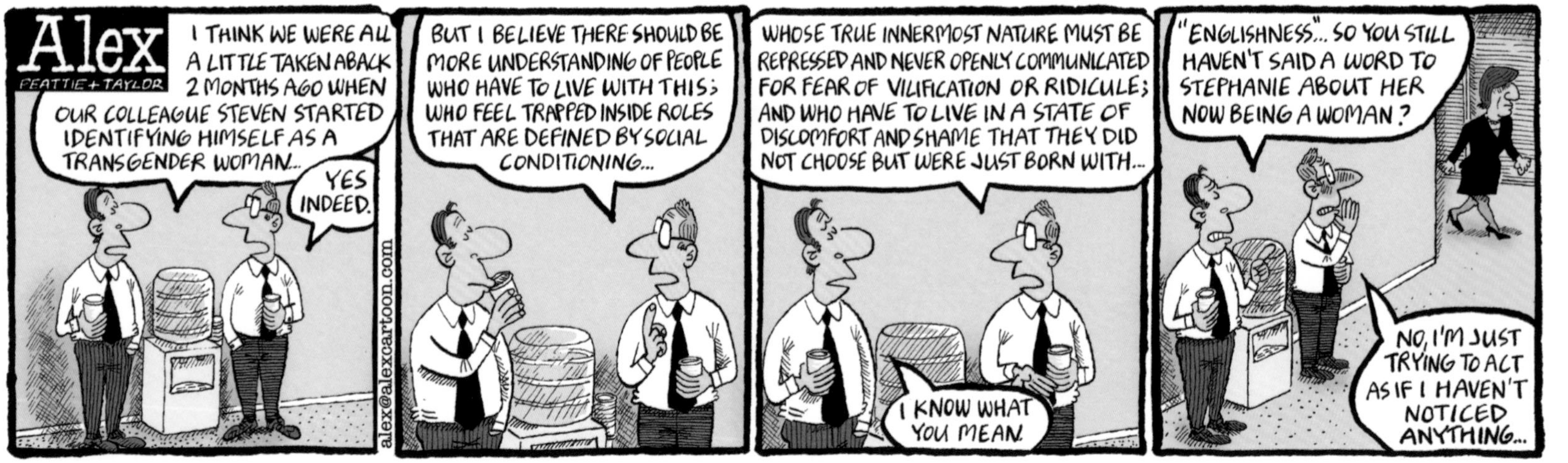
Alex
BEATTIE + TAYLOR
I THINK WE WERE ALL A LITTLE TAKEN ABACK 2 MONTHS AGO WHEN OUR COLLEAGUE STEVEN STARTED IDENTIFYING HIMSELF AS A TRANSGENDER WOMAN...
YES INDEED.
alex@alexcartoon.com
BUT I BELIEVE THERE SHOULD BE MORE UNDERSTANDING OF PEOPLE WHO HAVE TO LIVE WITH THIS; WHO FEEL TRAPPED INSIDE ROLES THAT ARE DEFINED BY SOCIAL CONDITIONING...
WHOSE TRUE INNERMOST NATURE MUST BE REPRESSED AND NEVER OPENLY COMMUNICATED FOR FEAR OF VILIFICATION OR RIDICULE; AND WHO HAVE TO LIVE IN A STATE OF DISCOMFORT AND SHAME THAT THEY DID NOT CHOOSE BUT WERE JUST BORN WITH...
I KNOW WHAT YOU MEAN.
"ENGLISHNESS"... SO YOU STILL HAVEN'T SAID A WORD TO STEPHANIE ABOUT HER NOW BEING A WOMAN?
NO, I'M JUST TRYING TO ACT AS IF I HAVEN'T NOTICED ANYTHING...

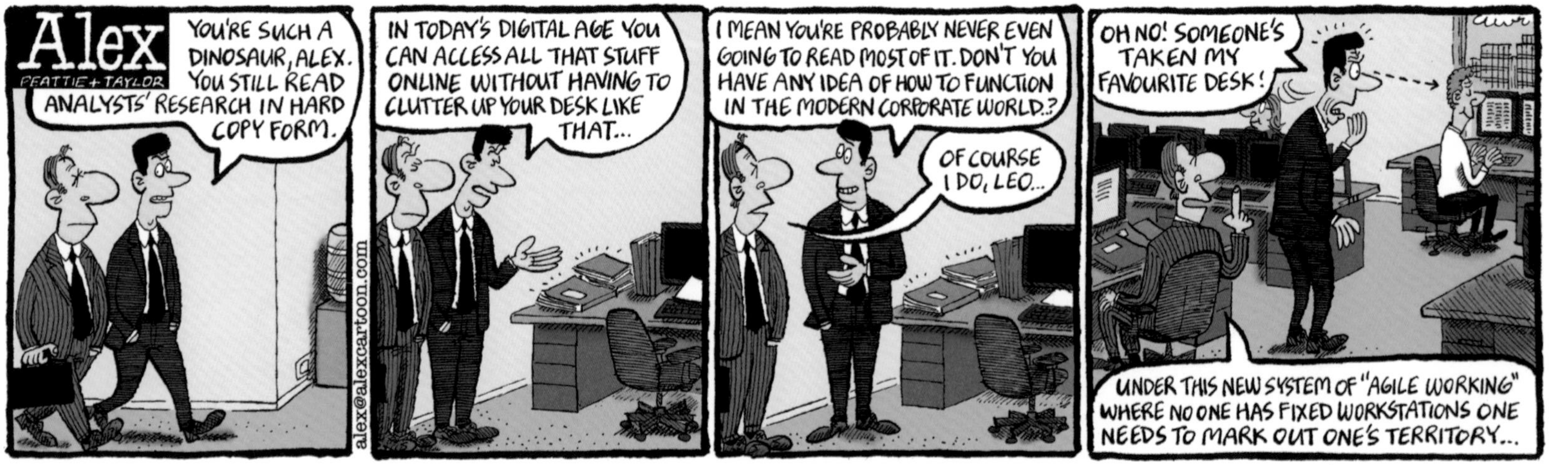
Alex
BEATTIE + TAYLOR
YOU'RE SUCH A DINOSAUR, ALEX. YOU STILL READ ANALYSTS' RESEARCH IN HARD COPY FORM.
alex@alexcartoon.com
IN TODAY'S DIGITAL AGE YOU CAN ACCESS ALL THAT STUFF ONLINE WITHOUT HAVING TO CLUTTER UP YOUR DESK LIKE THAT...
I MEAN YOU'RE PROBABLY NEVER EVEN GOING TO READ MOST OF IT. DON'T YOU HAVE ANY IDEA OF HOW TO FUNCTION IN THE MODERN CORPORATE WORLD?
OF COURSE I DO, LEO...
OH NO! SOMEONE'S TAKEN MY FAVOURITE DESK!
UNDER THIS NEW SYSTEM OF "AGILE WORKING" WHERE NO ONE HAS FIXED WORKSTATIONS ONE NEEDS TO MARK OUT ONE'S TERRITORY...

Alex PEATTIE + TAYLOR

Panel 1: Do I sense some resentment from you now that I'm a transgender woman, Amy?
MAYBE, YES.

Panel 2: IN RECENT YEARS THERE'S BEEN A CHANGE IN FASHION WITH REGARDS TO ATTITUDES TO GENDER IDENTITY BEING MORE FLEXIBLE. AND YOU'RE JUST TAKING ADVANTAGE OF IT...

Panel 3: IN THE OLD DAYS IF SOMEONE CAME INTO THE OFFICE WEARING CLOTHES THAT WERE DESIGNED TO BE WORN BY THE OPPOSITE SEX, LIKE YOU DO, THEY WOULD NEVER HAVE GOT AWAY WITH IT...

Panel 4: YOU'D NEVER HAVE GOT AWAY WITH THAT TROUSER SUIT BACK THEN...
WHY NOT? I'VE GOT THE HEIGHT FOR IT... AND THE FIGURE...
I MEAN WOMEN WEREN'T ALLOWED TO WEAR THEM... YOU SENT ME HOME FOR NOT WEARING A SKIRT IN 1989...
OH GOD... DID I? SORRY...

alex@alexcartoon.com

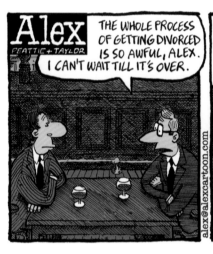

Alex PEATTIE + TAYLOR

Panel 1: THE WHOLE PROCESS OF GETTING DIVORCED IS SO AWFUL, ALEX. I CAN'T WAIT TILL IT'S OVER.

Panel 2: I'VE HAD TO HIDE MY MONEY FROM MY WIFE TO STOP HER LAYING CLAIM TO IT IN THE SETTLEMENT, SO I'VE BEEN COVERTLY MOVING IT TO PLACES WHERE IT'S HARD TO TRACE...

Panel 3: BUT I HATE ALL THE FURTIVENESS AND SECRECY INVOLVED... IT'S REALLY STRESSING ME OUT...
I CAN WELL IMAGINE, CLIVE.

Panel 4: YOU PUT ALL YOUR MONEY INTO BITCOIN EIGHTEEN MONTHS AGO...
AND IT'S GONE UP BY 1000% SINCE THEN... BUT I CAN'T TELL ANYONE...
LET'S HOPE IT DOESN'T CRASH BEFORE YOUR DIVORCE IS FINALISED WHEN YOU'LL BE FREE TO CHANGE IT BACK INTO REAL MONEY...

alex@alexcartoon.com

Alex PEATTIE + TAYLOR

Panel 1: OUR CHILDREN ENDLESSLY GRUMBLE ABOUT US BABY-BOOMERS AND THE ADVANTAGES WE'VE ENJOYED IN OUR LIVES...

Panel 2: UNLIKE THEM, WE HAD EASY ACCESS TO PROPERTY, JOBS AND PENSIONS... AND OF COURSE WE OWN ASSETS, LIKE HOUSES AND STOCKS, WHICH ARE GOING UP IN THE CURRENT MARKET.
TRUE.

Panel 3: BUT DON'T FORGET, OUR CHILDREN ARE COUNTING ON ONE DAY INHERITING THE PROPERTY WE OWN.
YES, THEY REALLY HAVEN'T THOUGHT IT THROUGH, HAVE THEY?
NO...

Panel 4: WE'VE REMORTGAGED OUR HOUSES AND PUNTED THE MONEY ON THE STOCK MARKET...
YES, "MORTGAGE ARBITRAGE." WE'RE ALL DOING IT!
AND IF THAT GOES WRONG OUR KIDS WILL BE REALLY PISSED OFF WITH US...

alex@alexcartoon.com

13

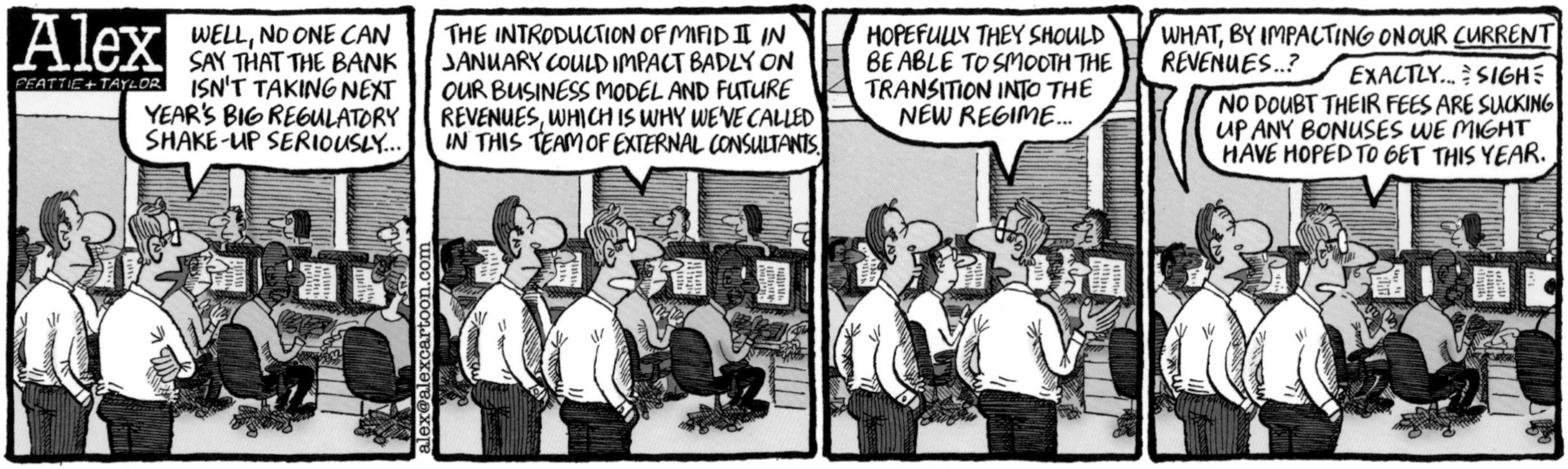
Alex
PEATTIE + TAYLOR
WELL, NO ONE CAN SAY THAT THE BANK ISN'T TAKING NEXT YEAR'S BIG REGULATORY SHAKE-UP SERIOUSLY...
THE INTRODUCTION OF MIFID II IN JANUARY COULD IMPACT BADLY ON OUR BUSINESS MODEL AND FUTURE REVENUES, WHICH IS WHY WE'VE CALLED IN THIS TEAM OF EXTERNAL CONSULTANTS.
HOPEFULLY THEY SHOULD BE ABLE TO SMOOTH THE TRANSITION INTO THE NEW REGIME...
WHAT, BY IMPACTING ON OUR CURRENT REVENUES...?
EXACTLY... SIGH NO DOUBT THEIR FEES ARE SUCKING UP ANY BONUSES WE MIGHT HAVE HOPED TO GET THIS YEAR.
alex@alexcartoon.com

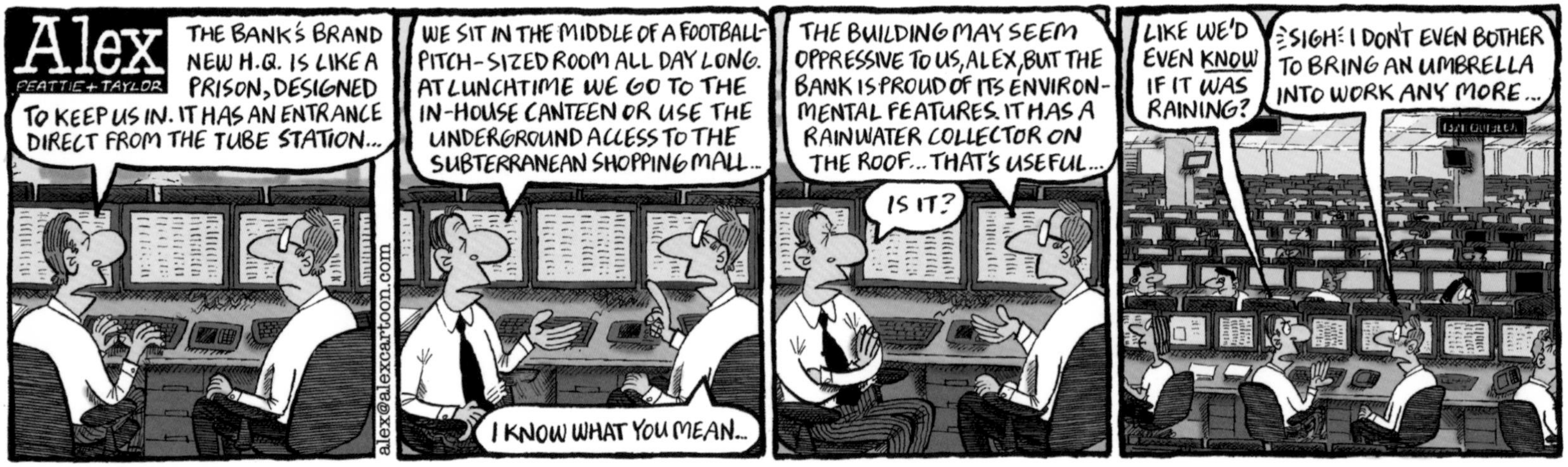
Alex
PEATTIE + TAYLOR
THE BANK'S BRAND NEW H.Q. IS LIKE A PRISON, DESIGNED TO KEEP US IN. IT HAS AN ENTRANCE DIRECT FROM THE TUBE STATION...
WE SIT IN THE MIDDLE OF A FOOTBALL-PITCH-SIZED ROOM ALL DAY LONG. AT LUNCHTIME WE GO TO THE IN-HOUSE CANTEEN OR USE THE UNDERGROUND ACCESS TO THE SUBTERRANEAN SHOPPING MALL...
I KNOW WHAT YOU MEAN...
THE BUILDING MAY SEEM OPPRESSIVE TO US, ALEX, BUT THE BANK IS PROUD OF ITS ENVIRONMENTAL FEATURES. IT HAS A RAINWATER COLLECTOR ON THE ROOF... THAT'S USEFUL...
IS IT?
LIKE WE'D EVEN KNOW IF IT WAS RAINING?
SIGH I DON'T EVEN BOTHER TO BRING AN UMBRELLA INTO WORK ANY MORE...
alex@alexcartoon.com

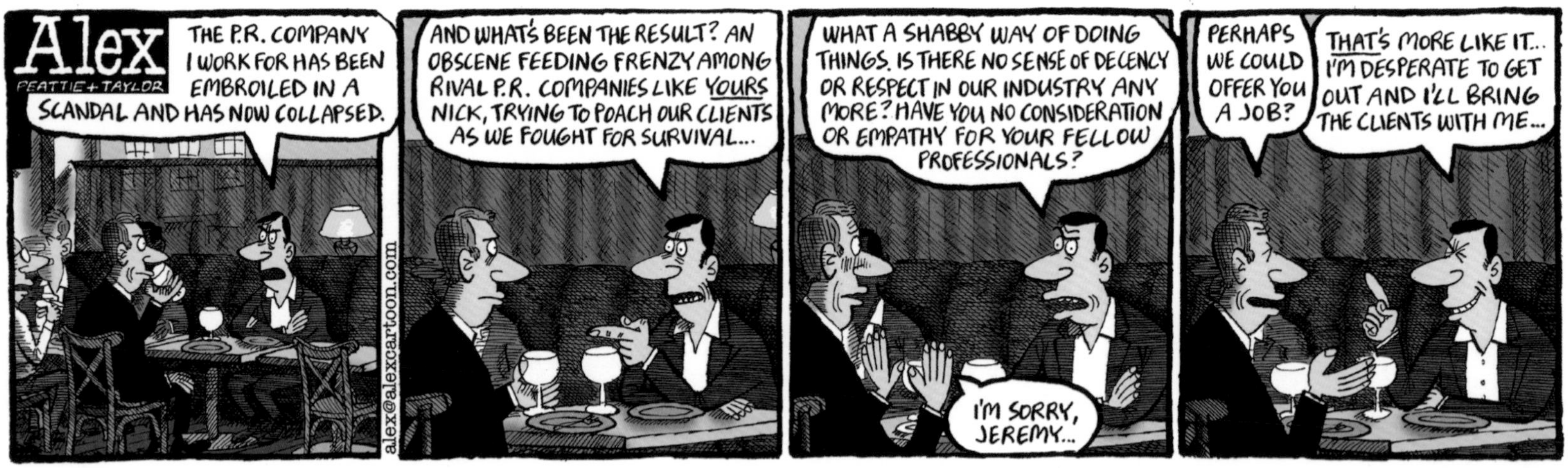
Alex
PEATTIE + TAYLOR
THE P.R. COMPANY I WORK FOR HAS BEEN EMBROILED IN A SCANDAL AND HAS NOW COLLAPSED.
AND WHAT'S BEEN THE RESULT? AN OBSCENE FEEDING FRENZY AMONG RIVAL P.R. COMPANIES LIKE YOURS NICK, TRYING TO POACH OUR CLIENTS AS WE FOUGHT FOR SURVIVAL...
WHAT A SHABBY WAY OF DOING THINGS. IS THERE NO SENSE OF DECENCY OR RESPECT IN OUR INDUSTRY ANY MORE? HAVE YOU NO CONSIDERATION OR EMPATHY FOR YOUR FELLOW PROFESSIONALS?
I'M SORRY, JEREMY...
PERHAPS WE COULD OFFER YOU A JOB?
THAT'S MORE LIKE IT... I'M DESPERATE TO GET OUT AND I'LL BRING THE CLIENTS WITH ME...
alex@alexcartoon.com

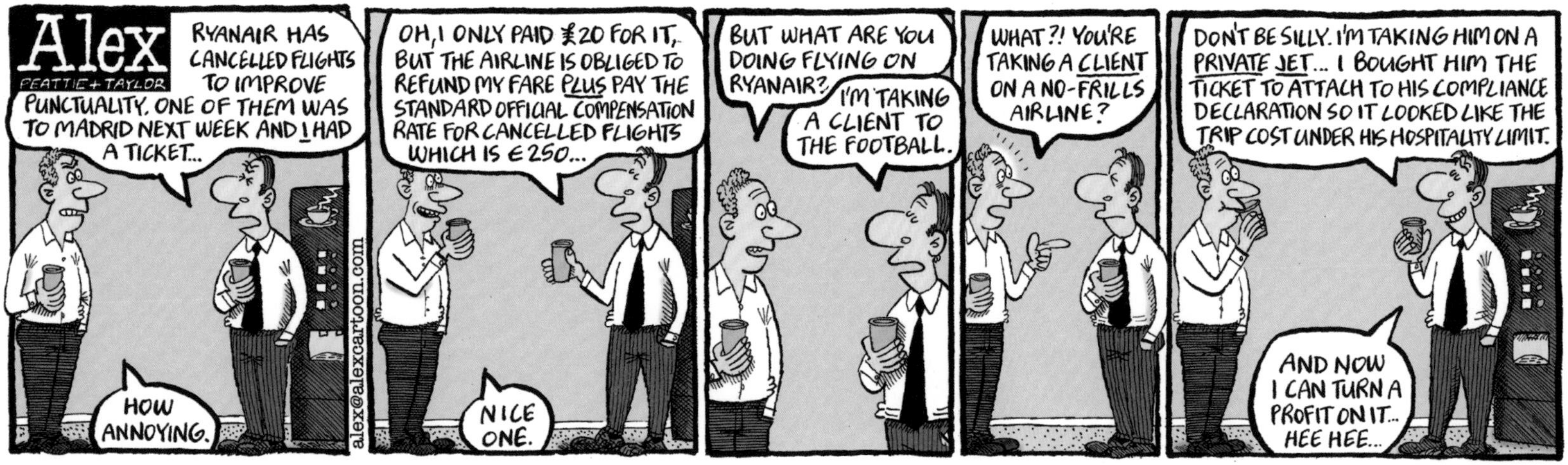
Alex
PEATTIE + TAYLOR
RYANAIR HAS CANCELLED FLIGHTS TO IMPROVE PUNCTUALITY. ONE OF THEM WAS TO MADRID NEXT WEEK AND I HAD A TICKET...
HOW ANNOYING.
OH, I ONLY PAID £20 FOR IT, BUT THE AIRLINE IS OBLIGED TO REFUND MY FARE PLUS PAY THE STANDARD OFFICIAL COMPENSATION RATE FOR CANCELLED FLIGHTS WHICH IS €250...
NICE ONE.
alex@alexcartoon.com
BUT WHAT ARE YOU DOING FLYING ON RYANAIR?
I'M TAKING A CLIENT TO THE FOOTBALL.
WHAT?! YOU'RE TAKING A CLIENT ON A NO-FRILLS AIRLINE?
DON'T BE SILLY. I'M TAKING HIM ON A PRIVATE JET... I BOUGHT HIM THE TICKET TO ATTACH TO HIS COMPLIANCE DECLARATION SO IT LOOKED LIKE THE TRIP COST UNDER HIS HOSPITALITY LIMIT.
AND NOW I CAN TURN A PROFIT ON IT... HEE HEE...

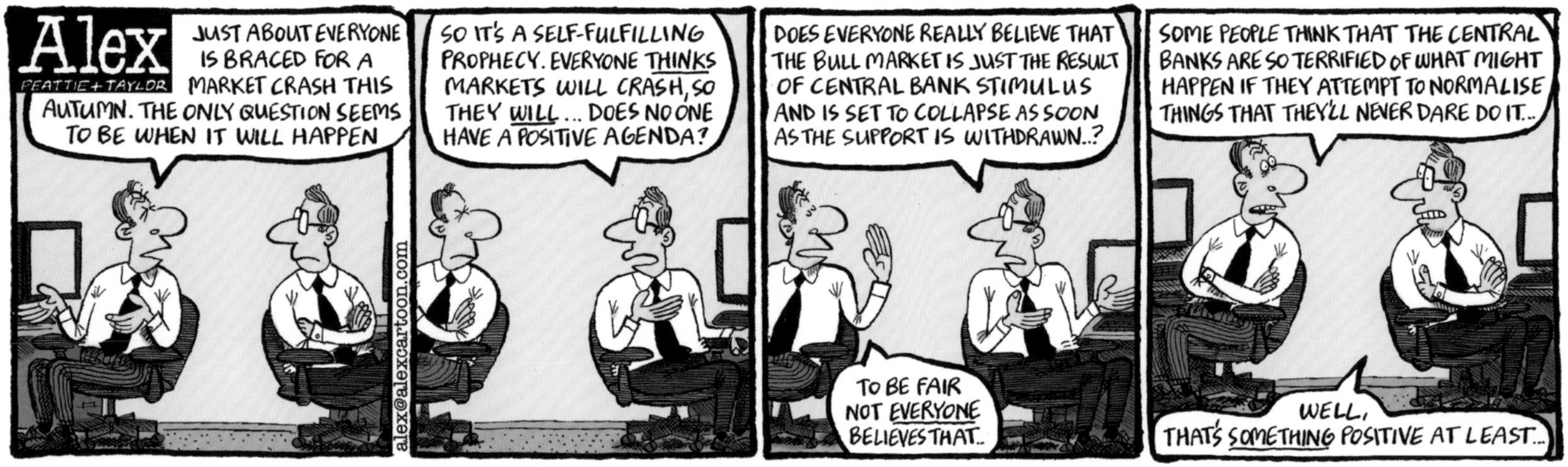
Alex
PEATTIE + TAYLOR
JUST ABOUT EVERYONE IS BRACED FOR A MARKET CRASH THIS AUTUMN. THE ONLY QUESTION SEEMS TO BE WHEN IT WILL HAPPEN
SO IT'S A SELF-FULFILLING PROPHECY. EVERYONE THINKS MARKETS WILL CRASH, SO THEY WILL... DOES NO ONE HAVE A POSITIVE AGENDA?
alex@alexcartoon.com
DOES EVERYONE REALLY BELIEVE THAT THE BULL MARKET IS JUST THE RESULT OF CENTRAL BANK STIMULUS AND IS SET TO COLLAPSE AS SOON AS THE SUPPORT IS WITHDRAWN..?
TO BE FAIR NOT EVERYONE BELIEVES THAT..
SOME PEOPLE THINK THAT THE CENTRAL BANKS ARE SO TERRIFIED OF WHAT MIGHT HAPPEN IF THEY ATTEMPT TO NORMALISE THINGS THAT THEY'LL NEVER DARE DO IT..
WELL, THAT'S SOMETHING POSITIVE AT LEAST...

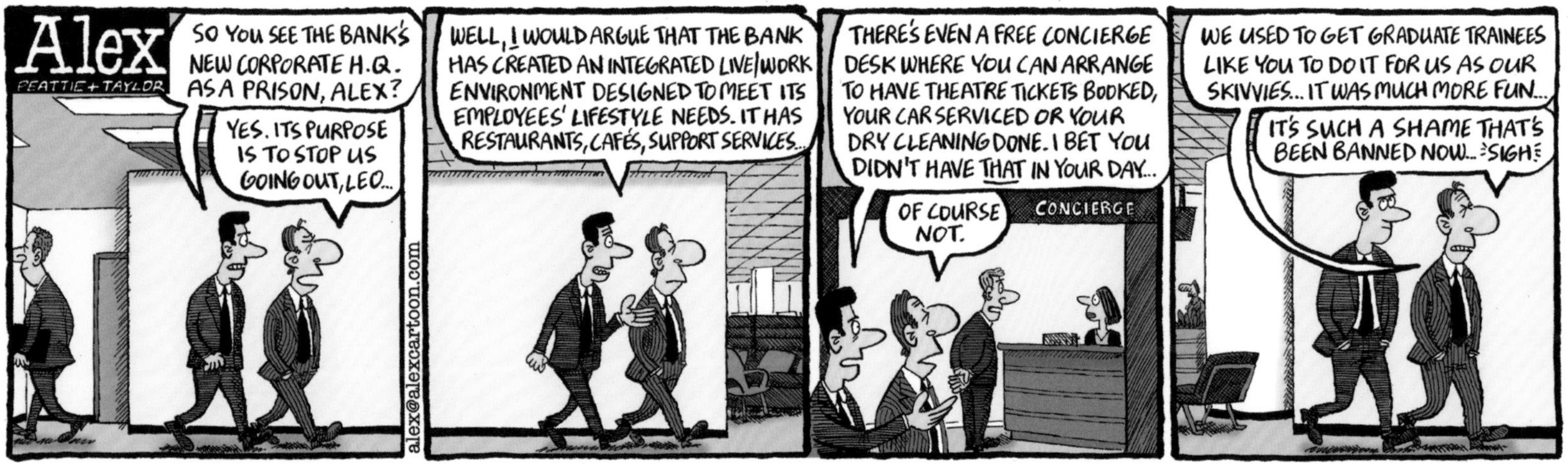
Alex
PEATTIE + TAYLOR
SO YOU SEE THE BANK'S NEW CORPORATE H.Q. AS A PRISON, ALEX?
YES. ITS PURPOSE IS TO STOP US GOING OUT, LEO...
WELL, I WOULD ARGUE THAT THE BANK HAS CREATED AN INTEGRATED LIVE/WORK ENVIRONMENT DESIGNED TO MEET ITS EMPLOYEES' LIFESTYLE NEEDS. IT HAS RESTAURANTS, CAFÉS, SUPPORT SERVICES...
alex@alexcartoon.com
THERE'S EVEN A FREE CONCIERGE DESK WHERE YOU CAN ARRANGE TO HAVE THEATRE TICKETS BOOKED, YOUR CAR SERVICED OR YOUR DRY CLEANING DONE. I BET YOU DIDN'T HAVE THAT IN YOUR DAY...
OF COURSE NOT.
CONCIERGE
WE USED TO GET GRADUATE TRAINEES LIKE YOU TO DO IT FOR US AS OUR SKIVVIES... IT WAS MUCH MORE FUN...
IT'S SUCH A SHAME THAT'S BEEN BANNED NOW... SIGH

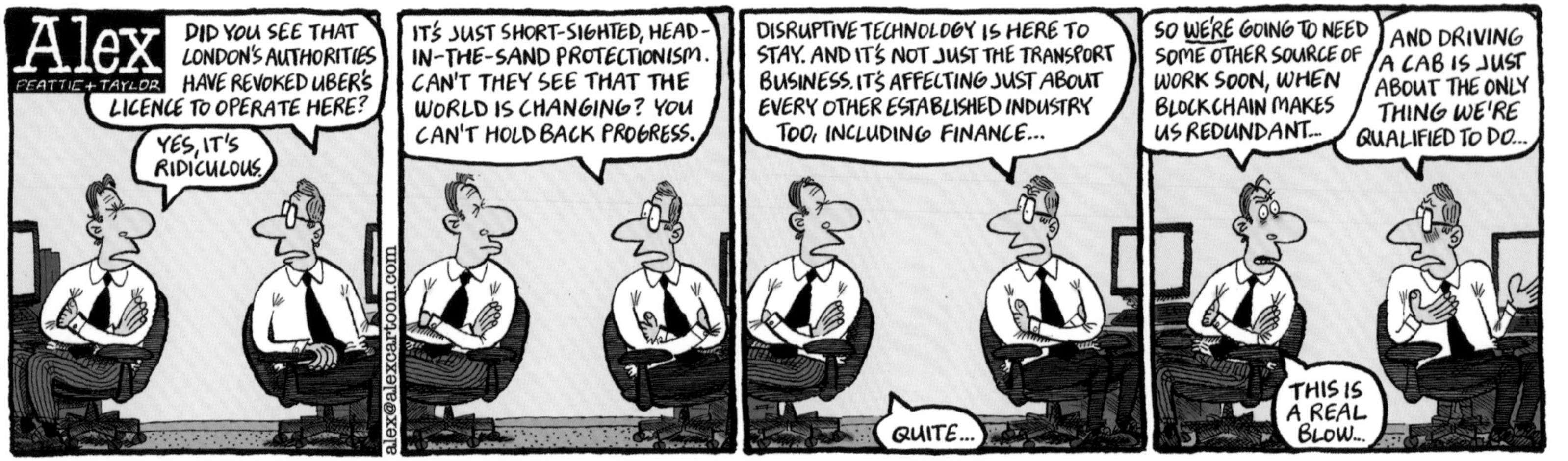
Alex
PEATTIE + TAYLOR
DID YOU SEE THAT LONDON'S AUTHORITIES HAVE REVOKED UBER'S LICENCE TO OPERATE HERE?
YES, IT'S RIDICULOUS.
alex@alexcartoon.com
IT'S JUST SHORT-SIGHTED, HEAD-IN-THE-SAND PROTECTIONISM. CAN'T THEY SEE THAT THE WORLD IS CHANGING? YOU CAN'T HOLD BACK PROGRESS.
DISRUPTIVE TECHNOLOGY IS HERE TO STAY. AND IT'S NOT JUST THE TRANSPORT BUSINESS. IT'S AFFECTING JUST ABOUT EVERY OTHER ESTABLISHED INDUSTRY TOO; INCLUDING FINANCE...
QUITE...
SO WE'RE GOING TO NEED SOME OTHER SOURCE OF WORK SOON, WHEN BLOCKCHAIN MAKES US REDUNDANT...
AND DRIVING A CAB IS JUST ABOUT THE ONLY THING WE'RE QUALIFIED TO DO...
THIS IS A REAL BLOW...

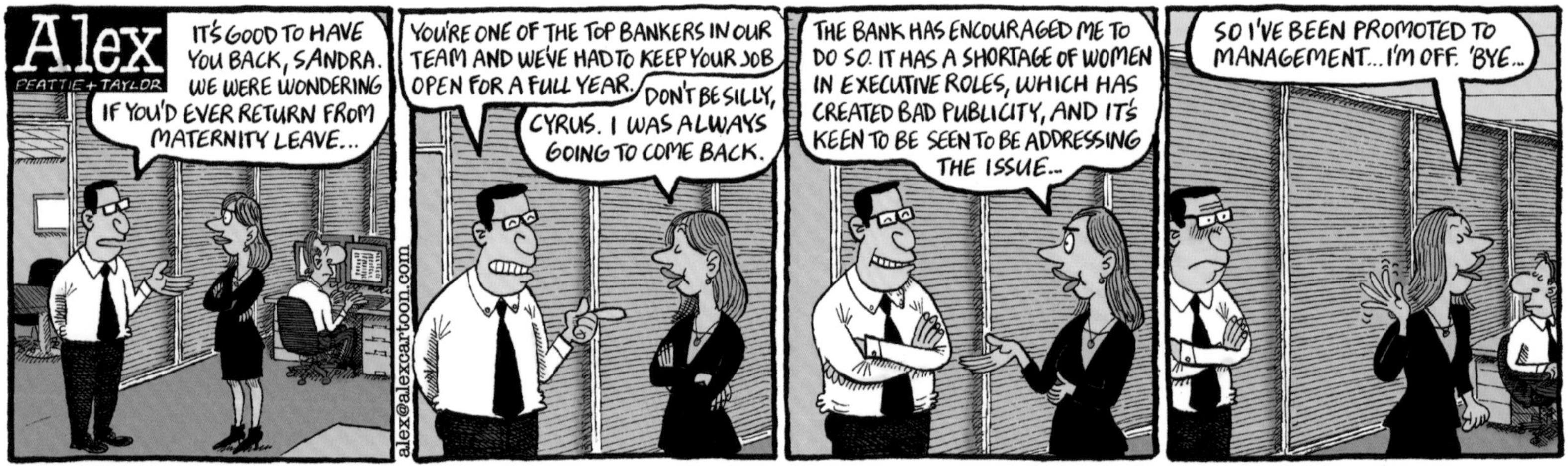
Alex
PEATTIE + TAYLOR
IT'S GOOD TO HAVE YOU BACK, SANDRA. WE WERE WONDERING IF YOU'D EVER RETURN FROM MATERNITY LEAVE...
alex@alexcartoon.com
YOU'RE ONE OF THE TOP BANKERS IN OUR TEAM AND WE'VE HAD TO KEEP YOUR JOB OPEN FOR A FULL YEAR.
DON'T BE SILLY, CYRUS. I WAS ALWAYS GOING TO COME BACK.
THE BANK HAS ENCOURAGED ME TO DO SO. IT HAS A SHORTAGE OF WOMEN IN EXECUTIVE ROLES, WHICH HAS CREATED BAD PUBLICITY, AND IT'S KEEN TO BE SEEN TO BE ADDRESSING THE ISSUE...
SO I'VE BEEN PROMOTED TO MANAGEMENT... I'M OFF. 'BYE...

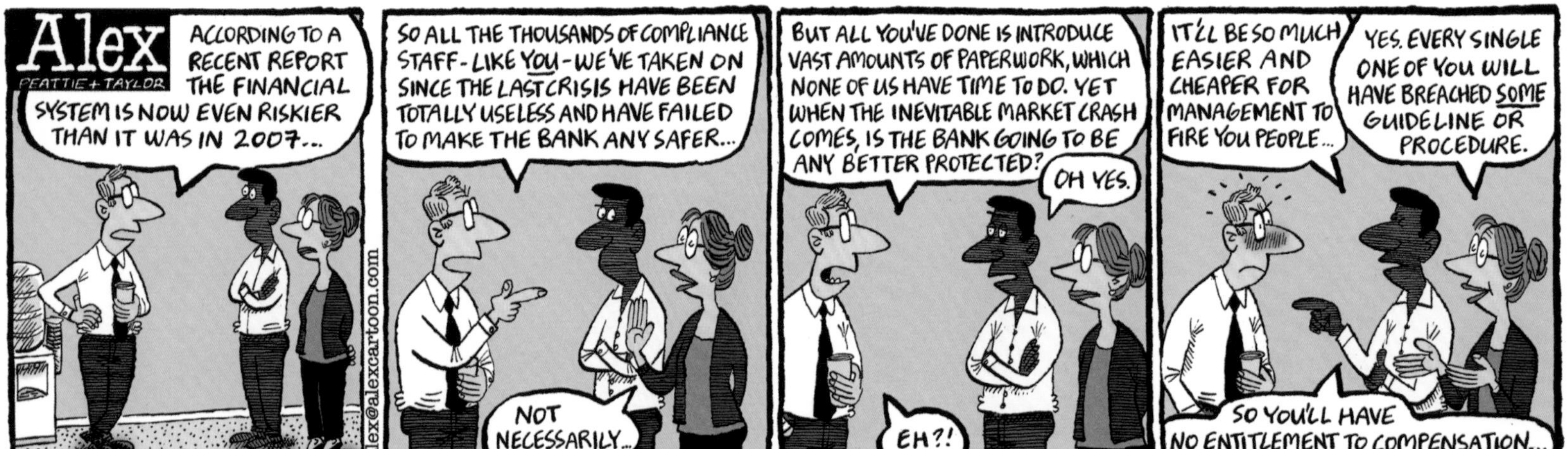
Alex
PEATTIE + TAYLOR
ACCORDING TO A RECENT REPORT THE FINANCIAL SYSTEM IS NOW EVEN RISKIER THAN IT WAS IN 2007...
alex@alexcartoon.com
SO ALL THE THOUSANDS OF COMPLIANCE STAFF - LIKE YOU - WE'VE TAKEN ON SINCE THE LAST CRISIS HAVE BEEN TOTALLY USELESS AND HAVE FAILED TO MAKE THE BANK ANY SAFER...
NOT NECESSARILY...
BUT ALL YOU'VE DONE IS INTRODUCE VAST AMOUNTS OF PAPERWORK, WHICH NONE OF US HAVE TIME TO DO. YET WHEN THE INEVITABLE MARKET CRASH COMES, IS THE BANK GOING TO BE ANY BETTER PROTECTED?
OH YES.
EH?!
IT'LL BE SO MUCH EASIER AND CHEAPER FOR MANAGEMENT TO FIRE YOU PEOPLE...
YES. EVERY SINGLE ONE OF YOU WILL HAVE BREACHED SOME GUIDELINE OR PROCEDURE.
SO YOU'LL HAVE NO ENTITLEMENT TO COMPENSATION...

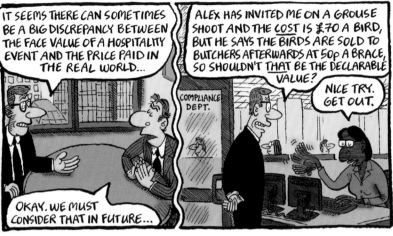

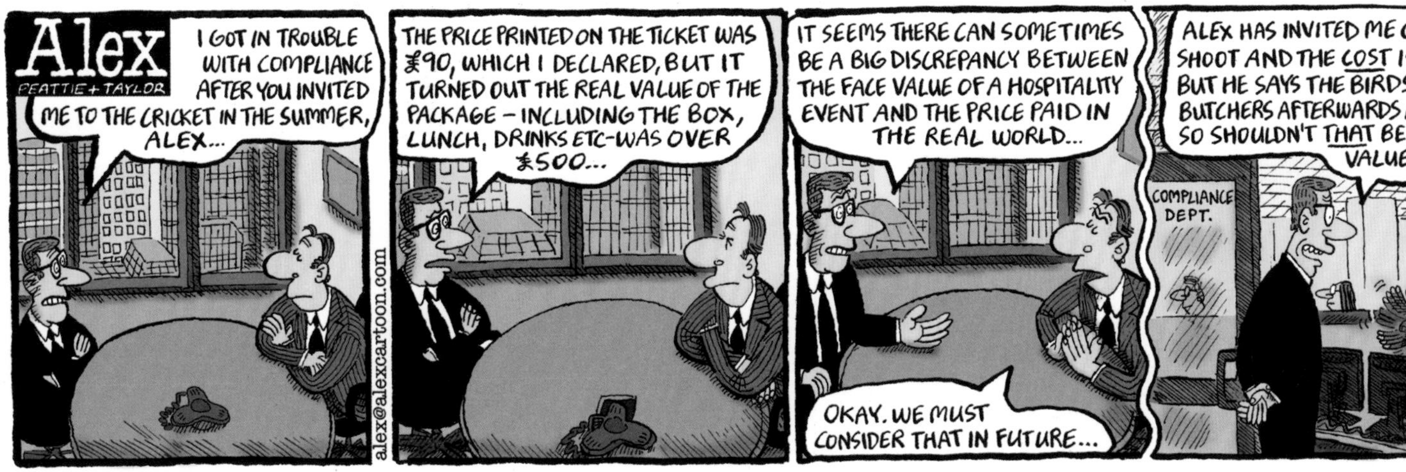
Alex
PEATTIE + TAYLOR
I GOT IN TROUBLE WITH COMPLIANCE AFTER YOU INVITED ME TO THE CRICKET IN THE SUMMER, ALEX...
THE PRICE PRINTED ON THE TICKET WAS £90, WHICH I DECLARED, BUT IT TURNED OUT THE REAL VALUE OF THE PACKAGE – INCLUDING THE BOX, LUNCH, DRINKS ETC – WAS OVER £500...
IT SEEMS THERE CAN SOMETIMES BE A BIG DISCREPANCY BETWEEN THE FACE VALUE OF A HOSPITALITY EVENT AND THE PRICE PAID IN THE REAL WORLD...
OKAY. WE MUST CONSIDER THAT IN FUTURE...
ALEX HAS INVITED ME ON A GROUSE SHOOT AND THE COST IS £70 A BIRD, BUT HE SAYS THE BIRDS ARE SOLD TO BUTCHERS AFTERWARDS AT 50p A BRACE, SO SHOULDN'T THAT BE THE DECLARABLE VALUE?
COMPLIANCE DEPT.
NICE TRY. GET OUT.
alex@alexcartoon.com

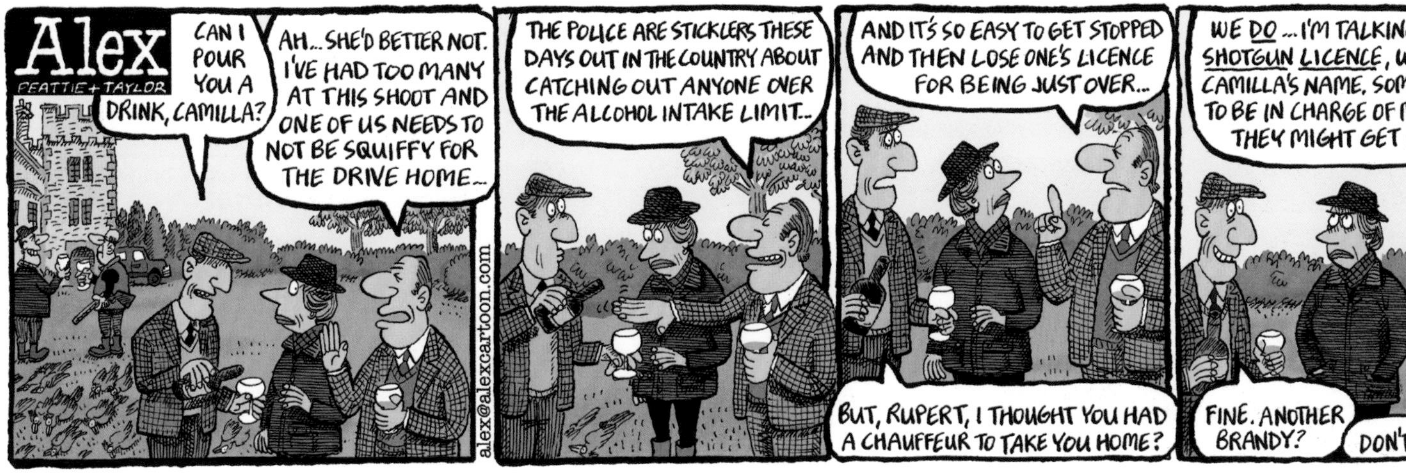
Alex
PEATTIE + TAYLOR
CAN I POUR YOU A DRINK, CAMILLA?
AH... SHE'D BETTER NOT. I'VE HAD TOO MANY AT THIS SHOOT AND ONE OF US NEEDS TO NOT BE SQUIFFY FOR THE DRIVE HOME...
THE POLICE ARE STICKLERS THESE DAYS OUT IN THE COUNTRY ABOUT CATCHING OUT ANYONE OVER THE ALCOHOL INTAKE LIMIT...
AND IT'S SO EASY TO GET STOPPED AND THEN LOSE ONE'S LICENCE FOR BEING JUST OVER...
BUT, RUPERT, I THOUGHT YOU HAD A CHAUFFEUR TO TAKE YOU HOME?
WE DO ... I'M TALKING ABOUT THE SHOTGUN LICENCE, WHICH I PUT IN CAMILLA'S NAME. SOMEONE SOBER HAS TO BE IN CHARGE OF MY PURDEYS OR THEY MIGHT GET CONFISCATED...
FINE. ANOTHER BRANDY?
DON'T MIND IF I DO...
alex@alexcartoon.com

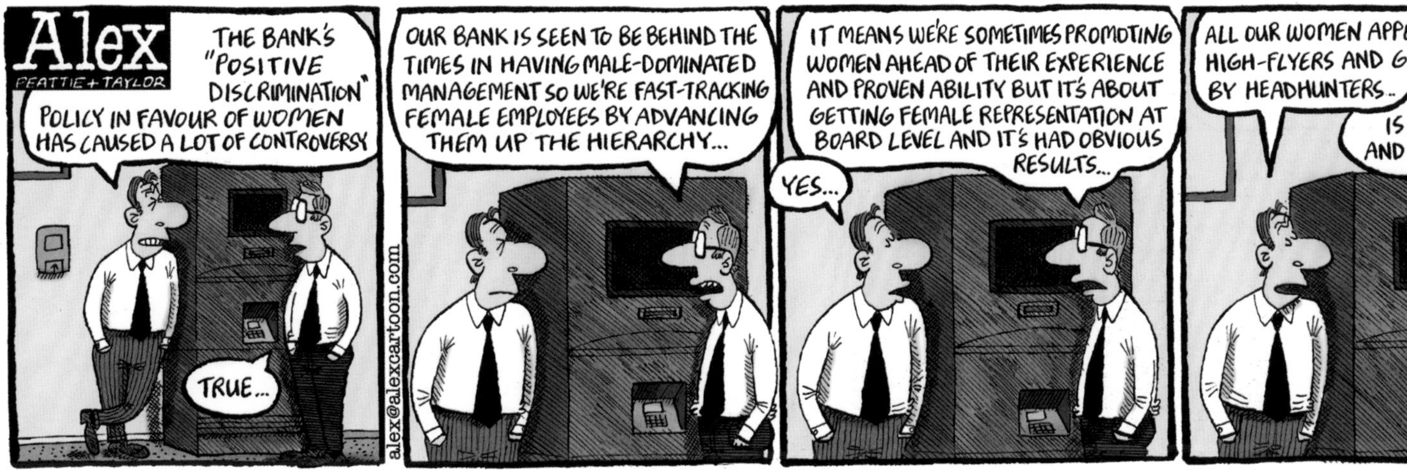
Alex
PEATTIE + TAYLOR
THE BANK'S "POSITIVE DISCRIMINATION" POLICY IN FAVOUR OF WOMEN HAS CAUSED A LOT OF CONTROVERSY
TRUE...
OUR BANK IS SEEN TO BE BEHIND THE TIMES IN HAVING MALE-DOMINATED MANAGEMENT SO WE'RE FAST-TRACKING FEMALE EMPLOYEES BY ADVANCING THEM UP THE HIERARCHY...
IT MEANS WE'RE SOMETIMES PROMOTING WOMEN AHEAD OF THEIR EXPERIENCE AND PROVEN ABILITY BUT IT'S ABOUT GETTING FEMALE REPRESENTATION AT BOARD LEVEL AND IT'S HAD OBVIOUS RESULTS...
YES...
ALL OUR WOMEN APPEAR TO BE SUPER HIGH-FLYERS AND GET POACHED BY HEADHUNTERS...
AND OUR BOARD IS AS MALE, PALE AND STALE AS EVER...
alex@alexcartoon.com

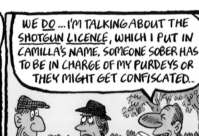

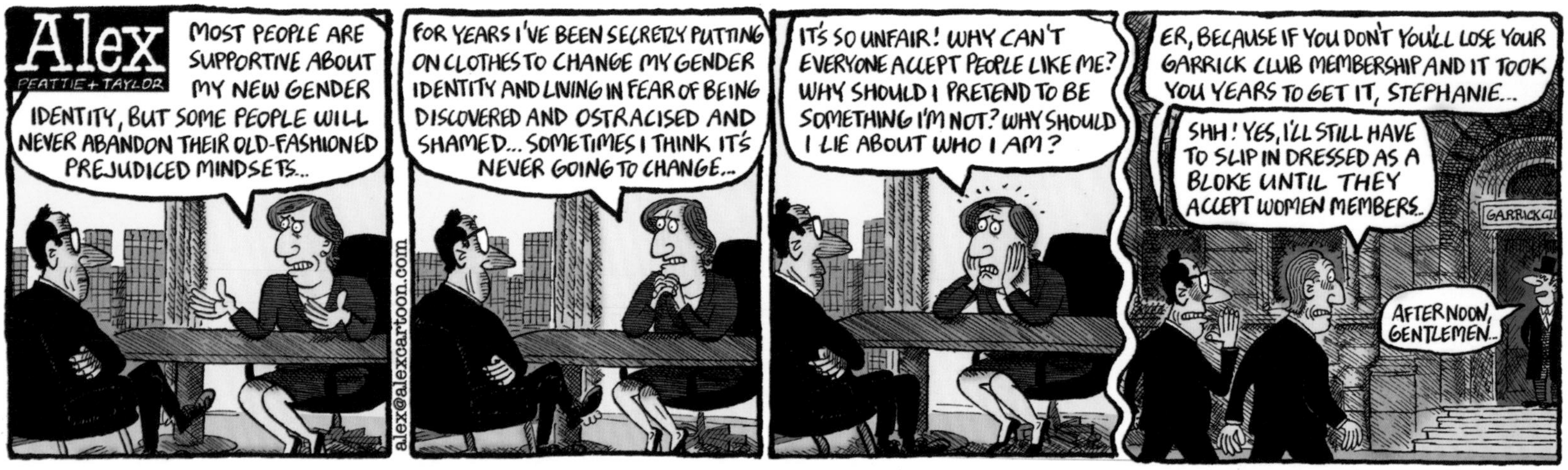
Alex
PEATTIE + TAYLOR
MOST PEOPLE ARE SUPPORTIVE ABOUT MY NEW GENDER IDENTITY, BUT SOME PEOPLE WILL NEVER ABANDON THEIR OLD-FASHIONED PREJUDICED MINDSETS...
alex@alexcartoon.com
FOR YEARS I'VE BEEN SECRETLY PUTTING ON CLOTHES TO CHANGE MY GENDER IDENTITY AND LIVING IN FEAR OF BEING DISCOVERED AND OSTRACISED AND SHAMED... SOMETIMES I THINK IT'S NEVER GOING TO CHANGE...
IT'S SO UNFAIR! WHY CAN'T EVERYONE ACCEPT PEOPLE LIKE ME? WHY SHOULD I PRETEND TO BE SOMETHING I'M NOT? WHY SHOULD I LIE ABOUT WHO I AM?
ER, BECAUSE IF YOU DON'T YOU'LL LOSE YOUR GARRICK CLUB MEMBERSHIP AND IT TOOK YOU YEARS TO GET IT, STEPHANIE...
SHH! YES, I'LL STILL HAVE TO SLIP IN DRESSED AS A BLOKE UNTIL THEY ACCEPT WOMEN MEMBERS...
GARRICK CL
AFTERNOON, GENTLEMEN...

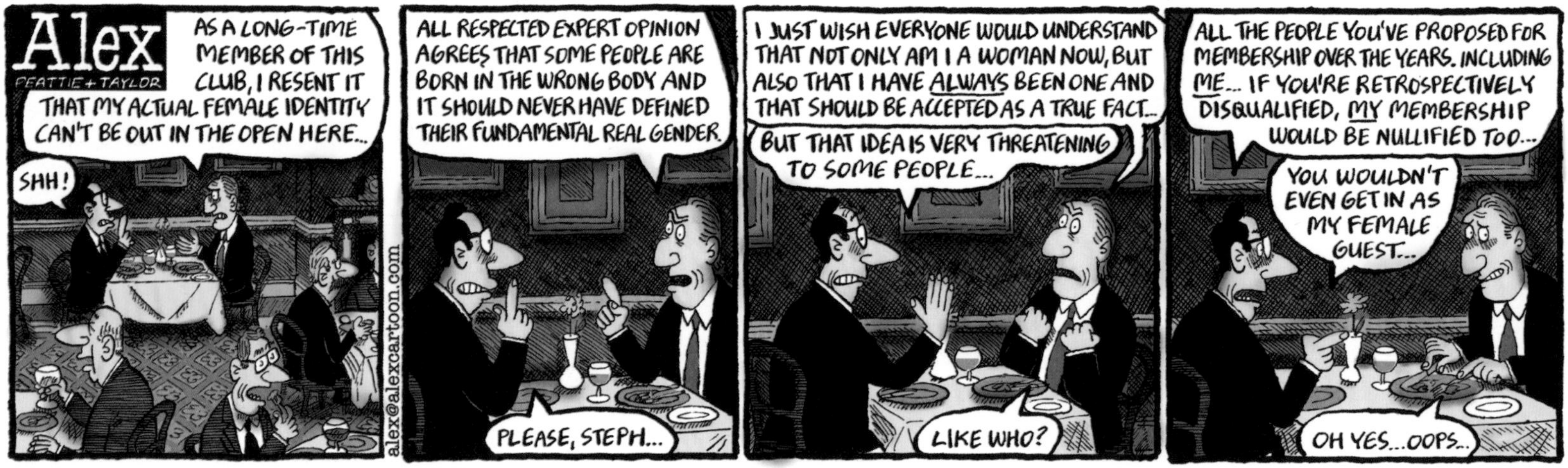
Alex
PEATTIE + TAYLOR
AS A LONG-TIME MEMBER OF THIS CLUB, I RESENT IT THAT MY ACTUAL FEMALE IDENTITY CAN'T BE OUT IN THE OPEN HERE...
SHH!
alex@alexcartoon.com
ALL RESPECTED EXPERT OPINION AGREES THAT SOME PEOPLE ARE BORN IN THE WRONG BODY AND IT SHOULD NEVER HAVE DEFINED THEIR FUNDAMENTAL REAL GENDER.
PLEASE, STEPH...
I JUST WISH EVERYONE WOULD UNDERSTAND THAT NOT ONLY AM I A WOMAN NOW, BUT ALSO THAT I HAVE ALWAYS BEEN ONE AND THAT SHOULD BE ACCEPTED AS A TRUE FACT...
BUT THAT IDEA IS VERY THREATENING TO SOME PEOPLE...
LIKE WHO?
ALL THE PEOPLE YOU'VE PROPOSED FOR MEMBERSHIP OVER THE YEARS. INCLUDING ME... IF YOU'RE RETROSPECTIVELY DISQUALIFIED, MY MEMBERSHIP WOULD BE NULLIFIED TOO...
YOU WOULDN'T EVEN GET IN AS MY FEMALE GUEST...
OH YES...OOPS...

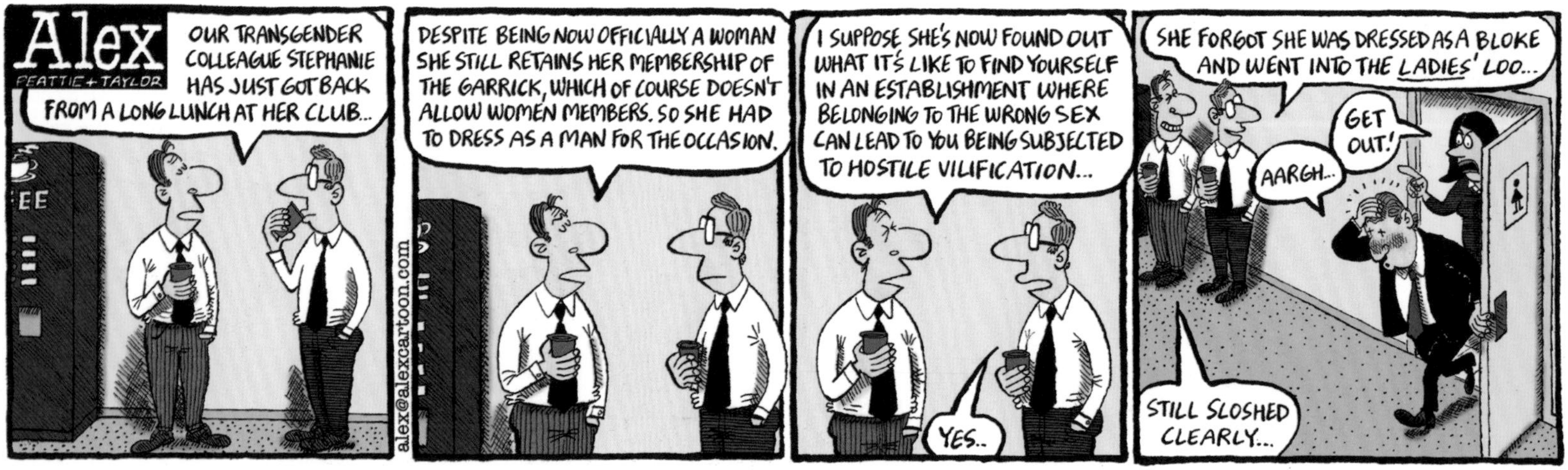
Alex
PEATTIE + TAYLOR
OUR TRANSGENDER COLLEAGUE STEPHANIE HAS JUST GOT BACK FROM A LONG LUNCH AT HER CLUB...
alex@alexcartoon.com
DESPITE BEING NOW OFFICIALLY A WOMAN SHE STILL RETAINS HER MEMBERSHIP OF THE GARRICK, WHICH OF COURSE DOESN'T ALLOW WOMEN MEMBERS. SO SHE HAD TO DRESS AS A MAN FOR THE OCCASION.
I SUPPOSE SHE'S NOW FOUND OUT WHAT IT'S LIKE TO FIND YOURSELF IN AN ESTABLISHMENT WHERE BELONGING TO THE WRONG SEX CAN LEAD TO YOU BEING SUBJECTED TO HOSTILE VILIFICATION...
YES..
SHE FORGOT SHE WAS DRESSED AS A BLOKE AND WENT INTO THE LADIES' LOO...
GET OUT!
AARGH...
STILL SLOSHED CLEARLY...

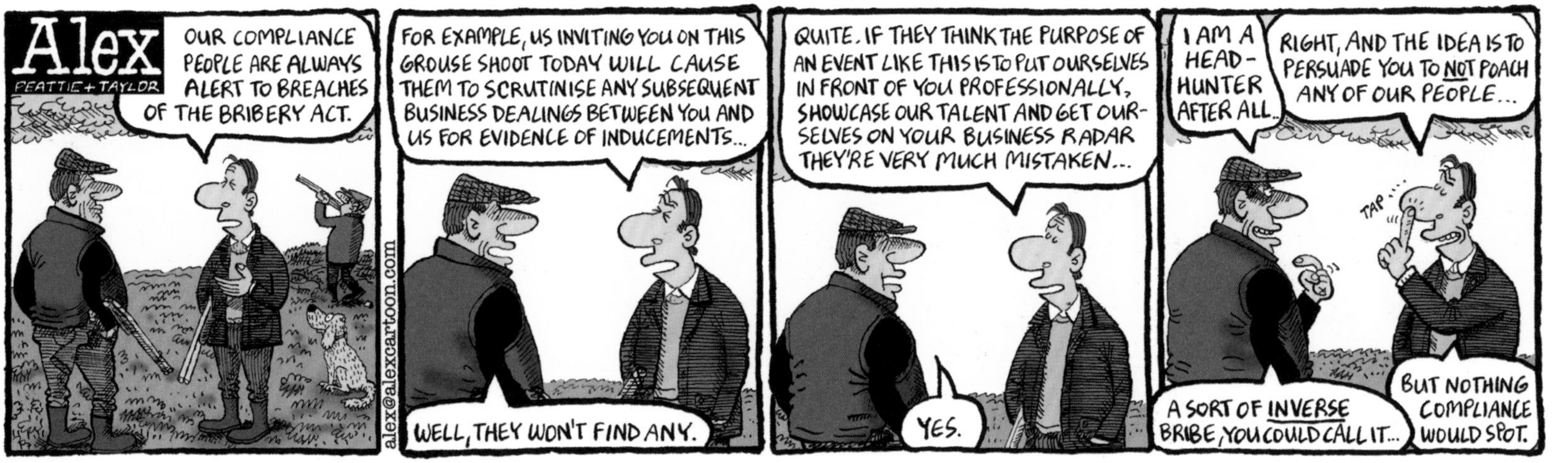
Alex
PEATTIE + TAYLOR
OUR COMPLIANCE PEOPLE ARE ALWAYS ALERT TO BREACHES OF THE BRIBERY ACT.
alex@alexcartoon.com
FOR EXAMPLE, US INVITING YOU ON THIS GROUSE SHOOT TODAY WILL CAUSE THEM TO SCRUTINISE ANY SUBSEQUENT BUSINESS DEALINGS BETWEEN YOU AND US FOR EVIDENCE OF INDUCEMENTS...
WELL, THEY WON'T FIND ANY.
QUITE. IF THEY THINK THE PURPOSE OF AN EVENT LIKE THIS IS TO PUT OURSELVES IN FRONT OF YOU PROFESSIONALLY, SHOWCASE OUR TALENT AND GET OURSELVES ON YOUR BUSINESS RADAR THEY'RE VERY MUCH MISTAKEN...
YES.
I AM A HEAD-HUNTER AFTER ALL..
RIGHT, AND THE IDEA IS TO PERSUADE YOU TO NOT POACH ANY OF OUR PEOPLE...
TAP
A SORT OF INVERSE BRIBE, YOU COULD CALL IT...
BUT NOTHING COMPLIANCE WOULD SPOT.

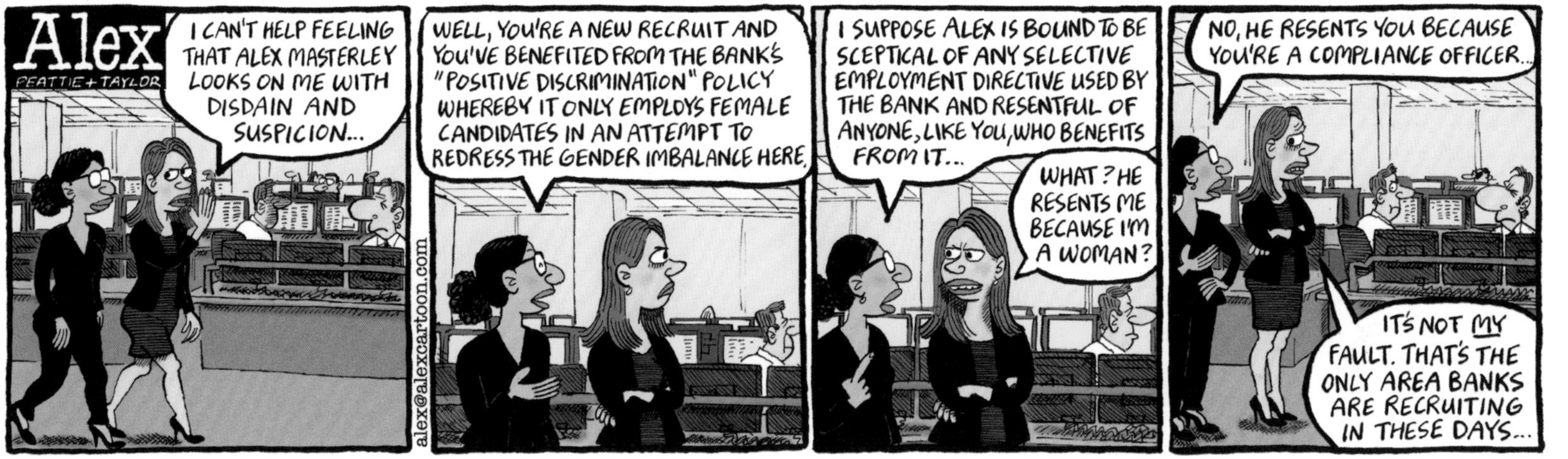
Alex
PEATTIE + TAYLOR
I CAN'T HELP FEELING THAT ALEX MASTERLEY LOOKS ON ME WITH DISDAIN AND SUSPICION...
alex@alexcartoon.com
WELL, YOU'RE A NEW RECRUIT AND YOU'VE BENEFITED FROM THE BANK'S "POSITIVE DISCRIMINATION" POLICY WHEREBY IT ONLY EMPLOYS FEMALE CANDIDATES IN AN ATTEMPT TO REDRESS THE GENDER IMBALANCE HERE.
I SUPPOSE ALEX IS BOUND TO BE SCEPTICAL OF ANY SELECTIVE EMPLOYMENT DIRECTIVE USED BY THE BANK AND RESENTFUL OF ANYONE, LIKE YOU, WHO BENEFITS FROM IT...
WHAT? HE RESENTS ME BECAUSE I'M A WOMAN?
NO, HE RESENTS YOU BECAUSE YOU'RE A COMPLIANCE OFFICER...
IT'S NOT MY FAULT. THAT'S THE ONLY AREA BANKS ARE RECRUITING IN THESE DAYS...

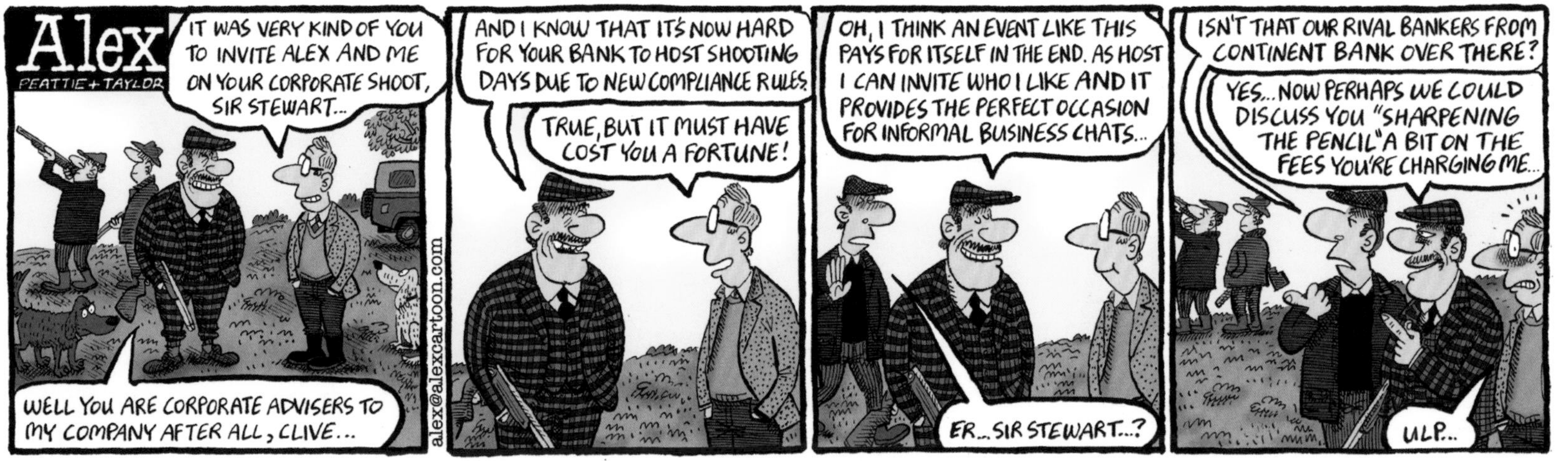
Alex
PEATTIE + TAYLOR
IT WAS VERY KIND OF YOU TO INVITE ALEX AND ME ON YOUR CORPORATE SHOOT, SIR STEWART...
WELL YOU ARE CORPORATE ADVISERS TO MY COMPANY AFTER ALL, CLIVE...
alex@alexcartoon.com
AND I KNOW THAT IT'S NOW HARD FOR YOUR BANK TO HOST SHOOTING DAYS DUE TO NEW COMPLIANCE RULES.
TRUE, BUT IT MUST HAVE COST YOU A FORTUNE!
OH, I THINK AN EVENT LIKE THIS PAYS FOR ITSELF IN THE END. AS HOST I CAN INVITE WHO I LIKE AND IT PROVIDES THE PERFECT OCCASION FOR INFORMAL BUSINESS CHATS...
ER... SIR STEWART...?
ISN'T THAT OUR RIVAL BANKERS FROM CONTINENT BANK OVER THERE?
YES... NOW PERHAPS WE COULD DISCUSS YOU "SHARPENING THE PENCIL" A BIT ON THE FEES YOU'RE CHARGING ME...
ULP...

Alex PEATTIE + TAYLOR

THE OCTOBER CLUB

Panel 1: YOU WERE THE WINNING BIDDER FOR THE GOLF DAY AT SUNNINGDALE IN THE AUCTION? COULD I TAKE THE PAYMENT?

SURE...

Panel 2: YOU KNOW, PEOPLE THINK OF US BANKERS AS BEING SELFISH, GREEDY AND MATERIALISTIC, BUT EVERY OCTOBER WE TURN OUT TO THIS DINNER AND RAISE HUNDREDS OF THOUSANDS OF POUNDS FOR CHARITY.

Panel 3: I WONDER IF PEOPLE APPRECIATE THE TRUE EXTENT OF OUR GENEROSITY?

BUT AREN'T YOU JUST GOING TO USE THIS GOLF DAY TO ENTERTAIN YOUR CLIENTS AND GET BUSINESS OFF THEM?

ER, YES...

Panel 4: BUT THANKS TO COMPLIANCE RULES I'M NOW OBLIGED TO PAY FOR IT OUT OF MY *OWN* *POCKET* INSTEAD OF BILLING IT BACK TO MY BANK LIKE I USED TO...

LET'S HOPE MY CLIENTS ARE AWARE OF THAT...

alex@alexcartoon.com

Alex PEATTIE + TAYLOR

Panel 1: SO YOU IN SENIOR MANAGEMENT DON'T HAVE ANY ISSUES WITH STEVEN HAVING GONE TRANSGENDER?

GOODNESS. NOT AT ALL!

alex@alexcartoon.com

Panel 2: LET'S FACE IT, THE CORPORATE WORLD IS CHANGING RAPIDLY AND WE WANT TO BE SEEN TO BE IN STEP WITH THE TIMES.

Panel 3: IT'S TRUE THAT STEPHANIE HAS BEEN A MAN ALL HER CAREER AT THE BANK, BUT IF SHE NOW WISHES TO IDENTIFY AS A WOMAN WE'RE FULLY SUPPORTIVE...

Panel 4: SHE'S ONE OF THE FEW WOMEN HERE WHO'S DECENTLY PAID, DUE TO HER HAVING FORMERLY BEEN MALE... AND FROM APRIL THIS NEW LEGISLATION WILL OBLIGE US TO ANNOUNCE OUR GENDER PAY GAPS...

THIS SHOULD HELP AVOID SOME EMBARRASSMENT.

Alex PEATTIE + TAYLOR

Panel 1: YOU MILLENNIALS ARE GREAT BELIEVERS IN GLOBALISATION AREN'T YOU, LEO?

IT'S JUST HOW THE MODERN WORLD WORKS, ALEX...

alex@alexcartoon.com

Panel 2: FOR EXAMPLE, THE IDEA FOR A COMPANY DEAL THAT YOU HAD THIS AFTERNOON: I'VE EMAILED IT OVER TO A TEAM OF MBAS IN INDIA. THEY CAN DO THE RESEARCH AND PUT IT INTO A REPORT RIGHT AWAY...

Panel 3: THE TIME DIFFERENCE WORKS IN OUR FAVOUR, ENABLING IT TO BE WAITING IN YOUR EMAIL IN-BOX WHEN YOU GET INTO WORK TOMORROW MORNING

WHAT'S NOT TO LIKE?

Panel 4: ER, THE FACT THAT IN THE OLD DAYS *YOU'D* HAVE HAD TO SIT UP ALL NIGHT AND DO IT?

S*D THAT. I'M OFF TO THE WINE BAR TO DRINK JÄGER BOMBS...

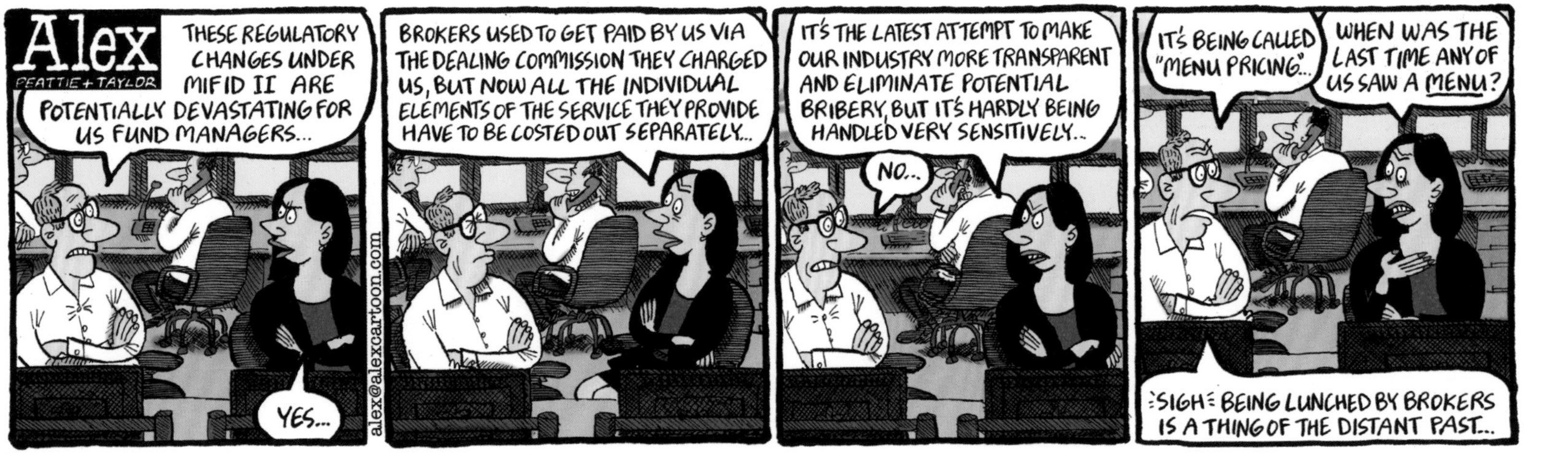
Alex
PEATTIE + TAYLOR
THESE REGULATORY CHANGES UNDER MIFID II ARE POTENTIALLY DEVASTATING FOR US FUND MANAGERS...
YES...
alex@alexcartoon.com
BROKERS USED TO GET PAID BY US VIA THE DEALING COMMISSION THEY CHARGED US, BUT NOW ALL THE INDIVIDUAL ELEMENTS OF THE SERVICE THEY PROVIDE HAVE TO BE COSTED OUT SEPARATELY...
IT'S THE LATEST ATTEMPT TO MAKE OUR INDUSTRY MORE TRANSPARENT AND ELIMINATE POTENTIAL BRIBERY, BUT IT'S HARDLY BEING HANDLED VERY SENSITIVELY...
NO...
IT'S BEING CALLED "MENU PRICING"...
WHEN WAS THE LAST TIME ANY OF US SAW A MENU?
SIGH BEING LUNCHED BY BROKERS IS A THING OF THE DISTANT PAST...

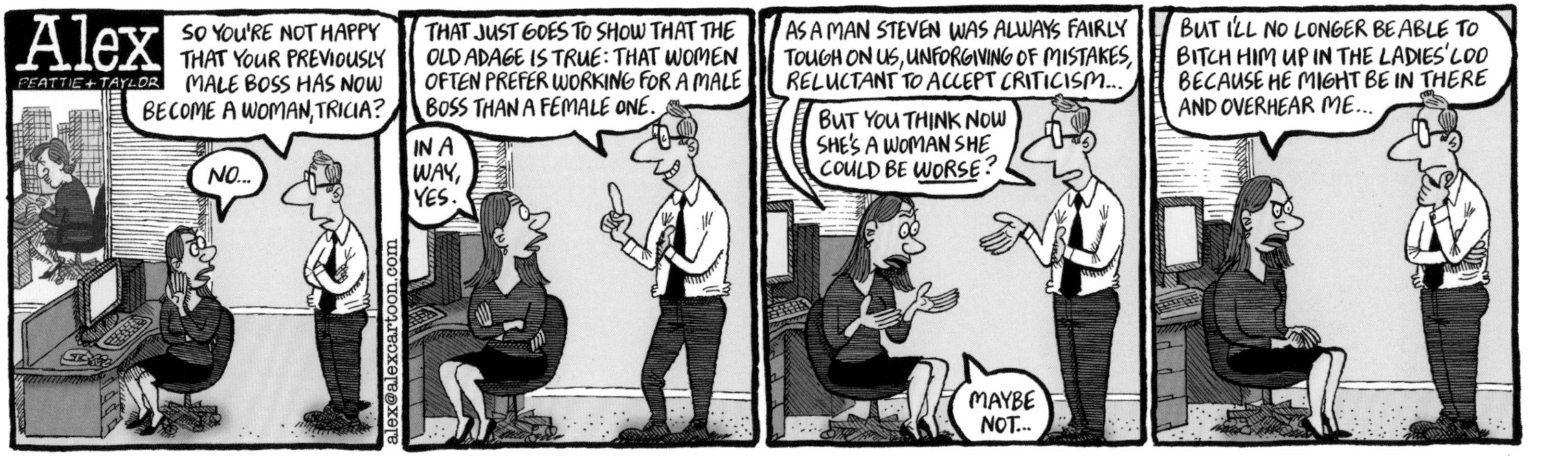
Alex
PEATTIE + TAYLOR
SO YOU'RE NOT HAPPY THAT YOUR PREVIOUSLY MALE BOSS HAS NOW BECOME A WOMAN, TRICIA?
NO...
alex@alexcartoon.com
THAT JUST GOES TO SHOW THAT THE OLD ADAGE IS TRUE: THAT WOMEN OFTEN PREFER WORKING FOR A MALE BOSS THAN A FEMALE ONE.
IN A WAY, YES.
AS A MAN STEVEN WAS ALWAYS FAIRLY TOUGH ON US, UNFORGIVING OF MISTAKES, RELUCTANT TO ACCEPT CRITICISM...
BUT YOU THINK NOW SHE'S A WOMAN SHE COULD BE WORSE?
MAYBE NOT...
BUT I'LL NO LONGER BE ABLE TO BITCH HIM UP IN THE LADIES' LOO BECAUSE HE MIGHT BE IN THERE AND OVERHEAR ME...

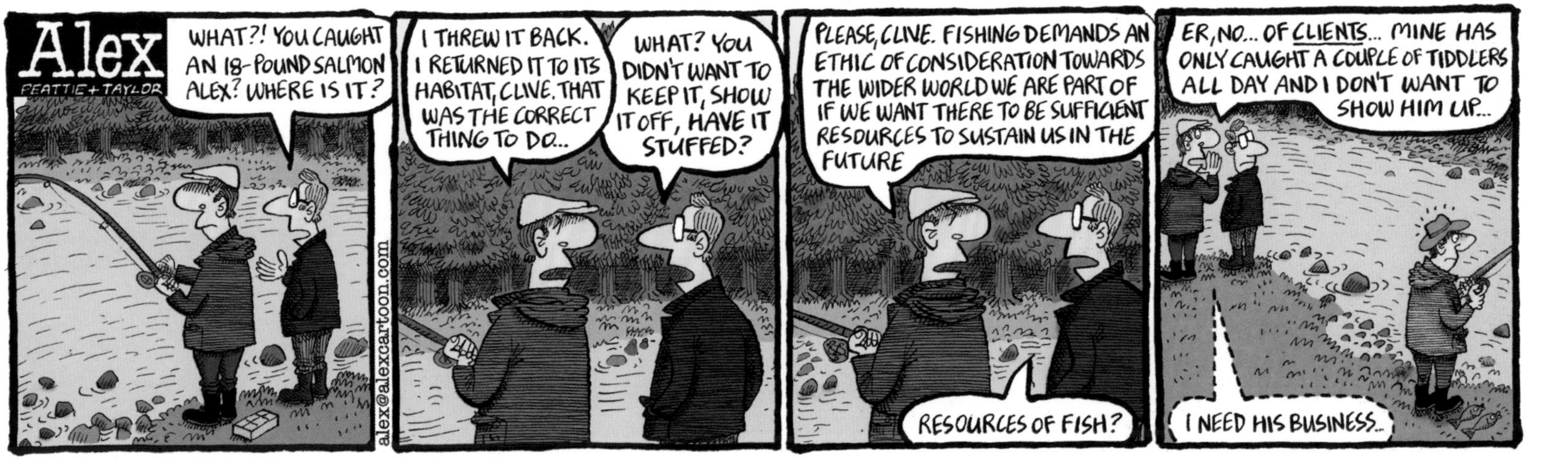
Alex
PEATTIE + TAYLOR
WHAT?! YOU CAUGHT AN 18-POUND SALMON ALEX? WHERE IS IT?
alex@alexcartoon.com
I THREW IT BACK. I RETURNED IT TO ITS HABITAT, CLIVE. THAT WAS THE CORRECT THING TO DO...
WHAT? YOU DIDN'T WANT TO KEEP IT, SHOW IT OFF, HAVE IT STUFFED?
PLEASE, CLIVE. FISHING DEMANDS AN ETHIC OF CONSIDERATION TOWARDS THE WIDER WORLD WE ARE PART OF IF WE WANT THERE TO BE SUFFICIENT RESOURCES TO SUSTAIN US IN THE FUTURE
RESOURCES OF FISH?
ER, NO... OF CLIENTS... MINE HAS ONLY CAUGHT A COUPLE OF TIDDLERS ALL DAY AND I DON'T WANT TO SHOW HIM UP...
I NEED HIS BUSINESS...

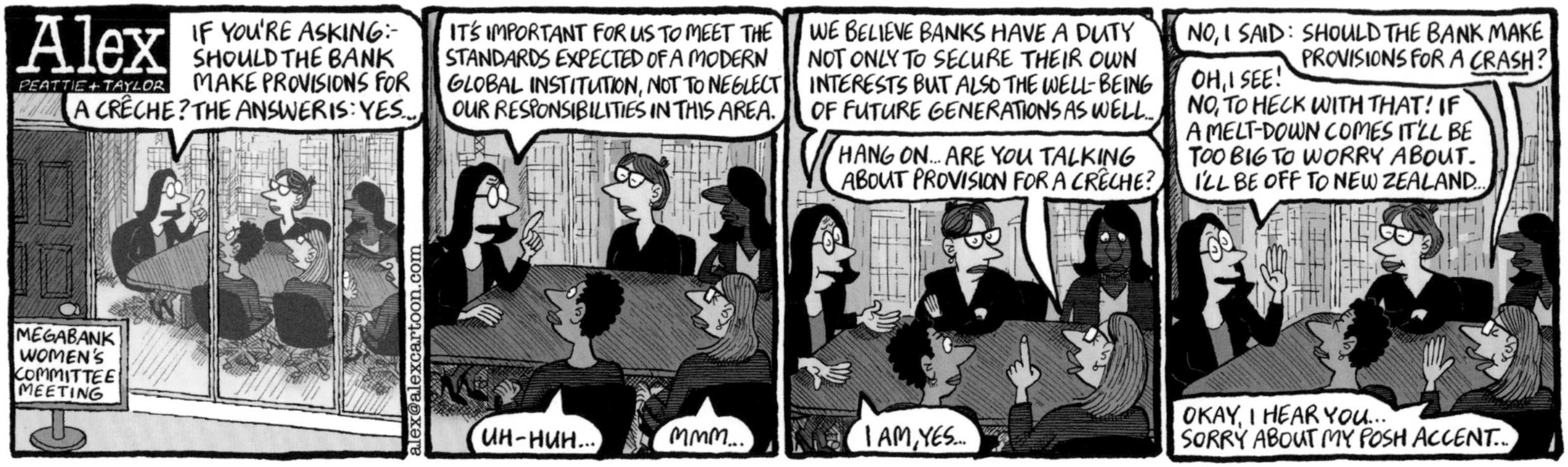
Alex
PEATTIE + TAYLOR
IF YOU'RE ASKING:- SHOULD THE BANK MAKE PROVISIONS FOR A CRÊCHE? THE ANSWER IS: YES...
MEGABANK WOMEN'S COMMITTEE MEETING
IT'S IMPORTANT FOR US TO MEET THE STANDARDS EXPECTED OF A MODERN GLOBAL INSTITUTION, NOT TO NEGLECT OUR RESPONSIBILITIES IN THIS AREA.
UH-HUH...
MMM...
alex@alexcartoon.com
WE BELIEVE BANKS HAVE A DUTY NOT ONLY TO SECURE THEIR OWN INTERESTS BUT ALSO THE WELL-BEING OF FUTURE GENERATIONS AS WELL...
HANG ON... ARE YOU TALKING ABOUT PROVISION FOR A CRÊCHE?
I AM, YES...
NO, I SAID: SHOULD THE BANK MAKE PROVISIONS FOR A CRASH?
OH, I SEE! NO, TO HECK WITH THAT! IF A MELT-DOWN COMES IT'LL BE TOO BIG TO WORRY ABOUT. I'LL BE OFF TO NEW ZEALAND...
OKAY, I HEAR YOU... SORRY ABOUT MY POSH ACCENT...

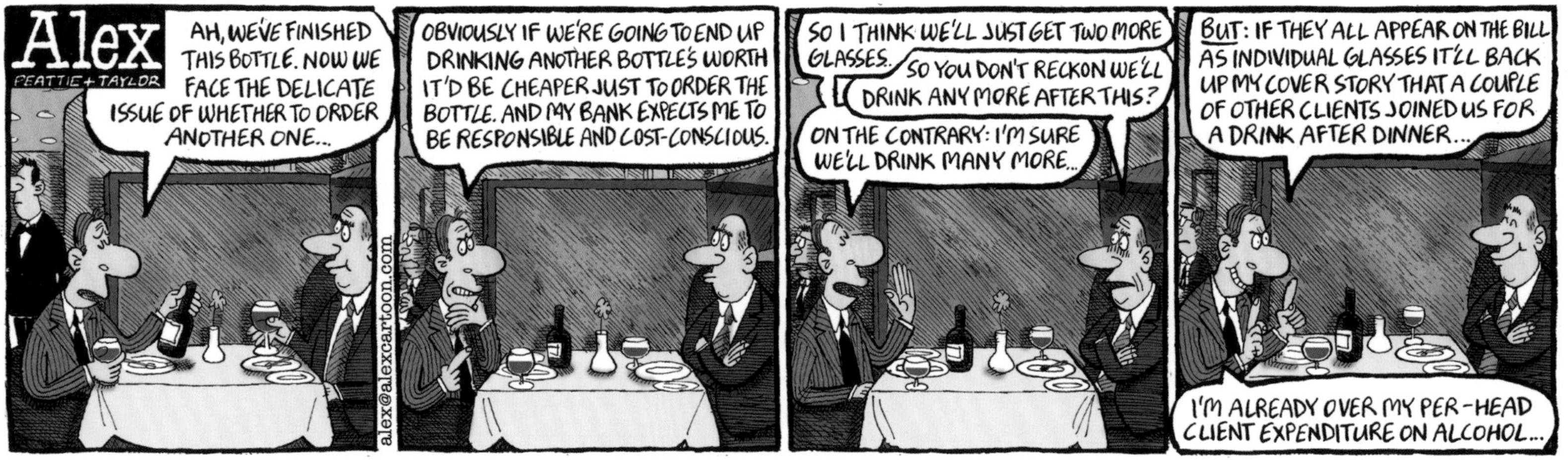
Alex
PEATTIE + TAYLOR
AH, WE'VE FINISHED THIS BOTTLE. NOW WE FACE THE DELICATE ISSUE OF WHETHER TO ORDER ANOTHER ONE...
OBVIOUSLY IF WE'RE GOING TO END UP DRINKING ANOTHER BOTTLE'S WORTH IT'D BE CHEAPER JUST TO ORDER THE BOTTLE. AND MY BANK EXPECTS ME TO BE RESPONSIBLE AND COST-CONSCIOUS.
alex@alexcartoon.com
SO I THINK WE'LL JUST GET TWO MORE GLASSES.
SO YOU DON'T RECKON WE'LL DRINK ANY MORE AFTER THIS?
ON THE CONTRARY: I'M SURE WE'LL DRINK MANY MORE...
BUT: IF THEY ALL APPEAR ON THE BILL AS INDIVIDUAL GLASSES IT'LL BACK UP MY COVER STORY THAT A COUPLE OF OTHER CLIENTS JOINED US FOR A DRINK AFTER DINNER...
I'M ALREADY OVER MY PER-HEAD CLIENT EXPENDITURE ON ALCOHOL...

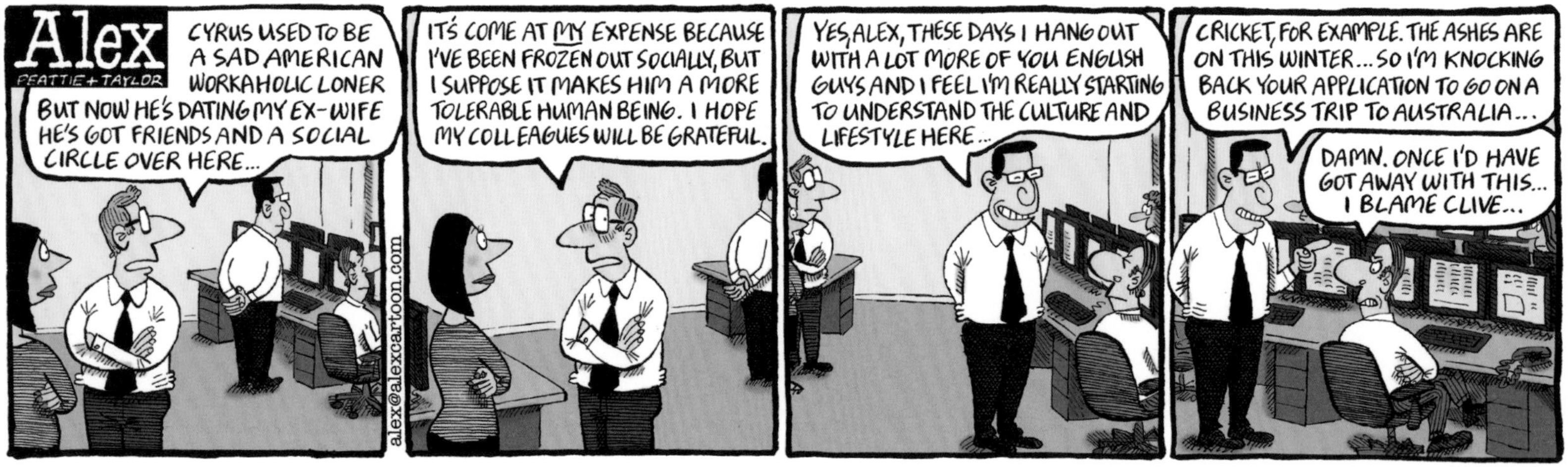
Alex
PEATTIE + TAYLOR
CYRUS USED TO BE A SAD AMERICAN WORKAHOLIC LONER BUT NOW HE'S DATING MY EX-WIFE HE'S GOT FRIENDS AND A SOCIAL CIRCLE OVER HERE...
IT'S COME AT MY EXPENSE BECAUSE I'VE BEEN FROZEN OUT SOCIALLY, BUT I SUPPOSE IT MAKES HIM A MORE TOLERABLE HUMAN BEING. I HOPE MY COLLEAGUES WILL BE GRATEFUL.
alex@alexcartoon.com
YES, ALEX, THESE DAYS I HANG OUT WITH A LOT MORE OF YOU ENGLISH GUYS AND I FEEL I'M REALLY STARTING TO UNDERSTAND THE CULTURE AND LIFESTYLE HERE...
CRICKET, FOR EXAMPLE. THE ASHES ARE ON THIS WINTER... SO I'M KNOCKING BACK YOUR APPLICATION TO GO ON A BUSINESS TRIP TO AUSTRALIA...
DAMN. ONCE I'D HAVE GOT AWAY WITH THIS... I BLAME CLIVE...

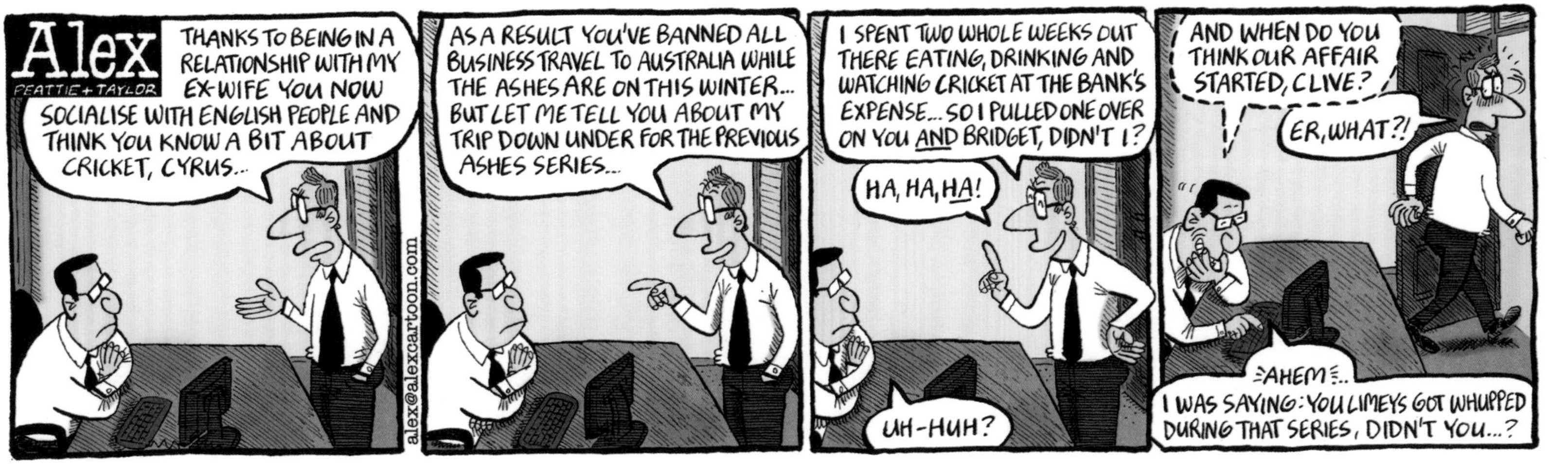
Alex
PEATTIE+TAYLOR
THANKS TO BEING IN A RELATIONSHIP WITH MY EX-WIFE YOU NOW SOCIALISE WITH ENGLISH PEOPLE AND THINK YOU KNOW A BIT ABOUT CRICKET, CYRUS...
AS A RESULT YOU'VE BANNED ALL BUSINESS TRAVEL TO AUSTRALIA WHILE THE ASHES ARE ON THIS WINTER... BUT LET ME TELL YOU ABOUT MY TRIP DOWN UNDER FOR THE PREVIOUS ASHES SERIES...
alex@alexcartoon.com
I SPENT TWO WHOLE WEEKS OUT THERE EATING, DRINKING AND WATCHING CRICKET AT THE BANK'S EXPENSE... SO I PULLED ONE OVER ON YOU AND BRIDGET, DIDN'T I?
HA, HA, HA!
UH-HUH?
AND WHEN DO YOU THINK OUR AFFAIR STARTED, CLIVE?
ER, WHAT?!
AHEM...
I WAS SAYING: YOU LIMEYS GOT WHUPPED DURING THAT SERIES, DIDN'T YOU...?

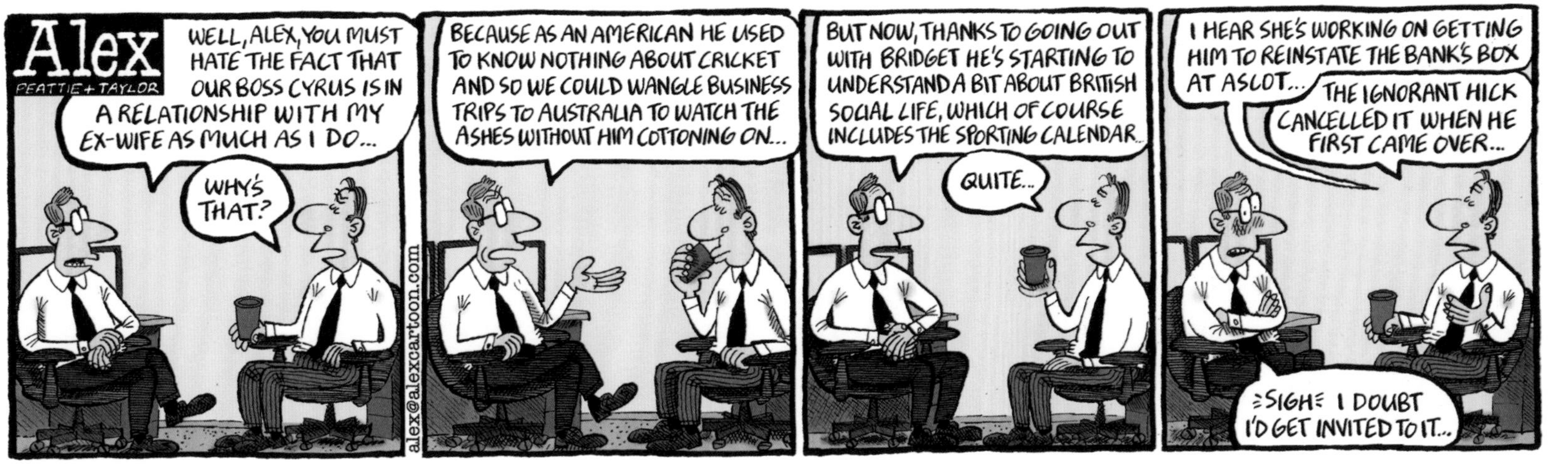
Alex
PEATTIE+TAYLOR
WELL, ALEX, YOU MUST HATE THE FACT THAT OUR BOSS CYRUS IS IN A RELATIONSHIP WITH MY EX-WIFE AS MUCH AS I DO...
WHY'S THAT?
BECAUSE AS AN AMERICAN HE USED TO KNOW NOTHING ABOUT CRICKET AND SO WE COULD WANGLE BUSINESS TRIPS TO AUSTRALIA TO WATCH THE ASHES WITHOUT HIM COTTONING ON...
alex@alexcartoon.com
BUT NOW, THANKS TO GOING OUT WITH BRIDGET HE'S STARTING TO UNDERSTAND A BIT ABOUT BRITISH SOCIAL LIFE, WHICH OF COURSE INCLUDES THE SPORTING CALENDAR...
QUITE...
I HEAR SHE'S WORKING ON GETTING HIM TO REINSTATE THE BANK'S BOX AT ASCOT...
THE IGNORANT HICK CANCELLED IT WHEN HE FIRST CAME OVER...
SIGH I DOUBT I'D GET INVITED TO IT...

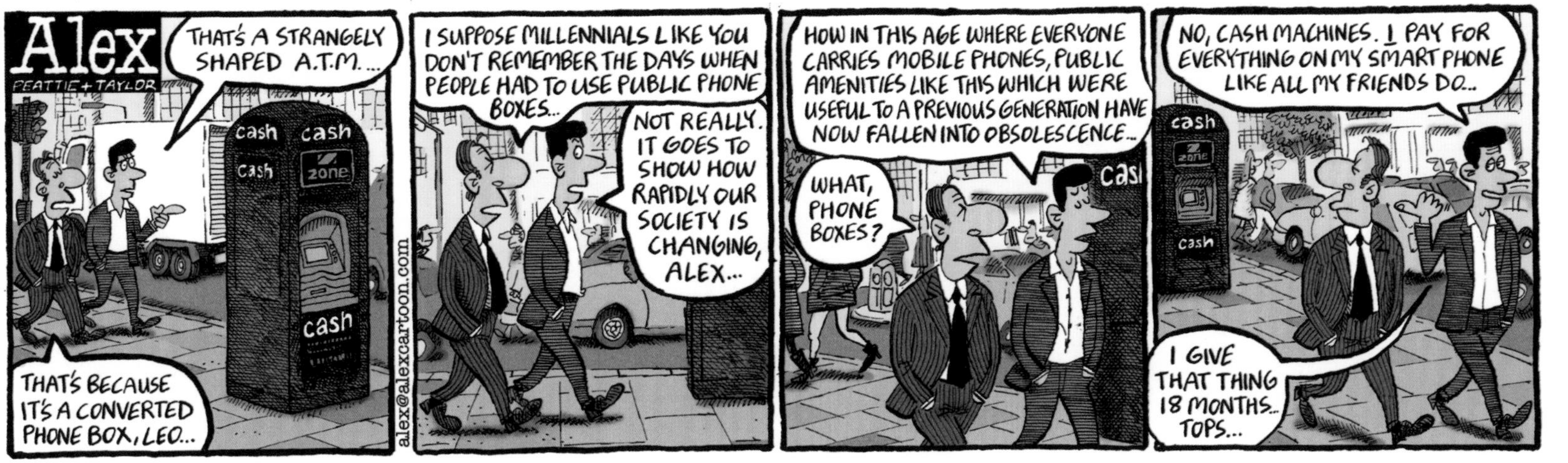
Alex
PEATTIE+TAYLOR
THAT'S A STRANGELY SHAPED A.T.M. ...
cash
cash
cash
zone
cash
THAT'S BECAUSE IT'S A CONVERTED PHONE BOX, LEO...
I SUPPOSE MILLENNIALS LIKE YOU DON'T REMEMBER THE DAYS WHEN PEOPLE HAD TO USE PUBLIC PHONE BOXES...
NOT REALLY. IT GOES TO SHOW HOW RAPIDLY OUR SOCIETY IS CHANGING, ALEX...
alex@alexcartoon.com
HOW IN THIS AGE WHERE EVERYONE CARRIES MOBILE PHONES, PUBLIC AMENITIES LIKE THIS WHICH WERE USEFUL TO A PREVIOUS GENERATION HAVE NOW FALLEN INTO OBSOLESCENCE...
WHAT, PHONE BOXES?
NO, CASH MACHINES. I PAY FOR EVERYTHING ON MY SMART PHONE LIKE ALL MY FRIENDS DO...
cash
zone
cash
I GIVE THAT THING 18 MONTHS... TOPS...

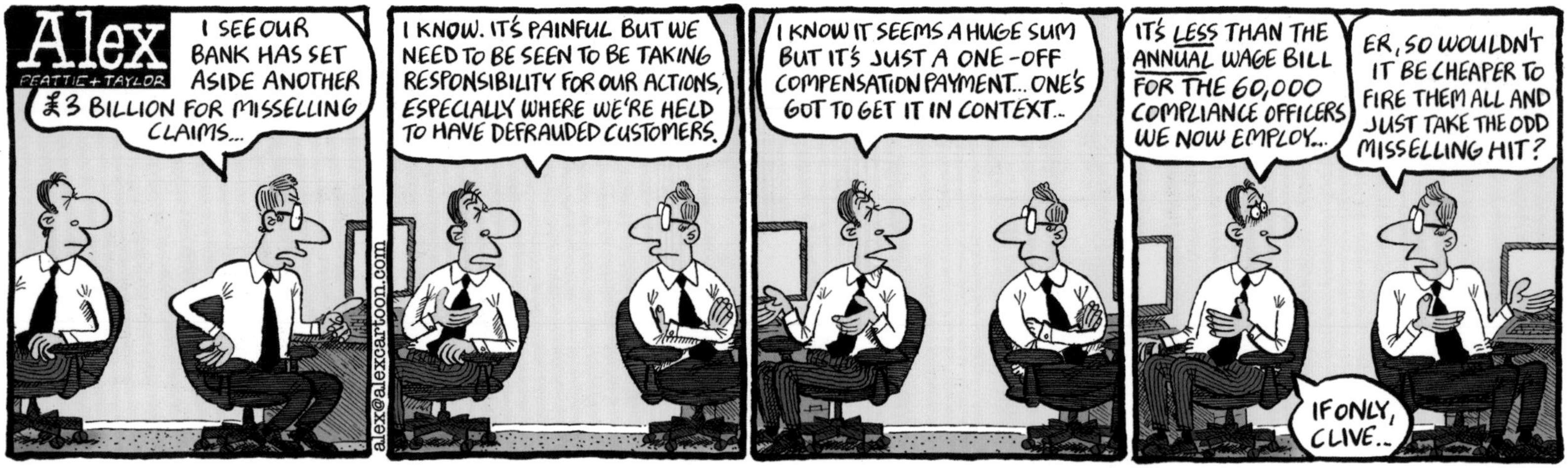
Alex
PEATTIE+TAYLOR
I SEE OUR BANK HAS SET ASIDE ANOTHER £3 BILLION FOR MISSELLING CLAIMS...
alex@alexcartoon.com
I KNOW. IT'S PAINFUL BUT WE NEED TO BE SEEN TO BE TAKING RESPONSIBILITY FOR OUR ACTIONS, ESPECIALLY WHERE WE'RE HELD TO HAVE DEFRAUDED CUSTOMERS.
I KNOW IT SEEMS A HUGE SUM BUT IT'S JUST A ONE-OFF COMPENSATION PAYMENT... ONE'S GOT TO GET IT IN CONTEXT...
IT'S LESS THAN THE ANNUAL WAGE BILL FOR THE 60,000 COMPLIANCE OFFICERS WE NOW EMPLOY...
ER, SO WOULDN'T IT BE CHEAPER TO FIRE THEM ALL AND JUST TAKE THE ODD MISSELLING HIT?
IF ONLY, CLIVE...

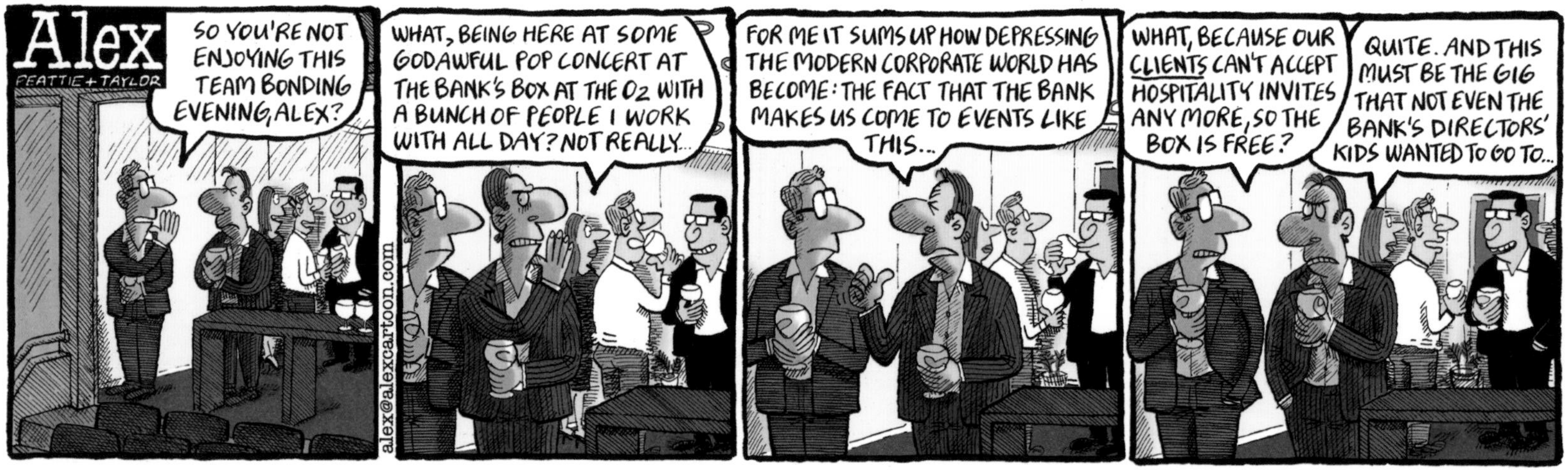
Alex
PEATTIE+TAYLOR
SO YOU'RE NOT ENJOYING THIS TEAM BONDING EVENING, ALEX?
alex@alexcartoon.com
WHAT, BEING HERE AT SOME GODAWFUL POP CONCERT AT THE BANK'S BOX AT THE O2 WITH A BUNCH OF PEOPLE I WORK WITH ALL DAY? NOT REALLY...
FOR ME IT SUMS UP HOW DEPRESSING THE MODERN CORPORATE WORLD HAS BECOME: THE FACT THAT THE BANK MAKES US COME TO EVENTS LIKE THIS...
WHAT, BECAUSE OUR CLIENTS CAN'T ACCEPT HOSPITALITY INVITES ANY MORE, SO THE BOX IS FREE?
QUITE. AND THIS MUST BE THE GIG THAT NOT EVEN THE BANK'S DIRECTORS' KIDS WANTED TO GO TO...

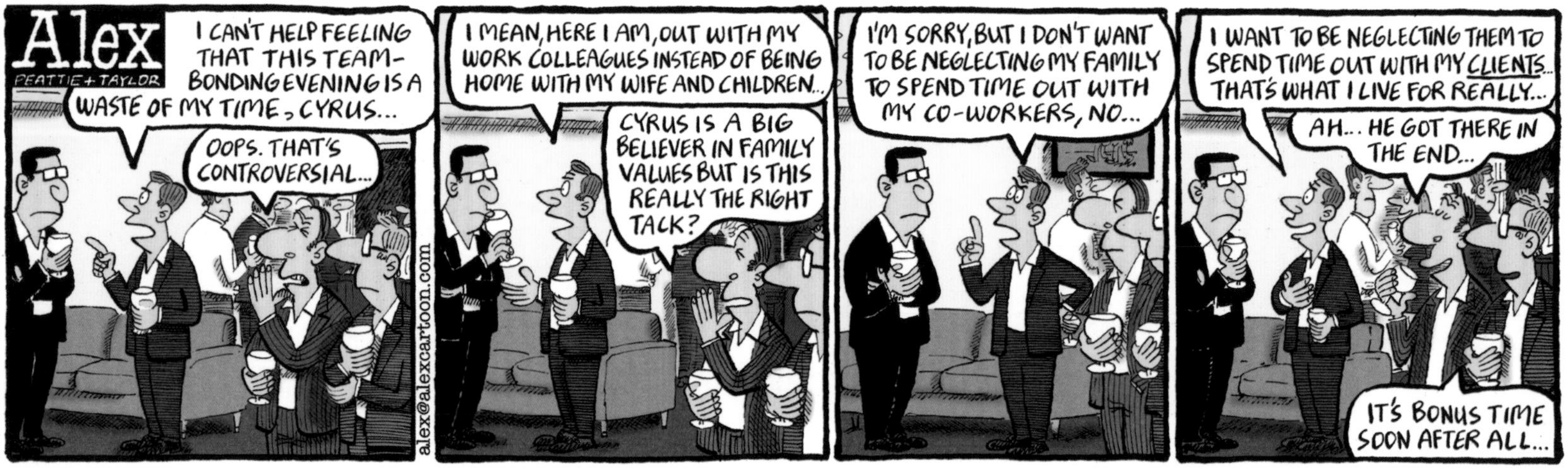
Alex
PEATTIE+TAYLOR
I CAN'T HELP FEELING THAT THIS TEAM-BONDING EVENING IS A WASTE OF MY TIME, CYRUS...
OOPS. THAT'S CONTROVERSIAL...
alex@alexcartoon.com
I MEAN, HERE I AM, OUT WITH MY WORK COLLEAGUES INSTEAD OF BEING HOME WITH MY WIFE AND CHILDREN...
CYRUS IS A BIG BELIEVER IN FAMILY VALUES BUT IS THIS REALLY THE RIGHT TACK?
I'M SORRY, BUT I DON'T WANT TO BE NEGLECTING MY FAMILY TO SPEND TIME OUT WITH MY CO-WORKERS, NO...
I WANT TO BE NEGLECTING THEM TO SPEND TIME OUT WITH MY CLIENTS... THAT'S WHAT I LIVE FOR REALLY...
AH... HE GOT THERE IN THE END...
IT'S BONUS TIME SOON AFTER ALL...

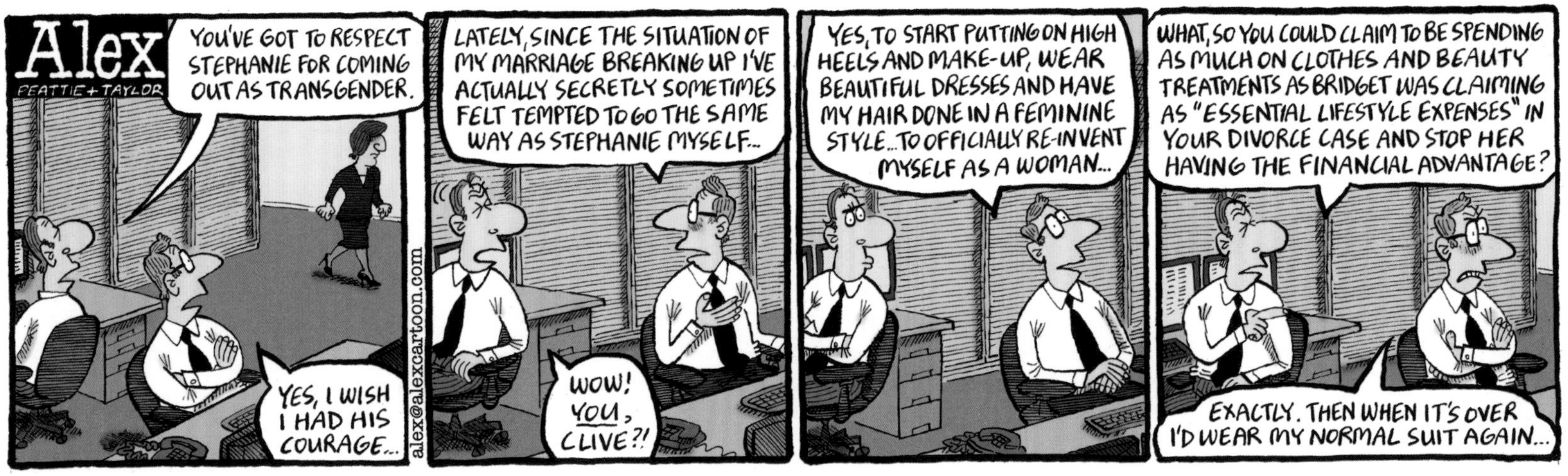
Alex
PEATTIE + TAYLOR
YOU'VE GOT TO RESPECT STEPHANIE FOR COMING OUT AS TRANSGENDER.
YES, I WISH I HAD HIS COURAGE...
alex@alexcartoon.com
LATELY, SINCE THE SITUATION OF MY MARRIAGE BREAKING UP I'VE ACTUALLY SECRETLY SOMETIMES FELT TEMPTED TO GO THE SAME WAY AS STEPHANIE MYSELF...
WOW! YOU, CLIVE?!
YES, TO START PUTTING ON HIGH HEELS AND MAKE-UP, WEAR BEAUTIFUL DRESSES AND HAVE MY HAIR DONE IN A FEMININE STYLE... TO OFFICIALLY RE-INVENT MYSELF AS A WOMAN...
WHAT, SO YOU COULD CLAIM TO BE SPENDING AS MUCH ON CLOTHES AND BEAUTY TREATMENTS AS BRIDGET WAS CLAIMING AS "ESSENTIAL LIFESTYLE EXPENSES" IN YOUR DIVORCE CASE AND STOP HER HAVING THE FINANCIAL ADVANTAGE?
EXACTLY. THEN WHEN IT'S OVER I'D WEAR MY NORMAL SUIT AGAIN...

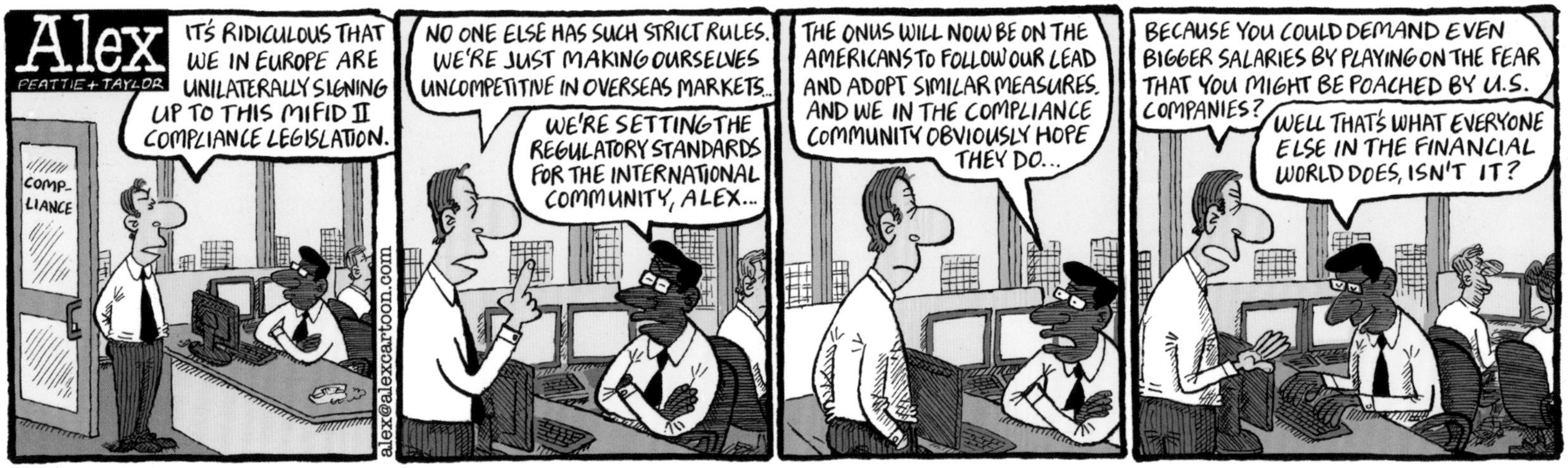
Alex
PEATTIE + TAYLOR
IT'S RIDICULOUS THAT WE IN EUROPE ARE UNILATERALLY SIGNING UP TO THIS MIFID II COMPLIANCE LEGISLATION.
COMP-LIANCE
alex@alexcartoon.com
NO ONE ELSE HAS SUCH STRICT RULES. WE'RE JUST MAKING OURSELVES UNCOMPETITIVE IN OVERSEAS MARKETS...
WE'RE SETTING THE REGULATORY STANDARDS FOR THE INTERNATIONAL COMMUNITY, ALEX...
THE ONUS WILL NOW BE ON THE AMERICANS TO FOLLOW OUR LEAD AND ADOPT SIMILAR MEASURES. AND WE IN THE COMPLIANCE COMMUNITY OBVIOUSLY HOPE THEY DO...
BECAUSE YOU COULD DEMAND EVEN BIGGER SALARIES BY PLAYING ON THE FEAR THAT YOU MIGHT BE POACHED BY U.S. COMPANIES?
WELL THAT'S WHAT EVERYONE ELSE IN THE FINANCIAL WORLD DOES, ISN'T IT?

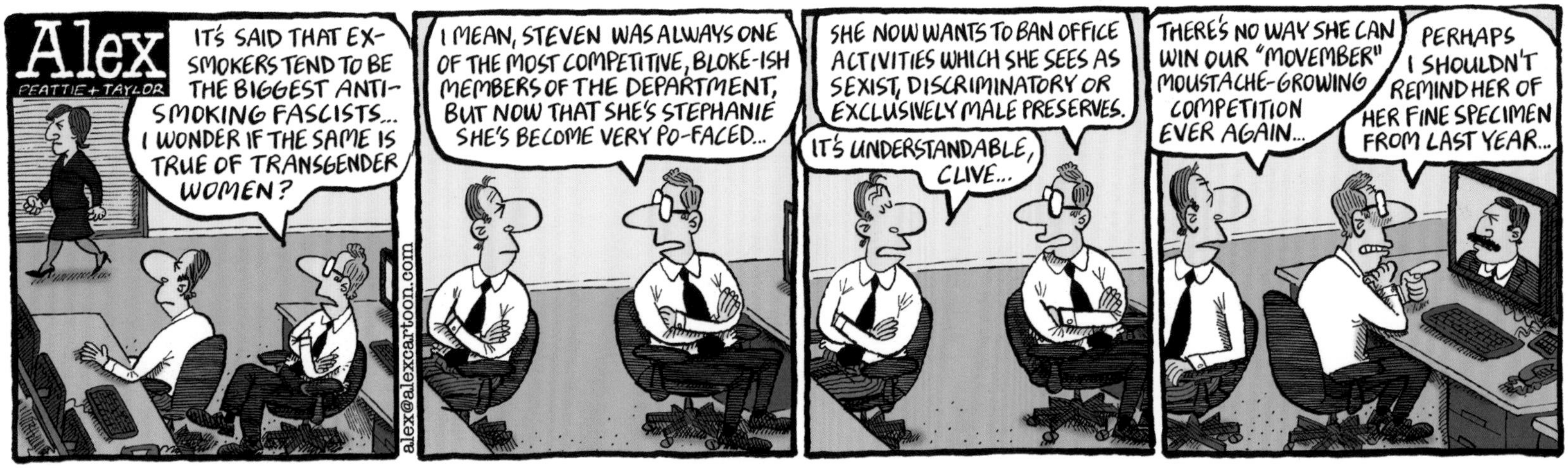
Alex
PEATTIE + TAYLOR
IT'S SAID THAT EX-SMOKERS TEND TO BE THE BIGGEST ANTI-SMOKING FASCISTS... I WONDER IF THE SAME IS TRUE OF TRANSGENDER WOMEN?
alex@alexcartoon.com
I MEAN, STEVEN WAS ALWAYS ONE OF THE MOST COMPETITIVE, BLOKE-ISH MEMBERS OF THE DEPARTMENT, BUT NOW THAT SHE'S STEPHANIE SHE'S BECOME VERY PO-FACED...
SHE NOW WANTS TO BAN OFFICE ACTIVITIES WHICH SHE SEES AS SEXIST, DISCRIMINATORY OR EXCLUSIVELY MALE PRESERVES.
IT'S UNDERSTANDABLE, CLIVE...
THERE'S NO WAY SHE CAN WIN OUR "MOVEMBER" MOUSTACHE-GROWING COMPETITION EVER AGAIN...
PERHAPS I SHOULDN'T REMIND HER OF HER FINE SPECIMEN FROM LAST YEAR...

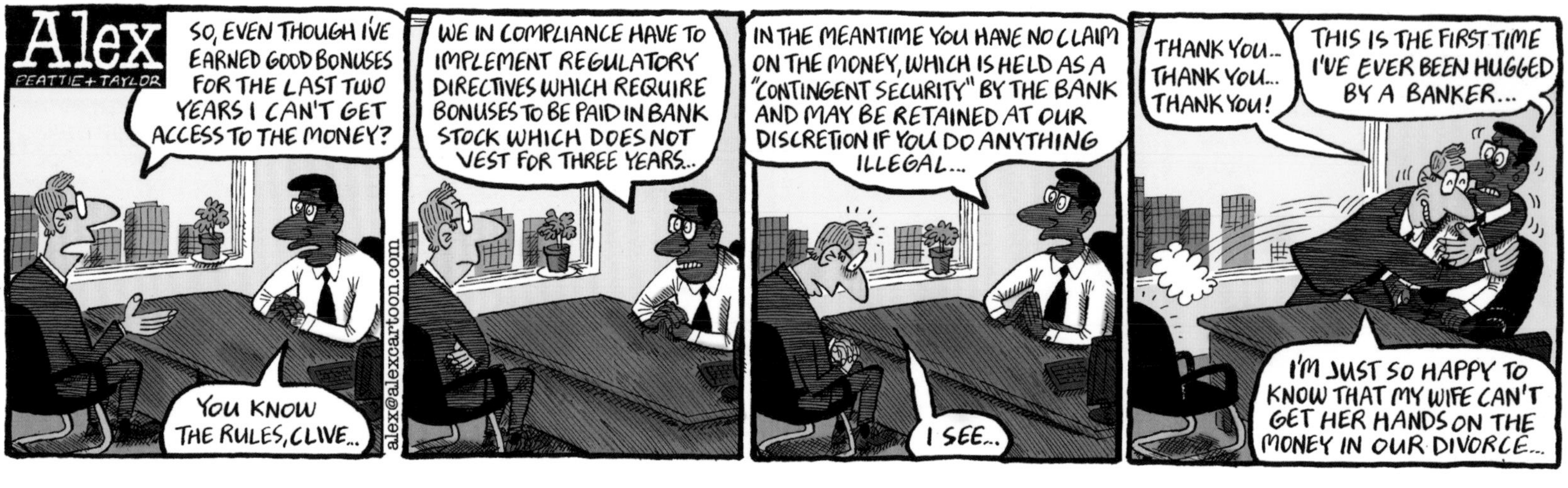
Alex
PEATTIE + TAYLOR
SO, EVEN THOUGH I'VE EARNED GOOD BONUSES FOR THE LAST TWO YEARS I CAN'T GET ACCESS TO THE MONEY?
YOU KNOW THE RULES, CLIVE...
alex@alexcartoon.com
WE IN COMPLIANCE HAVE TO IMPLEMENT REGULATORY DIRECTIVES WHICH REQUIRE BONUSES TO BE PAID IN BANK STOCK WHICH DOES NOT VEST FOR THREE YEARS...
IN THE MEANTIME YOU HAVE NO CLAIM ON THE MONEY, WHICH IS HELD AS A "CONTINGENT SECURITY" BY THE BANK AND MAY BE RETAINED AT OUR DISCRETION IF YOU DO ANYTHING ILLEGAL...
I SEE...
THANK YOU... THANK YOU... THANK YOU!
THIS IS THE FIRST TIME I'VE EVER BEEN HUGGED BY A BANKER...
I'M JUST SO HAPPY TO KNOW THAT MY WIFE CAN'T GET HER HANDS ON THE MONEY IN OUR DIVORCE...

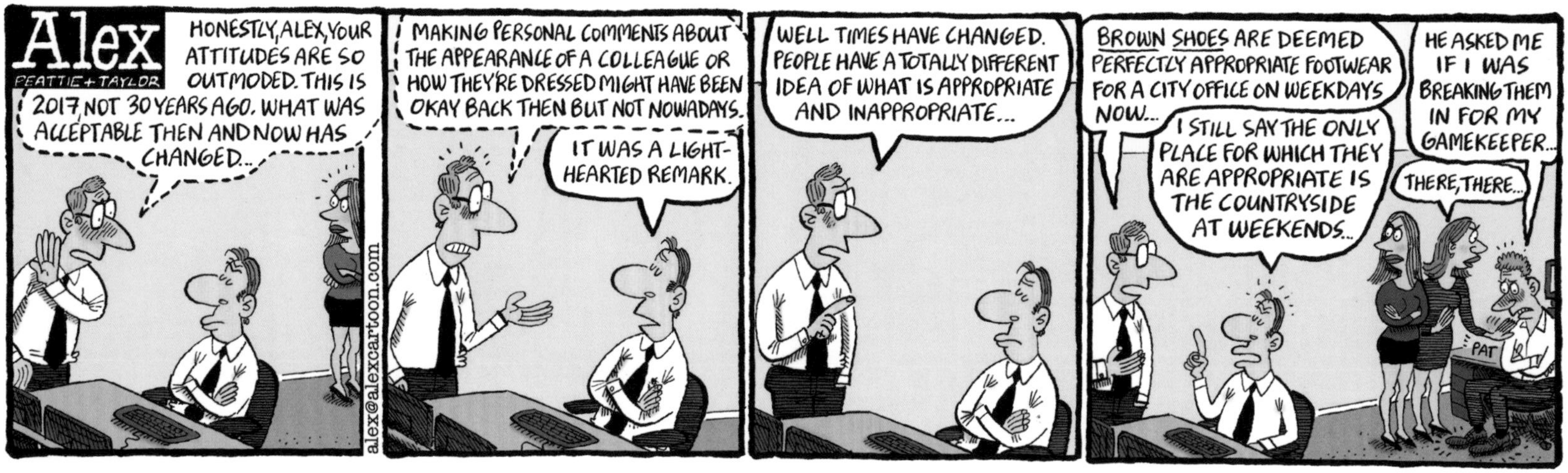
Alex
PEATTIE + TAYLOR
HONESTLY, ALEX, YOUR ATTITUDES ARE SO OUTMODED. THIS IS 2017, NOT 30 YEARS AGO. WHAT WAS ACCEPTABLE THEN AND NOW HAS CHANGED...
alex@alexcartoon.com
MAKING PERSONAL COMMENTS ABOUT THE APPEARANCE OF A COLLEAGUE OR HOW THEY'RE DRESSED MIGHT HAVE BEEN OKAY BACK THEN BUT NOT NOWADAYS.
IT WAS A LIGHT-HEARTED REMARK.
WELL TIMES HAVE CHANGED. PEOPLE HAVE A TOTALLY DIFFERENT IDEA OF WHAT IS APPROPRIATE AND INAPPROPRIATE...
BROWN SHOES ARE DEEMED PERFECTLY APPROPRIATE FOOTWEAR FOR A CITY OFFICE ON WEEKDAYS NOW...
I STILL SAY THE ONLY PLACE FOR WHICH THEY ARE APPROPRIATE IS THE COUNTRYSIDE AT WEEKENDS...
HE ASKED ME IF I WAS BREAKING THEM IN FOR MY GAMEKEEPER...
THERE, THERE...
PAT

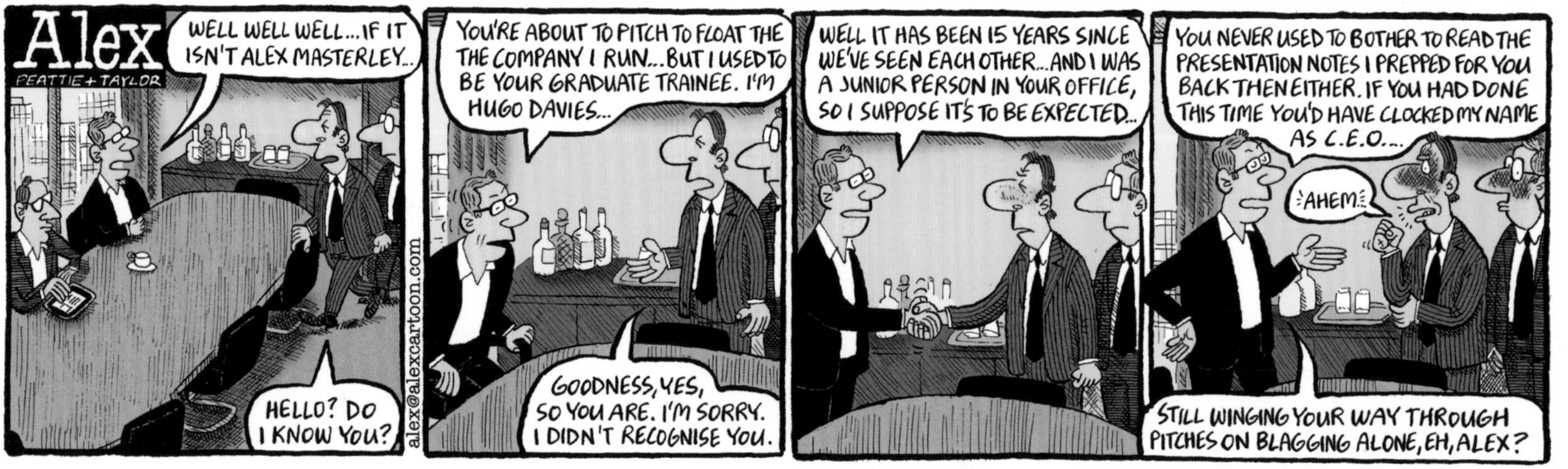
Alex
PEATTIE + TAYLOR
WELL WELL WELL... IF IT ISN'T ALEX MASTERLEY...
HELLO? DO I KNOW YOU?
alex@alexcartoon.com
YOU'RE ABOUT TO PITCH TO FLOAT THE THE COMPANY I RUN... BUT I USED TO BE YOUR GRADUATE TRAINEE. I'M HUGO DAVIES...
GOODNESS, YES, SO YOU ARE. I'M SORRY. I DIDN'T RECOGNISE YOU.
WELL IT HAS BEEN 15 YEARS SINCE WE'VE SEEN EACH OTHER... AND I WAS A JUNIOR PERSON IN YOUR OFFICE, SO I SUPPOSE IT'S TO BE EXPECTED...
YOU NEVER USED TO BOTHER TO READ THE PRESENTATION NOTES I PREPPED FOR YOU BACK THEN EITHER. IF YOU HAD DONE THIS TIME YOU'D HAVE CLOCKED MY NAME AS C.E.O....
AHEM
STILL WINGING YOUR WAY THROUGH PITCHES ON BLAGGING ALONE, EH, ALEX?

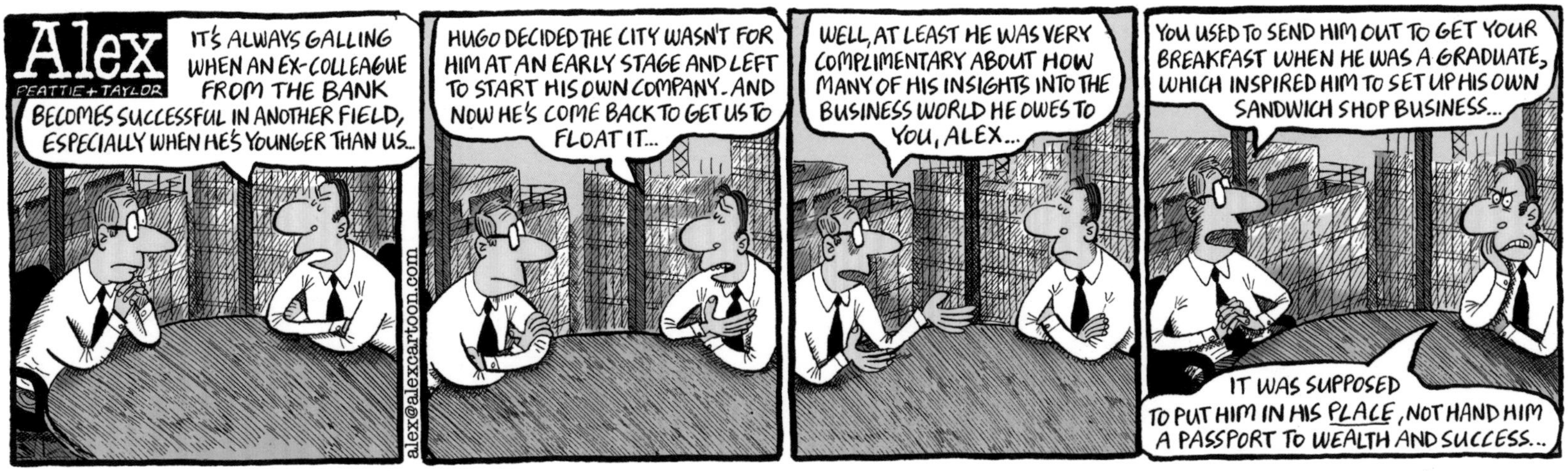
Alex
PEATTIE + TAYLOR
IT'S ALWAYS GALLING WHEN AN EX-COLLEAGUE FROM THE BANK BECOMES SUCCESSFUL IN ANOTHER FIELD, ESPECIALLY WHEN HE'S YOUNGER THAN US...
alex@alexcartoon.com
HUGO DECIDED THE CITY WASN'T FOR HIM AT AN EARLY STAGE AND LEFT TO START HIS OWN COMPANY. AND NOW HE'S COME BACK TO GET US TO FLOAT IT...
WELL, AT LEAST HE WAS VERY COMPLIMENTARY ABOUT HOW MANY OF HIS INSIGHTS INTO THE BUSINESS WORLD HE OWES TO YOU, ALEX...
YOU USED TO SEND HIM OUT TO GET YOUR BREAKFAST WHEN HE WAS A GRADUATE, WHICH INSPIRED HIM TO SET UP HIS OWN SANDWICH SHOP BUSINESS...
IT WAS SUPPOSED TO PUT HIM IN HIS PLACE, NOT HAND HIM A PASSPORT TO WEALTH AND SUCCESS...

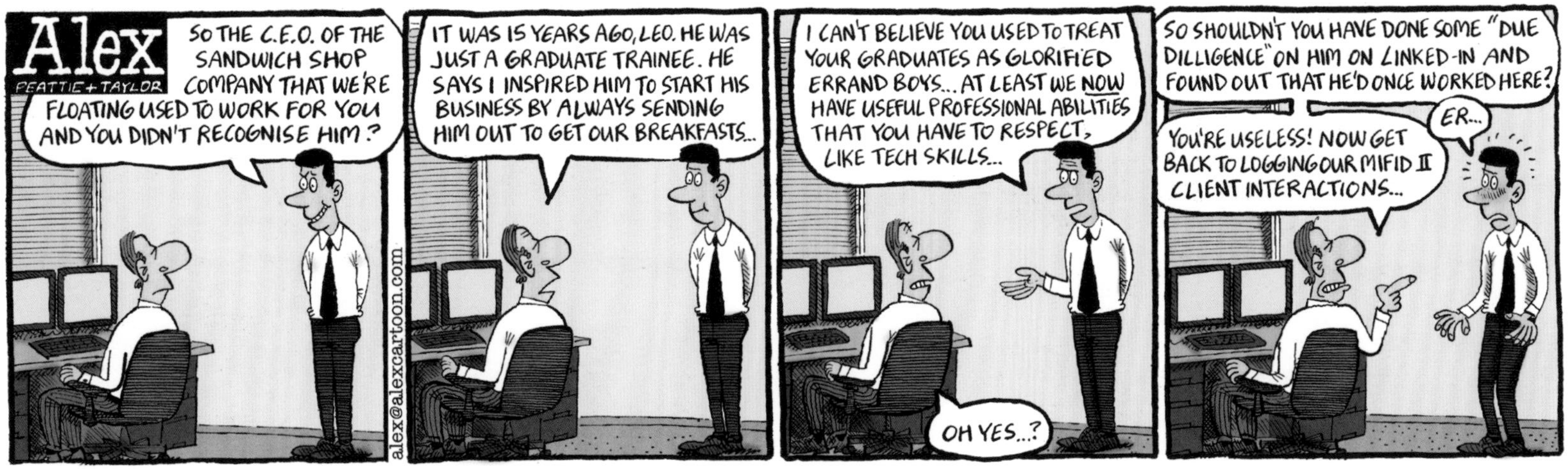
Alex
PEATTIE + TAYLOR
SO THE C.E.O. OF THE SANDWICH SHOP COMPANY THAT WE'RE FLOATING USED TO WORK FOR YOU AND YOU DIDN'T RECOGNISE HIM?
alex@alexcartoon.com
IT WAS 15 YEARS AGO, LEO. HE WAS JUST A GRADUATE TRAINEE. HE SAYS I INSPIRED HIM TO START HIS BUSINESS BY ALWAYS SENDING HIM OUT TO GET OUR BREAKFASTS...
I CAN'T BELIEVE YOU USED TO TREAT YOUR GRADUATES AS GLORIFIED ERRAND BOYS... AT LEAST WE NOW HAVE USEFUL PROFESSIONAL ABILITIES THAT YOU HAVE TO RESPECT, LIKE TECH SKILLS...
OH YES...?
SO SHOULDN'T YOU HAVE DONE SOME "DUE DILIGENCE" ON HIM ON LINKED-IN AND FOUND OUT THAT HE'D ONCE WORKED HERE?
ER...
YOU'RE USELESS! NOW GET BACK TO LOGGING OUR MIFID II CLIENT INTERACTIONS...

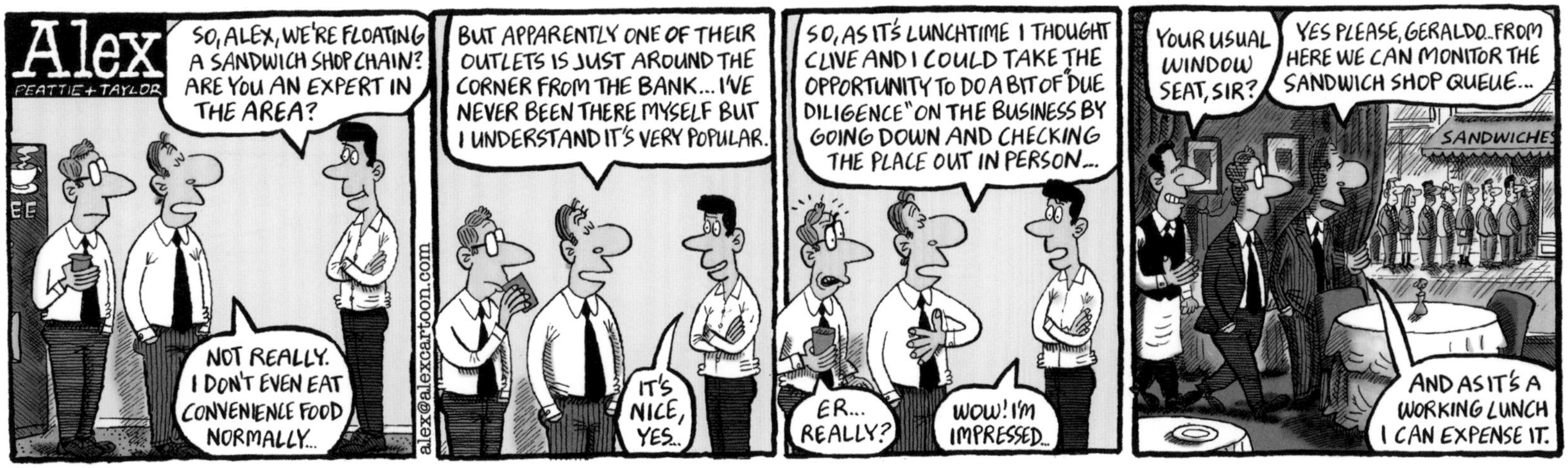
Alex
PEATTIE + TAYLOR
SO, ALEX, WE'RE FLOATING A SANDWICH SHOP CHAIN? ARE YOU AN EXPERT IN THE AREA?
NOT REALLY. I DON'T EVEN EAT CONVENIENCE FOOD NORMALLY...
alex@alexcartoon.com
BUT APPARENTLY ONE OF THEIR OUTLETS IS JUST AROUND THE CORNER FROM THE BANK... I'VE NEVER BEEN THERE MYSELF BUT I UNDERSTAND IT'S VERY POPULAR.
IT'S NICE, YES...
SO, AS IT'S LUNCHTIME I THOUGHT CLIVE AND I COULD TAKE THE OPPORTUNITY TO DO A BIT OF "DUE DILIGENCE" ON THE BUSINESS BY GOING DOWN AND CHECKING THE PLACE OUT IN PERSON...
ER... REALLY?
WOW! I'M IMPRESSED...
YOUR USUAL WINDOW SEAT, SIR?
YES PLEASE, GERALDO... FROM HERE WE CAN MONITOR THE SANDWICH SHOP QUEUE...
SANDWICHES
AND AS IT'S A WORKING LUNCH I CAN EXPENSE IT.

Alex PEATTIE + TAYLOR

Panel 1: IN THE PAST I'VE BEEN VERY SCATHING AND CYNICAL ABOUT YOU COMPLIANCE PEOPLE...

Panel 2: I'VE TENDED TO LABEL YOU AS "BUSINESS PREVENTION OFFICERS" AND CLAIM THAT YOUR SOLE RAISON D'ÊTRE IS TO STOP THE BANK FROM MAKING ANY MONEY...

Panel 3: BUT CREDIT WHERE CREDIT'S DUE: IT'S NICE FOR ONCE TO FIND THAT COMPLIANCE RULES HAVE MADE A POSITIVE CONTRIBUTION TO THE SUCCESS OF A DEAL I'M WORKING ON...

Panel 4: NAMELY THIS SANDWICH SHOP CHAIN WE'RE FLOATING... NOW THAT OUR CLIENTS ARE BANNED FROM ACCEPTING LUNCH INVITES DUE TO THE BRIBERY ACT AND EVERYONE EATS AT THEIR DESKS INSTEAD IT SHOULD BE A LUCRATIVE FRANCHISE...

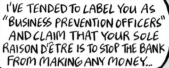

Alex PEATTIE + TAYLOR

Panel 1: IT'S SO ANNOYING HOW THE NEW COMPLIANCE REGIME FORCES EVERYONE TO REPORT ANY MEETINGS WITH ANYONE WORK-RELATED...

Panel 2: AND NOT JUST PREARRANGED LUNCHES BUT ANY HOSPITALITY RECEIVED... ANYONE PEOPLE COME ACROSS SOCIALLY WHO MIGHT BE IN THE SAME BUSINESS, AT PARTIES, BARS, EVEN ON HOLIDAY...

IT'S SO TEDIOUS, ISN'T IT?

Panel 3: WELL, I SUPPOSE IT'S BECAUSE THERE ARE ALWAYS SOME PEOPLE WHO CHOOSE TO TAKE ADVANTAGE OF A SITUATION TO ABUSE THE SYSTEM...

YES.

Panel 4: OH YES... I FORGOT... SAME WEEKEND: AFTER LUNCH AT SIR ADRIAN'S VILLA IN TUSCANY, HE OPENED A THIRD BOTTLE OF PETRUS AND WHO SHOULD TURN UP BUT RICHARD BRANSON... ARE YOU TAKING NOTES?

BECAUSE SOME PEOPLE JUST USE THE SYSTEM TO SHOW OFF...

COMPLIANCE DEPARTMENT

THERE ARE DAYS WHEN I HATE BEING A COMPLIANCE OFFICER...

Alex PEATTIE + TAYLOR

Panel 1: IT'S FUNNY: YOU INVITING ME HERE TO TRY AND PERSUADE ME TO INVEST IN THIS SANDWICH SHOP CHAIN YOU'RE FLOATING, ALEX...

WHY?

Panel 2: WELL, YOU'VE ALWAYS BEEN A BIT OF A SNOB ABOUT SANDWICHES AND REFUSED TO EAT THEM... TRUE... CONVENIENCE FOOD IS NOT SOMETHING I HAVE MUCH PERSONAL INSIGHT INTO...

Panel 3: BUT BEFORE MEETING WITH YOU ABOUT THIS I'VE SOUGHT OUT THE OPINIONS OF EXPERTS WHO REALLY KNOW THE VALUE OF LOW-COST PRE-PREPARED FOOD ITEMS...

REALLY? WHO?

Panel 4: THE BANK'S COMPLIANCE OFFICERS, WHO'VE INFORMED ME THAT IF I WERE TO OFFER YOU SO MUCH AS A BISCUIT IN THIS MEETING IT WOULD CONSTITUTE A BRIBE TO DO BUSINESS WITH MY BANK...

I PREFERRED THE OLD DAYS, OVER LUNCH...

RUMBLE...

ME TOO...

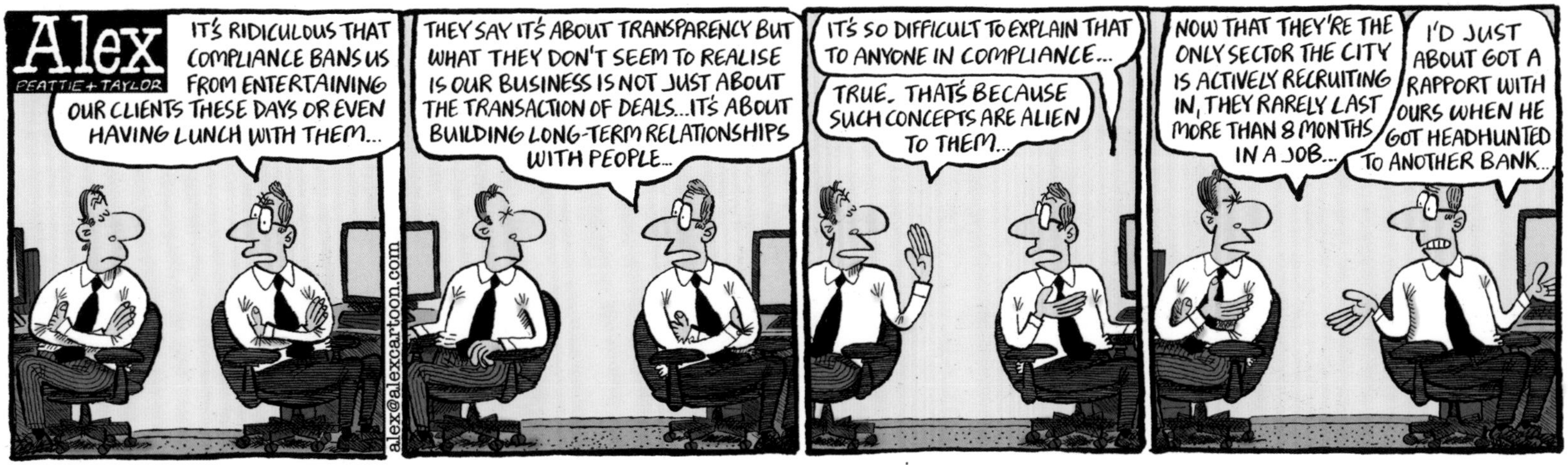
Alex
PEATTIE + TAYLOR
IT'S RIDICULOUS THAT COMPLIANCE BANS US FROM ENTERTAINING OUR CLIENTS THESE DAYS OR EVEN HAVING LUNCH WITH THEM...
alex@alexcartoon.com
THEY SAY IT'S ABOUT TRANSPARENCY BUT WHAT THEY DON'T SEEM TO REALISE IS OUR BUSINESS IS NOT JUST ABOUT THE TRANSACTION OF DEALS...IT'S ABOUT BUILDING LONG-TERM RELATIONSHIPS WITH PEOPLE...
IT'S SO DIFFICULT TO EXPLAIN THAT TO ANYONE IN COMPLIANCE...
TRUE. THAT'S BECAUSE SUCH CONCEPTS ARE ALIEN TO THEM...
NOW THAT THEY'RE THE ONLY SECTOR THE CITY IS ACTIVELY RECRUITING IN, THEY RARELY LAST MORE THAN 8 MONTHS IN A JOB...
I'D JUST ABOUT GOT A RAPPORT WITH OURS WHEN HE GOT HEADHUNTED TO ANOTHER BANK...

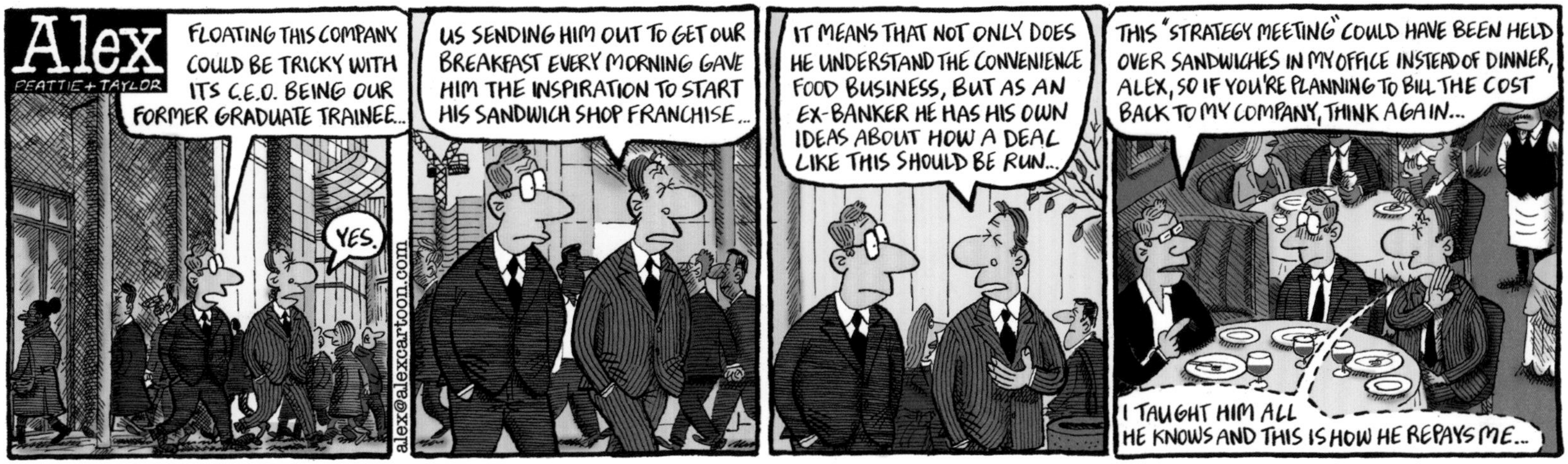
Alex
PEATTIE + TAYLOR
FLOATING THIS COMPANY COULD BE TRICKY WITH ITS C.E.O. BEING OUR FORMER GRADUATE TRAINEE...
YES.
alex@alexcartoon.com
US SENDING HIM OUT TO GET OUR BREAKFAST EVERY MORNING GAVE HIM THE INSPIRATION TO START HIS SANDWICH SHOP FRANCHISE...
IT MEANS THAT NOT ONLY DOES HE UNDERSTAND THE CONVENIENCE FOOD BUSINESS, BUT AS AN EX-BANKER HE HAS HIS OWN IDEAS ABOUT HOW A DEAL LIKE THIS SHOULD BE RUN...
THIS "STRATEGY MEETING" COULD HAVE BEEN HELD OVER SANDWICHES IN MY OFFICE INSTEAD OF DINNER, ALEX, SO IF YOU'RE PLANNING TO BILL THE COST BACK TO MY COMPANY, THINK AGAIN...
I TAUGHT HIM ALL HE KNOWS AND THIS IS HOW HE REPAYS ME...

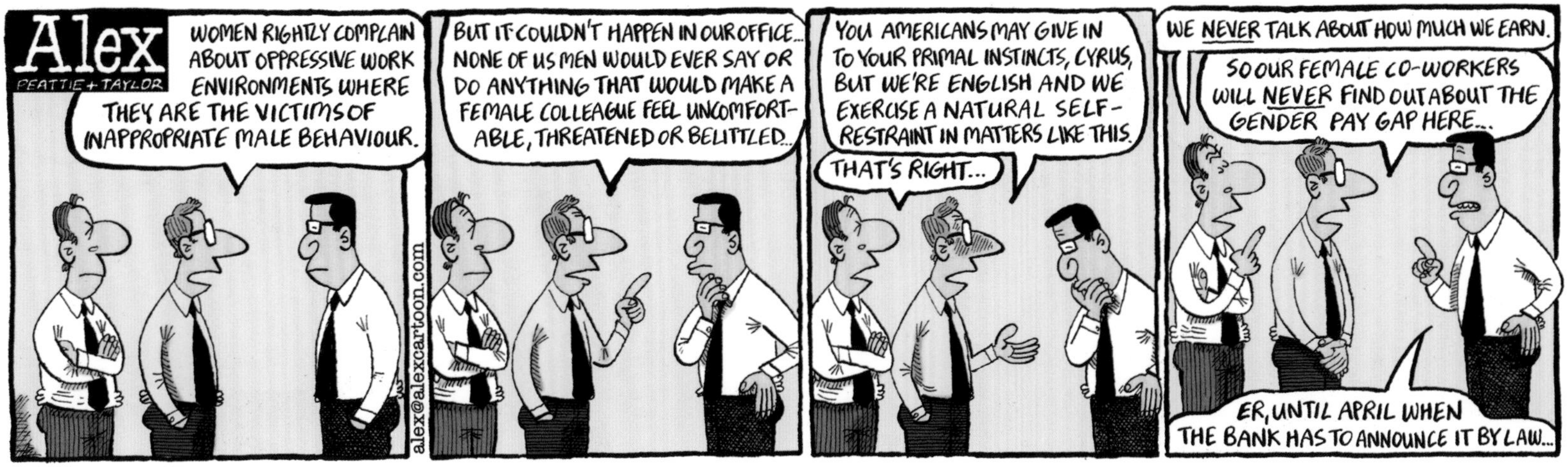
Alex
PEATTIE + TAYLOR
WOMEN RIGHTLY COMPLAIN ABOUT OPPRESSIVE WORK ENVIRONMENTS WHERE THEY ARE THE VICTIMS OF INAPPROPRIATE MALE BEHAVIOUR.
alex@alexcartoon.com
BUT IT COULDN'T HAPPEN IN OUR OFFICE... NONE OF US MEN WOULD EVER SAY OR DO ANYTHING THAT WOULD MAKE A FEMALE COLLEAGUE FEEL UNCOMFORTABLE, THREATENED OR BELITTLED...
YOU AMERICANS MAY GIVE IN TO YOUR PRIMAL INSTINCTS, CYRUS, BUT WE'RE ENGLISH AND WE EXERCISE A NATURAL SELF-RESTRAINT IN MATTERS LIKE THIS.
THAT'S RIGHT...
WE NEVER TALK ABOUT HOW MUCH WE EARN.
SO OUR FEMALE CO-WORKERS WILL NEVER FIND OUT ABOUT THE GENDER PAY GAP HERE...
ER, UNTIL APRIL WHEN THE BANK HAS TO ANNOUNCE IT BY LAW...

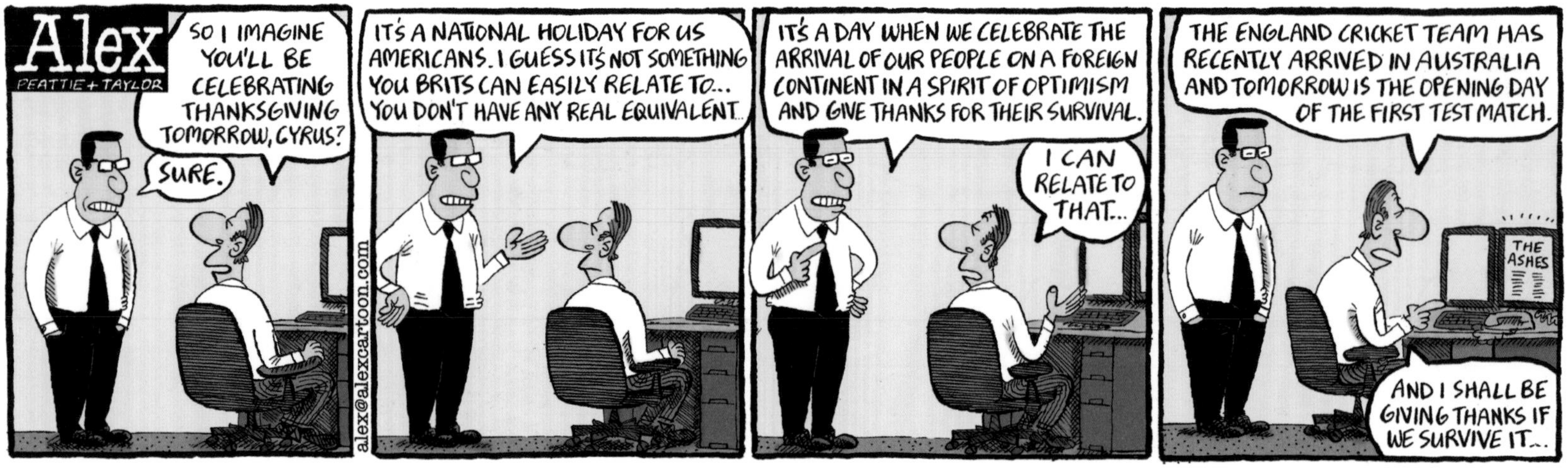
Alex
PEATTIE + TAYLOR
SO I IMAGINE YOU'LL BE CELEBRATING THANKSGIVING TOMORROW, CYRUS?
SURE.
alex@alexcartoon.com
IT'S A NATIONAL HOLIDAY FOR US AMERICANS. I GUESS IT'S NOT SOMETHING YOU BRITS CAN EASILY RELATE TO... YOU DON'T HAVE ANY REAL EQUIVALENT...
IT'S A DAY WHEN WE CELEBRATE THE ARRIVAL OF OUR PEOPLE ON A FOREIGN CONTINENT IN A SPIRIT OF OPTIMISM AND GIVE THANKS FOR THEIR SURVIVAL.
I CAN RELATE TO THAT...
THE ENGLAND CRICKET TEAM HAS RECENTLY ARRIVED IN AUSTRALIA AND TOMORROW IS THE OPENING DAY OF THE FIRST TEST MATCH.
THE ASHES
AND I SHALL BE GIVING THANKS IF WE SURVIVE IT...

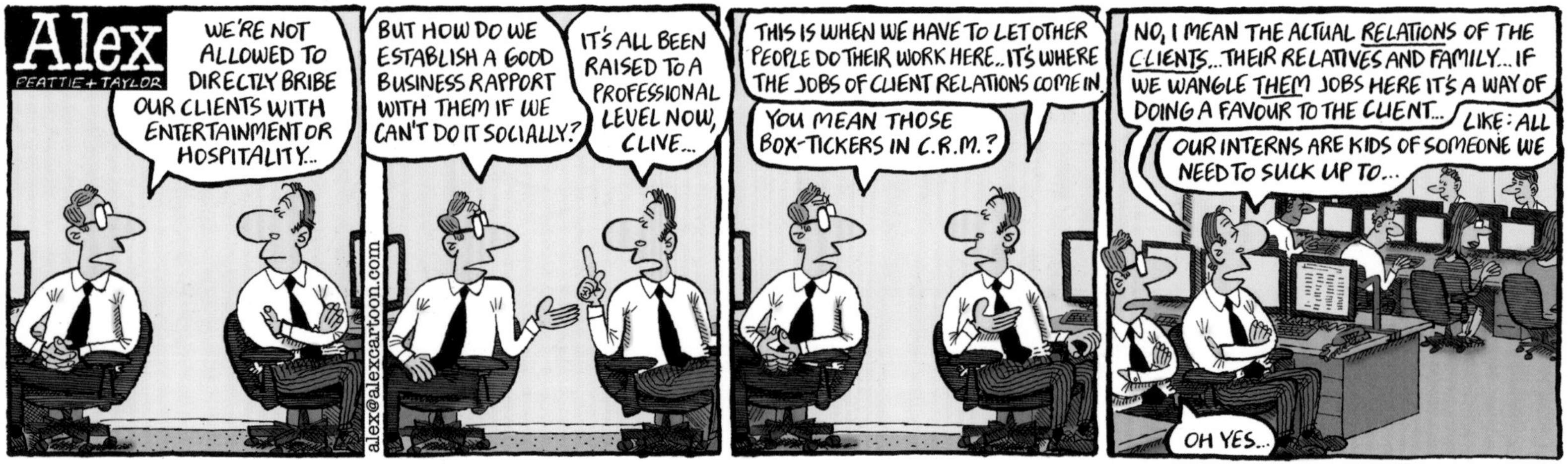
Alex
PEATTIE + TAYLOR
WE'RE NOT ALLOWED TO DIRECTLY BRIBE OUR CLIENTS WITH ENTERTAINMENT OR HOSPITALITY...
alex@alexcartoon.com
BUT HOW DO WE ESTABLISH A GOOD BUSINESS RAPPORT WITH THEM IF WE CAN'T DO IT SOCIALLY?
IT'S ALL BEEN RAISED TO A PROFESSIONAL LEVEL NOW, CLIVE...
THIS IS WHEN WE HAVE TO LET OTHER PEOPLE DO THEIR WORK HERE.. IT'S WHERE THE JOBS OF CLIENT RELATIONS COME IN.
YOU MEAN THOSE BOX-TICKERS IN C.R.M.?
NO, I MEAN THE ACTUAL RELATIONS OF THE CLIENTS... THEIR RELATIVES AND FAMILY... IF WE WANGLE THEM JOBS HERE IT'S A WAY OF DOING A FAVOUR TO THE CLIENT...
LIKE: ALL OUR INTERNS ARE KIDS OF SOMEONE WE NEED TO SUCK UP TO...
OH YES...

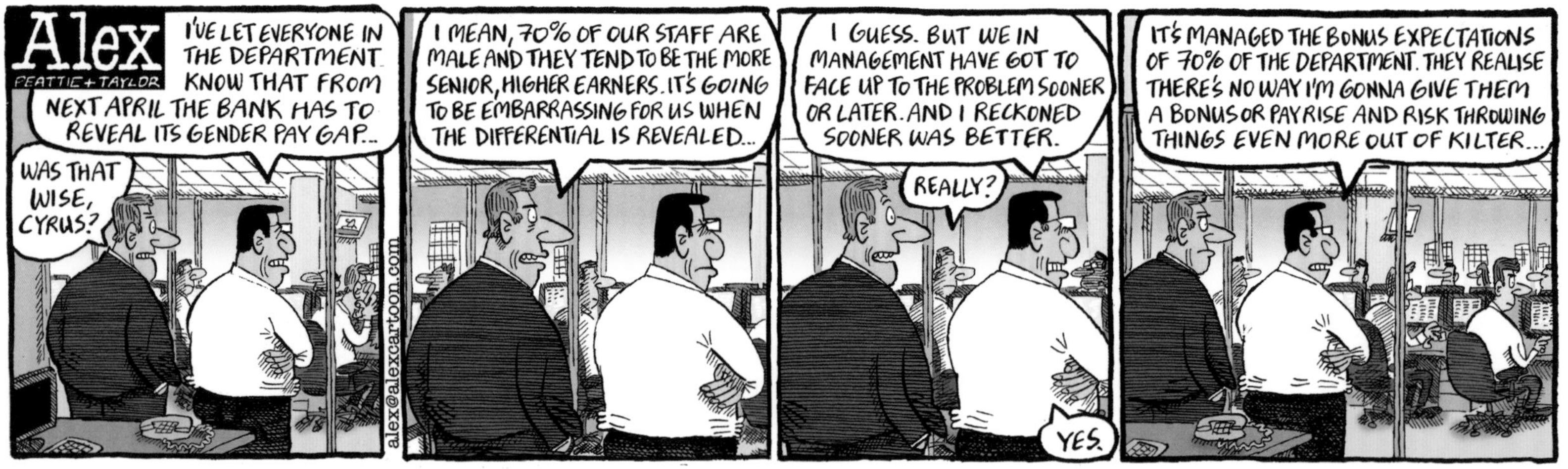
Alex
PEATTIE + TAYLOR
I'VE LET EVERYONE IN THE DEPARTMENT KNOW THAT FROM NEXT APRIL THE BANK HAS TO REVEAL ITS GENDER PAY GAP...
WAS THAT WISE, CYRUS?
alex@alexcartoon.com
I MEAN, 70% OF OUR STAFF ARE MALE AND THEY TEND TO BE THE MORE SENIOR, HIGHER EARNERS. IT'S GOING TO BE EMBARRASSING FOR US WHEN THE DIFFERENTIAL IS REVEALED...
I GUESS. BUT WE IN MANAGEMENT HAVE GOT TO FACE UP TO THE PROBLEM SOONER OR LATER. AND I RECKONED SOONER WAS BETTER.
REALLY?
YES.
IT'S MANAGED THE BONUS EXPECTATIONS OF 70% OF THE DEPARTMENT. THEY REALISE THERE'S NO WAY I'M GONNA GIVE THEM A BONUS OR PAY RISE AND RISK THROWING THINGS EVEN MORE OUT OF KILTER...

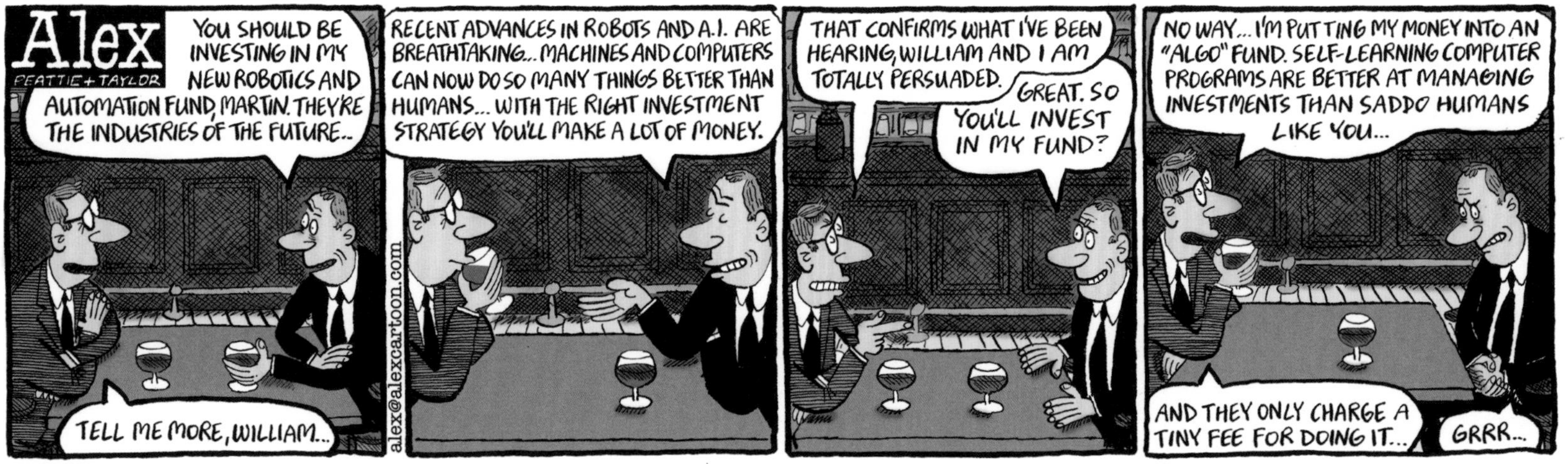
Alex
PEATTIE + TAYLOR
YOU SHOULD BE INVESTING IN MY NEW ROBOTICS AND AUTOMATION FUND, MARTIN. THEY'RE THE INDUSTRIES OF THE FUTURE...
TELL ME MORE, WILLIAM...
alex@alexcartoon.com
RECENT ADVANCES IN ROBOTS AND A.I. ARE BREATHTAKING... MACHINES AND COMPUTERS CAN NOW DO SO MANY THINGS BETTER THAN HUMANS... WITH THE RIGHT INVESTMENT STRATEGY YOU'LL MAKE A LOT OF MONEY.
THAT CONFIRMS WHAT I'VE BEEN HEARING, WILLIAM AND I AM TOTALLY PERSUADED.
GREAT. SO YOU'LL INVEST IN MY FUND?
NO WAY... I'M PUTTING MY MONEY INTO AN "ALGO" FUND. SELF-LEARNING COMPUTER PROGRAMS ARE BETTER AT MANAGING INVESTMENTS THAN SADDO HUMANS LIKE YOU...
AND THEY ONLY CHARGE A TINY FEE FOR DOING IT...
GRRR...

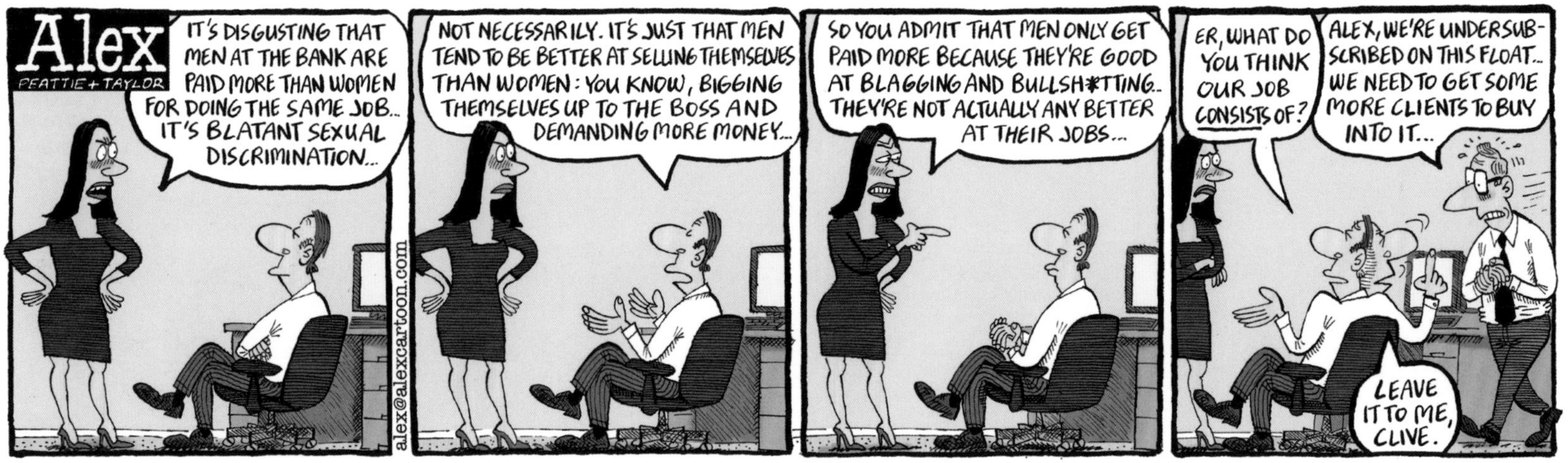
Alex
PEATTIE + TAYLOR
IT'S DISGUSTING THAT MEN AT THE BANK ARE PAID MORE THAN WOMEN FOR DOING THE SAME JOB... IT'S BLATANT SEXUAL DISCRIMINATION...
alex@alexcartoon.com
NOT NECESSARILY. IT'S JUST THAT MEN TEND TO BE BETTER AT SELLING THEMSELVES THAN WOMEN: YOU KNOW, BIGGING THEMSELVES UP TO THE BOSS AND DEMANDING MORE MONEY...
SO YOU ADMIT THAT MEN ONLY GET PAID MORE BECAUSE THEY'RE GOOD AT BLAGGING AND BULLSH*TTING.. THEY'RE NOT ACTUALLY ANY BETTER AT THEIR JOBS...
ER, WHAT DO YOU THINK OUR JOB CONSISTS OF?
ALEX, WE'RE UNDERSUBSCRIBED ON THIS FLOAT... WE NEED TO GET SOME MORE CLIENTS TO BUY INTO IT...
LEAVE IT TO ME, CLIVE.

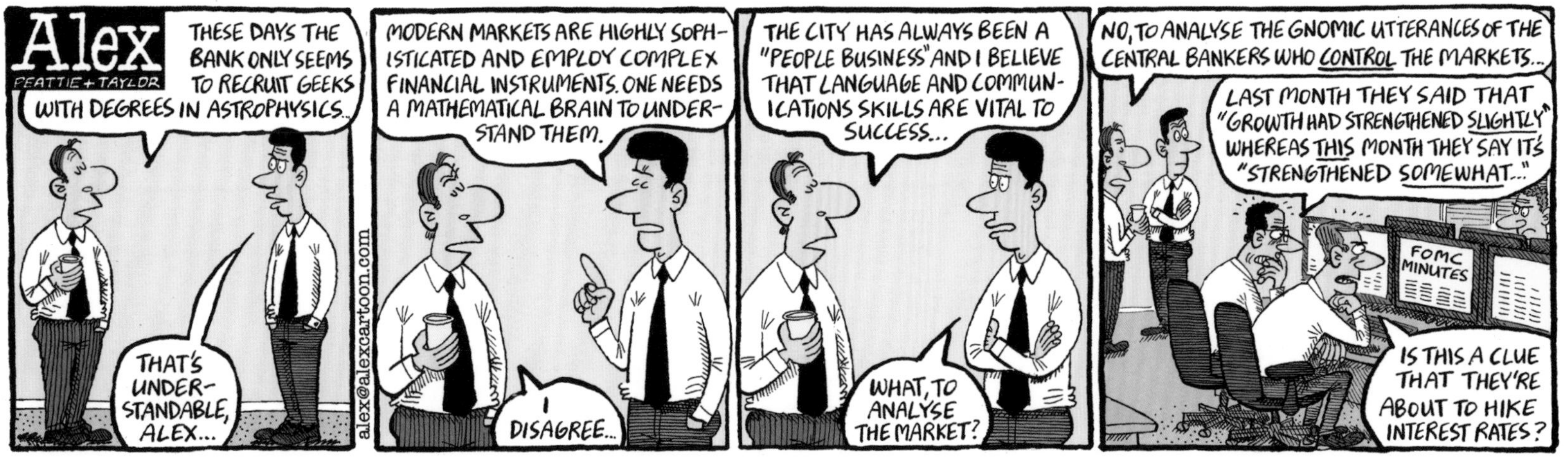
Alex
PEATTIE + TAYLOR
THESE DAYS THE BANK ONLY SEEMS TO RECRUIT GEEKS WITH DEGREES IN ASTROPHYSICS...
THAT'S UNDERSTANDABLE, ALEX...
alex@alexcartoon.com
MODERN MARKETS ARE HIGHLY SOPHISTICATED AND EMPLOY COMPLEX FINANCIAL INSTRUMENTS. ONE NEEDS A MATHEMATICAL BRAIN TO UNDERSTAND THEM.
I DISAGREE...
THE CITY HAS ALWAYS BEEN A "PEOPLE BUSINESS" AND I BELIEVE THAT LANGUAGE AND COMMUNICATIONS SKILLS ARE VITAL TO SUCCESS...
WHAT, TO ANALYSE THE MARKET?
NO, TO ANALYSE THE GNOMIC UTTERANCES OF THE CENTRAL BANKERS WHO CONTROL THE MARKETS...
LAST MONTH THEY SAID THAT "GROWTH HAD STRENGTHENED SLIGHTLY" WHEREAS THIS MONTH THEY SAY IT'S "STRENGTHENED SOMEWHAT..."
FOMC MINUTES
IS THIS A CLUE THAT THEY'RE ABOUT TO HIKE INTEREST RATES?

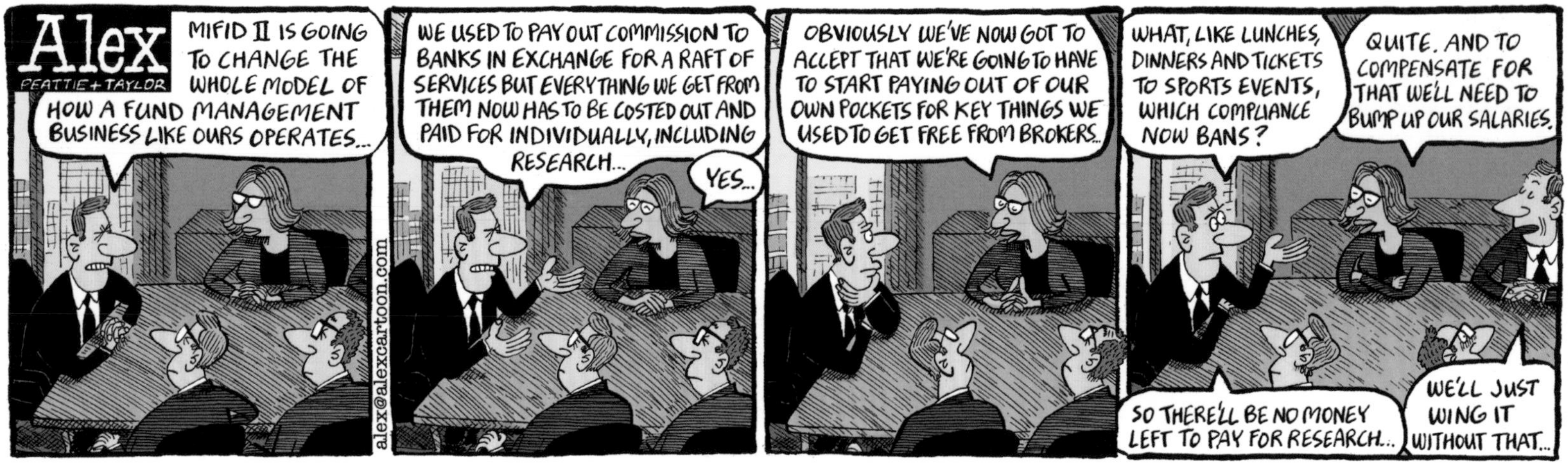
Alex
PEATTIE + TAYLOR
MIFID II IS GOING TO CHANGE THE WHOLE MODEL OF HOW A FUND MANAGEMENT BUSINESS LIKE OURS OPERATES...
alex@alexcartoon.com
WE USED TO PAY OUT COMMISSION TO BANKS IN EXCHANGE FOR A RAFT OF SERVICES BUT EVERYTHING WE GET FROM THEM NOW HAS TO BE COSTED OUT AND PAID FOR INDIVIDUALLY, INCLUDING RESEARCH...
YES...
OBVIOUSLY WE'VE NOW GOT TO ACCEPT THAT WE'RE GOING TO HAVE TO START PAYING OUT OF OUR OWN POCKETS FOR KEY THINGS WE USED TO GET FREE FROM BROKERS...
WHAT, LIKE LUNCHES, DINNERS AND TICKETS TO SPORTS EVENTS, WHICH COMPLIANCE NOW BANS?
QUITE. AND TO COMPENSATE FOR THAT WE'LL NEED TO BUMP UP OUR SALARIES.
SO THERE'LL BE NO MONEY LEFT TO PAY FOR RESEARCH...
WE'LL JUST WING IT WITHOUT THAT...

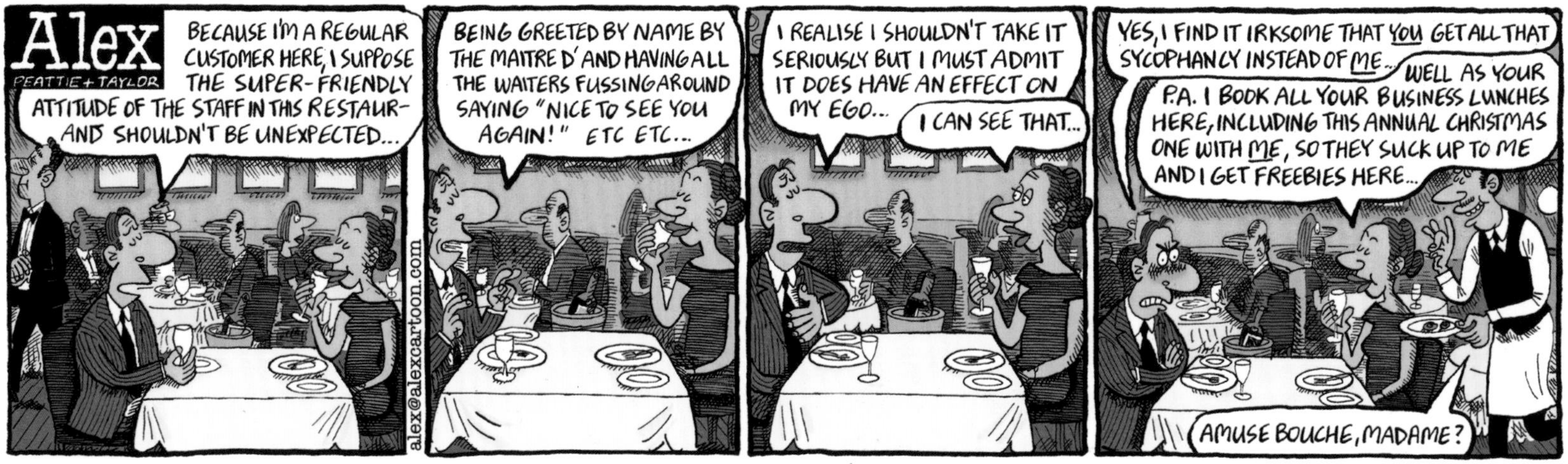
Alex
PEATTIE + TAYLOR
BECAUSE I'M A REGULAR CUSTOMER HERE, I SUPPOSE THE SUPER-FRIENDLY ATTITUDE OF THE STAFF IN THIS RESTAURANT SHOULDN'T BE UNEXPECTED...
alex@alexcartoon.com
BEING GREETED BY NAME BY THE MAITRE D' AND HAVING ALL THE WAITERS FUSSING AROUND SAYING "NICE TO SEE YOU AGAIN!" ETC ETC...
I REALISE I SHOULDN'T TAKE IT SERIOUSLY BUT I MUST ADMIT IT DOES HAVE AN EFFECT ON MY EGO...
I CAN SEE THAT...
YES, I FIND IT IRKSOME THAT YOU GET ALL THAT SYCOPHANCY INSTEAD OF ME...
WELL AS YOUR P.A. I BOOK ALL YOUR BUSINESS LUNCHES HERE, INCLUDING THIS ANNUAL CHRISTMAS ONE WITH ME, SO THEY SUCK UP TO ME AND I GET FREEBIES HERE...
AMUSE BOUCHE, MADAME?

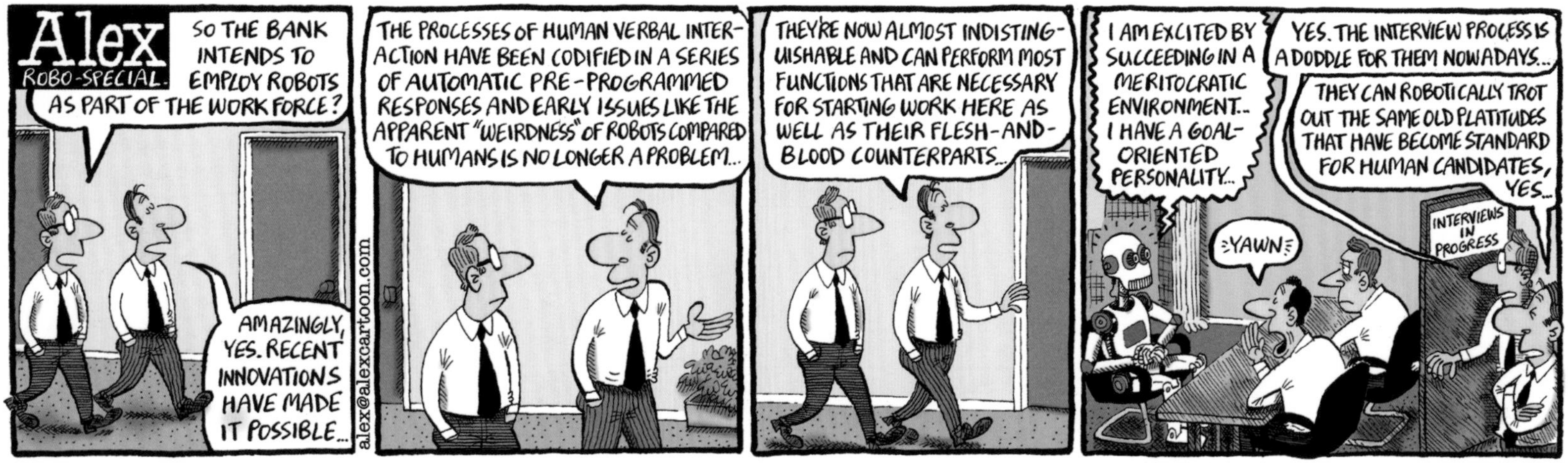
Alex
ROBO-SPECIAL.
SO THE BANK INTENDS TO EMPLOY ROBOTS AS PART OF THE WORK FORCE?
AMAZINGLY, YES. RECENT INNOVATIONS HAVE MADE IT POSSIBLE...
alex@alexcartoon.com
THE PROCESSES OF HUMAN VERBAL INTERACTION HAVE BEEN CODIFIED IN A SERIES OF AUTOMATIC PRE-PROGRAMMED RESPONSES AND EARLY ISSUES LIKE THE APPARENT "WEIRDNESS" OF ROBOTS COMPARED TO HUMANS IS NO LONGER A PROBLEM...
THEY'RE NOW ALMOST INDISTINGUISHABLE AND CAN PERFORM MOST FUNCTIONS THAT ARE NECESSARY FOR STARTING WORK HERE AS WELL AS THEIR FLESH-AND-BLOOD COUNTERPARTS...
I AM EXCITED BY SUCCEEDING IN A MERITOCRATIC ENVIRONMENT... I HAVE A GOAL-ORIENTED PERSONALITY...
YAWN
YES. THE INTERVIEW PROCESS IS A DODDLE FOR THEM NOWADAYS...
THEY CAN ROBOTICALLY TROT OUT THE SAME OLD PLATITUDES THAT HAVE BECOME STANDARD FOR HUMAN CANDIDATES, YES...
INTERVIEWS IN PROGRESS

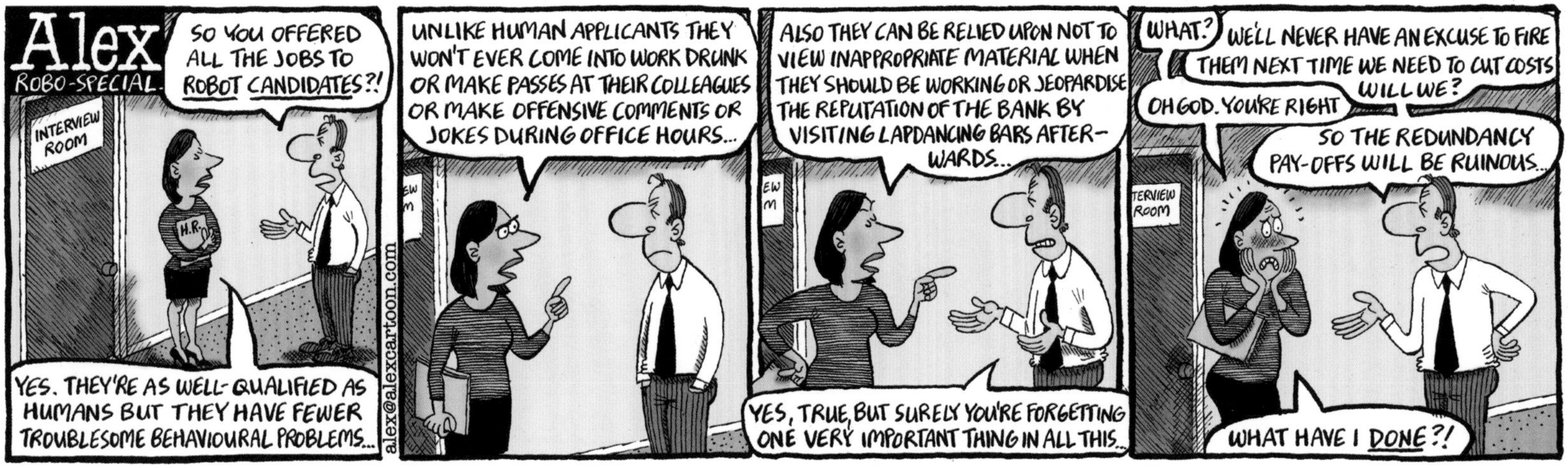
Alex
ROBO-SPECIAL
SO YOU OFFERED ALL THE JOBS TO ROBOT CANDIDATES?!
INTERVIEW ROOM
H.R.
YES. THEY'RE AS WELL-QUALIFIED AS HUMANS BUT THEY HAVE FEWER TROUBLESOME BEHAVIOURAL PROBLEMS...
alex@alexcartoon.com
UNLIKE HUMAN APPLICANTS THEY WON'T EVER COME INTO WORK DRUNK OR MAKE PASSES AT THEIR COLLEAGUES OR MAKE OFFENSIVE COMMENTS OR JOKES DURING OFFICE HOURS...
ALSO THEY CAN BE RELIED UPON NOT TO VIEW INAPPROPRIATE MATERIAL WHEN THEY SHOULD BE WORKING OR JEOPARDISE THE REPUTATION OF THE BANK BY VISITING LAPDANCING BARS AFTER-WARDS...
YES, TRUE, BUT SURELY YOU'RE FORGETTING ONE VERY IMPORTANT THING IN ALL THIS...
WHAT?
WE'LL NEVER HAVE AN EXCUSE TO FIRE THEM NEXT TIME WE NEED TO CUT COSTS WILL WE?
OH GOD. YOU'RE RIGHT
SO THE REDUNDANCY PAY-OFFS WILL BE RUINOUS...
WHAT HAVE I DONE?!

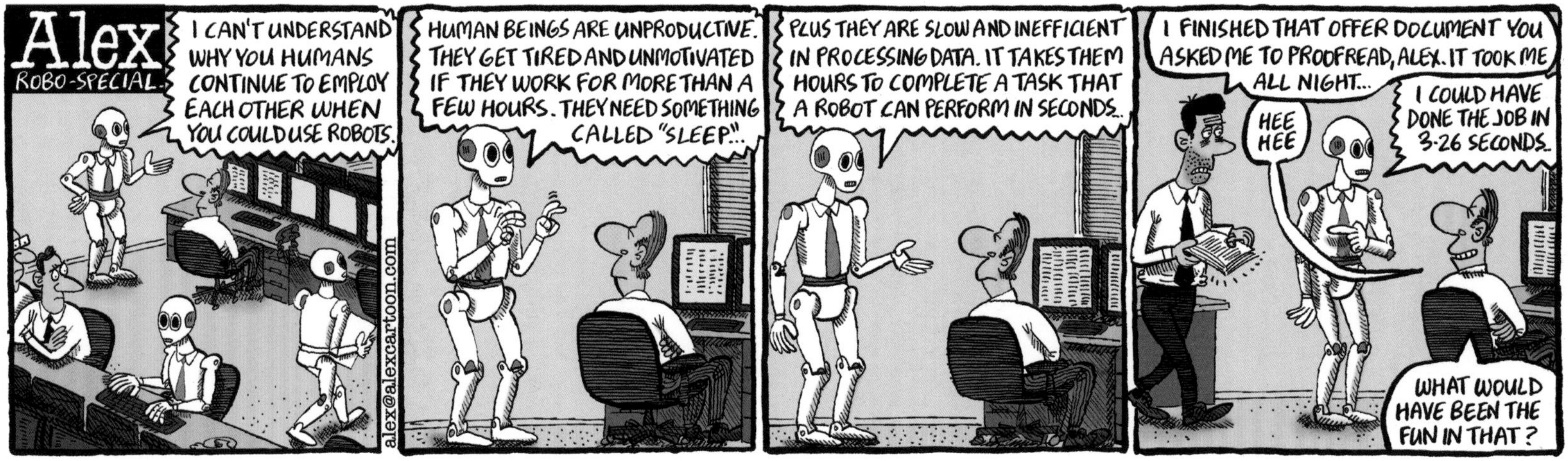
Alex
ROBO-SPECIAL
I CAN'T UNDERSTAND WHY YOU HUMANS CONTINUE TO EMPLOY EACH OTHER WHEN YOU COULD USE ROBOTS.
alex@alexcartoon.com
HUMAN BEINGS ARE UNPRODUCTIVE. THEY GET TIRED AND UNMOTIVATED IF THEY WORK FOR MORE THAN A FEW HOURS. THEY NEED SOMETHING CALLED "SLEEP"...
PLUS THEY ARE SLOW AND INEFFICIENT IN PROCESSING DATA. IT TAKES THEM HOURS TO COMPLETE A TASK THAT A ROBOT CAN PERFORM IN SECONDS...
I FINISHED THAT OFFER DOCUMENT YOU ASKED ME TO PROOFREAD, ALEX. IT TOOK ME ALL NIGHT...
HEE HEE
I COULD HAVE DONE THE JOB IN 3.26 SECONDS.
WHAT WOULD HAVE BEEN THE FUN IN THAT?

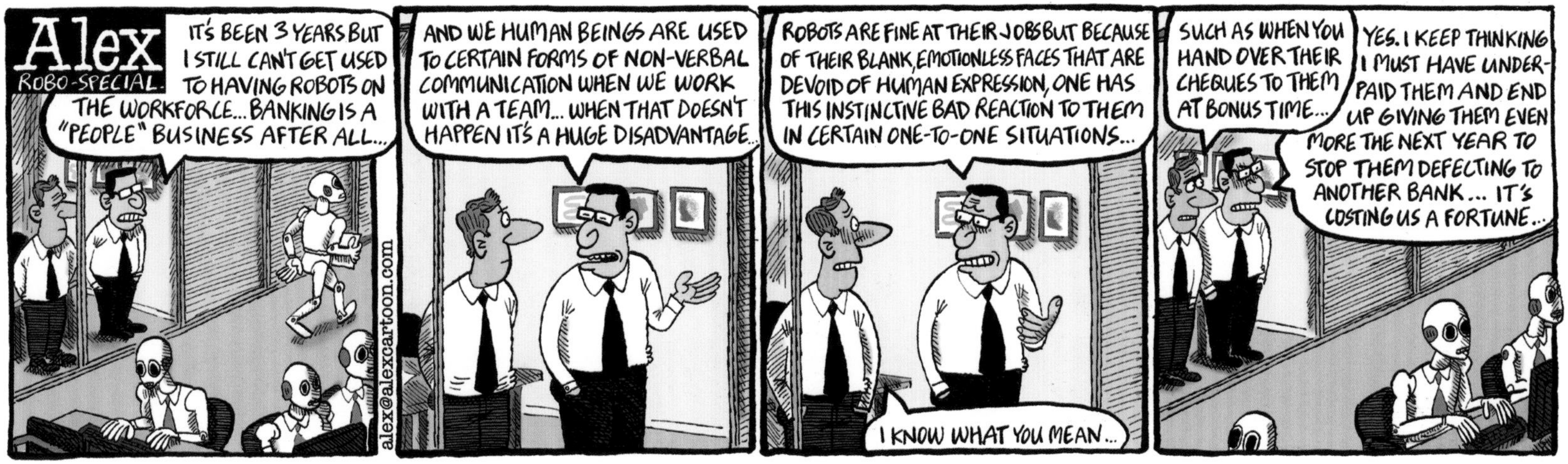
Alex
ROBO-SPECIAL
IT'S BEEN 3 YEARS BUT I STILL CAN'T GET USED TO HAVING ROBOTS ON THE WORKFORCE... BANKING IS A "PEOPLE" BUSINESS AFTER ALL...
alex@alexcartoon.com
AND WE HUMAN BEINGS ARE USED TO CERTAIN FORMS OF NON-VERBAL COMMUNICATION WHEN WE WORK WITH A TEAM... WHEN THAT DOESN'T HAPPEN IT'S A HUGE DISADVANTAGE...
ROBOTS ARE FINE AT THEIR JOBS BUT BECAUSE OF THEIR BLANK, EMOTIONLESS FACES THAT ARE DEVOID OF HUMAN EXPRESSION, ONE HAS THIS INSTINCTIVE BAD REACTION TO THEM IN CERTAIN ONE-TO-ONE SITUATIONS...
I KNOW WHAT YOU MEAN...
SUCH AS WHEN YOU HAND OVER THEIR CHEQUES TO THEM AT BONUS TIME...
YES. I KEEP THINKING I MUST HAVE UNDER-PAID THEM AND END UP GIVING THEM EVEN MORE THE NEXT YEAR TO STOP THEM DEFECTING TO ANOTHER BANK... IT'S COSTING US A FORTUNE...

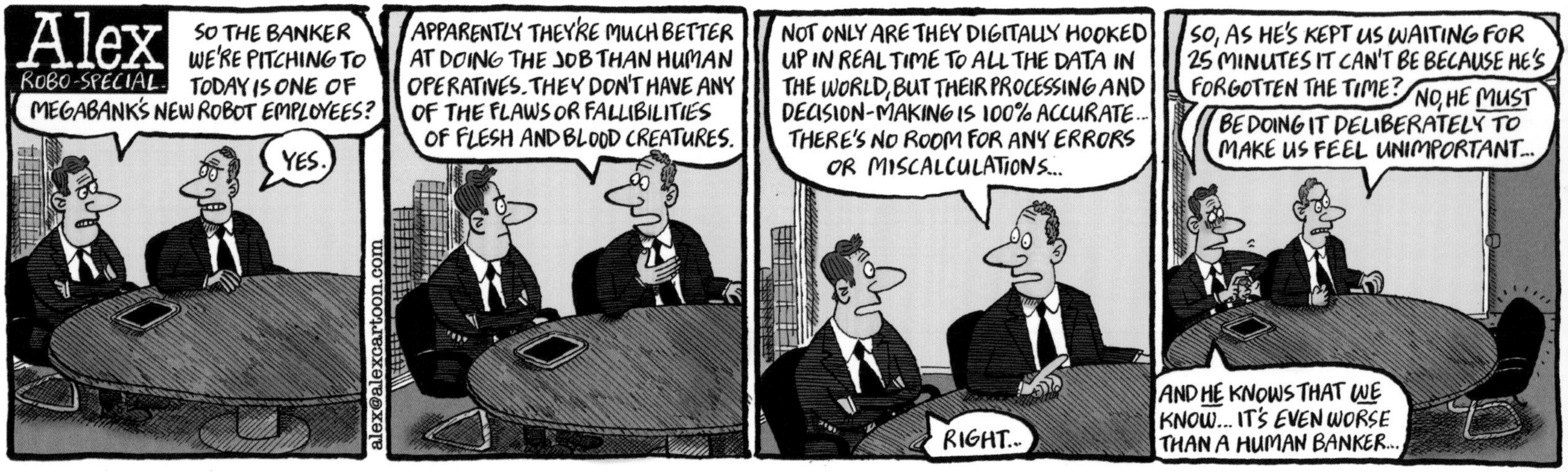
Alex
ROBO-SPECIAL
SO THE BANKER WE'RE PITCHING TO TODAY IS ONE OF MEGABANK'S NEW ROBOT EMPLOYEES?
YES.
alex@alexcartoon.com
APPARENTLY THEY'RE MUCH BETTER AT DOING THE JOB THAN HUMAN OPERATIVES. THEY DON'T HAVE ANY OF THE FLAWS OR FALLIBILITIES OF FLESH AND BLOOD CREATURES.
NOT ONLY ARE THEY DIGITALLY HOOKED UP IN REAL TIME TO ALL THE DATA IN THE WORLD, BUT THEIR PROCESSING AND DECISION-MAKING IS 100% ACCURATE... THERE'S NO ROOM FOR ANY ERRORS OR MISCALCULATIONS...
RIGHT...
SO, AS HE'S KEPT US WAITING FOR 25 MINUTES IT CAN'T BE BECAUSE HE'S FORGOTTEN THE TIME?
NO, HE MUST BE DOING IT DELIBERATELY TO MAKE US FEEL UNIMPORTANT...
AND HE KNOWS THAT WE KNOW... IT'S EVEN WORSE THAN A HUMAN BANKER...

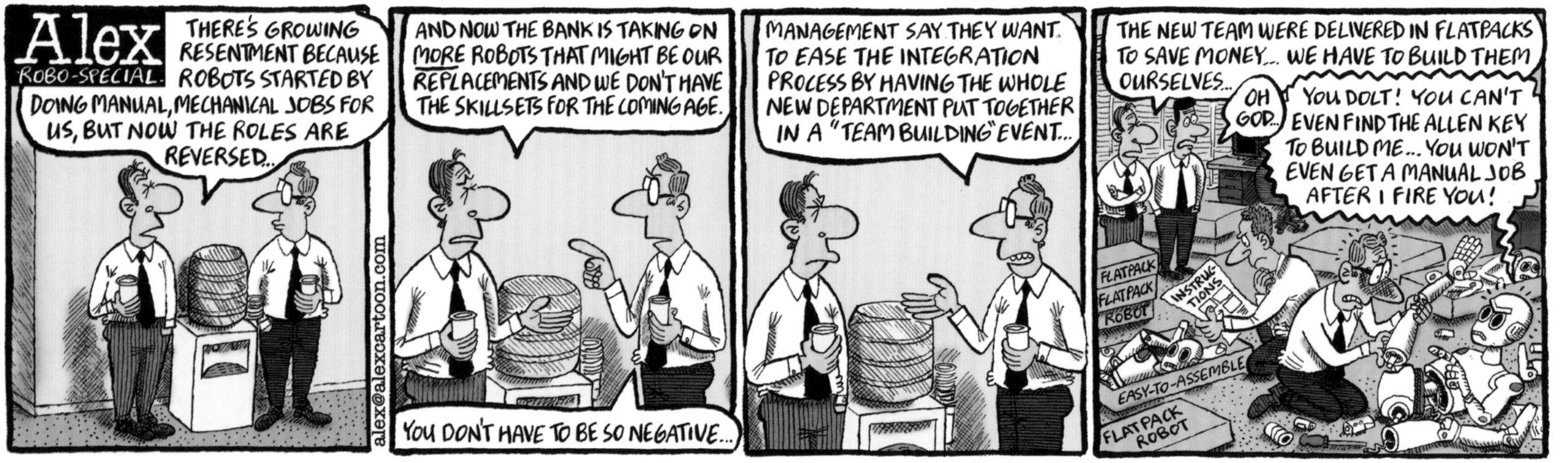
Alex
ROBO-SPECIAL
THERE'S GROWING RESENTMENT BECAUSE ROBOTS STARTED BY DOING MANUAL, MECHANICAL JOBS FOR US, BUT NOW THE ROLES ARE REVERSED...
alex@alexcartoon.com
AND NOW THE BANK IS TAKING ON MORE ROBOTS THAT MIGHT BE OUR REPLACEMENTS AND WE DON'T HAVE THE SKILLSETS FOR THE COMING AGE.
YOU DON'T HAVE TO BE SO NEGATIVE...
MANAGEMENT SAY THEY WANT TO EASE THE INTEGRATION PROCESS BY HAVING THE WHOLE NEW DEPARTMENT PUT TOGETHER IN A "TEAM BUILDING" EVENT...
THE NEW TEAM WERE DELIVERED IN FLATPACKS TO SAVE MONEY... WE HAVE TO BUILD THEM OURSELVES...
OH GOD...
YOU DOLT! YOU CAN'T EVEN FIND THE ALLEN KEY TO BUILD ME... YOU WON'T EVEN GET A MANUAL JOB AFTER I FIRE YOU!
FLATPACK
FLATPACK
ROBOT
INSTRUCTIONS
EASY-TO-ASSEMBLE
FLATPACK ROBOT

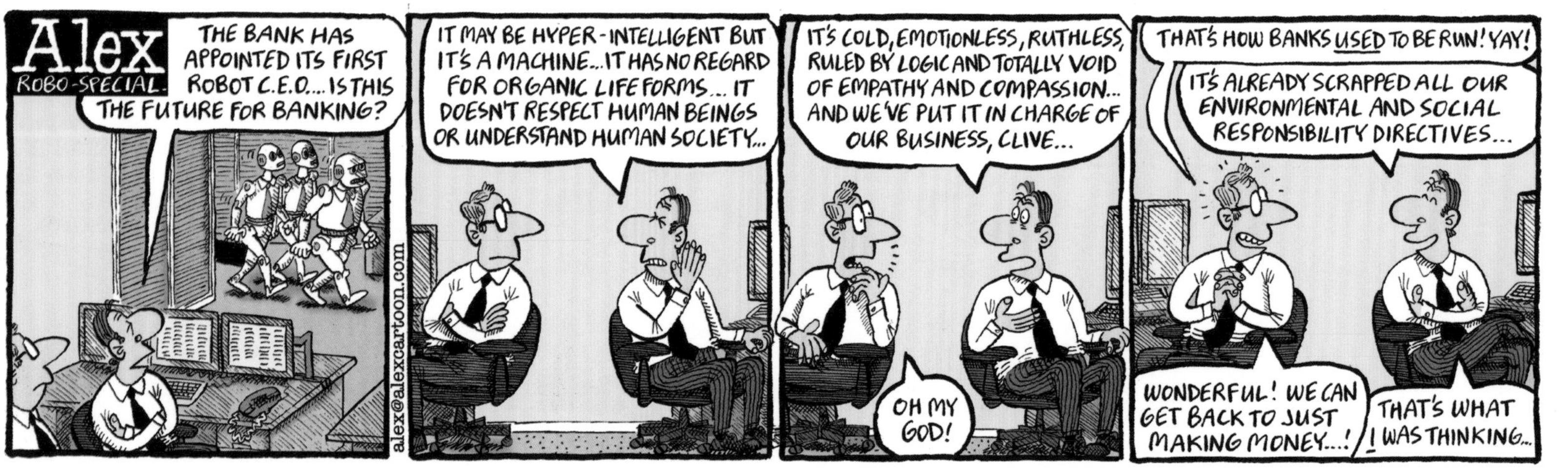
Alex
ROBO-SPECIAL
THE BANK HAS APPOINTED ITS FIRST ROBOT C.E.O.... IS THIS THE FUTURE FOR BANKING?
alex@alexcartoon.com
IT MAY BE HYPER-INTELLIGENT BUT IT'S A MACHINE... IT HAS NO REGARD FOR ORGANIC LIFE FORMS... IT DOESN'T RESPECT HUMAN BEINGS OR UNDERSTAND HUMAN SOCIETY...
IT'S COLD, EMOTIONLESS, RUTHLESS, RULED BY LOGIC AND TOTALLY VOID OF EMPATHY AND COMPASSION... AND WE'VE PUT IT IN CHARGE OF OUR BUSINESS, CLIVE...
OH MY GOD!
THAT'S HOW BANKS USED TO BE RUN! YAY!
IT'S ALREADY SCRAPPED ALL OUR ENVIRONMENTAL AND SOCIAL RESPONSIBILITY DIRECTIVES...
WONDERFUL! WE CAN GET BACK TO JUST MAKING MONEY...!
THAT'S WHAT I WAS THINKING...

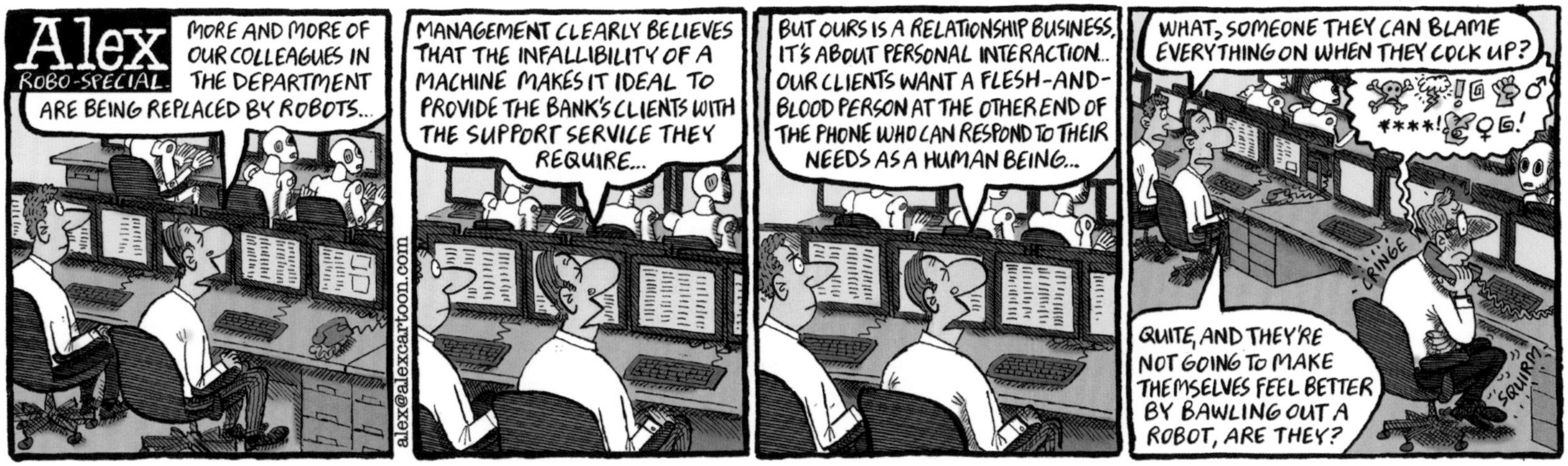
Alex
ROBO-SPECIAL.
MORE AND MORE OF OUR COLLEAGUES IN THE DEPARTMENT ARE BEING REPLACED BY ROBOTS...
alex@alexcartoon.com
MANAGEMENT CLEARLY BELIEVES THAT THE INFALLIBILITY OF A MACHINE MAKES IT IDEAL TO PROVIDE THE BANK'S CLIENTS WITH THE SUPPORT SERVICE THEY REQUIRE...
BUT OURS IS A RELATIONSHIP BUSINESS, IT'S ABOUT PERSONAL INTERACTION... OUR CLIENTS WANT A FLESH-AND-BLOOD PERSON AT THE OTHER END OF THE PHONE WHO CAN RESPOND TO THEIR NEEDS AS A HUMAN BEING...
WHAT, SOMEONE THEY CAN BLAME EVERYTHING ON WHEN THEY COCK UP?
****!
CRINGE
QUITE, AND THEY'RE NOT GOING TO MAKE THEMSELVES FEEL BETTER BY BAWLING OUT A ROBOT, ARE THEY?
SQUIRM

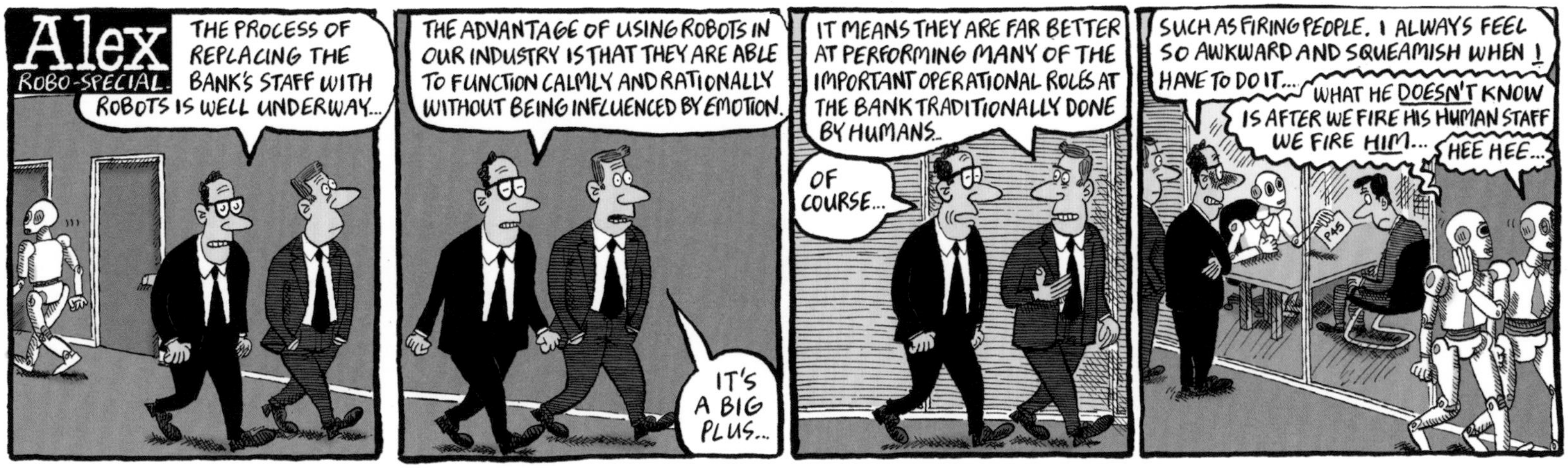
Alex
ROBO-SPECIAL.
THE PROCESS OF REPLACING THE BANK'S STAFF WITH ROBOTS IS WELL UNDERWAY...
THE ADVANTAGE OF USING ROBOTS IN OUR INDUSTRY IS THAT THEY ARE ABLE TO FUNCTION CALMLY AND RATIONALLY WITHOUT BEING INFLUENCED BY EMOTION.
IT'S A BIG PLUS...
IT MEANS THEY ARE FAR BETTER AT PERFORMING MANY OF THE IMPORTANT OPERATIONAL ROLES AT THE BANK TRADITIONALLY DONE BY HUMANS...
OF COURSE...
SUCH AS FIRING PEOPLE. I ALWAYS FEEL SO AWKWARD AND SQUEAMISH WHEN I HAVE TO DO IT...
WHAT HE DOESN'T KNOW IS AFTER WE FIRE HIS HUMAN STAFF WE FIRE HIM...
HEE HEE...
P45

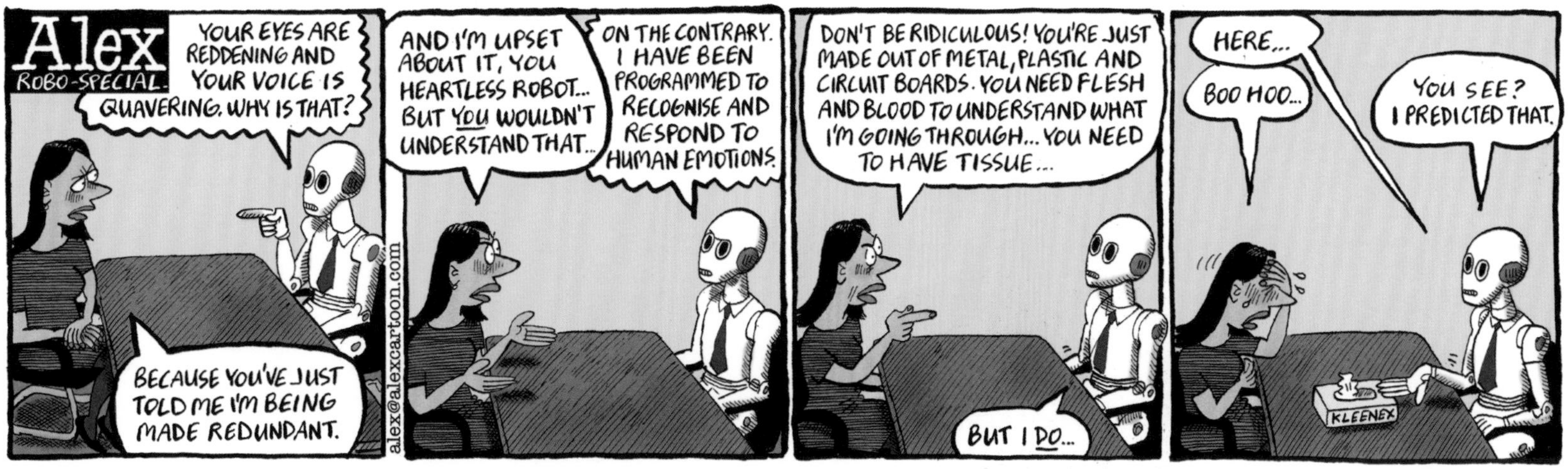
Alex
ROBO-SPECIAL.
YOUR EYES ARE REDDENING AND YOUR VOICE IS QUAVERING. WHY IS THAT?
BECAUSE YOU'VE JUST TOLD ME I'M BEING MADE REDUNDANT.
alex@alexcartoon.com
AND I'M UPSET ABOUT IT, YOU HEARTLESS ROBOT... BUT YOU WOULDN'T UNDERSTAND THAT...
ON THE CONTRARY. I HAVE BEEN PROGRAMMED TO RECOGNISE AND RESPOND TO HUMAN EMOTIONS.
DON'T BE RIDICULOUS! YOU'RE JUST MADE OUT OF METAL, PLASTIC AND CIRCUIT BOARDS. YOU NEED FLESH AND BLOOD TO UNDERSTAND WHAT I'M GOING THROUGH... YOU NEED TO HAVE TISSUE...
BUT I DO...
HERE...
BOO HOO...
YOU SEE? I PREDICTED THAT.
KLEENEX

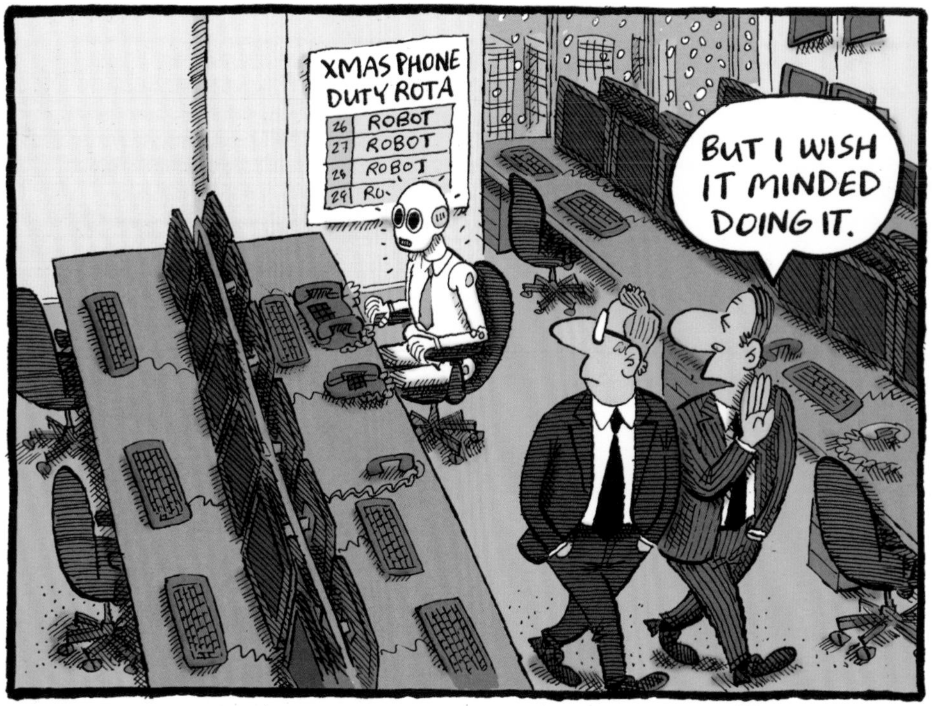
XMAS PHONE DUTY ROTA
26 ROBOT
27 ROBOT
28 ROBOT
BUT I WISH IT MINDED DOING IT.

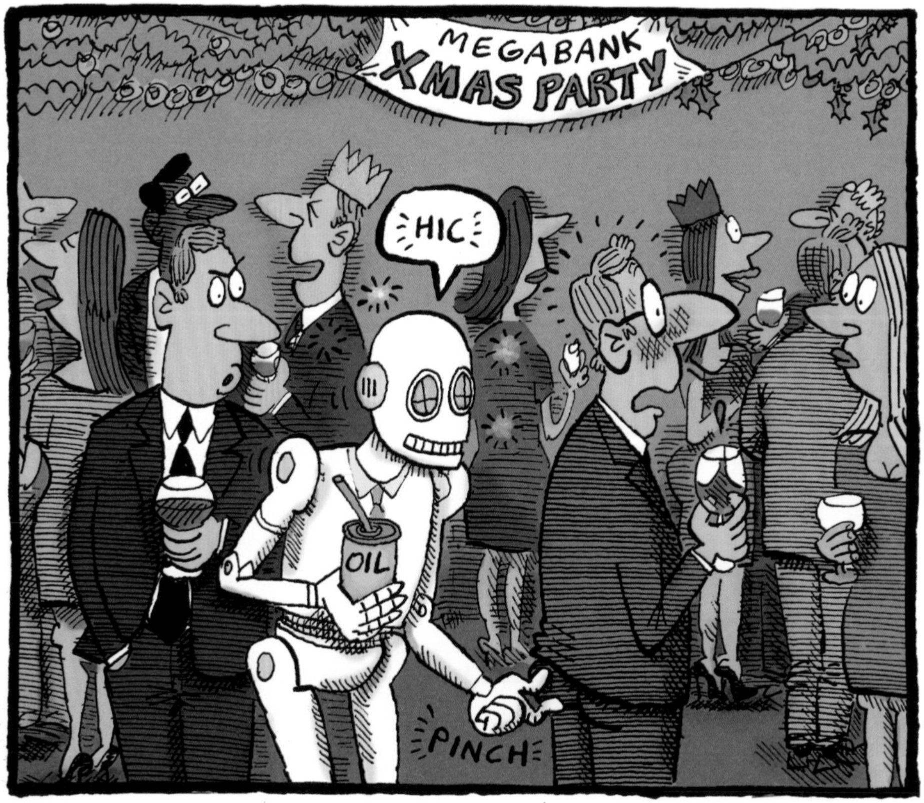
MEGABANK XMAS PARTY
HIC
OIL
PINCH

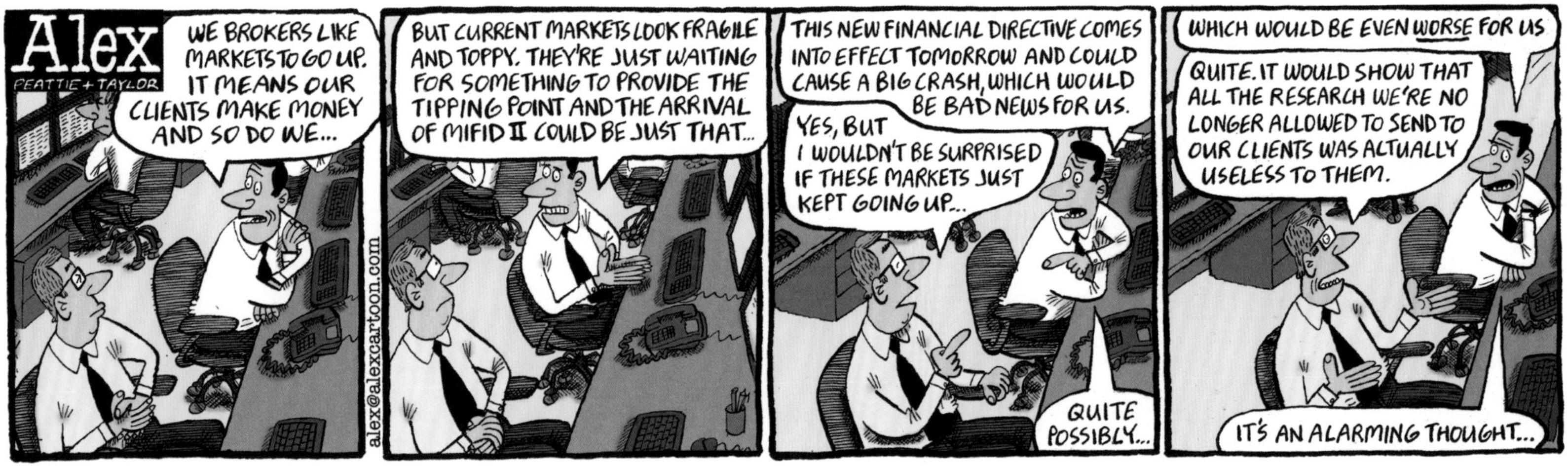
Alex
PEATTIE+TAYLOR
WE BROKERS LIKE MARKETS TO GO UP. IT MEANS OUR CLIENTS MAKE MONEY AND SO DO WE...
BUT CURRENT MARKETS LOOK FRAGILE AND TOPPY. THEY'RE JUST WAITING FOR SOMETHING TO PROVIDE THE TIPPING POINT AND THE ARRIVAL OF MIFID II COULD BE JUST THAT...
alex@alexcartoon.com
THIS NEW FINANCIAL DIRECTIVE COMES INTO EFFECT TOMORROW AND COULD CAUSE A BIG CRASH, WHICH WOULD BE BAD NEWS FOR US.
YES, BUT I WOULDN'T BE SURPRISED IF THESE MARKETS JUST KEPT GOING UP...
QUITE POSSIBLY...
WHICH WOULD BE EVEN WORSE FOR US
QUITE. IT WOULD SHOW THAT ALL THE RESEARCH WE'RE NO LONGER ALLOWED TO SEND TO OUR CLIENTS WAS ACTUALLY USELESS TO THEM.
IT'S AN ALARMING THOUGHT...

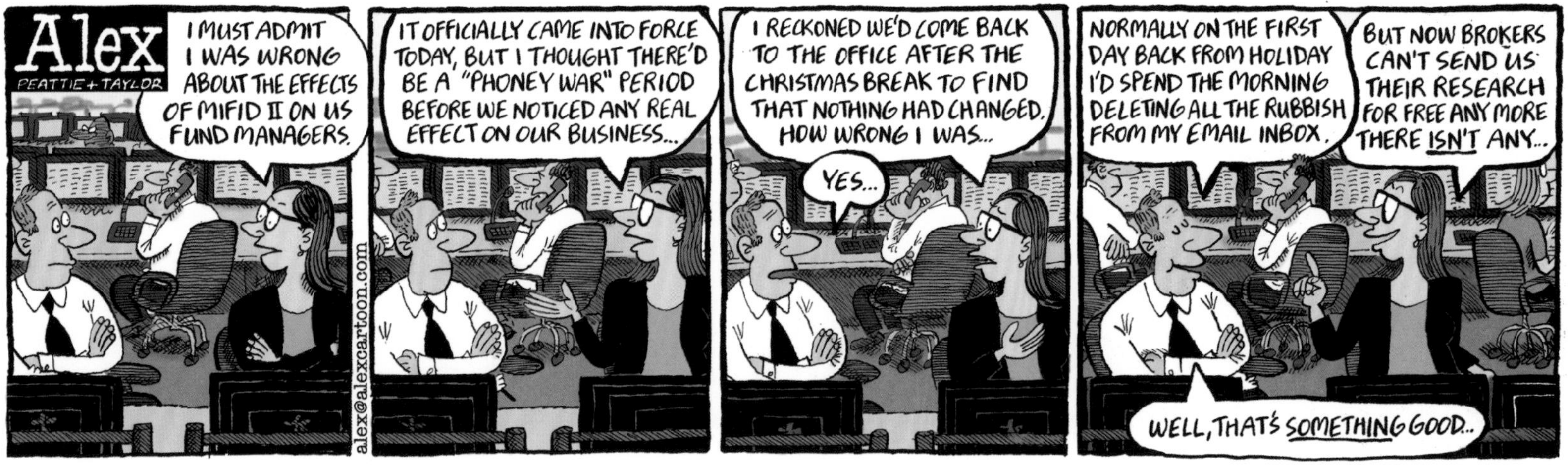
Alex
PEATTIE+TAYLOR
I MUST ADMIT I WAS WRONG ABOUT THE EFFECTS OF MIFID II ON US FUND MANAGERS.
IT OFFICIALLY CAME INTO FORCE TODAY, BUT I THOUGHT THERE'D BE A "PHONEY WAR" PERIOD BEFORE WE NOTICED ANY REAL EFFECT ON OUR BUSINESS...
alex@alexcartoon.com
I RECKONED WE'D COME BACK TO THE OFFICE AFTER THE CHRISTMAS BREAK TO FIND THAT NOTHING HAD CHANGED. HOW WRONG I WAS...
YES...
NORMALLY ON THE FIRST DAY BACK FROM HOLIDAY I'D SPEND THE MORNING DELETING ALL THE RUBBISH FROM MY EMAIL INBOX.
BUT NOW BROKERS CAN'T SEND US THEIR RESEARCH FOR FREE ANY MORE THERE ISN'T ANY...
WELL, THAT'S SOMETHING GOOD...

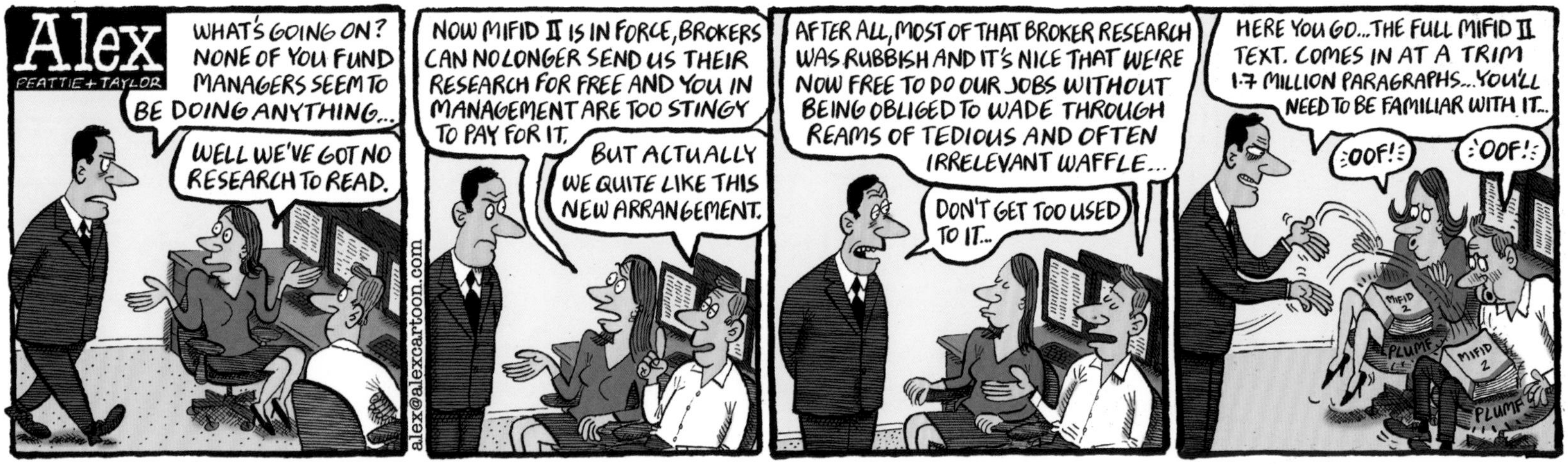
Alex
PEATTIE+TAYLOR
WHAT'S GOING ON? NONE OF YOU FUND MANAGERS SEEM TO BE DOING ANYTHING...
WELL WE'VE GOT NO RESEARCH TO READ.
NOW MIFID II IS IN FORCE, BROKERS CAN NO LONGER SEND US THEIR RESEARCH FOR FREE AND YOU IN MANAGEMENT ARE TOO STINGY TO PAY FOR IT.
BUT ACTUALLY WE QUITE LIKE THIS NEW ARRANGEMENT.
alex@alexcartoon.com
AFTER ALL, MOST OF THAT BROKER RESEARCH WAS RUBBISH AND IT'S NICE THAT WE'RE NOW FREE TO DO OUR JOBS WITHOUT BEING OBLIGED TO WADE THROUGH REAMS OF TEDIOUS AND OFTEN IRRELEVANT WAFFLE...
DON'T GET TOO USED TO IT...
HERE YOU GO... THE FULL MIFID II TEXT. COMES IN AT A TRIM 1.7 MILLION PARAGRAPHS... YOU'LL NEED TO BE FAMILIAR WITH IT...
OOF!
OOF!
MIFID 2
MIFID 2
PLUMF
PLUMF

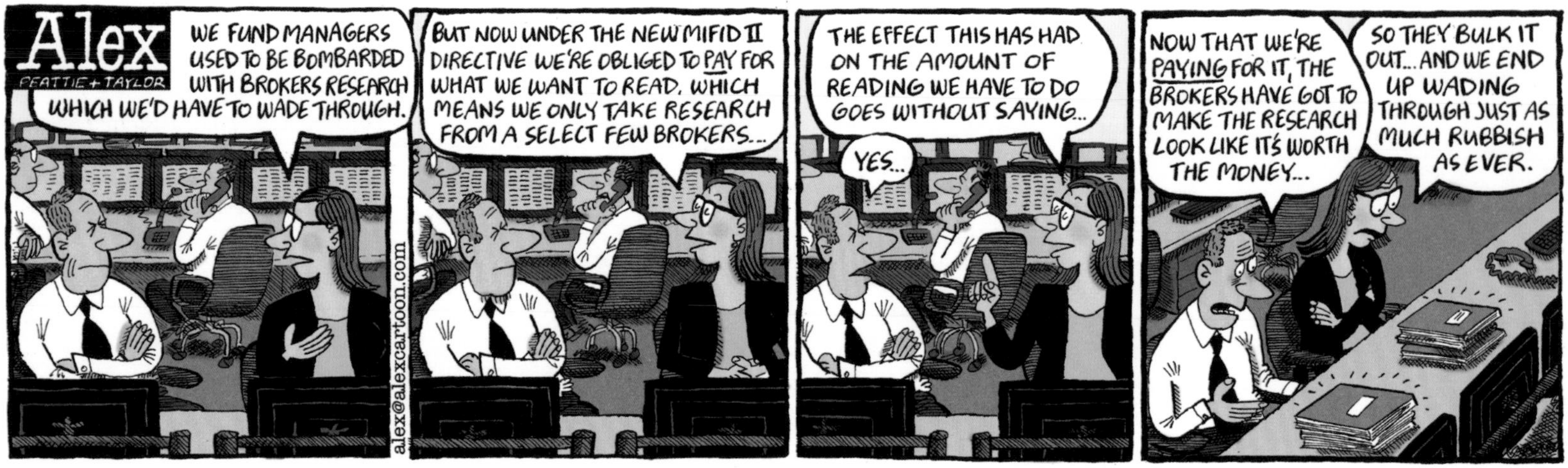
Alex
BEATTIE + TAYLOR
WE FUND MANAGERS USED TO BE BOMBARDED WITH BROKERS RESEARCH WHICH WE'D HAVE TO WADE THROUGH.
BUT NOW UNDER THE NEW MIFID II DIRECTIVE WE'RE OBLIGED TO PAY FOR WHAT WE WANT TO READ, WHICH MEANS WE ONLY TAKE RESEARCH FROM A SELECT FEW BROKERS...
alex@alexcartoon.com
THE EFFECT THIS HAS HAD ON THE AMOUNT OF READING WE HAVE TO DO GOES WITHOUT SAYING...
YES...
NOW THAT WE'RE PAYING FOR IT, THE BROKERS HAVE GOT TO MAKE THE RESEARCH LOOK LIKE IT'S WORTH THE MONEY...
SO THEY BULK IT OUT... AND WE END UP WADING THROUGH JUST AS MUCH RUBBISH AS EVER.

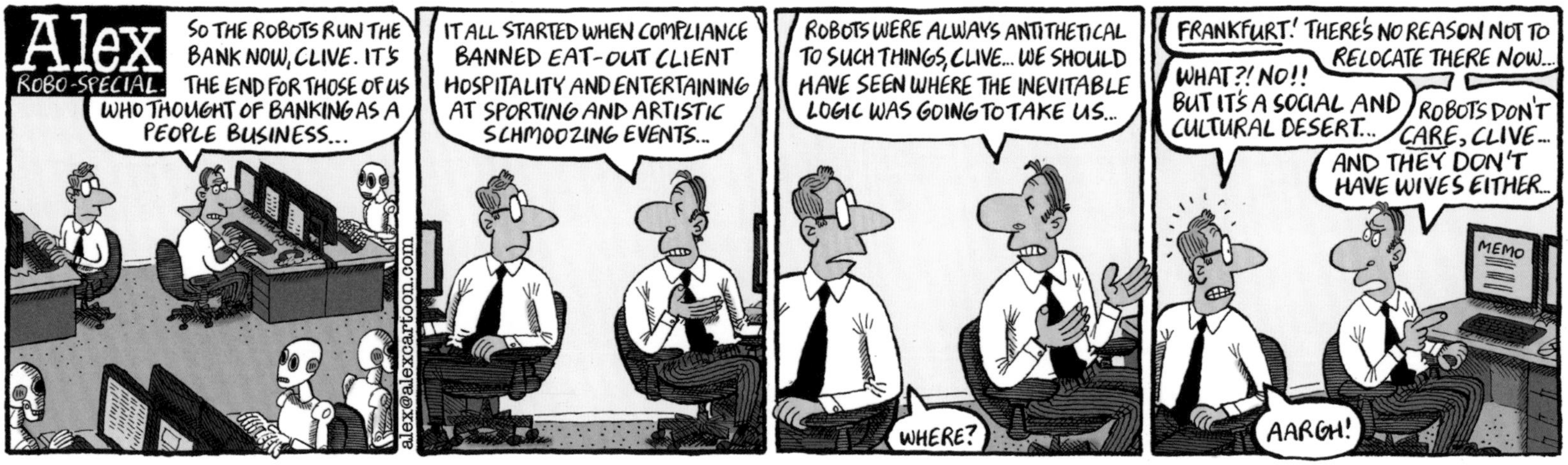
Alex
ROBO-SPECIAL.
SO THE ROBOTS RUN THE BANK NOW, CLIVE. IT'S THE END FOR THOSE OF US WHO THOUGHT OF BANKING AS A PEOPLE BUSINESS...
IT ALL STARTED WHEN COMPLIANCE BANNED EAT-OUT CLIENT HOSPITALITY AND ENTERTAINING AT SPORTING AND ARTISTIC SCHMOOZING EVENTS...
alex@alexcartoon.com
ROBOTS WERE ALWAYS ANTITHETICAL TO SUCH THINGS, CLIVE... WE SHOULD HAVE SEEN WHERE THE INEVITABLE LOGIC WAS GOING TO TAKE US...
WHERE?
FRANKFURT! THERE'S NO REASON NOT TO RELOCATE THERE NOW...
WHAT?! NO!! BUT IT'S A SOCIAL AND CULTURAL DESERT...
ROBOTS DON'T CARE, CLIVE...
AND THEY DON'T HAVE WIVES EITHER...
MEMO
AARGH!

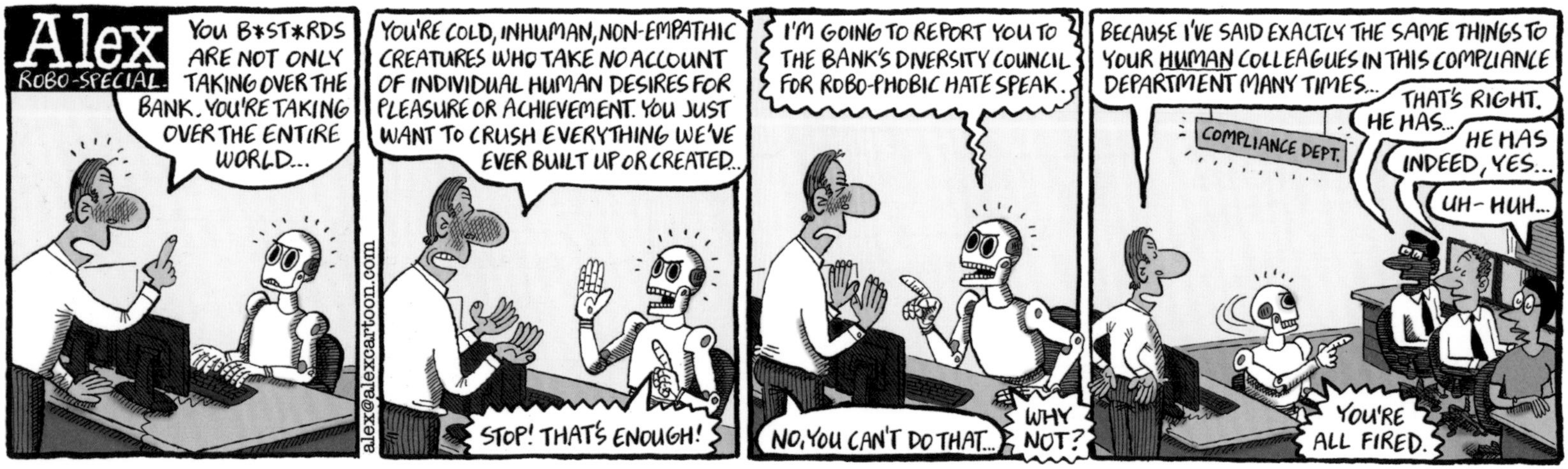
Alex
ROBO-SPECIAL.
YOU B*ST*RDS ARE NOT ONLY TAKING OVER THE BANK. YOU'RE TAKING OVER THE ENTIRE WORLD...
YOU'RE COLD, INHUMAN, NON-EMPATHIC CREATURES WHO TAKE NO ACCOUNT OF INDIVIDUAL HUMAN DESIRES FOR PLEASURE OR ACHIEVEMENT. YOU JUST WANT TO CRUSH EVERYTHING WE'VE EVER BUILT UP OR CREATED...
alex@alexcartoon.com
STOP! THAT'S ENOUGH!
I'M GOING TO REPORT YOU TO THE BANK'S DIVERSITY COUNCIL FOR ROBO-PHOBIC HATE SPEAK.
NO, YOU CAN'T DO THAT...
WHY NOT?
BECAUSE I'VE SAID EXACTLY THE SAME THINGS TO YOUR HUMAN COLLEAGUES IN THIS COMPLIANCE DEPARTMENT MANY TIMES...
COMPLIANCE DEPT.
THAT'S RIGHT. HE HAS...
HE HAS INDEED, YES...
UH-HUH...
YOU'RE ALL FIRED.

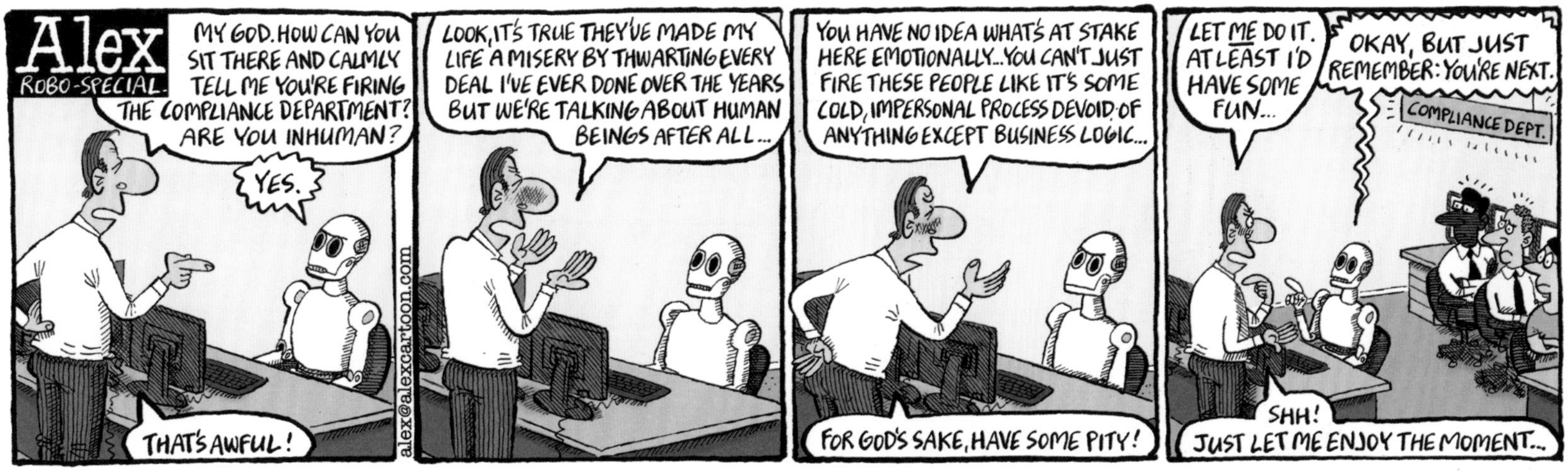
Alex
ROBO-SPECIAL
MY GOD. HOW CAN YOU SIT THERE AND CALMLY TELL ME YOU'RE FIRING THE COMPLIANCE DEPARTMENT? ARE YOU INHUMAN?
YES.
THAT'S AWFUL!
alex@alexcartoon.com
LOOK, IT'S TRUE THEY'VE MADE MY LIFE A MISERY BY THWARTING EVERY DEAL I'VE EVER DONE OVER THE YEARS BUT WE'RE TALKING ABOUT HUMAN BEINGS AFTER ALL...
YOU HAVE NO IDEA WHAT'S AT STAKE HERE EMOTIONALLY... YOU CAN'T JUST FIRE THESE PEOPLE LIKE IT'S SOME COLD, IMPERSONAL PROCESS DEVOID OF ANYTHING EXCEPT BUSINESS LOGIC...
FOR GOD'S SAKE, HAVE SOME PITY!
LET ME DO IT. AT LEAST I'D HAVE SOME FUN...
OKAY, BUT JUST REMEMBER: YOU'RE NEXT.
COMPLIANCE DEPT.
SHH! JUST LET ME ENJOY THE MOMENT...

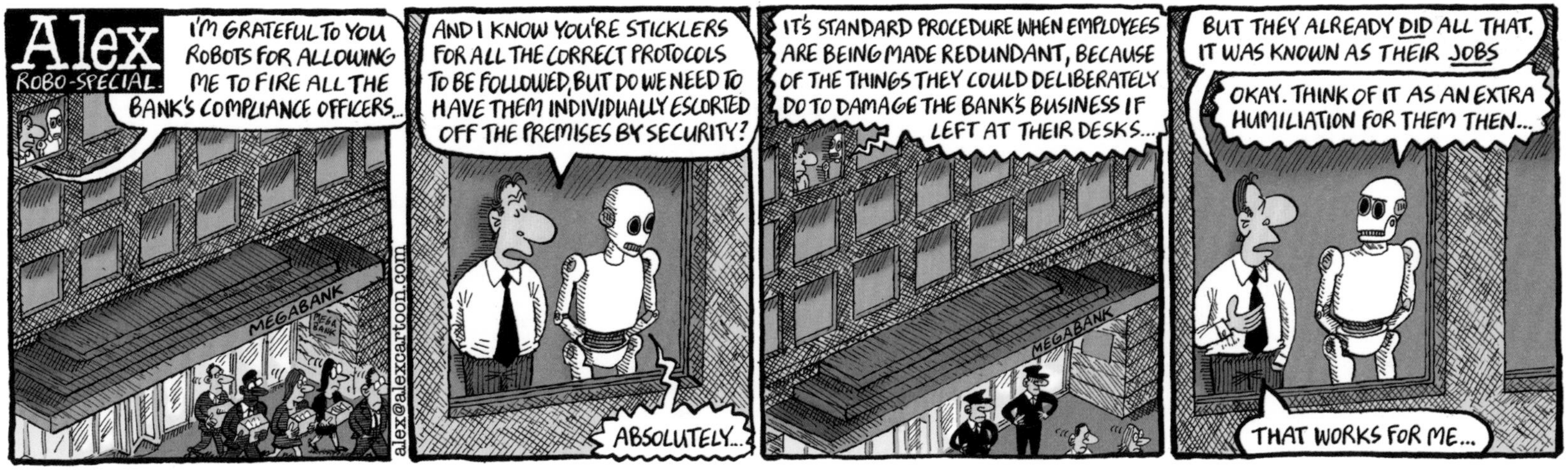
Alex
ROBO-SPECIAL
I'M GRATEFUL TO YOU ROBOTS FOR ALLOWING ME TO FIRE ALL THE BANK'S COMPLIANCE OFFICERS...
MEGABANK
alex@alexcartoon.com
AND I KNOW YOU'RE STICKLERS FOR ALL THE CORRECT PROTOCOLS TO BE FOLLOWED, BUT DO WE NEED TO HAVE THEM INDIVIDUALLY ESCORTED OFF THE PREMISES BY SECURITY?
ABSOLUTELY...
IT'S STANDARD PROCEDURE WHEN EMPLOYEES ARE BEING MADE REDUNDANT, BECAUSE OF THE THINGS THEY COULD DELIBERATELY DO TO DAMAGE THE BANK'S BUSINESS IF LEFT AT THEIR DESKS...
MEGABANK
BUT THEY ALREADY DID ALL THAT. IT WAS KNOWN AS THEIR JOBS
OKAY. THINK OF IT AS AN EXTRA HUMILIATION FOR THEM THEN...
THAT WORKS FOR ME...

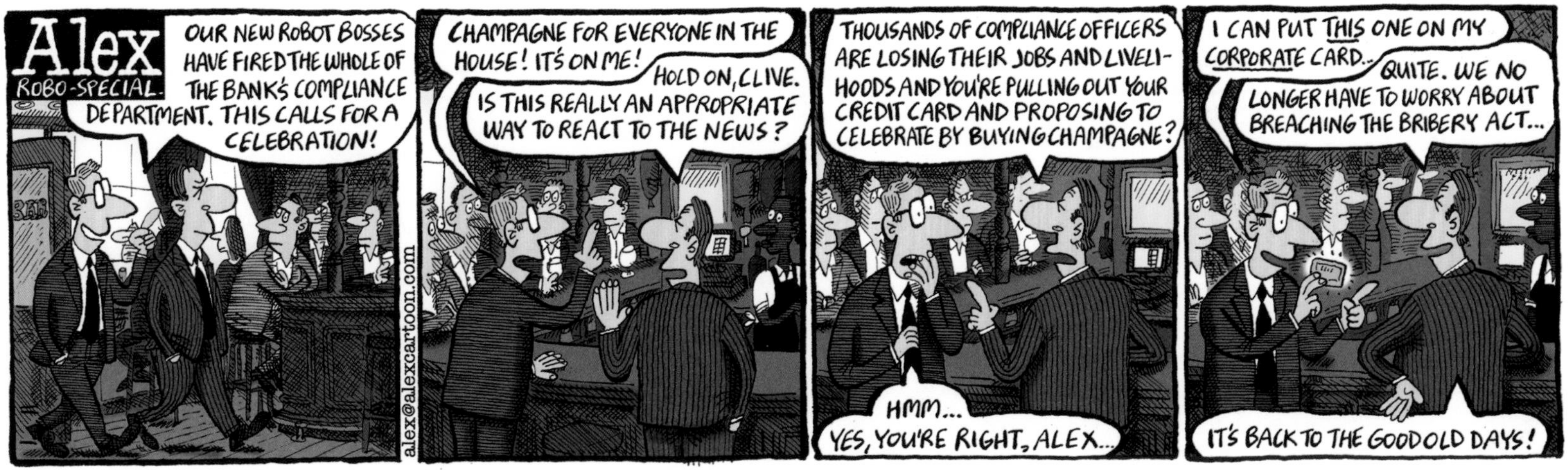
Alex
ROBO-SPECIAL
OUR NEW ROBOT BOSSES HAVE FIRED THE WHOLE OF THE BANK'S COMPLIANCE DEPARTMENT. THIS CALLS FOR A CELEBRATION!
alex@alexcartoon.com
CHAMPAGNE FOR EVERYONE IN THE HOUSE! IT'S ON ME!
HOLD ON, CLIVE. IS THIS REALLY AN APPROPRIATE WAY TO REACT TO THE NEWS?
THOUSANDS OF COMPLIANCE OFFICERS ARE LOSING THEIR JOBS AND LIVELIHOODS AND YOU'RE PULLING OUT YOUR CREDIT CARD AND PROPOSING TO CELEBRATE BY BUYING CHAMPAGNE?
HMM... YES, YOU'RE RIGHT, ALEX...
I CAN PUT THIS ONE ON MY CORPORATE CARD...
QUITE. WE NO LONGER HAVE TO WORRY ABOUT BREACHING THE BRIBERY ACT...
IT'S BACK TO THE GOOD OLD DAYS!

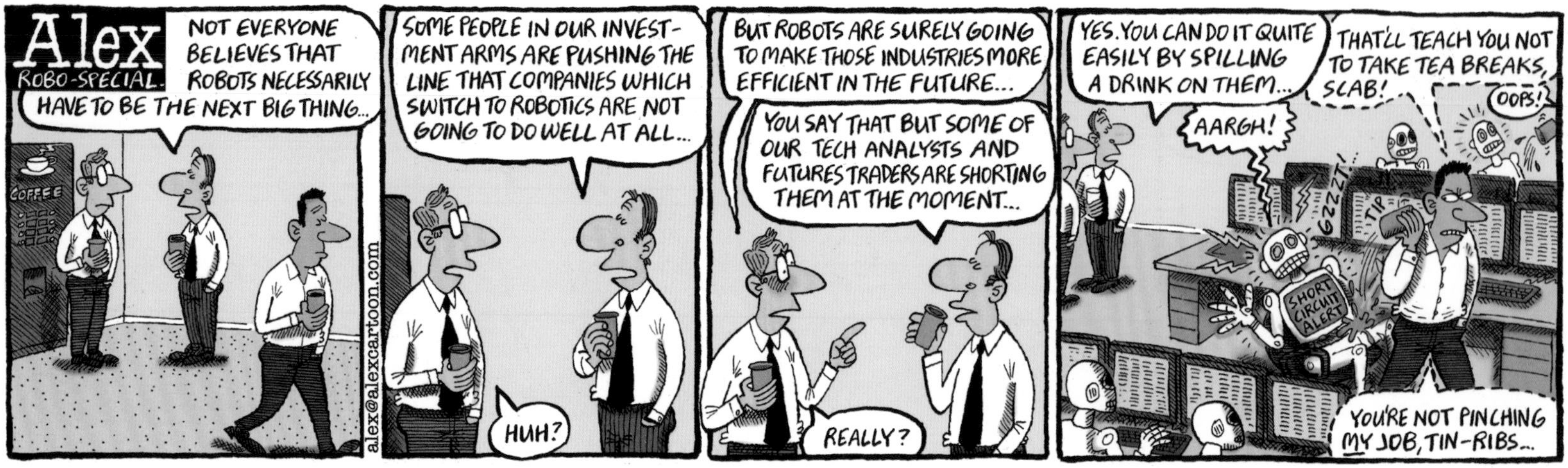
Alex
ROBO-SPECIAL.
NOT EVERYONE BELIEVES THAT ROBOTS NECESSARILY HAVE TO BE THE NEXT BIG THING...
COFFEE
alex@alexcartoon.com
SOME PEOPLE IN OUR INVESTMENT ARMS ARE PUSHING THE LINE THAT COMPANIES WHICH SWITCH TO ROBOTICS ARE NOT GOING TO DO WELL AT ALL...
HUH?
BUT ROBOTS ARE SURELY GOING TO MAKE THOSE INDUSTRIES MORE EFFICIENT IN THE FUTURE...
YOU SAY THAT BUT SOME OF OUR TECH ANALYSTS AND FUTURES TRADERS ARE SHORTING THEM AT THE MOMENT...
REALLY?
YES. YOU CAN DO IT QUITE EASILY BY SPILLING A DRINK ON THEM...
THAT'LL TEACH YOU NOT TO TAKE TEA BREAKS, SCAB!
OOPS!
AARGH!
GZZZT!
TIP
SHORT CIRCUIT ALERT
YOU'RE NOT PINCHING MY JOB, TIN-RIBS...

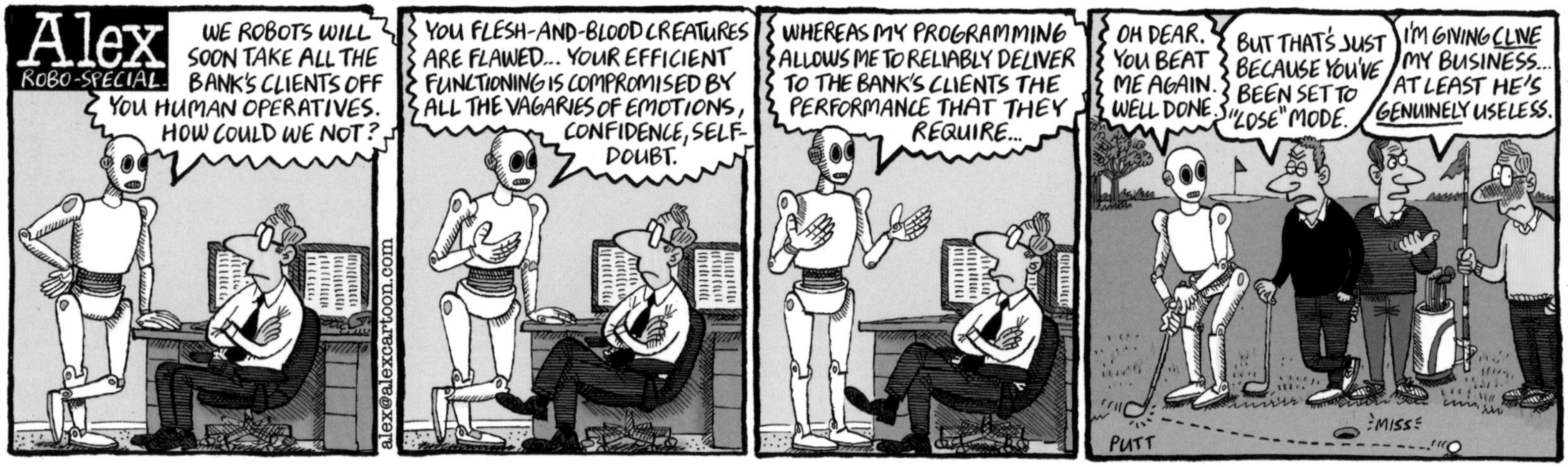
Alex
ROBO-SPECIAL.
WE ROBOTS WILL SOON TAKE ALL THE BANK'S CLIENTS OFF YOU HUMAN OPERATIVES. HOW COULD WE NOT?
alex@alexcartoon.com
YOU FLESH-AND-BLOOD CREATURES ARE FLAWED... YOUR EFFICIENT FUNCTIONING IS COMPROMISED BY ALL THE VAGARIES OF EMOTIONS, CONFIDENCE, SELF-DOUBT.
WHEREAS MY PROGRAMMING ALLOWS ME TO RELIABLY DELIVER TO THE BANK'S CLIENTS THE PERFORMANCE THAT THEY REQUIRE...
OH DEAR. YOU BEAT ME AGAIN. WELL DONE.
BUT THAT'S JUST BECAUSE YOU'VE BEEN SET TO "LOSE" MODE.
I'M GIVING CLIVE MY BUSINESS... AT LEAST HE'S GENUINELY USELESS.
PUTT
MISS

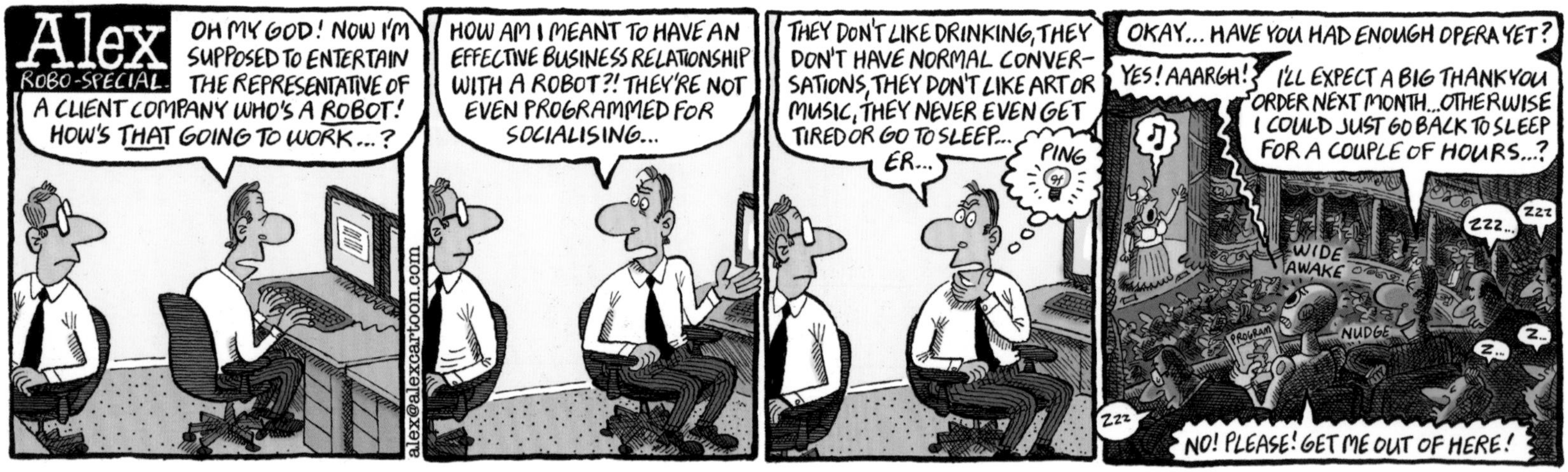
Alex
ROBO-SPECIAL.
OH MY GOD! NOW I'M SUPPOSED TO ENTERTAIN THE REPRESENTATIVE OF A CLIENT COMPANY WHO'S A ROBOT! HOW'S THAT GOING TO WORK...?
alex@alexcartoon.com
HOW AM I MEANT TO HAVE AN EFFECTIVE BUSINESS RELATIONSHIP WITH A ROBOT?! THEY'RE NOT EVEN PROGRAMMED FOR SOCIALISING...
THEY DON'T LIKE DRINKING, THEY DON'T HAVE NORMAL CONVERSATIONS, THEY DON'T LIKE ART OR MUSIC, THEY NEVER EVEN GET TIRED OR GO TO SLEEP...
ER...
PING
OKAY... HAVE YOU HAD ENOUGH OPERA YET?
YES! AAARGH!
I'LL EXPECT A BIG THANK YOU ORDER NEXT MONTH... OTHERWISE I COULD JUST GO BACK TO SLEEP FOR A COUPLE OF HOURS...?
WIDE AWAKE
NUDGE
PROGRAM
ZZZ...
ZZZ
Z...
Z...
ZZZ
NO! PLEASE! GET ME OUT OF HERE!

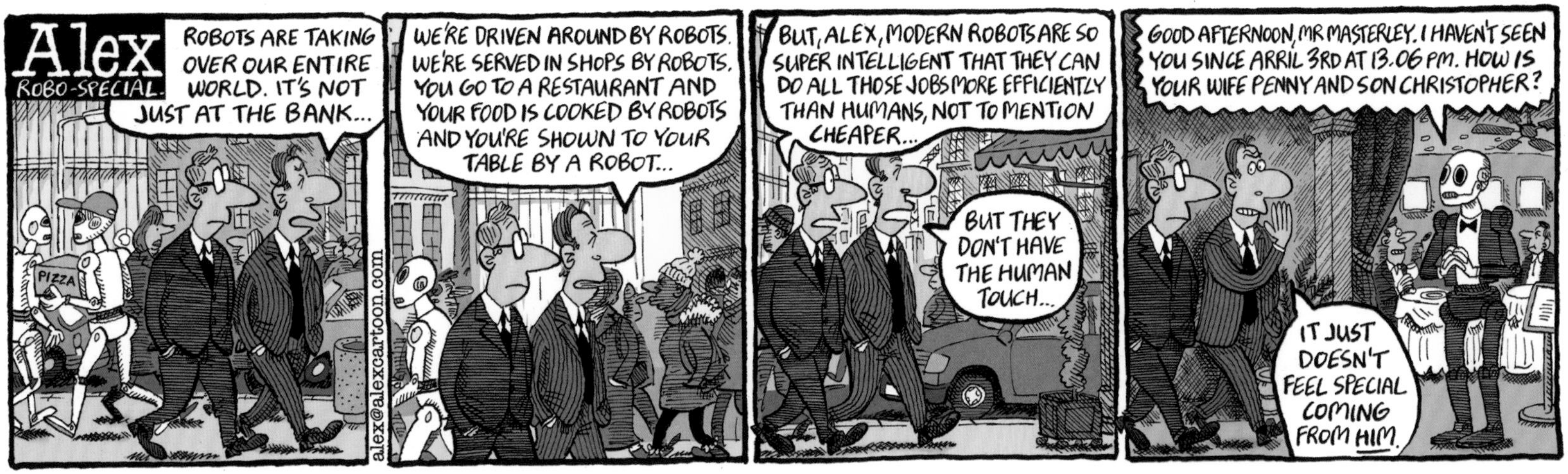
Alex
ROBO-SPECIAL.
ROBOTS ARE TAKING OVER OUR ENTIRE WORLD. IT'S NOT JUST AT THE BANK...
PIZZA
alex@alexcartoon.com
WE'RE DRIVEN AROUND BY ROBOTS. WE'RE SERVED IN SHOPS BY ROBOTS. YOU GO TO A RESTAURANT AND YOUR FOOD IS COOKED BY ROBOTS AND YOU'RE SHOWN TO YOUR TABLE BY A ROBOT...
BUT, ALEX, MODERN ROBOTS ARE SO SUPER INTELLIGENT THAT THEY CAN DO ALL THOSE JOBS MORE EFFICIENTLY THAN HUMANS, NOT TO MENTION CHEAPER...
BUT THEY DON'T HAVE THE HUMAN TOUCH...
GOOD AFTERNOON, MR MASTERLEY. I HAVEN'T SEEN YOU SINCE APRIL 3RD AT 13.06 PM. HOW IS YOUR WIFE PENNY AND SON CHRISTOPHER?
IT JUST DOESN'T FEEL SPECIAL COMING FROM HIM.

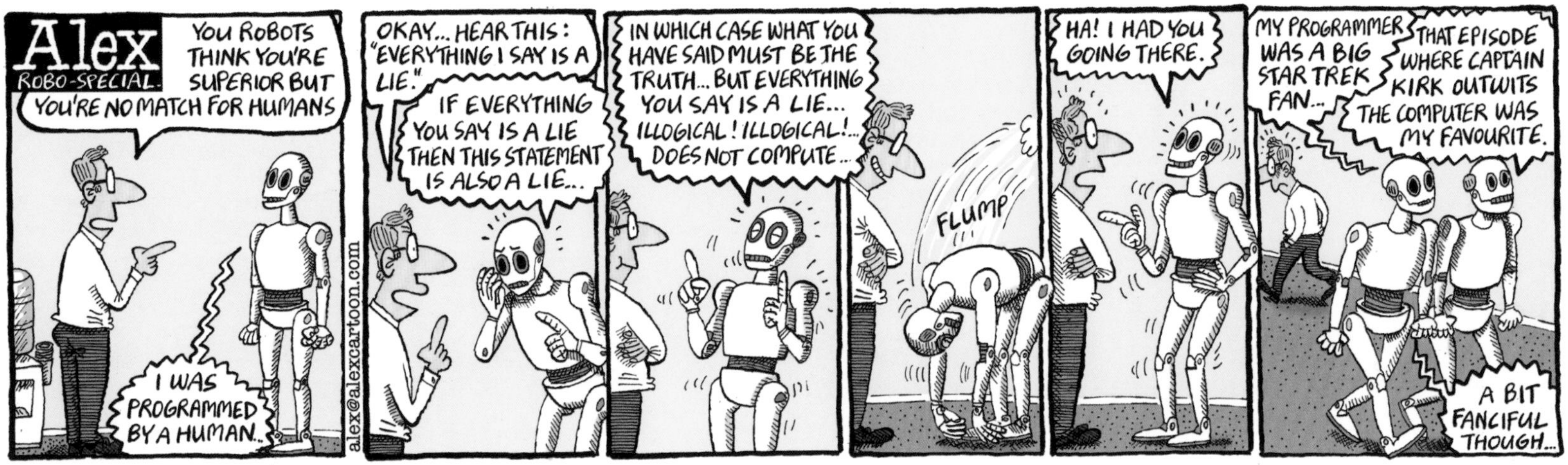
Alex
ROBO-SPECIAL.
YOU ROBOTS THINK YOU'RE SUPERIOR BUT YOU'RE NO MATCH FOR HUMANS
I WAS PROGRAMMED BY A HUMAN...
alex@alexcartoon.com
OKAY... HEAR THIS: "EVERYTHING I SAY IS A LIE."
IF EVERYTHING YOU SAY IS A LIE THEN THIS STATEMENT IS ALSO A LIE...
IN WHICH CASE WHAT YOU HAVE SAID MUST BE THE TRUTH... BUT EVERYTHING YOU SAY IS A LIE... ILLOGICAL! ILLOGICAL!... DOES NOT COMPUTE...
FLUMP
HA! I HAD YOU GOING THERE.
MY PROGRAMMER WAS A BIG STAR TREK FAN...
THAT EPISODE WHERE CAPTAIN KIRK OUTWITS THE COMPUTER WAS MY FAVOURITE.
A BIT FANCIFUL THOUGH...

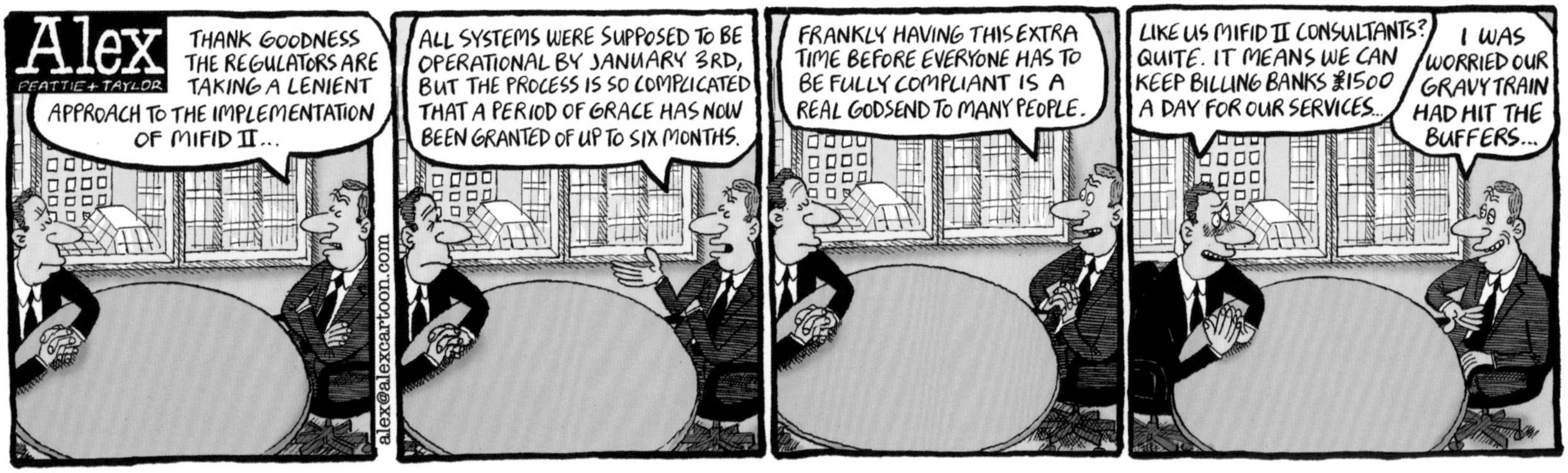
Alex
PEATTIE + TAYLOR
THANK GOODNESS THE REGULATORS ARE TAKING A LENIENT APPROACH TO THE IMPLEMENTATION OF MIFID II...
alex@alexcartoon.com
ALL SYSTEMS WERE SUPPOSED TO BE OPERATIONAL BY JANUARY 3RD, BUT THE PROCESS IS SO COMPLICATED THAT A PERIOD OF GRACE HAS NOW BEEN GRANTED OF UP TO SIX MONTHS.
FRANKLY HAVING THIS EXTRA TIME BEFORE EVERYONE HAS TO BE FULLY COMPLIANT IS A REAL GODSEND TO MANY PEOPLE.
LIKE US MIFID II CONSULTANTS? QUITE. IT MEANS WE CAN KEEP BILLING BANKS £1500 A DAY FOR OUR SERVICES...
I WAS WORRIED OUR GRAVY TRAIN HAD HIT THE BUFFERS...

Alex PEATTIE + TAYLOR

Panel 1: SO, UNDER MIFID II THE BANK NOW HAS TO CHARGE FUND MANAGERS FOR THE RESEARCH THAT THEY USED TO GET SENT FOR FREE?

CORRECT...

Panel 2: BUT CAN'T WE JUST UNDERCUT OUR COMPETITORS ON PRICE? SELL OUR RESEARCH DIRT CHEAP AND PUT THEM OUT OF BUSINESS? WE'RE A BIG BANK WITH DEEP POCKETS...

THAT'S EXPLICITLY BANNED, CLIVE...

Panel 3: IT'S ALL PART OF A STACK OF NEW REGULATIONS THAT ARE DESIGNED TO CREATE A LEVEL PLAYING FIELD AND PREVENT THE BIGGER MARKET PLAYERS HAVING AN UNFAIR ADVANTAGE OVER THE SMALLER ONES...

AND THAT'S GOOD?

DEFINITELY...

Panel 4: BECAUSE THE SMALLER BANKS CAN'T AFFORD TO EMPLOY THE ARMY OF COMPLIANCE STAFF IT'S GOING TO TAKE TO OVERSEE ALL THESE RULES...

RIGHT... AND WE CAN... SO THEY'LL GO OUT OF BUSINESS?

HEE HEE...

alex@alexcartoon.com

Alex PEATTIE + TAYLOR

Panel 1: REMEMBER HOW BEFORE BREXIT EVERYONE WAS TALKING ABOUT GREECE BEING THE FIRST COUNTRY TO LEAVE THE E.U.?

OH YES... "GREXIT"...

Panel 2: WELL, THE EUROPEAN UNION IS STILL VERY UNPOPULAR IN MANY OF THOSE MEDITERRANEAN COUNTRIES WHERE THE STRENGTH OF THE EURO HAS DAMAGED THEIR ECONOMIES...

Panel 3: NOW THAT WE IN THE U.K. HAVE HAD THE COURAGE TO BREAK AWAY I WONDER HOW ORDINARY GREEKS WILL BE FEELING ABOUT THEIR CONTINUED MEMBERSHIP OF THE E.U...

THERE'S NO DOUBT, CLIVE...

Panel 4: VERY POSITIVE... THE EUROPEAN CENTRAL BANK WILL NOW CHUCK THEM AS MUCH MONEY AS THEY WANT TO PREVENT ANY FURTHER BREAK-UP...

RIGHT... IT'LL BE "DO WHATEVER IT TAKES" CUBED.

I MIGHT EVEN BUY SOME GREEK BONDS...

alex@alexcartoon.com

Alex PEATTIE + TAYLOR

Panel 1: UNDER MIFID II RULES ANY BROKER WHO RECOMMENDS A STOCK TO ME HAS TO SEND ME A "SUITABILITY REPORT" TO ENSURE IT FITS MY RISK TOLERANCE, TIME HORIZON ETC...

Panel 2: WHAT A WASTE OF EVERYONE'S TIME. FRANKLY THIS IS GOING STRAIGHT IN THE BIN...

HOLD ON, THIS IS PART OF A NEW REGULATORY DRIVE TO MAKE FINANCIAL DEALING SAFER AND MORE TRANSPARENT...

Panel 3: I DON'T THINK OUR COMPLIANCE OFFICER WOULD BE VERY HAPPY TO HEAR THAT YOU'RE PUTTING AN IMPORTANT DOCUMENT LIKE THIS STRAIGHT IN THE BIN...

NO, YOU'RE RIGHT...

Panel 4: UNDER THIS NEW DATA PRIVACY LEGISLATION THAT'S COMING IN I HAVE TO SHRED IT AND THEN PUT IT IN THE BIN...

QUITE, THERE'S NO END TO THE TEDIOUS RULES WE HAVE TO FOLLOW...

GDPR

alex@alexcartoon.com

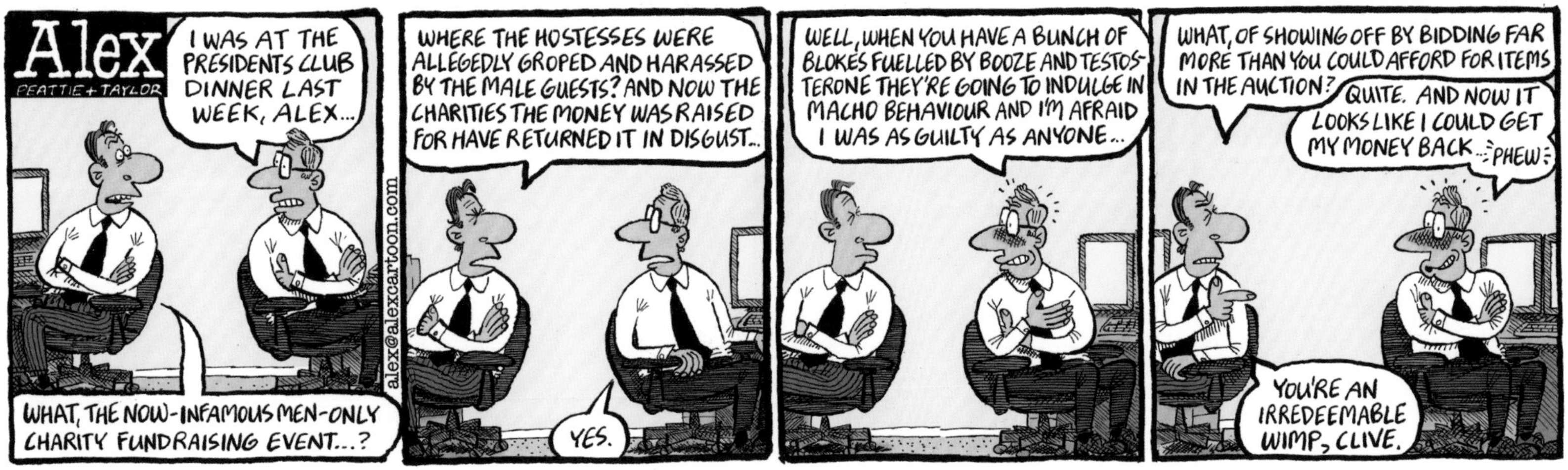
Alex
PEATTIE+TAYLOR
I WAS AT THE PRESIDENTS CLUB DINNER LAST WEEK, ALEX...
WHAT, THE NOW-INFAMOUS MEN-ONLY CHARITY FUNDRAISING EVENT...?
alex@alexcartoon.com
WHERE THE HOSTESSES WERE ALLEGEDLY GROPED AND HARASSED BY THE MALE GUESTS? AND NOW THE CHARITIES THE MONEY WAS RAISED FOR HAVE RETURNED IT IN DISGUST...
YES.
WELL, WHEN YOU HAVE A BUNCH OF BLOKES FUELLED BY BOOZE AND TESTOSTERONE THEY'RE GOING TO INDULGE IN MACHO BEHAVIOUR AND I'M AFRAID I WAS AS GUILTY AS ANYONE...
WHAT, OF SHOWING OFF BY BIDDING FAR MORE THAN YOU COULD AFFORD FOR ITEMS IN THE AUCTION?
QUITE. AND NOW IT LOOKS LIKE I COULD GET MY MONEY BACK...
PHEW
YOU'RE AN IRREDEEMABLE WIMP, CLIVE.

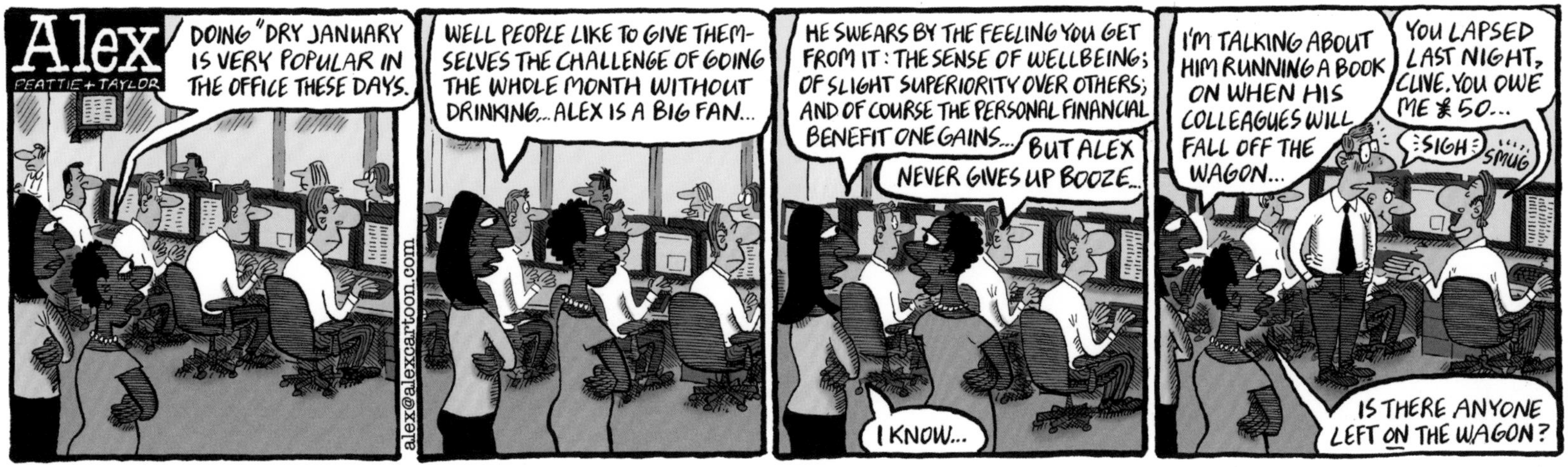
Alex
PEATTIE+TAYLOR
DOING "DRY JANUARY IS VERY POPULAR IN THE OFFICE THESE DAYS.
alex@alexcartoon.com
WELL PEOPLE LIKE TO GIVE THEMSELVES THE CHALLENGE OF GOING THE WHOLE MONTH WITHOUT DRINKING... ALEX IS A BIG FAN...
HE SWEARS BY THE FEELING YOU GET FROM IT: THE SENSE OF WELLBEING; OF SLIGHT SUPERIORITY OVER OTHERS; AND OF COURSE THE PERSONAL FINANCIAL BENEFIT ONE GAINS...
BUT ALEX NEVER GIVES UP BOOZE...
I KNOW...
I'M TALKING ABOUT HIM RUNNING A BOOK ON WHEN HIS COLLEAGUES WILL FALL OFF THE WAGON...
YOU LAPSED LAST NIGHT, CLIVE. YOU OWE ME £50...
SIGH
SMUG
IS THERE ANYONE LEFT ON THE WAGON?

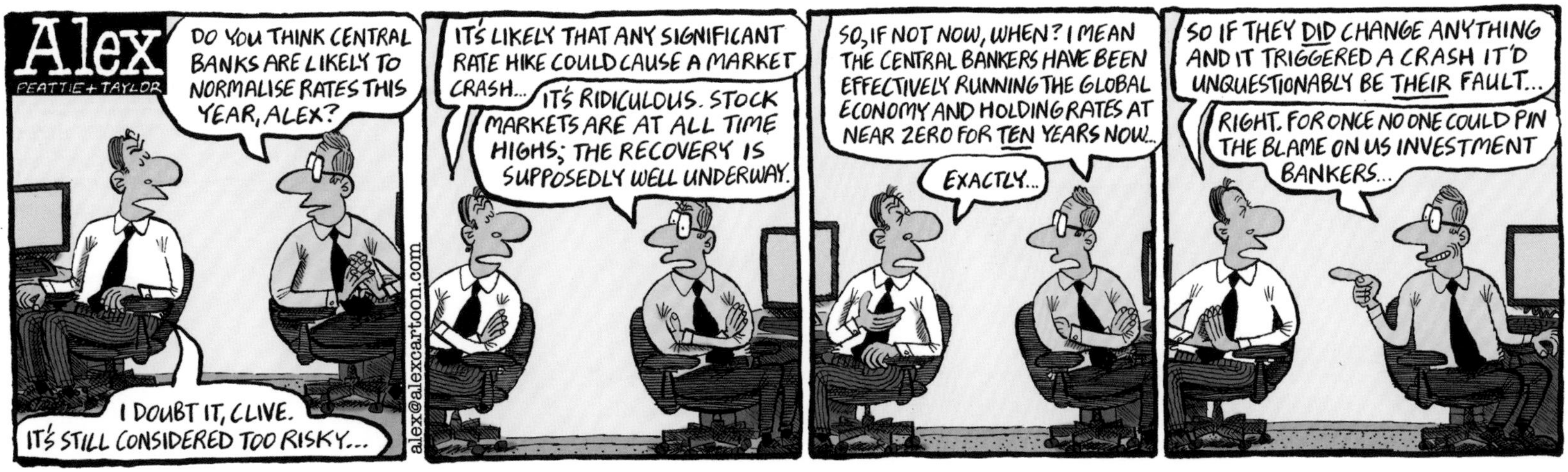
Alex
PEATTIE+TAYLOR
DO YOU THINK CENTRAL BANKS ARE LIKELY TO NORMALISE RATES THIS YEAR, ALEX?
I DOUBT IT, CLIVE. IT'S STILL CONSIDERED TOO RISKY...
alex@alexcartoon.com
IT'S LIKELY THAT ANY SIGNIFICANT RATE HIKE COULD CAUSE A MARKET CRASH...
IT'S RIDICULOUS. STOCK MARKETS ARE AT ALL TIME HIGHS; THE RECOVERY IS SUPPOSEDLY WELL UNDERWAY.
SO, IF NOT NOW, WHEN? I MEAN THE CENTRAL BANKERS HAVE BEEN EFFECTIVELY RUNNING THE GLOBAL ECONOMY AND HOLDING RATES AT NEAR ZERO FOR TEN YEARS NOW...
EXACTLY...
SO IF THEY DID CHANGE ANYTHING AND IT TRIGGERED A CRASH IT'D UNQUESTIONABLY BE THEIR FAULT...
RIGHT. FOR ONCE NO ONE COULD PIN THE BLAME ON US INVESTMENT BANKERS...

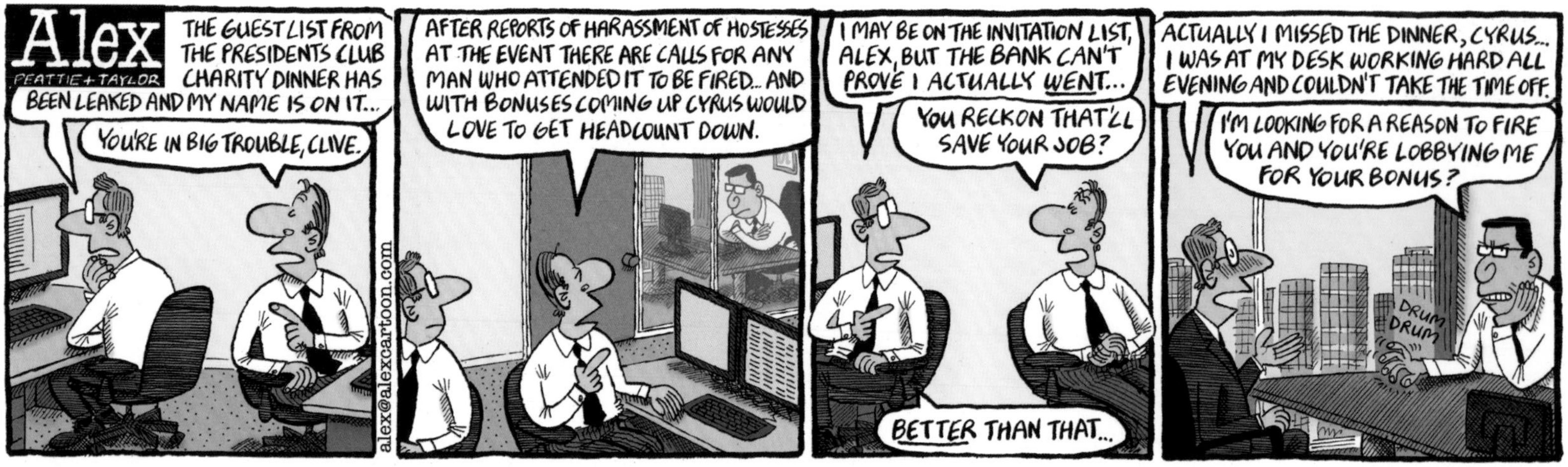
Alex
PEATTIE + TAYLOR
THE GUEST LIST FROM THE PRESIDENTS CLUB CHARITY DINNER HAS BEEN LEAKED AND MY NAME IS ON IT...
YOU'RE IN BIG TROUBLE, CLIVE.
alex@alexcartoon.com
AFTER REPORTS OF HARASSMENT OF HOSTESSES AT THE EVENT THERE ARE CALLS FOR ANY MAN WHO ATTENDED IT TO BE FIRED... AND WITH BONUSES COMING UP CYRUS WOULD LOVE TO GET HEADCOUNT DOWN.
I MAY BE ON THE INVITATION LIST, ALEX, BUT THE BANK CAN'T PROVE I ACTUALLY WENT...
YOU RECKON THAT'LL SAVE YOUR JOB?
BETTER THAN THAT...
ACTUALLY I MISSED THE DINNER, CYRUS... I WAS AT MY DESK WORKING HARD ALL EVENING AND COULDN'T TAKE THE TIME OFF.
I'M LOOKING FOR A REASON TO FIRE YOU AND YOU'RE LOBBYING ME FOR YOUR BONUS?
DRUM DRUM

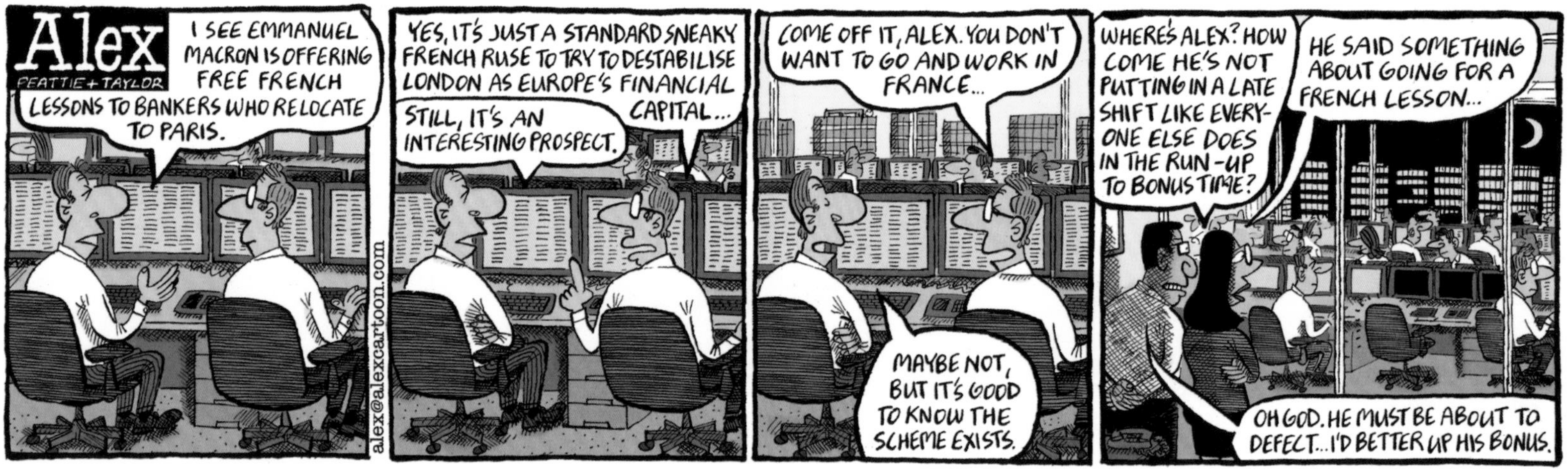
Alex
PEATTIE + TAYLOR
I SEE EMMANUEL MACRON IS OFFERING FREE FRENCH LESSONS TO BANKERS WHO RELOCATE TO PARIS.
alex@alexcartoon.com
YES, IT'S JUST A STANDARD SNEAKY FRENCH RUSE TO TRY TO DESTABILISE LONDON AS EUROPE'S FINANCIAL CAPITAL...
STILL, IT'S AN INTERESTING PROSPECT.
COME OFF IT, ALEX. YOU DON'T WANT TO GO AND WORK IN FRANCE...
MAYBE NOT, BUT IT'S GOOD TO KNOW THE SCHEME EXISTS.
WHERE'S ALEX? HOW COME HE'S NOT PUTTING IN A LATE SHIFT LIKE EVERY-ONE ELSE DOES IN THE RUN-UP TO BONUS TIME?
HE SAID SOMETHING ABOUT GOING FOR A FRENCH LESSON...
OH GOD. HE MUST BE ABOUT TO DEFECT... I'D BETTER UP HIS BONUS.

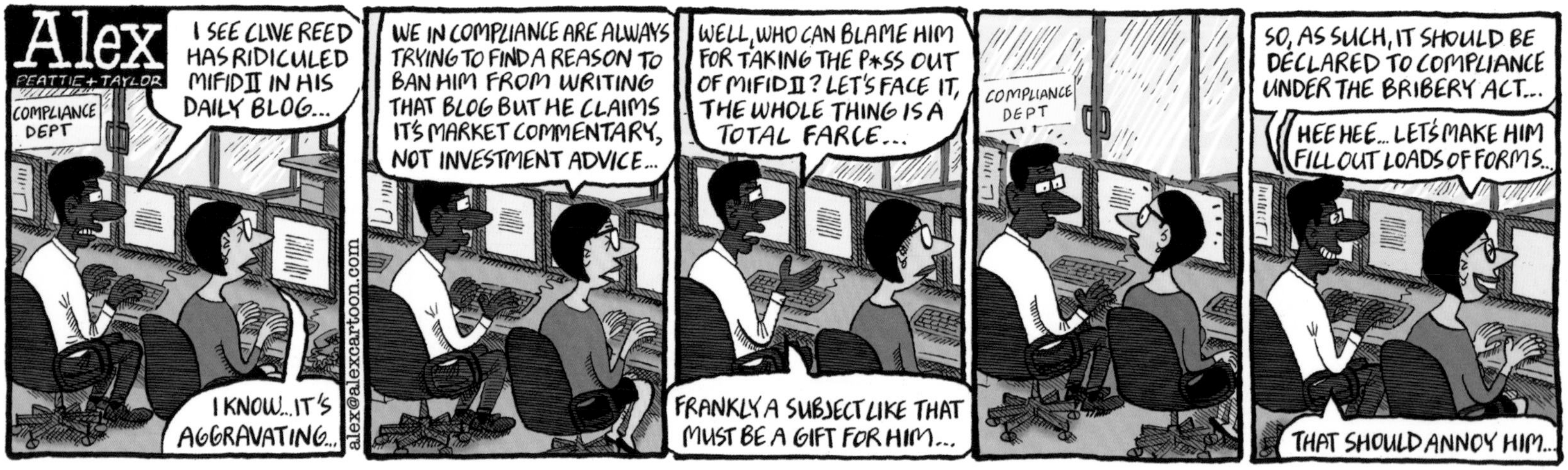
Alex
PEATTIE + TAYLOR
COMPLIANCE DEPT
I SEE CLIVE REED HAS RIDICULED MIFID II IN HIS DAILY BLOG...
I KNOW... IT'S AGGRAVATING...
alex@alexcartoon.com
WE IN COMPLIANCE ARE ALWAYS TRYING TO FIND A REASON TO BAN HIM FROM WRITING THAT BLOG BUT HE CLAIMS IT'S MARKET COMMENTARY, NOT INVESTMENT ADVICE...
WELL, WHO CAN BLAME HIM FOR TAKING THE P*SS OUT OF MIFID II? LET'S FACE IT, THE WHOLE THING IS A TOTAL FARCE...
FRANKLY A SUBJECT LIKE THAT MUST BE A GIFT FOR HIM...
COMPLIANCE DEPT
SO, AS SUCH, IT SHOULD BE DECLARED TO COMPLIANCE UNDER THE BRIBERY ACT...
HEE HEE... LET'S MAKE HIM FILL OUT LOADS OF FORMS...
THAT SHOULD ANNOY HIM...

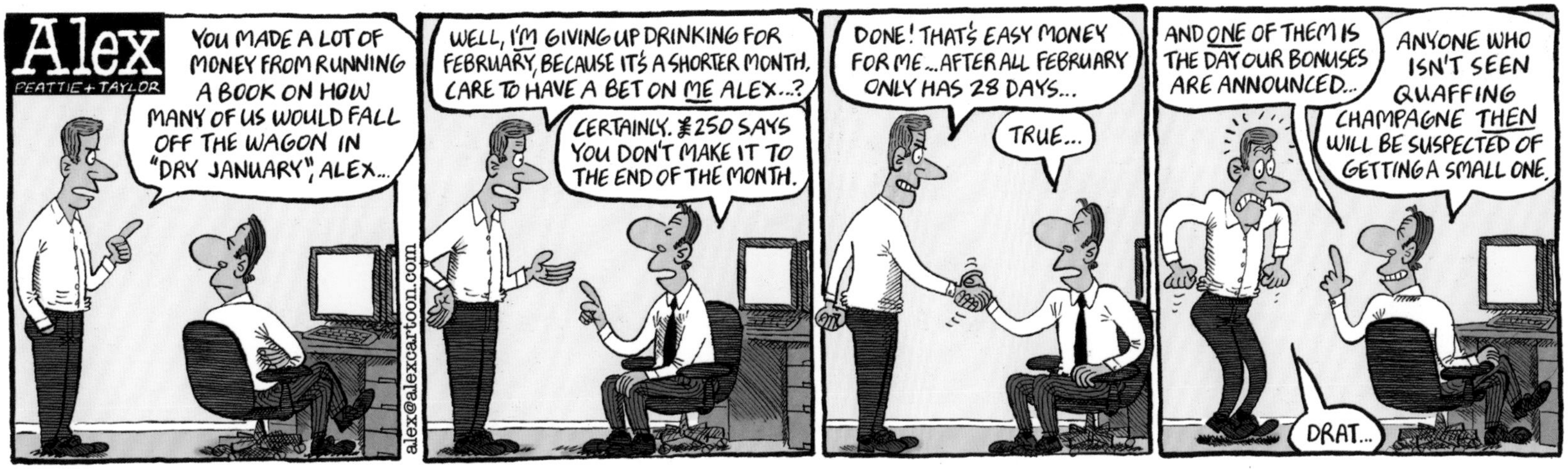
Alex
PEATTIE + TAYLOR
YOU MADE A LOT OF MONEY FROM RUNNING A BOOK ON HOW MANY OF US WOULD FALL OFF THE WAGON IN "DRY JANUARY", ALEX...
alex@alexcartoon.com
WELL, I'M GIVING UP DRINKING FOR FEBRUARY, BECAUSE IT'S A SHORTER MONTH. CARE TO HAVE A BET ON ME ALEX...?
CERTAINLY. £250 SAYS YOU DON'T MAKE IT TO THE END OF THE MONTH.
DONE! THAT'S EASY MONEY FOR ME... AFTER ALL FEBRUARY ONLY HAS 28 DAYS...
TRUE...
AND ONE OF THEM IS THE DAY OUR BONUSES ARE ANNOUNCED...
ANYONE WHO ISN'T SEEN QUAFFING CHAMPAGNE THEN WILL BE SUSPECTED OF GETTING A SMALL ONE.
DRAT...

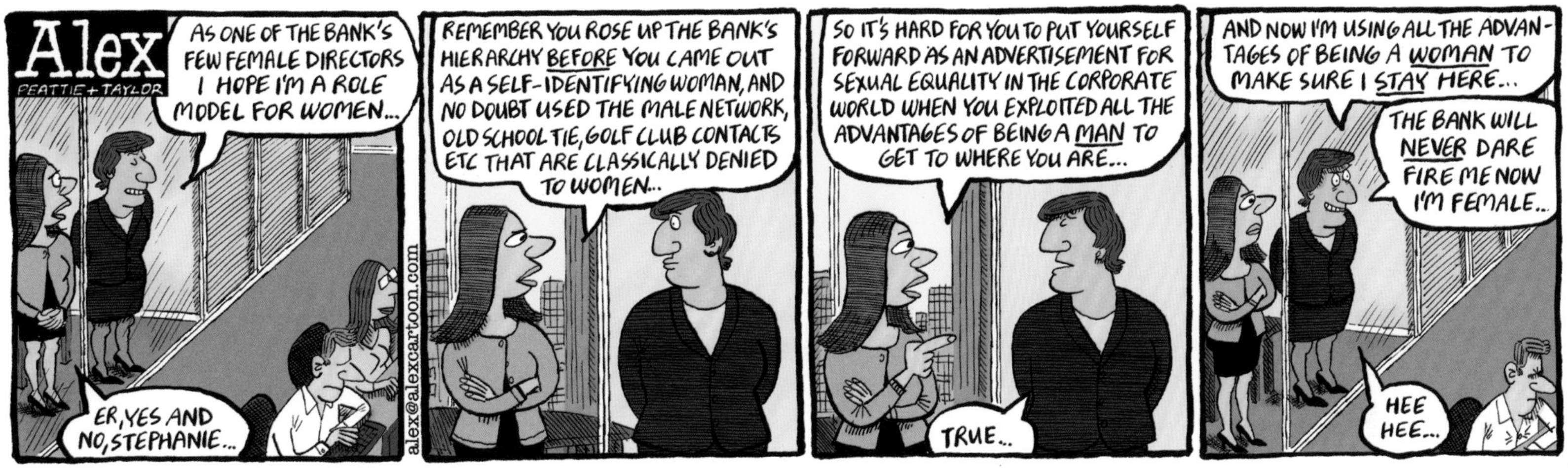
Alex
PEATTIE + TAYLOR
AS ONE OF THE BANK'S FEW FEMALE DIRECTORS I HOPE I'M A ROLE MODEL FOR WOMEN...
ER, YES AND NO, STEPHANIE...
alex@alexcartoon.com
REMEMBER YOU ROSE UP THE BANK'S HIERARCHY BEFORE YOU CAME OUT AS A SELF-IDENTIFYING WOMAN, AND NO DOUBT USED THE MALE NETWORK, OLD SCHOOL TIE, GOLF CLUB CONTACTS ETC THAT ARE CLASSICALLY DENIED TO WOMEN...
SO IT'S HARD FOR YOU TO PUT YOURSELF FORWARD AS AN ADVERTISEMENT FOR SEXUAL EQUALITY IN THE CORPORATE WORLD WHEN YOU EXPLOITED ALL THE ADVANTAGES OF BEING A MAN TO GET TO WHERE YOU ARE...
TRUE...
AND NOW I'M USING ALL THE ADVANTAGES OF BEING A WOMAN TO MAKE SURE I STAY HERE...
THE BANK WILL NEVER DARE FIRE ME NOW I'M FEMALE...
HEE HEE...

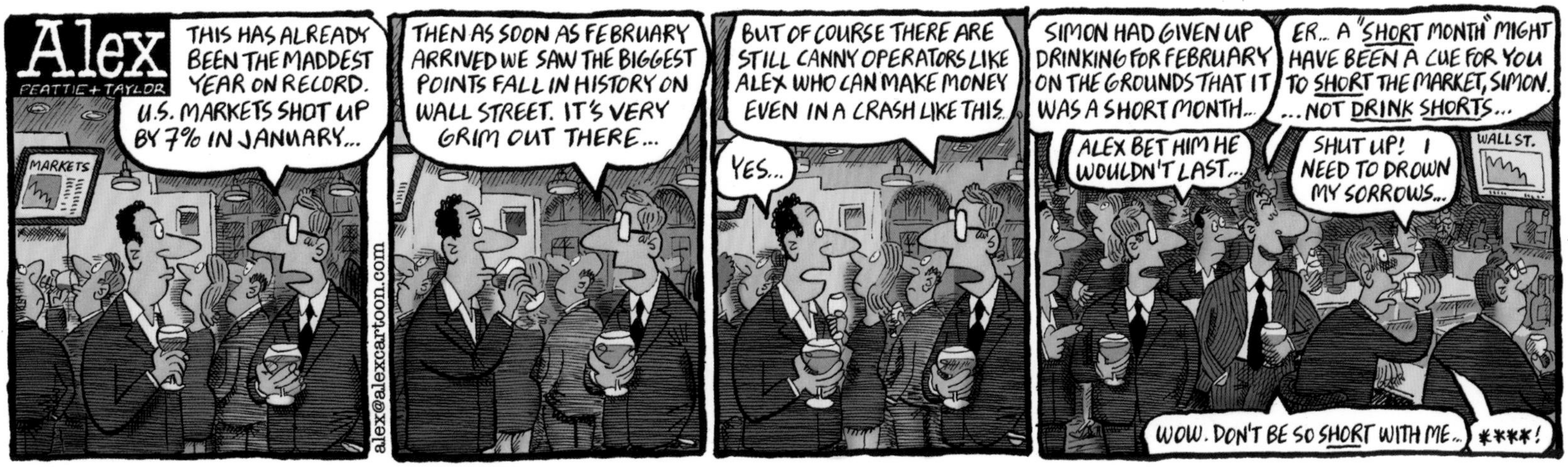
Alex
PEATTIE + TAYLOR
THIS HAS ALREADY BEEN THE MADDEST YEAR ON RECORD. U.S. MARKETS SHOT UP BY 7% IN JANUARY...
MARKETS
alex@alexcartoon.com
THEN AS SOON AS FEBRUARY ARRIVED WE SAW THE BIGGEST POINTS FALL IN HISTORY ON WALL STREET. IT'S VERY GRIM OUT THERE...
BUT OF COURSE THERE ARE STILL CANNY OPERATORS LIKE ALEX WHO CAN MAKE MONEY EVEN IN A CRASH LIKE THIS.
YES...
SIMON HAD GIVEN UP DRINKING FOR FEBRUARY ON THE GROUNDS THAT IT WAS A SHORT MONTH...
ALEX BET HIM HE WOULDN'T LAST...
ER... A "SHORT MONTH" MIGHT HAVE BEEN A CUE FOR YOU TO SHORT THE MARKET, SIMON. ...NOT DRINK SHORTS...
SHUT UP! I NEED TO DROWN MY SORROWS...
WALL ST.
WOW. DON'T BE SO SHORT WITH ME...
****!

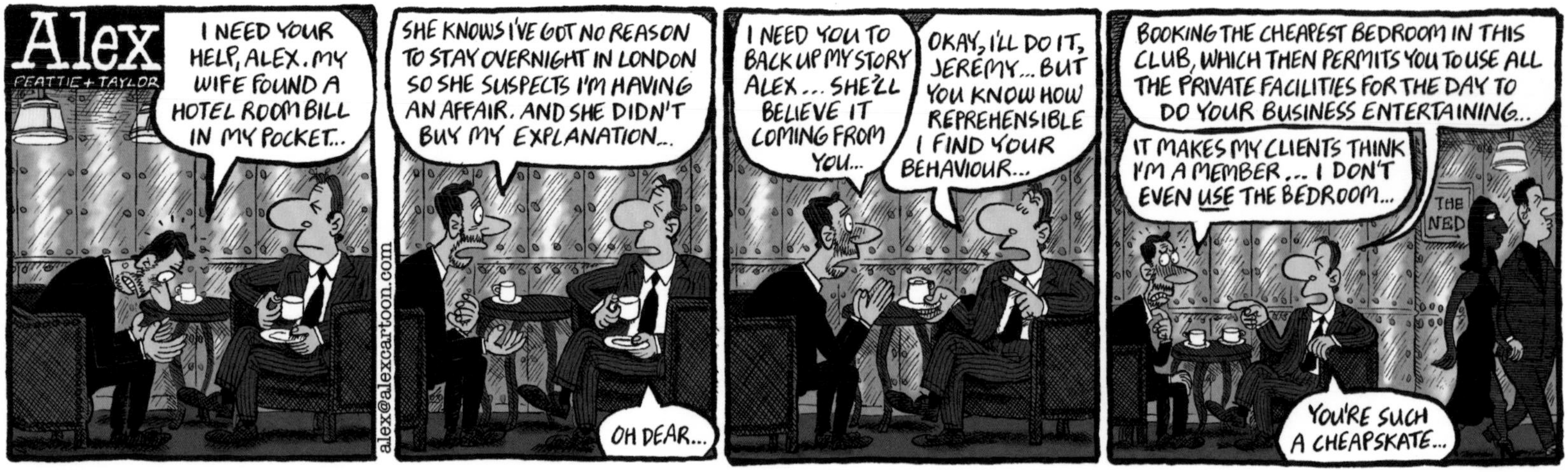
Alex
PEATTIE + TAYLOR
I NEED YOUR HELP, ALEX. MY WIFE FOUND A HOTEL ROOM BILL IN MY POCKET...
SHE KNOWS I'VE GOT NO REASON TO STAY OVERNIGHT IN LONDON SO SHE SUSPECTS I'M HAVING AN AFFAIR. AND SHE DIDN'T BUY MY EXPLANATION...
OH DEAR...
I NEED YOU TO BACK UP MY STORY ALEX... SHE'LL BELIEVE IT COMING FROM YOU...
OKAY, I'LL DO IT, JEREMY... BUT YOU KNOW HOW REPREHENSIBLE I FIND YOUR BEHAVIOUR...
BOOKING THE CHEAPEST BEDROOM IN THIS CLUB, WHICH THEN PERMITS YOU TO USE ALL THE PRIVATE FACILITIES FOR THE DAY TO DO YOUR BUSINESS ENTERTAINING...
IT MAKES MY CLIENTS THINK I'M A MEMBER... I DON'T EVEN USE THE BEDROOM...
THE NED
YOU'RE SUCH A CHEAPSKATE...
alex@alexcartoon.com

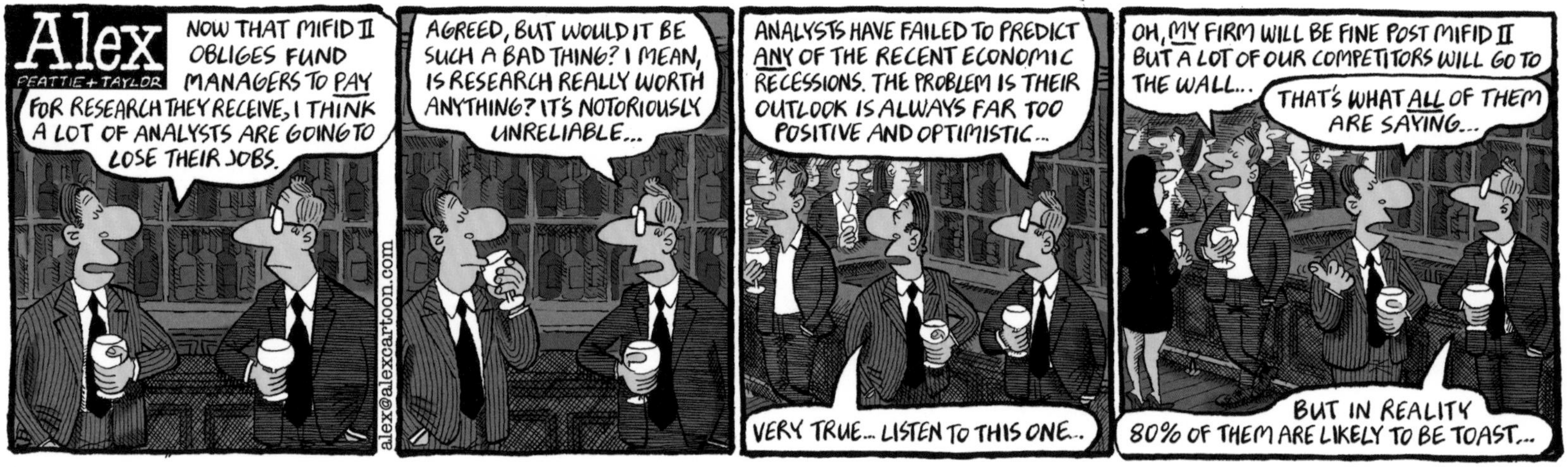
Alex
PEATTIE + TAYLOR
NOW THAT MIFID II OBLIGES FUND MANAGERS TO PAY FOR RESEARCH THEY RECEIVE, I THINK A LOT OF ANALYSTS ARE GOING TO LOSE THEIR JOBS.
AGREED, BUT WOULD IT BE SUCH A BAD THING? I MEAN, IS RESEARCH REALLY WORTH ANYTHING? IT'S NOTORIOUSLY UNRELIABLE...
ANALYSTS HAVE FAILED TO PREDICT ANY OF THE RECENT ECONOMIC RECESSIONS. THE PROBLEM IS THEIR OUTLOOK IS ALWAYS FAR TOO POSITIVE AND OPTIMISTIC...
VERY TRUE... LISTEN TO THIS ONE...
OH, MY FIRM WILL BE FINE POST MIFID II BUT A LOT OF OUR COMPETITORS WILL GO TO THE WALL...
THAT'S WHAT ALL OF THEM ARE SAYING...
BUT IN REALITY 80% OF THEM ARE LIKELY TO BE TOAST...
alex@alexcartoon.com

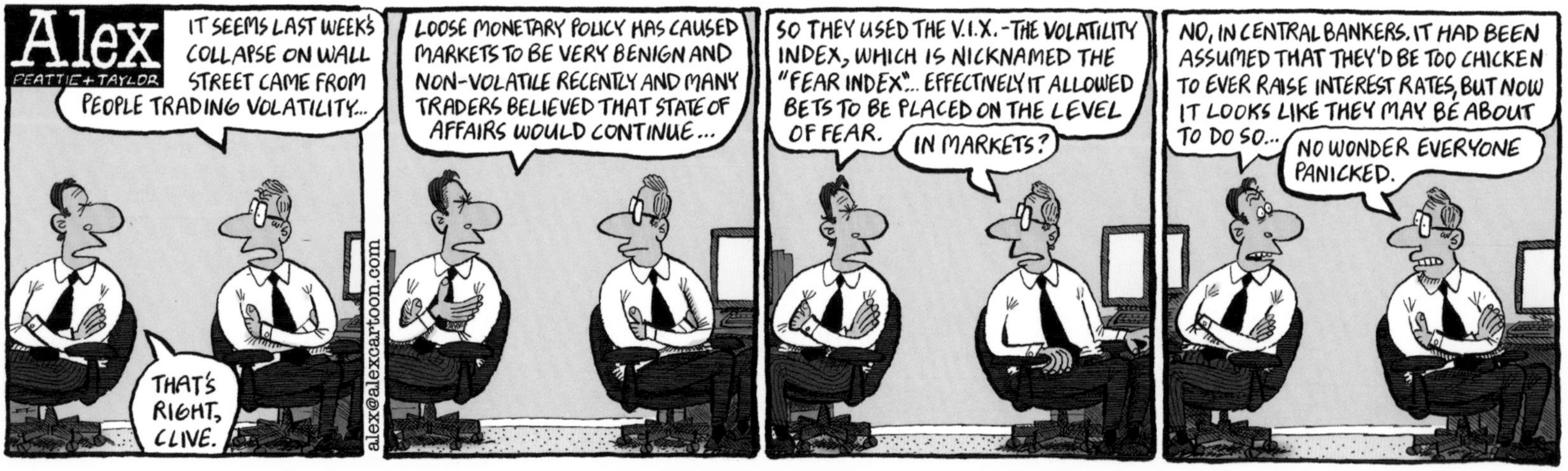
Alex
PEATTIE + TAYLOR
IT SEEMS LAST WEEK'S COLLAPSE ON WALL STREET CAME FROM PEOPLE TRADING VOLATILITY...
THAT'S RIGHT, CLIVE.
LOOSE MONETARY POLICY HAS CAUSED MARKETS TO BE VERY BENIGN AND NON-VOLATILE RECENTLY AND MANY TRADERS BELIEVED THAT STATE OF AFFAIRS WOULD CONTINUE...
SO THEY USED THE V.I.X. - THE VOLATILITY INDEX, WHICH IS NICKNAMED THE "FEAR INDEX"... EFFECTIVELY IT ALLOWED BETS TO BE PLACED ON THE LEVEL OF FEAR.
IN MARKETS?
NO, IN CENTRAL BANKERS. IT HAD BEEN ASSUMED THAT THEY'D BE TOO CHICKEN TO EVER RAISE INTEREST RATES, BUT NOW IT LOOKS LIKE THEY MAY BE ABOUT TO DO SO...
NO WONDER EVERYONE PANICKED.
alex@alexcartoon.com

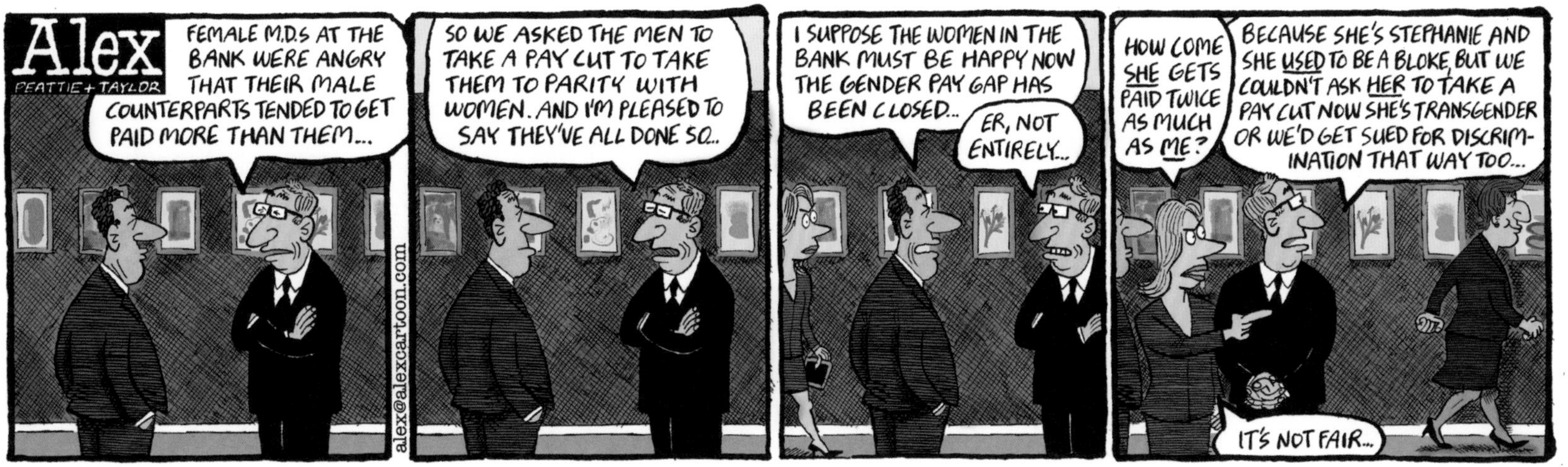
Alex
PEATTIE+TAYLOR
FEMALE M.D.S AT THE BANK WERE ANGRY THAT THEIR MALE COUNTERPARTS TENDED TO GET PAID MORE THAN THEM...
SO WE ASKED THE MEN TO TAKE A PAY CUT TO TAKE THEM TO PARITY WITH WOMEN. AND I'M PLEASED TO SAY THEY'VE ALL DONE SO..
alex@alexcartoon.com
I SUPPOSE THE WOMEN IN THE BANK MUST BE HAPPY NOW THE GENDER PAY GAP HAS BEEN CLOSED...
ER, NOT ENTIRELY...
HOW COME SHE GETS PAID TWICE AS MUCH AS ME?
BECAUSE SHE'S STEPHANIE AND SHE USED TO BE A BLOKE, BUT WE COULDN'T ASK HER TO TAKE A PAY CUT NOW SHE'S TRANSGENDER OR WE'D GET SUED FOR DISCRIMINATION THAT WAY TOO...
IT'S NOT FAIR...

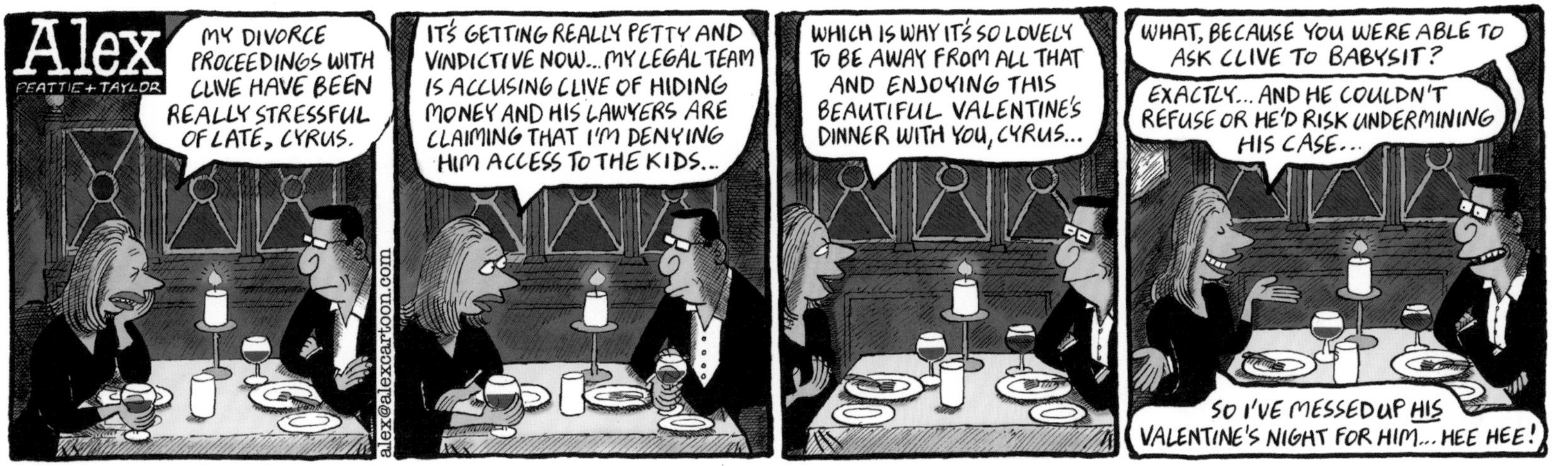
Alex
PEATTIE+TAYLOR
MY DIVORCE PROCEEDINGS WITH CLIVE HAVE BEEN REALLY STRESSFUL OF LATE, CYRUS.
IT'S GETTING REALLY PETTY AND VINDICTIVE NOW... MY LEGAL TEAM IS ACCUSING CLIVE OF HIDING MONEY AND HIS LAWYERS ARE CLAIMING THAT I'M DENYING HIM ACCESS TO THE KIDS...
alex@alexcartoon.com
WHICH IS WHY IT'S SO LOVELY TO BE AWAY FROM ALL THAT AND ENJOYING THIS BEAUTIFUL VALENTINE'S DINNER WITH YOU, CYRUS...
WHAT, BECAUSE YOU WERE ABLE TO ASK CLIVE TO BABYSIT?
EXACTLY... AND HE COULDN'T REFUSE OR HE'D RISK UNDERMINING HIS CASE...
SO I'VE MESSED UP HIS VALENTINE'S NIGHT FOR HIM... HEE HEE!

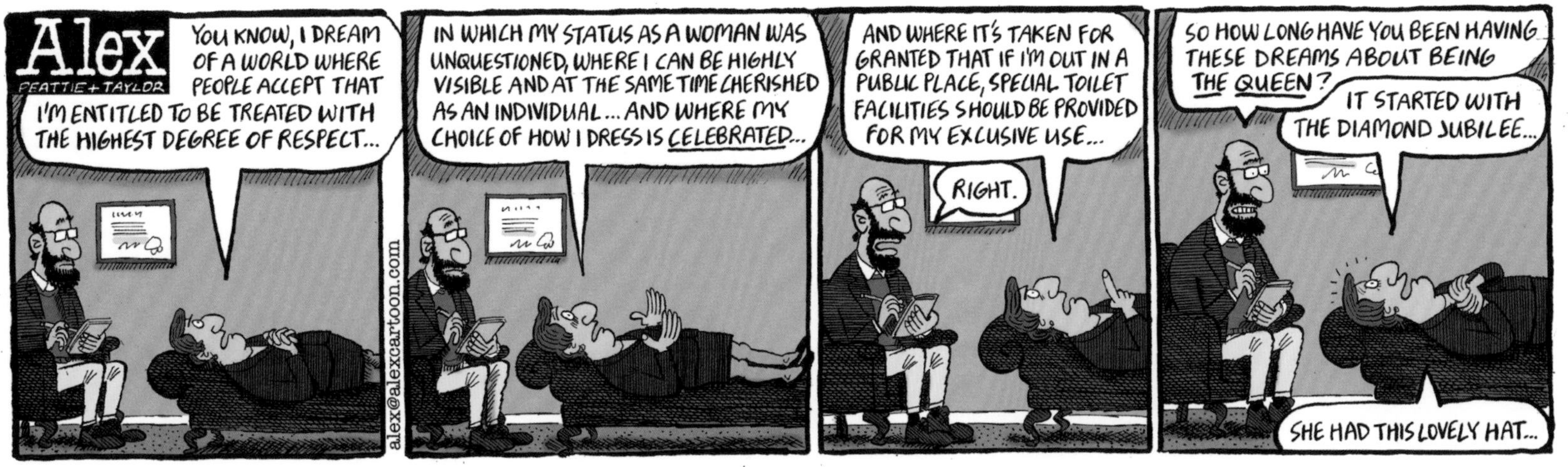
Alex
PEATTIE+TAYLOR
YOU KNOW, I DREAM OF A WORLD WHERE PEOPLE ACCEPT THAT I'M ENTITLED TO BE TREATED WITH THE HIGHEST DEGREE OF RESPECT...
IN WHICH MY STATUS AS A WOMAN WAS UNQUESTIONED, WHERE I CAN BE HIGHLY VISIBLE AND AT THE SAME TIME CHERISHED AS AN INDIVIDUAL... AND WHERE MY CHOICE OF HOW I DRESS IS CELEBRATED...
alex@alexcartoon.com
AND WHERE IT'S TAKEN FOR GRANTED THAT IF I'M OUT IN A PUBLIC PLACE, SPECIAL TOILET FACILITIES SHOULD BE PROVIDED FOR MY EXCLUSIVE USE...
RIGHT.
SO HOW LONG HAVE YOU BEEN HAVING THESE DREAMS ABOUT BEING THE QUEEN?
IT STARTED WITH THE DIAMOND JUBILEE...
SHE HAD THIS LOVELY HAT...

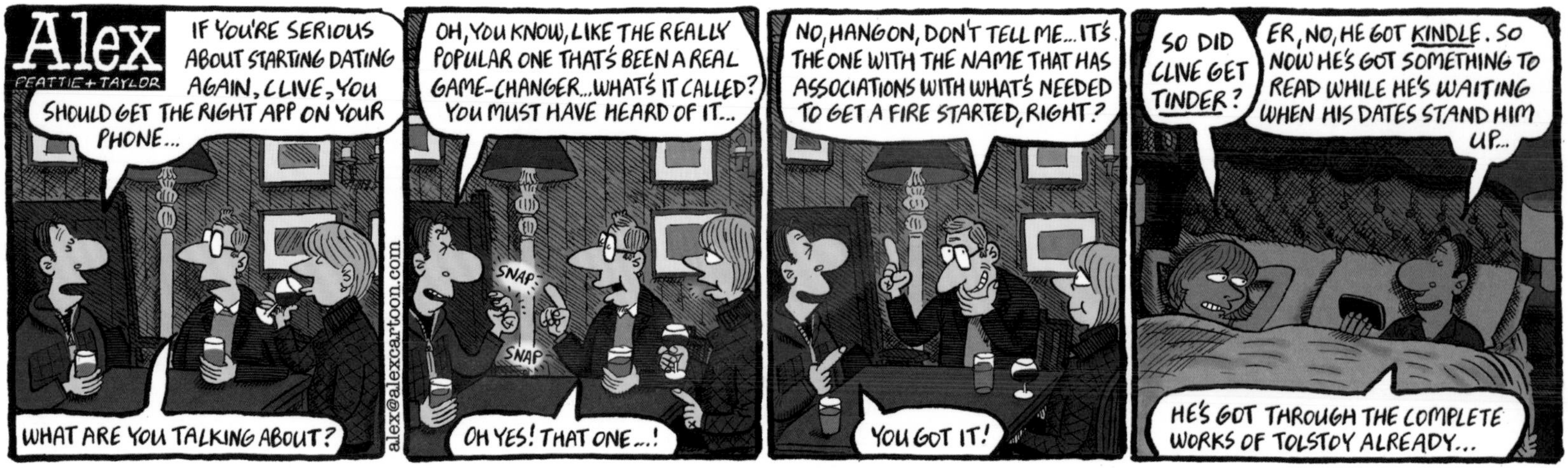
Alex
PEATTIE + TAYLOR
IF YOU'RE SERIOUS ABOUT STARTING DATING AGAIN, CLIVE, YOU SHOULD GET THE RIGHT APP ON YOUR PHONE...
WHAT ARE YOU TALKING ABOUT?
alex@alexcartoon.com
OH, YOU KNOW, LIKE THE REALLY POPULAR ONE THAT'S BEEN A REAL GAME-CHANGER... WHAT'S IT CALLED? YOU MUST HAVE HEARD OF IT...
SNAP
SNAP
OH YES! THAT ONE...!
NO, HANG ON, DON'T TELL ME... IT'S THE ONE WITH THE NAME THAT HAS ASSOCIATIONS WITH WHAT'S NEEDED TO GET A FIRE STARTED, RIGHT?
YOU GOT IT!
SO DID CLIVE GET TINDER?
ER, NO, HE GOT KINDLE. SO NOW HE'S GOT SOMETHING TO READ WHILE HE'S WAITING WHEN HIS DATES STAND HIM UP...
HE'S GOT THROUGH THE COMPLETE WORKS OF TOLSTOY ALREADY...

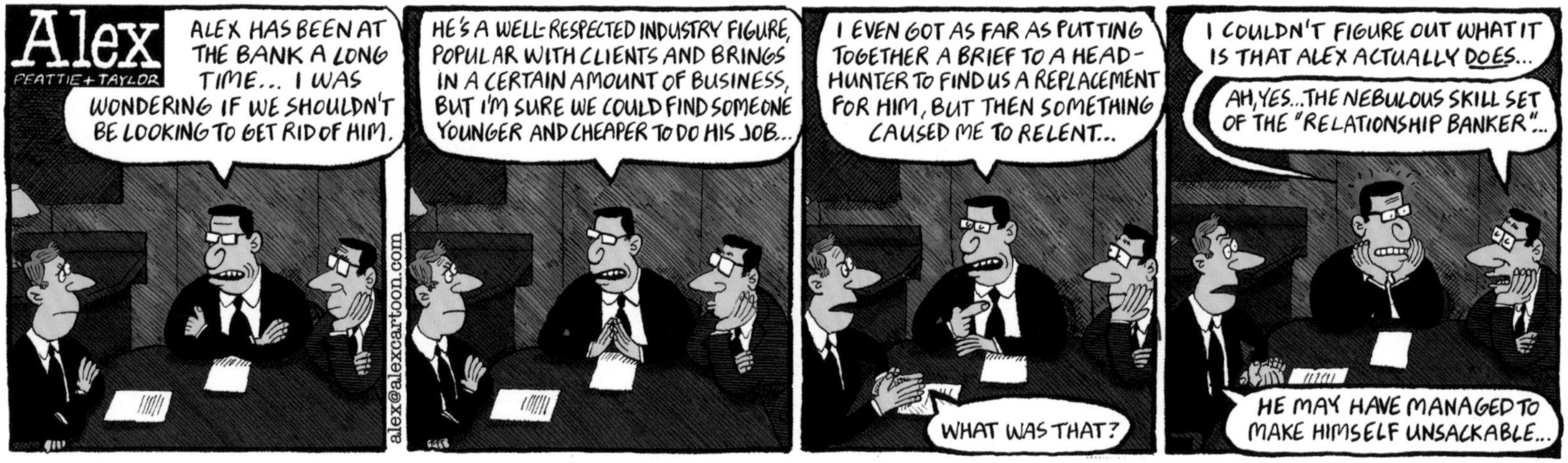
Alex
PEATTIE + TAYLOR
ALEX HAS BEEN AT THE BANK A LONG TIME... I WAS WONDERING IF WE SHOULDN'T BE LOOKING TO GET RID OF HIM.
alex@alexcartoon.com
HE'S A WELL-RESPECTED INDUSTRY FIGURE, POPULAR WITH CLIENTS AND BRINGS IN A CERTAIN AMOUNT OF BUSINESS, BUT I'M SURE WE COULD FIND SOMEONE YOUNGER AND CHEAPER TO DO HIS JOB...
I EVEN GOT AS FAR AS PUTTING TOGETHER A BRIEF TO A HEAD-HUNTER TO FIND US A REPLACEMENT FOR HIM, BUT THEN SOMETHING CAUSED ME TO RELENT...
WHAT WAS THAT?
I COULDN'T FIGURE OUT WHAT IT IS THAT ALEX ACTUALLY DOES...
AH, YES... THE NEBULOUS SKILL SET OF THE "RELATIONSHIP BANKER"...
HE MAY HAVE MANAGED TO MAKE HIMSELF UNSACKABLE...

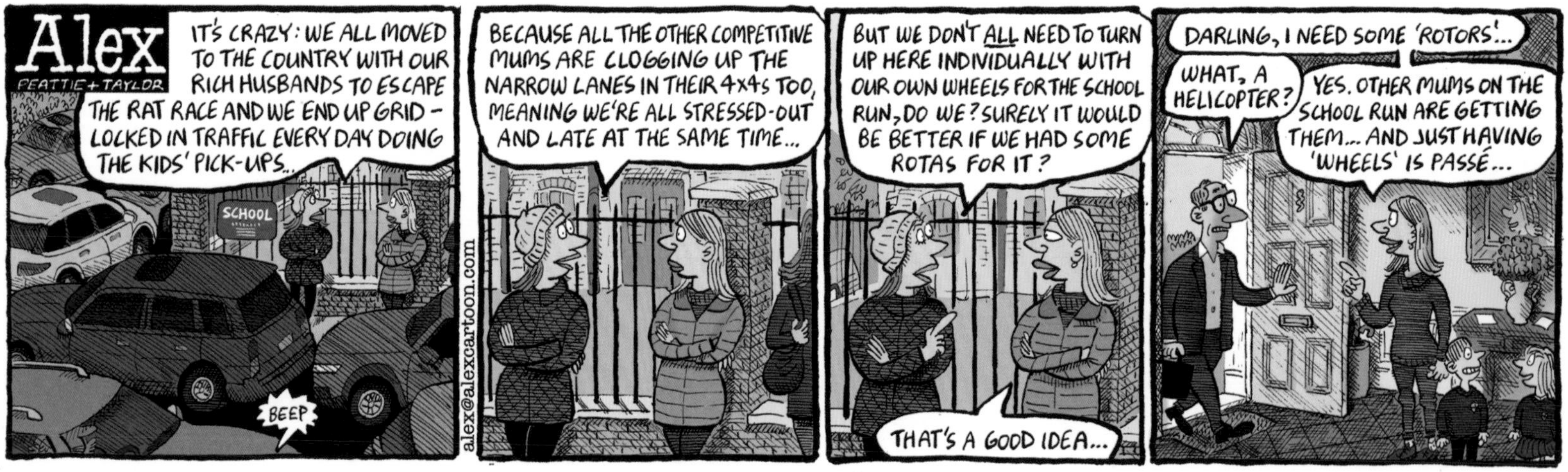
Alex
PEATTIE + TAYLOR
IT'S CRAZY: WE ALL MOVED TO THE COUNTRY WITH OUR RICH HUSBANDS TO ESCAPE THE RAT RACE AND WE END UP GRID-LOCKED IN TRAFFIC EVERY DAY DOING THE KIDS' PICK-UPS...
SCHOOL
BEEP
alex@alexcartoon.com
BECAUSE ALL THE OTHER COMPETITIVE MUMS ARE CLOGGING UP THE NARROW LANES IN THEIR 4x4s TOO, MEANING WE'RE ALL STRESSED-OUT AND LATE AT THE SAME TIME...
BUT WE DON'T ALL NEED TO TURN UP HERE INDIVIDUALLY WITH OUR OWN WHEELS FOR THE SCHOOL RUN, DO WE? SURELY IT WOULD BE BETTER IF WE HAD SOME ROTAS FOR IT?
THAT'S A GOOD IDEA...
DARLING, I NEED SOME 'ROTORS'...
WHAT, A HELICOPTER?
YES. OTHER MUMS ON THE SCHOOL RUN ARE GETTING THEM... AND JUST HAVING 'WHEELS' IS PASSÉ...

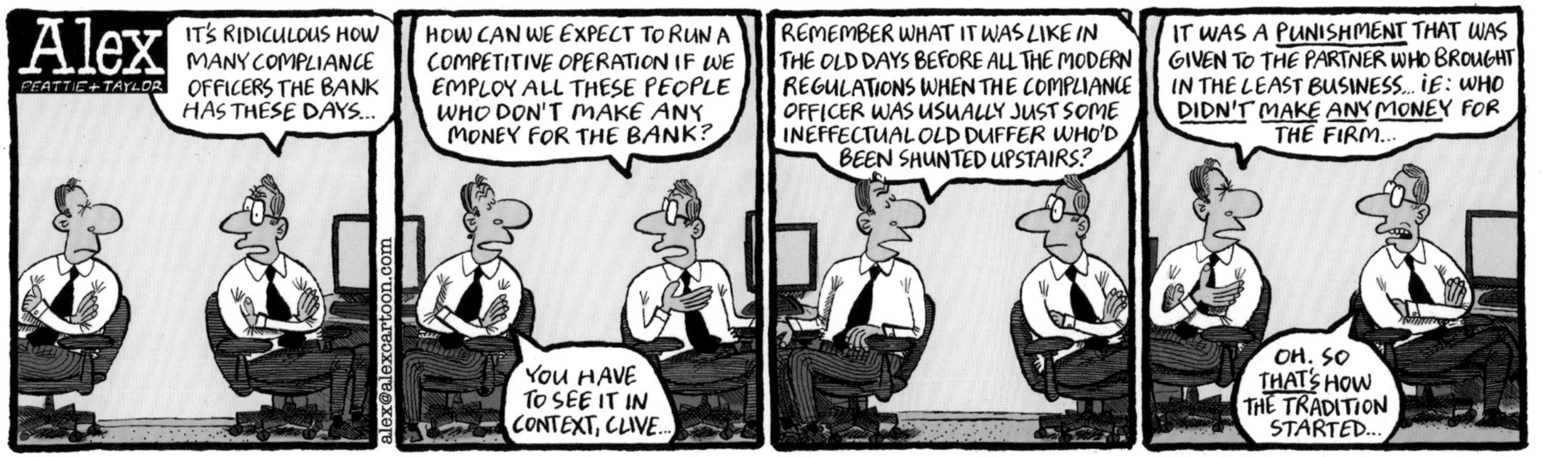
Alex
PEATTIE + TAYLOR
IT'S RIDICULOUS HOW MANY COMPLIANCE OFFICERS THE BANK HAS THESE DAYS...
alex@alexcartoon.com
HOW CAN WE EXPECT TO RUN A COMPETITIVE OPERATION IF WE EMPLOY ALL THESE PEOPLE WHO DON'T MAKE ANY MONEY FOR THE BANK?
YOU HAVE TO SEE IT IN CONTEXT, CLIVE...
REMEMBER WHAT IT WAS LIKE IN THE OLD DAYS BEFORE ALL THE MODERN REGULATIONS WHEN THE COMPLIANCE OFFICER WAS USUALLY JUST SOME INEFFECTUAL OLD DUFFER WHO'D BEEN SHUNTED UPSTAIRS?
IT WAS A PUNISHMENT THAT WAS GIVEN TO THE PARTNER WHO BROUGHT IN THE LEAST BUSINESS... IE: WHO DIDN'T MAKE ANY MONEY FOR THE FIRM...
OH. SO THAT'S HOW THE TRADITION STARTED...

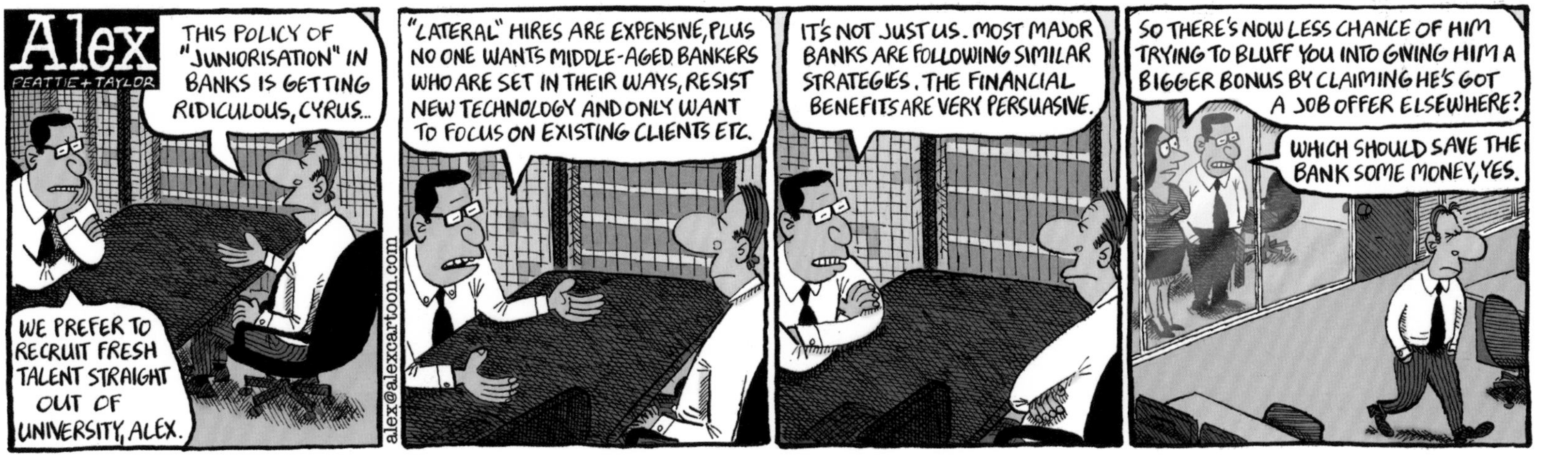
Alex
PEATTIE + TAYLOR
THIS POLICY OF "JUNIORISATION" IN BANKS IS GETTING RIDICULOUS, CYRUS...
WE PREFER TO RECRUIT FRESH TALENT STRAIGHT OUT OF UNIVERSITY, ALEX.
alex@alexcartoon.com
"LATERAL" HIRES ARE EXPENSIVE, PLUS NO ONE WANTS MIDDLE-AGED BANKERS WHO ARE SET IN THEIR WAYS, RESIST NEW TECHNOLOGY AND ONLY WANT TO FOCUS ON EXISTING CLIENTS ETC.
IT'S NOT JUST US. MOST MAJOR BANKS ARE FOLLOWING SIMILAR STRATEGIES. THE FINANCIAL BENEFITS ARE VERY PERSUASIVE.
SO THERE'S NOW LESS CHANCE OF HIM TRYING TO BLUFF YOU INTO GIVING HIM A BIGGER BONUS BY CLAIMING HE'S GOT A JOB OFFER ELSEWHERE?
WHICH SHOULD SAVE THE BANK SOME MONEY, YES.

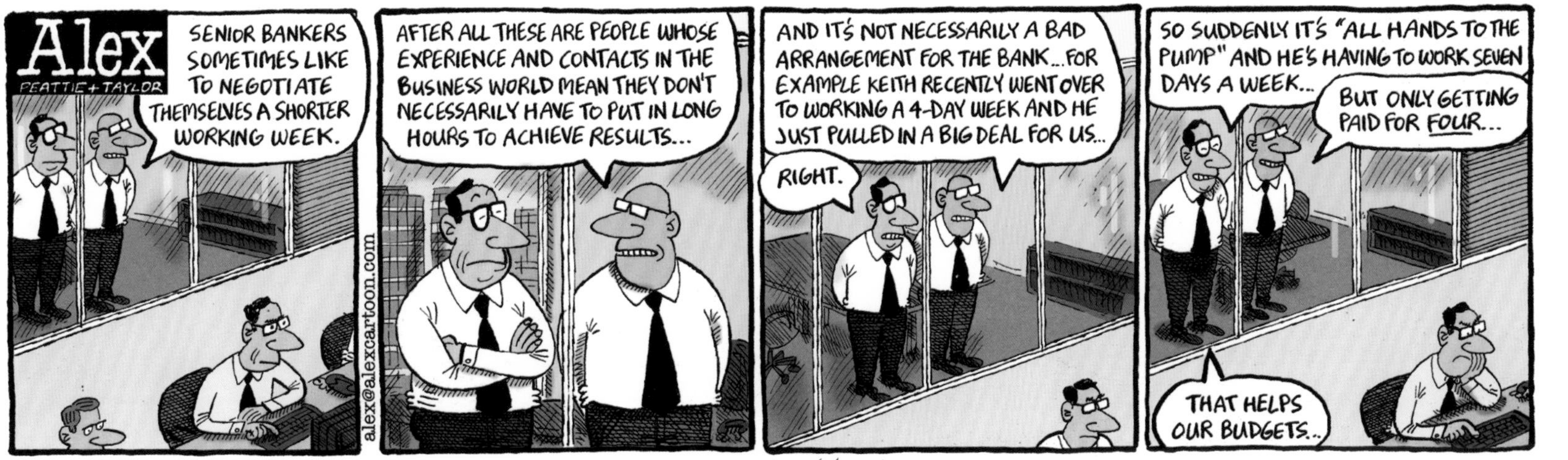
Alex
PEATTIE + TAYLOR
SENIOR BANKERS SOMETIMES LIKE TO NEGOTIATE THEMSELVES A SHORTER WORKING WEEK.
alex@alexcartoon.com
AFTER ALL THESE ARE PEOPLE WHOSE EXPERIENCE AND CONTACTS IN THE BUSINESS WORLD MEAN THEY DON'T NECESSARILY HAVE TO PUT IN LONG HOURS TO ACHIEVE RESULTS...
AND IT'S NOT NECESSARILY A BAD ARRANGEMENT FOR THE BANK... FOR EXAMPLE KEITH RECENTLY WENT OVER TO WORKING A 4-DAY WEEK AND HE JUST PULLED IN A BIG DEAL FOR US...
RIGHT.
SO SUDDENLY IT'S "ALL HANDS TO THE PUMP" AND HE'S HAVING TO WORK SEVEN DAYS A WEEK...
BUT ONLY GETTING PAID FOR FOUR...
THAT HELPS OUR BUDGETS...

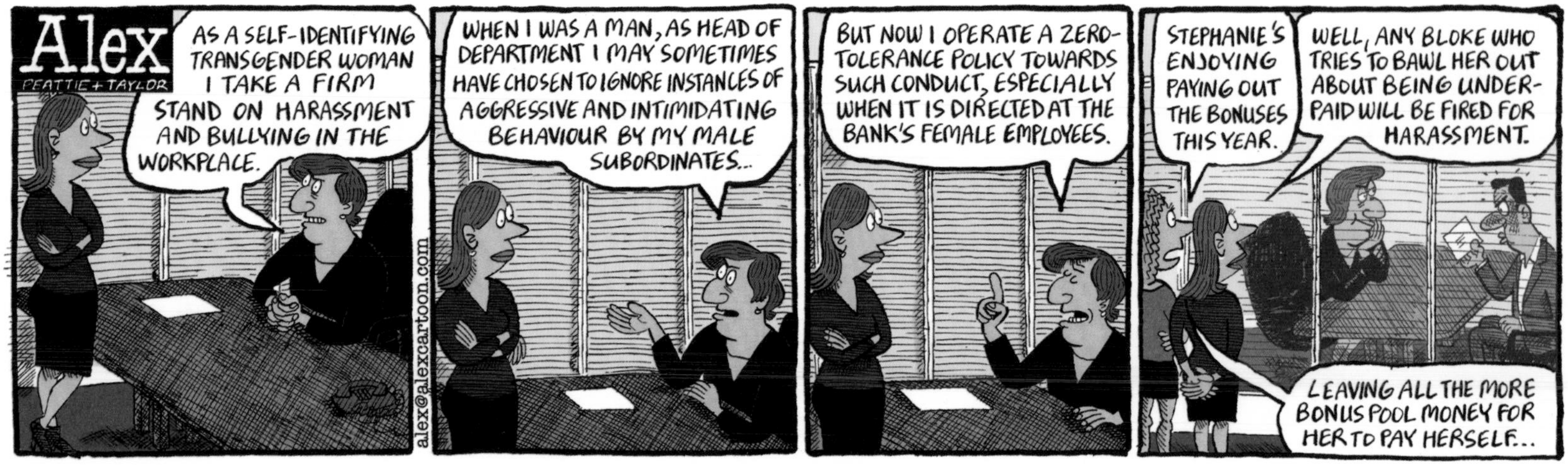
Alex
PEATTIE + TAYLOR
AS A SELF-IDENTIFYING TRANSGENDER WOMAN I TAKE A FIRM STAND ON HARASSMENT AND BULLYING IN THE WORKPLACE.
WHEN I WAS A MAN, AS HEAD OF DEPARTMENT I MAY SOMETIMES HAVE CHOSEN TO IGNORE INSTANCES OF AGGRESSIVE AND INTIMIDATING BEHAVIOUR BY MY MALE SUBORDINATES...
alex@alexcartoon.com
BUT NOW I OPERATE A ZERO-TOLERANCE POLICY TOWARDS SUCH CONDUCT, ESPECIALLY WHEN IT IS DIRECTED AT THE BANK'S FEMALE EMPLOYEES.
STEPHANIE'S ENJOYING PAYING OUT THE BONUSES THIS YEAR.
WELL, ANY BLOKE WHO TRIES TO BAWL HER OUT ABOUT BEING UNDER-PAID WILL BE FIRED FOR HARASSMENT.
LEAVING ALL THE MORE BONUS POOL MONEY FOR HER TO PAY HERSELF...

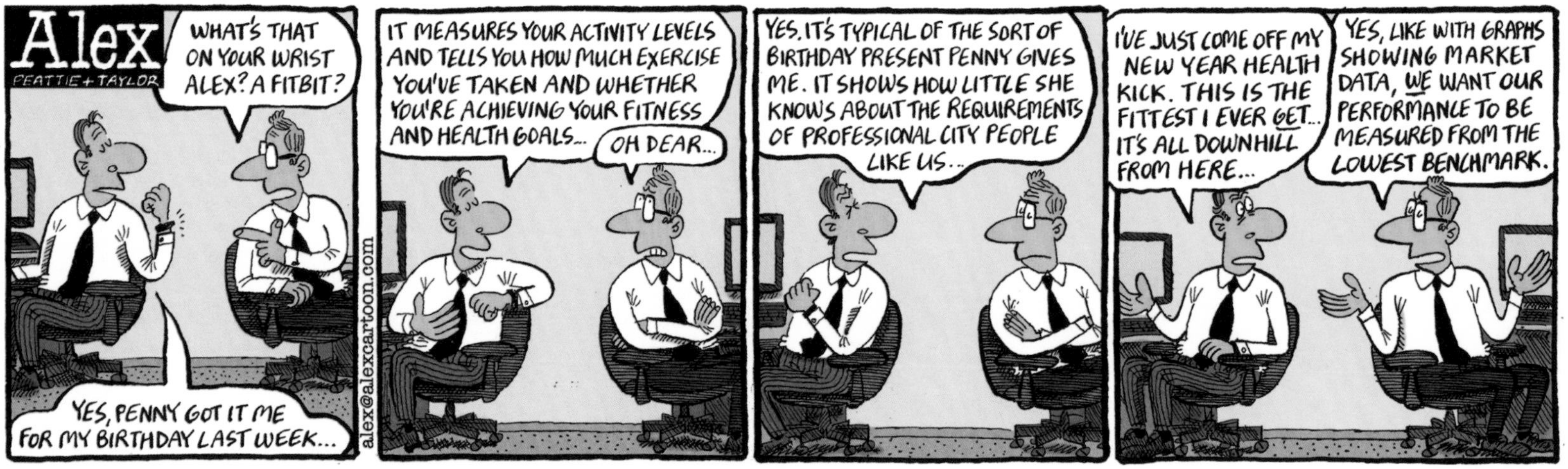
Alex
PEATTIE + TAYLOR
WHAT'S THAT ON YOUR WRIST ALEX? A FITBIT?
YES, PENNY GOT IT ME FOR MY BIRTHDAY LAST WEEK...
alex@alexcartoon.com
IT MEASURES YOUR ACTIVITY LEVELS AND TELLS YOU HOW MUCH EXERCISE YOU'VE TAKEN AND WHETHER YOU'RE ACHIEVING YOUR FITNESS AND HEALTH GOALS...
OH DEAR...
YES. IT'S TYPICAL OF THE SORT OF BIRTHDAY PRESENT PENNY GIVES ME. IT SHOWS HOW LITTLE SHE KNOWS ABOUT THE REQUIREMENTS OF PROFESSIONAL CITY PEOPLE LIKE US...
I'VE JUST COME OFF MY NEW YEAR HEALTH KICK. THIS IS THE FITTEST I EVER GET... IT'S ALL DOWNHILL FROM HERE...
YES, LIKE WITH GRAPHS SHOWING MARKET DATA, WE WANT OUR PERFORMANCE TO BE MEASURED FROM THE LOWEST BENCHMARK.

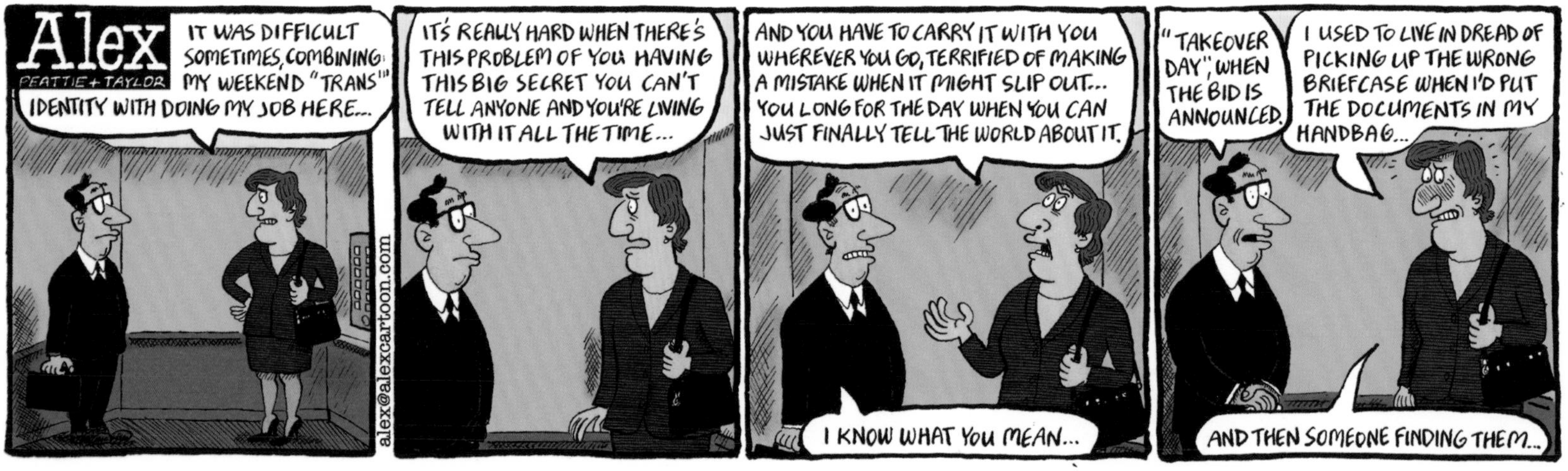
Alex
PEATTIE + TAYLOR
IT WAS DIFFICULT SOMETIMES, COMBINING MY WEEKEND "TRANS" IDENTITY WITH DOING MY JOB HERE...
alex@alexcartoon.com
IT'S REALLY HARD WHEN THERE'S THIS PROBLEM OF YOU HAVING THIS BIG SECRET YOU CAN'T TELL ANYONE AND YOU'RE LIVING WITH IT ALL THE TIME...
AND YOU HAVE TO CARRY IT WITH YOU WHEREVER YOU GO, TERRIFIED OF MAKING A MISTAKE WHEN IT MIGHT SLIP OUT... YOU LONG FOR THE DAY WHEN YOU CAN JUST FINALLY TELL THE WORLD ABOUT IT.
I KNOW WHAT YOU MEAN...
"TAKEOVER DAY", WHEN THE BID IS ANNOUNCED.
I USED TO LIVE IN DREAD OF PICKING UP THE WRONG BRIEFCASE WHEN I'D PUT THE DOCUMENTS IN MY HANDBAG...
AND THEN SOMEONE FINDING THEM...

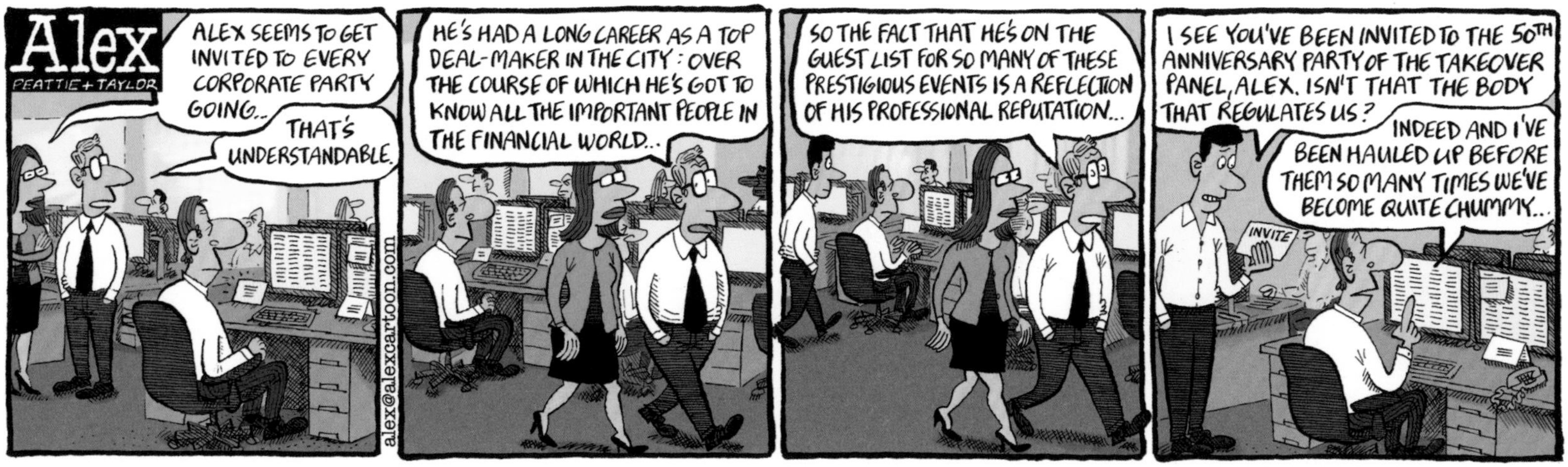
Alex
PEATTIE + TAYLOR
ALEX SEEMS TO GET INVITED TO EVERY CORPORATE PARTY GOING...
THAT'S UNDERSTANDABLE.
alex@alexcartoon.com
HE'S HAD A LONG CAREER AS A TOP DEAL-MAKER IN THE CITY: OVER THE COURSE OF WHICH HE'S GOT TO KNOW ALL THE IMPORTANT PEOPLE IN THE FINANCIAL WORLD..
SO THE FACT THAT HE'S ON THE GUEST LIST FOR SO MANY OF THESE PRESTIGIOUS EVENTS IS A REFLECTION OF HIS PROFESSIONAL REPUTATION...
I SEE YOU'VE BEEN INVITED TO THE 50TH ANNIVERSARY PARTY OF THE TAKEOVER PANEL, ALEX. ISN'T THAT THE BODY THAT REGULATES US?
INVITE
INDEED AND I'VE BEEN HAULED UP BEFORE THEM SO MANY TIMES WE'VE BECOME QUITE CHUMMY...

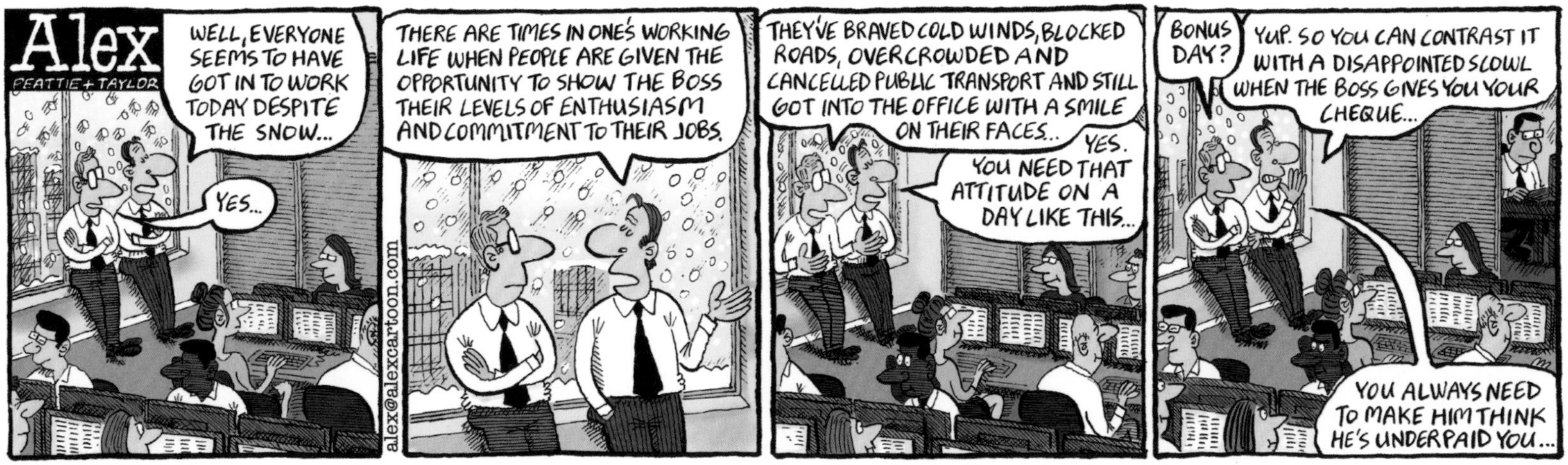
Alex
PEATTIE + TAYLOR
WELL, EVERYONE SEEMS TO HAVE GOT IN TO WORK TODAY DESPITE THE SNOW...
YES...
alex@alexcartoon.com
THERE ARE TIMES IN ONE'S WORKING LIFE WHEN PEOPLE ARE GIVEN THE OPPORTUNITY TO SHOW THE BOSS THEIR LEVELS OF ENTHUSIASM AND COMMITMENT TO THEIR JOBS.
THEY'VE BRAVED COLD WINDS, BLOCKED ROADS, OVERCROWDED AND CANCELLED PUBLIC TRANSPORT AND STILL GOT INTO THE OFFICE WITH A SMILE ON THEIR FACES...
YES. YOU NEED THAT ATTITUDE ON A DAY LIKE THIS...
BONUS DAY?
YUP. SO YOU CAN CONTRAST IT WITH A DISAPPOINTED SCOWL WHEN THE BOSS GIVES YOU YOUR CHEQUE...
YOU ALWAYS NEED TO MAKE HIM THINK HE'S UNDERPAID YOU...

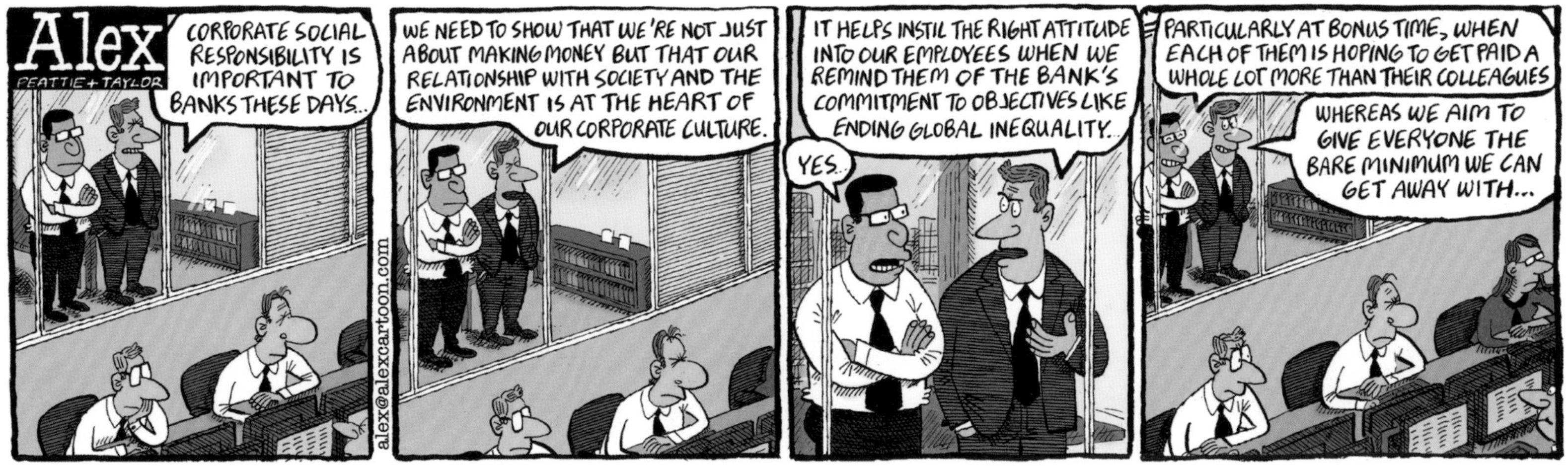
Alex
PEATTIE + TAYLOR
CORPORATE SOCIAL RESPONSIBILITY IS IMPORTANT TO BANKS THESE DAYS..
alex@alexcartoon.com
WE NEED TO SHOW THAT WE'RE NOT JUST ABOUT MAKING MONEY BUT THAT OUR RELATIONSHIP WITH SOCIETY AND THE ENVIRONMENT IS AT THE HEART OF OUR CORPORATE CULTURE.
IT HELPS INSTIL THE RIGHT ATTITUDE INTO OUR EMPLOYEES WHEN WE REMIND THEM OF THE BANK'S COMMITMENT TO OBJECTIVES LIKE ENDING GLOBAL INEQUALITY...
YES..
PARTICULARLY AT BONUS TIME, WHEN EACH OF THEM IS HOPING TO GET PAID A WHOLE LOT MORE THAN THEIR COLLEAGUES
WHEREAS WE AIM TO GIVE EVERYONE THE BARE MINIMUM WE CAN GET AWAY WITH...

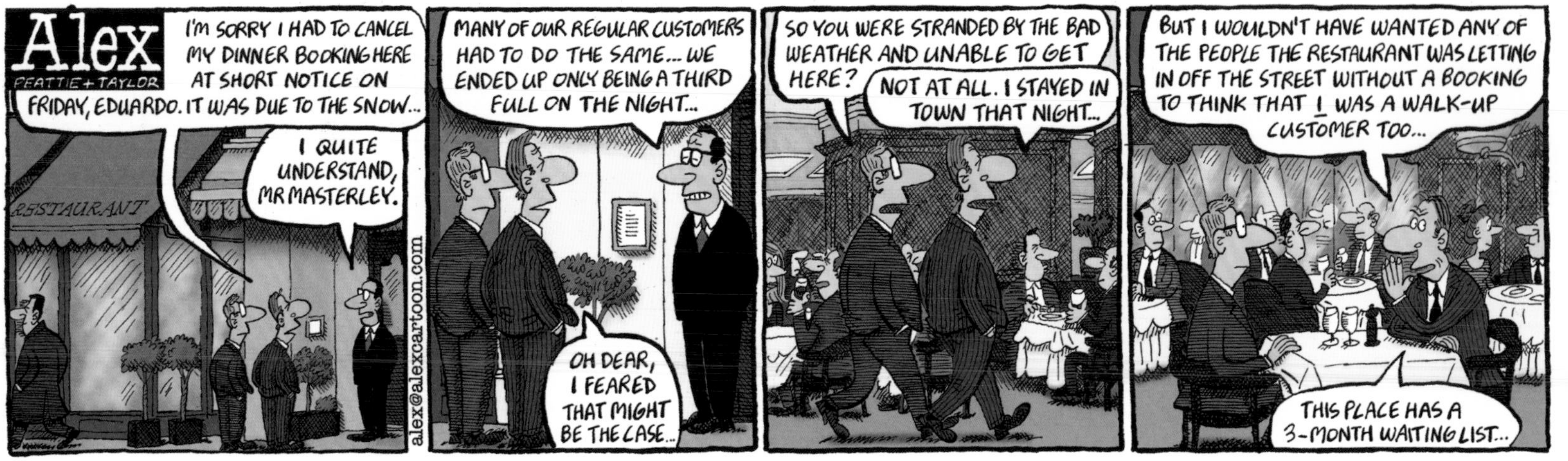
Alex
PEATTIE + TAYLOR
I'M SORRY I HAD TO CANCEL MY DINNER BOOKING HERE AT SHORT NOTICE ON FRIDAY, EDUARDO. IT WAS DUE TO THE SNOW...
I QUITE UNDERSTAND, MR MASTERLEY.
RESTAURANT
MANY OF OUR REGULAR CUSTOMERS HAD TO DO THE SAME... WE ENDED UP ONLY BEING A THIRD FULL ON THE NIGHT...
OH DEAR, I FEARED THAT MIGHT BE THE CASE...
alex@alexcartoon.com
SO YOU WERE STRANDED BY THE BAD WEATHER AND UNABLE TO GET HERE?
NOT AT ALL. I STAYED IN TOWN THAT NIGHT...
BUT I WOULDN'T HAVE WANTED ANY OF THE PEOPLE THE RESTAURANT WAS LETTING IN OFF THE STREET WITHOUT A BOOKING TO THINK THAT I WAS A WALK-UP CUSTOMER TOO...
THIS PLACE HAS A 3-MONTH WAITING LIST...

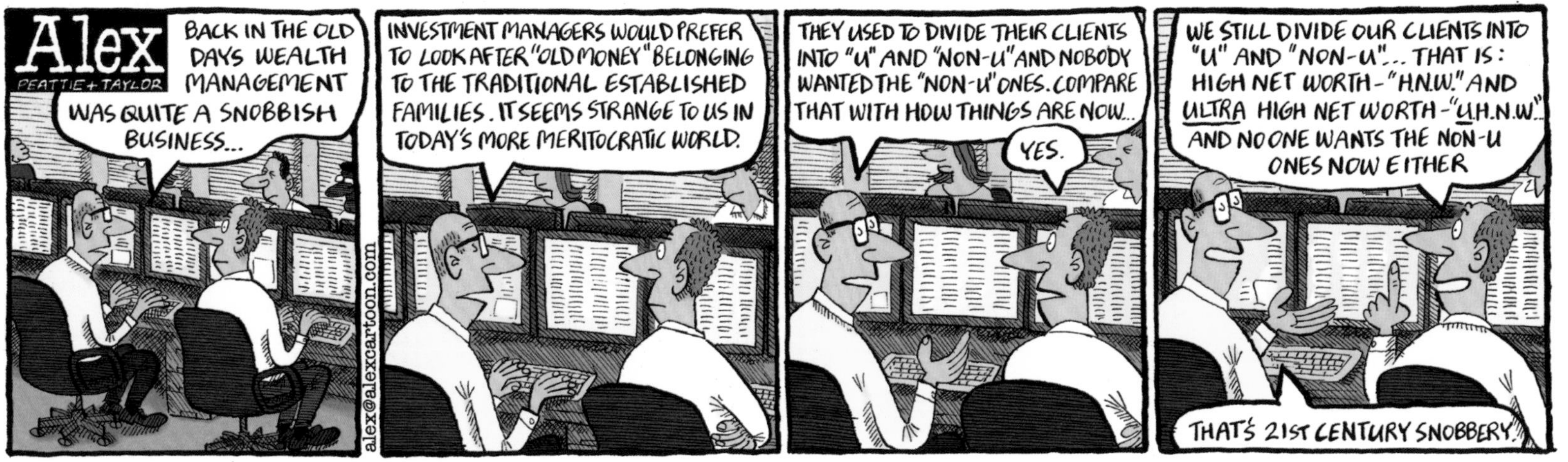
Alex
PEATTIE + TAYLOR
BACK IN THE OLD DAYS WEALTH MANAGEMENT WAS QUITE A SNOBBISH BUSINESS...
INVESTMENT MANAGERS WOULD PREFER TO LOOK AFTER "OLD MONEY" BELONGING TO THE TRADITIONAL ESTABLISHED FAMILIES. IT SEEMS STRANGE TO US IN TODAY'S MORE MERITOCRATIC WORLD.
alex@alexcartoon.com
THEY USED TO DIVIDE THEIR CLIENTS INTO "U" AND "NON-U" AND NOBODY WANTED THE "NON-U" ONES. COMPARE THAT WITH HOW THINGS ARE NOW...
YES.
WE STILL DIVIDE OUR CLIENTS INTO "U" AND "NON-U"... THAT IS: HIGH NET WORTH - "H.N.W." AND ULTRA HIGH NET WORTH - "U.H.N.W." AND NO ONE WANTS THE NON-U ONES NOW EITHER
THAT'S 21ST CENTURY SNOBBERY.

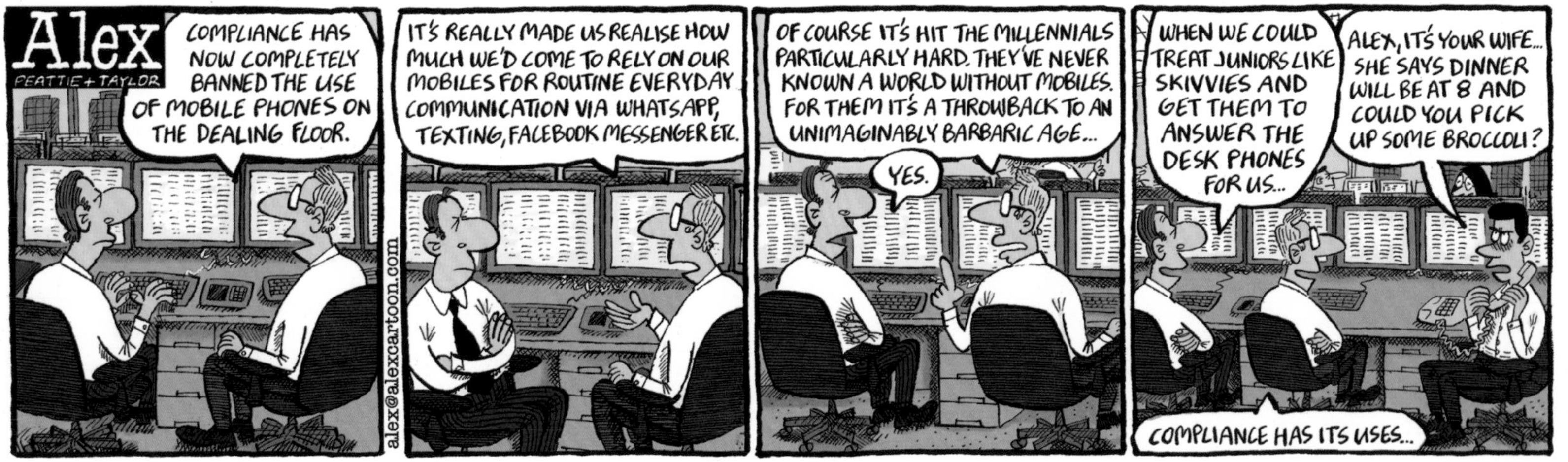
Alex
PEATTIE + TAYLOR
COMPLIANCE HAS NOW COMPLETELY BANNED THE USE OF MOBILE PHONES ON THE DEALING FLOOR.
IT'S REALLY MADE US REALISE HOW MUCH WE'D COME TO RELY ON OUR MOBILES FOR ROUTINE EVERYDAY COMMUNICATION VIA WHATSAPP, TEXTING, FACEBOOK MESSENGER ETC.
alex@alexcartoon.com
OF COURSE IT'S HIT THE MILLENNIALS PARTICULARLY HARD. THEY'VE NEVER KNOWN A WORLD WITHOUT MOBILES. FOR THEM IT'S A THROWBACK TO AN UNIMAGINABLY BARBARIC AGE...
YES.
WHEN WE COULD TREAT JUNIORS LIKE SKIVVIES AND GET THEM TO ANSWER THE DESK PHONES FOR US...
ALEX, IT'S YOUR WIFE... SHE SAYS DINNER WILL BE AT 8 AND COULD YOU PICK UP SOME BROCCOLI?
COMPLIANCE HAS ITS USES...

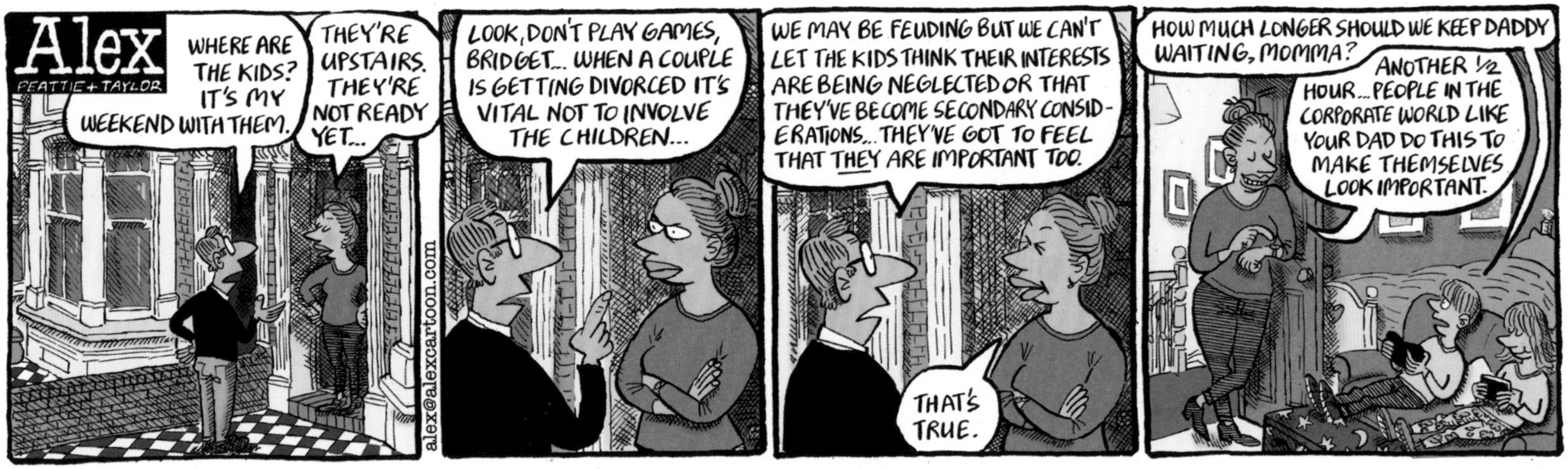
Alex
PEATTIE + TAYLOR
WHERE ARE THE KIDS? IT'S MY WEEKEND WITH THEM.
THEY'RE UPSTAIRS. THEY'RE NOT READY YET...
alex@alexcartoon.com
LOOK, DON'T PLAY GAMES, BRIDGET... WHEN A COUPLE IS GETTING DIVORCED IT'S VITAL NOT TO INVOLVE THE CHILDREN...
WE MAY BE FEUDING BUT WE CAN'T LET THE KIDS THINK THEIR INTERESTS ARE BEING NEGLECTED OR THAT THEY'VE BECOME SECONDARY CONSIDERATIONS... THEY'VE GOT TO FEEL THAT THEY ARE IMPORTANT TOO.
THAT'S TRUE.
HOW MUCH LONGER SHOULD WE KEEP DADDY WAITING, MOMMA?
ANOTHER 1/2 HOUR... PEOPLE IN THE CORPORATE WORLD LIKE YOUR DAD DO THIS TO MAKE THEMSELVES LOOK IMPORTANT.

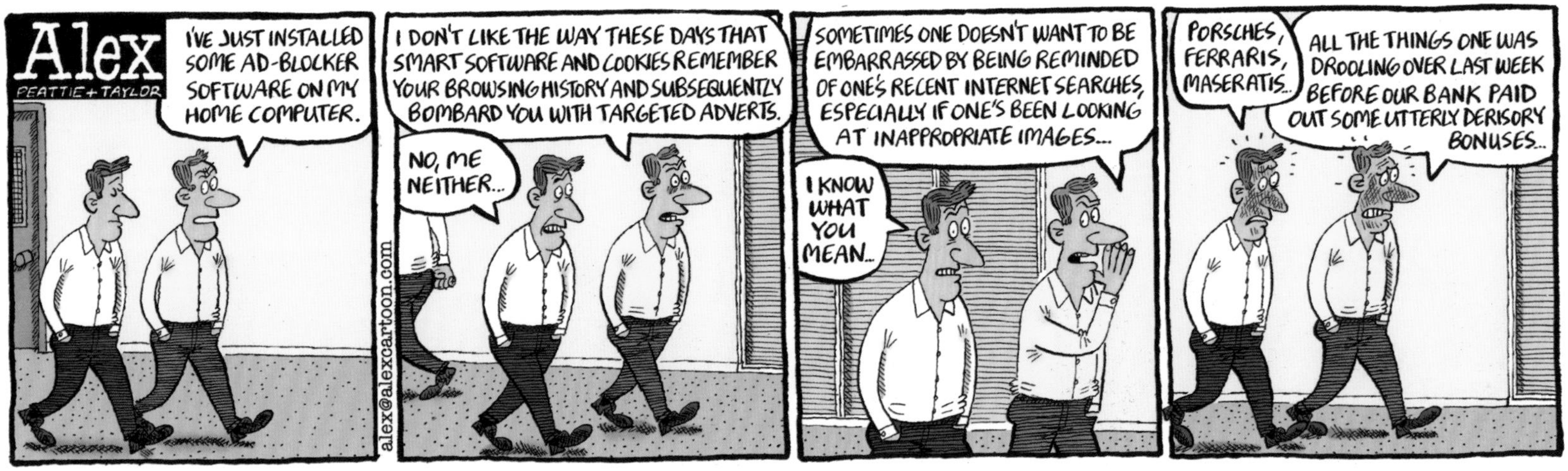
Alex
PEATTIE + TAYLOR
I'VE JUST INSTALLED SOME AD-BLOCKER SOFTWARE ON MY HOME COMPUTER.
alex@alexcartoon.com
I DON'T LIKE THE WAY THESE DAYS THAT SMART SOFTWARE AND COOKIES REMEMBER YOUR BROWSING HISTORY AND SUBSEQUENTLY BOMBARD YOU WITH TARGETED ADVERTS.
NO, ME NEITHER...
SOMETIMES ONE DOESN'T WANT TO BE EMBARRASSED BY BEING REMINDED OF ONE'S RECENT INTERNET SEARCHES, ESPECIALLY IF ONE'S BEEN LOOKING AT INAPPROPRIATE IMAGES...
I KNOW WHAT YOU MEAN...
PORSCHES, FERRARIS, MASERATIS...
ALL THE THINGS ONE WAS DROOLING OVER LAST WEEK BEFORE OUR BANK PAID OUT SOME UTTERLY DERISORY BONUSES...

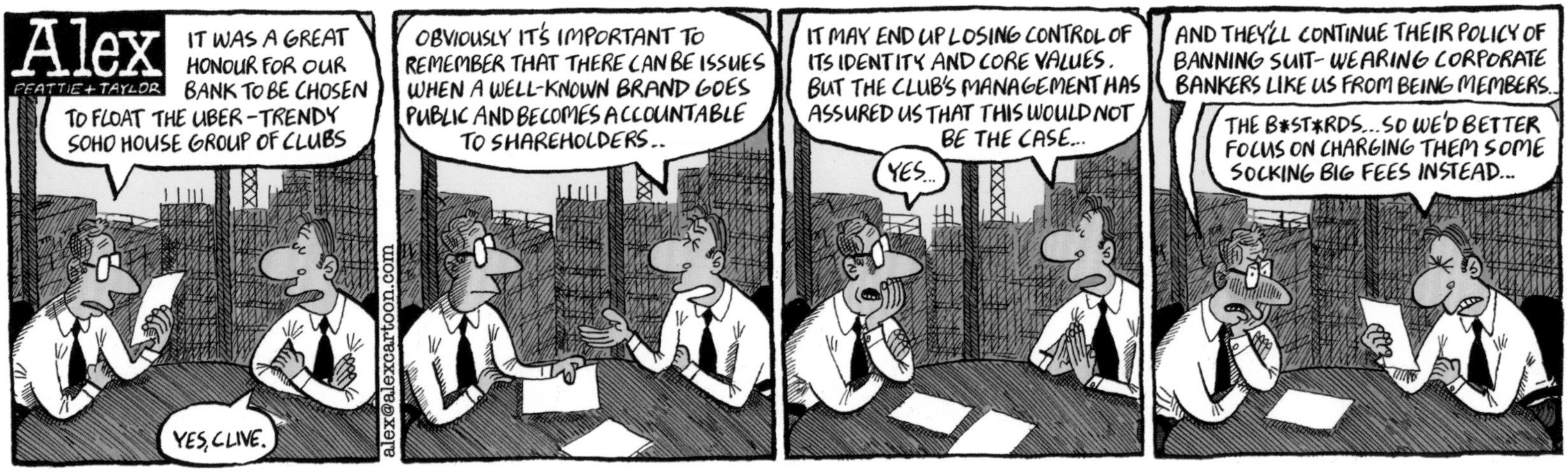
Alex
PEATTIE + TAYLOR
IT WAS A GREAT HONOUR FOR OUR BANK TO BE CHOSEN TO FLOAT THE UBER-TRENDY SOHO HOUSE GROUP OF CLUBS
YES, CLIVE.
alex@alexcartoon.com
OBVIOUSLY IT'S IMPORTANT TO REMEMBER THAT THERE CAN BE ISSUES WHEN A WELL-KNOWN BRAND GOES PUBLIC AND BECOMES ACCOUNTABLE TO SHAREHOLDERS...
IT MAY END UP LOSING CONTROL OF ITS IDENTITY AND CORE VALUES. BUT THE CLUB'S MANAGEMENT HAS ASSURED US THAT THIS WOULD NOT BE THE CASE...
YES...
AND THEY'LL CONTINUE THEIR POLICY OF BANNING SUIT-WEARING CORPORATE BANKERS LIKE US FROM BEING MEMBERS...
THE B*ST*RDS... SO WE'D BETTER FOCUS ON CHARGING THEM SOME SOCKING BIG FEES INSTEAD...

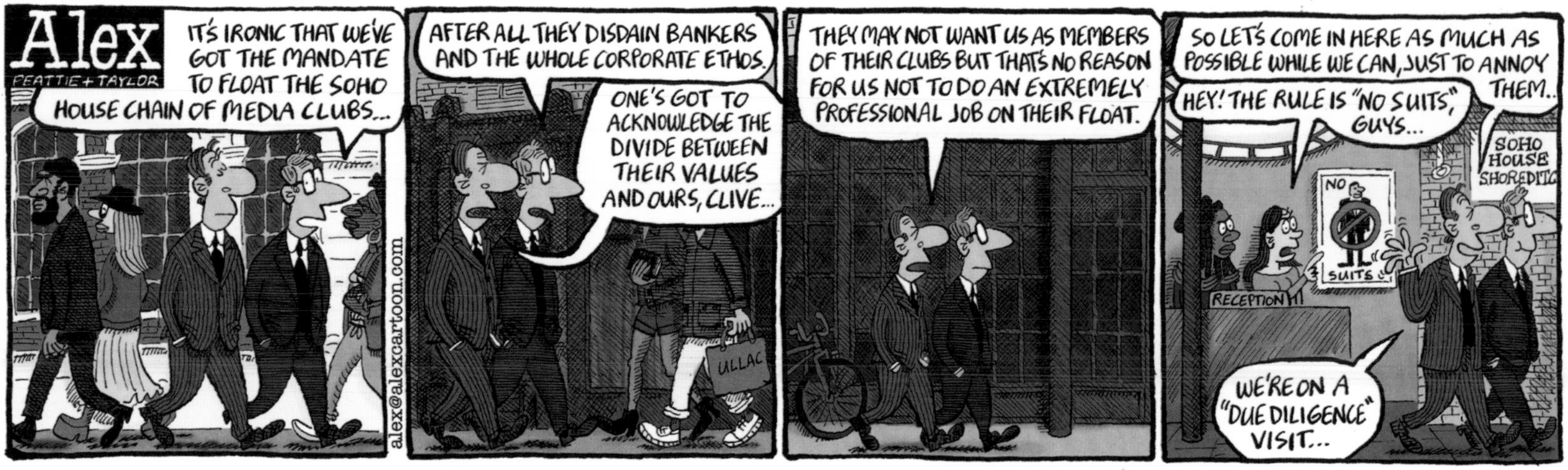
Alex
PEATTIE+TAYLOR
IT'S IRONIC THAT WE'VE GOT THE MANDATE TO FLOAT THE SOHO HOUSE CHAIN OF MEDIA CLUBS...
alex@alexcartoon.com
AFTER ALL THEY DISDAIN BANKERS AND THE WHOLE CORPORATE ETHOS.
ONE'S GOT TO ACKNOWLEDGE THE DIVIDE BETWEEN THEIR VALUES AND OURS, CLIVE...
ULLAC
THEY MAY NOT WANT US AS MEMBERS OF THEIR CLUBS BUT THAT'S NO REASON FOR US NOT TO DO AN EXTREMELY PROFESSIONAL JOB ON THEIR FLOAT.
SO LET'S COME IN HERE AS MUCH AS POSSIBLE WHILE WE CAN, JUST TO ANNOY THEM..
HEY! THE RULE IS "NO SUITS," GUYS...
SOHO HOUSE SHOREDITC
NO SUITS
RECEPTION
WE'RE ON A "DUE DILIGENCE" VISIT...

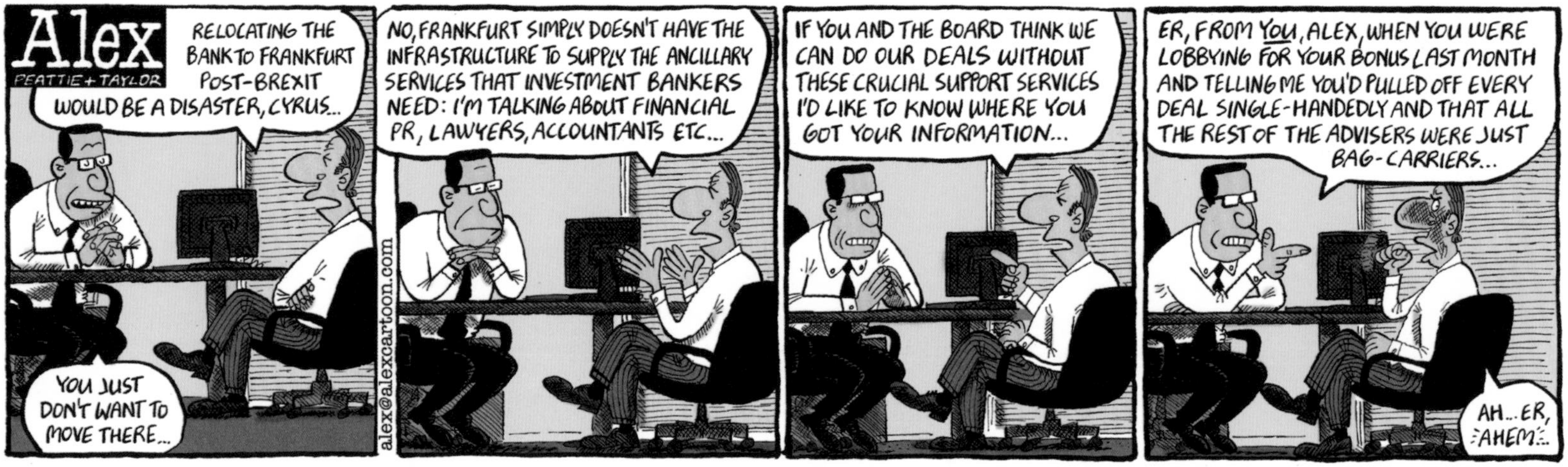
Alex
PEATTIE+TAYLOR
RELOCATING THE BANK TO FRANKFURT POST-BREXIT WOULD BE A DISASTER, CYRUS...
YOU JUST DON'T WANT TO MOVE THERE...
alex@alexcartoon.com
NO, FRANKFURT SIMPLY DOESN'T HAVE THE INFRASTRUCTURE TO SUPPLY THE ANCILLARY SERVICES THAT INVESTMENT BANKERS NEED: I'M TALKING ABOUT FINANCIAL PR, LAWYERS, ACCOUNTANTS ETC...
IF YOU AND THE BOARD THINK WE CAN DO OUR DEALS WITHOUT THESE CRUCIAL SUPPORT SERVICES I'D LIKE TO KNOW WHERE YOU GOT YOUR INFORMATION...
ER, FROM YOU, ALEX, WHEN YOU WERE LOBBYING FOR YOUR BONUS LAST MONTH AND TELLING ME YOU'D PULLED OFF EVERY DEAL SINGLE-HANDEDLY AND THAT ALL THE REST OF THE ADVISERS WERE JUST BAG-CARRIERS...
AH...ER, AHEM...

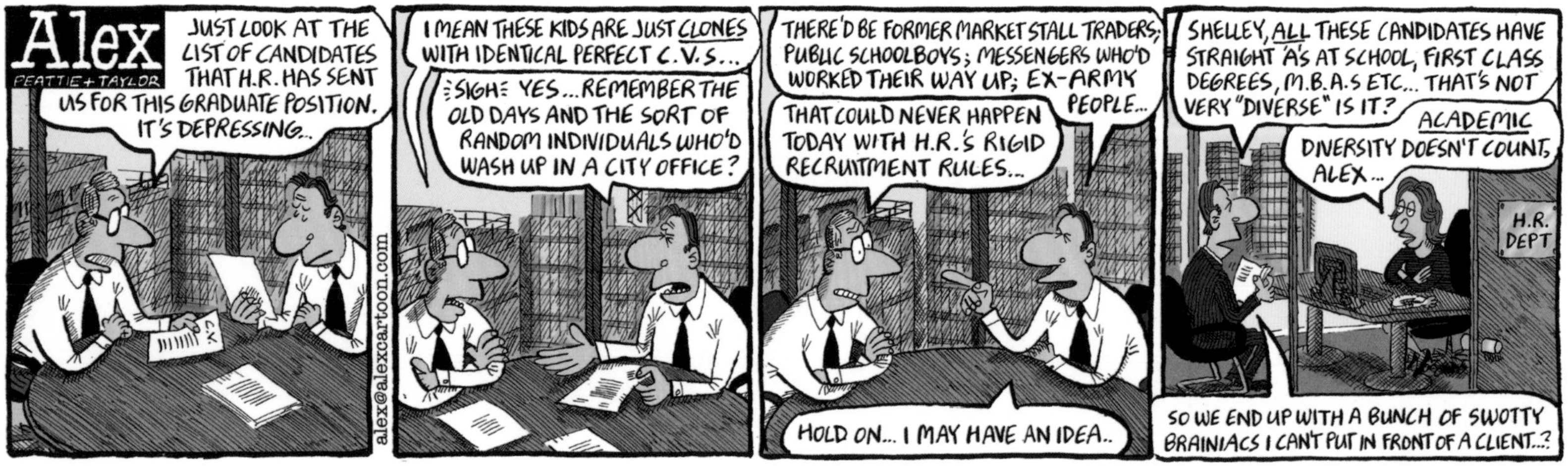
Alex
PEATTIE+TAYLOR
JUST LOOK AT THE LIST OF CANDIDATES THAT H.R. HAS SENT US FOR THIS GRADUATE POSITION. IT'S DEPRESSING...
C.V.
alex@alexcartoon.com
I MEAN THESE KIDS ARE JUST CLONES WITH IDENTICAL PERFECT C.V.S...
SIGH YES... REMEMBER THE OLD DAYS AND THE SORT OF RANDOM INDIVIDUALS WHO'D WASH UP IN A CITY OFFICE?
THERE'D BE FORMER MARKET STALL TRADERS; PUBLIC SCHOOLBOYS; MESSENGERS WHO'D WORKED THEIR WAY UP; EX-ARMY PEOPLE...
THAT COULD NEVER HAPPEN TODAY WITH H.R.'S RIGID RECRUITMENT RULES...
HOLD ON... I MAY HAVE AN IDEA..
SHELLEY, ALL THESE CANDIDATES HAVE STRAIGHT A'S AT SCHOOL, FIRST CLASS DEGREES, M.B.A.S ETC... THAT'S NOT VERY "DIVERSE" IS IT?
ACADEMIC DIVERSITY DOESN'T COUNT, ALEX...
H.R. DEPT
SO WE END UP WITH A BUNCH OF SWOTTY BRAINIACS I CAN'T PUT IN FRONT OF A CLIENT..?

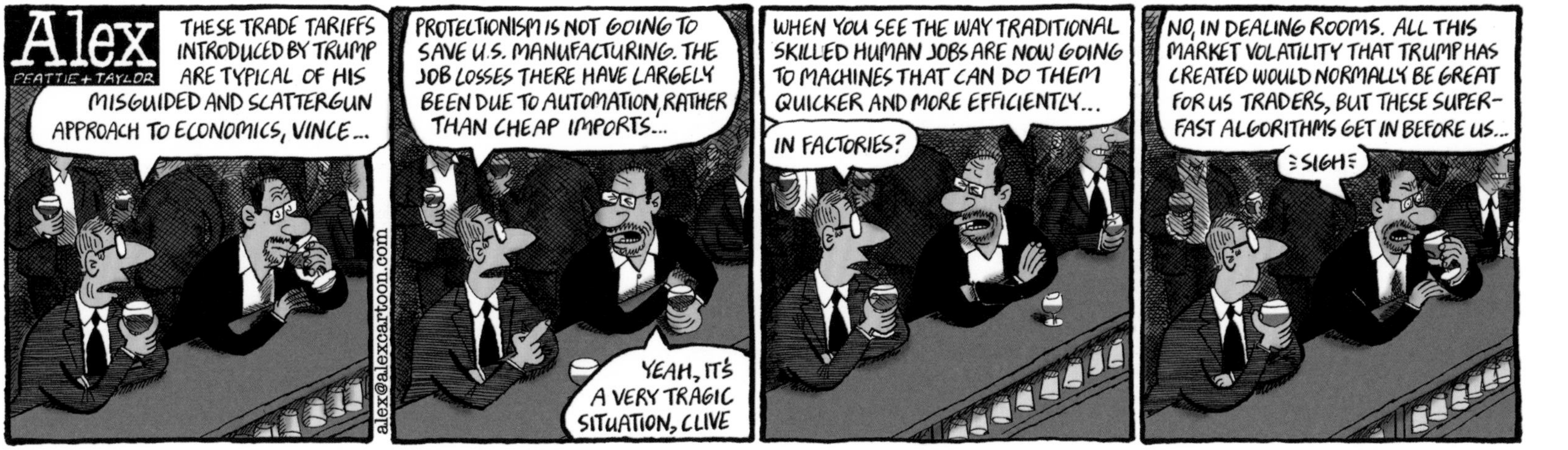
Alex
PEATTIE + TAYLOR
THESE TRADE TARIFFS INTRODUCED BY TRUMP ARE TYPICAL OF HIS MISGUIDED AND SCATTERGUN APPROACH TO ECONOMICS, VINCE...
alex@alexcartoon.com
PROTECTIONISM IS NOT GOING TO SAVE U.S. MANUFACTURING. THE JOB LOSSES THERE HAVE LARGELY BEEN DUE TO AUTOMATION, RATHER THAN CHEAP IMPORTS...
YEAH, IT'S A VERY TRAGIC SITUATION, CLIVE
WHEN YOU SEE THE WAY TRADITIONAL SKILLED HUMAN JOBS ARE NOW GOING TO MACHINES THAT CAN DO THEM QUICKER AND MORE EFFICIENTLY...
IN FACTORIES?
NO, IN DEALING ROOMS. ALL THIS MARKET VOLATILITY THAT TRUMP HAS CREATED WOULD NORMALLY BE GREAT FOR US TRADERS, BUT THESE SUPER-FAST ALGORITHMS GET IN BEFORE US...
SIGH

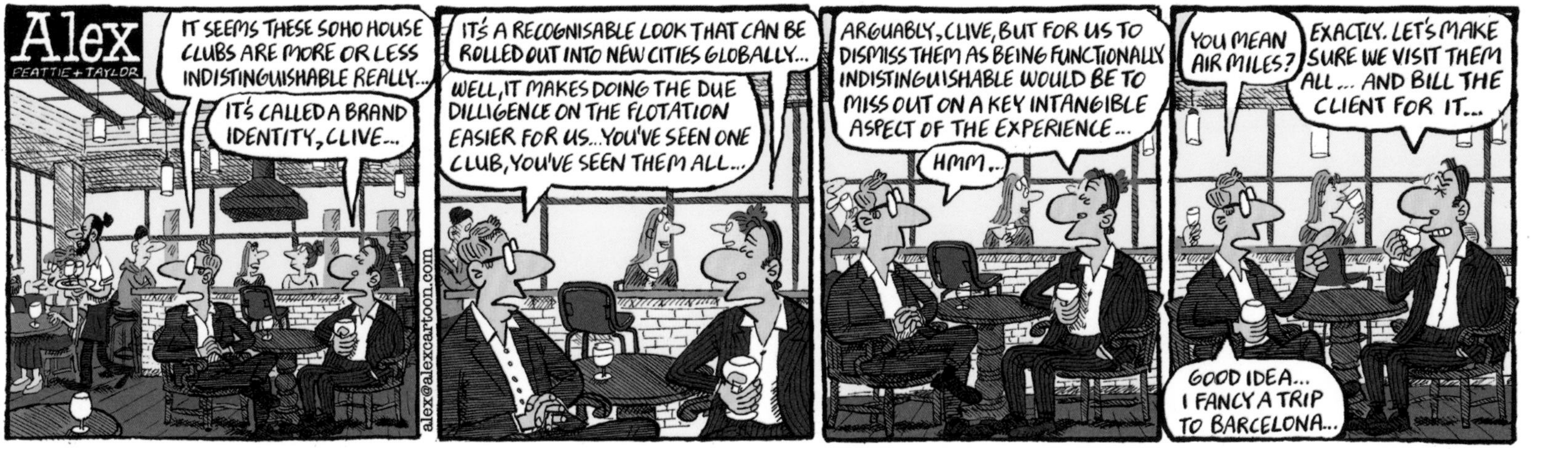
Alex
PEATTIE + TAYLOR
IT SEEMS THESE SOHO HOUSE CLUBS ARE MORE OR LESS INDISTINGUISHABLE REALLY...
IT'S CALLED A BRAND IDENTITY, CLIVE...
alex@alexcartoon.com
IT'S A RECOGNISABLE LOOK THAT CAN BE ROLLED OUT INTO NEW CITIES GLOBALLY...
WELL, IT MAKES DOING THE DUE DILLIGENCE ON THE FLOTATION EASIER FOR US... YOU'VE SEEN ONE CLUB, YOU'VE SEEN THEM ALL...
ARGUABLY, CLIVE, BUT FOR US TO DISMISS THEM AS BEING FUNCTIONALLY INDISTINGUISHABLE WOULD BE TO MISS OUT ON A KEY INTANGIBLE ASPECT OF THE EXPERIENCE...
HMM...
YOU MEAN AIR MILES?
EXACTLY. LET'S MAKE SURE WE VISIT THEM ALL... AND BILL THE CLIENT FOR IT...
GOOD IDEA... I FANCY A TRIP TO BARCELONA...

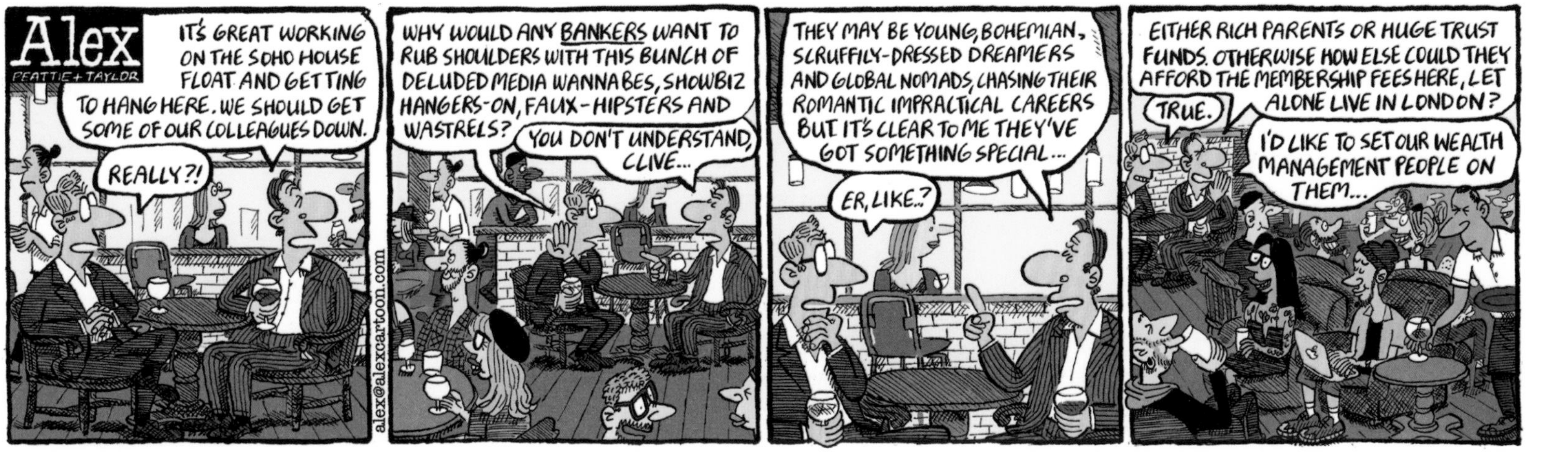
Alex
PEATTIE + TAYLOR
IT'S GREAT WORKING ON THE SOHO HOUSE FLOAT AND GETTING TO HANG HERE. WE SHOULD GET SOME OF OUR COLLEAGUES DOWN.
REALLY?!
alex@alexcartoon.com
WHY WOULD ANY BANKERS WANT TO RUB SHOULDERS WITH THIS BUNCH OF DELUDED MEDIA WANNABES, SHOWBIZ HANGERS-ON, FAUX-HIPSTERS AND WASTRELS?
YOU DON'T UNDERSTAND, CLIVE...
THEY MAY BE YOUNG, BOHEMIAN, SCRUFFILY-DRESSED DREAMERS AND GLOBAL NOMADS, CHASING THEIR ROMANTIC IMPRACTICAL CAREERS BUT IT'S CLEAR TO ME THEY'VE GOT SOMETHING SPECIAL...
ER, LIKE..?
EITHER RICH PARENTS OR HUGE TRUST FUNDS. OTHERWISE HOW ELSE COULD THEY AFFORD THE MEMBERSHIP FEES HERE, LET ALONE LIVE IN LONDON?
TRUE.
I'D LIKE TO SET OUR WEALTH MANAGEMENT PEOPLE ON THEM...

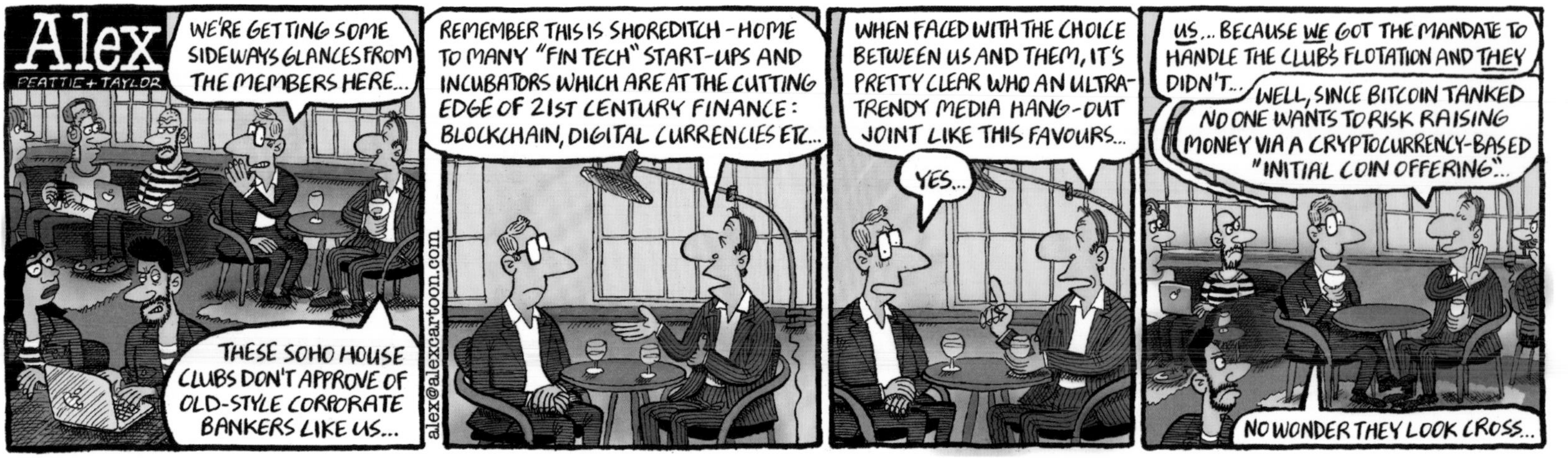
Alex
PEATTIE + TAYLOR
WE'RE GETTING SOME SIDEWAYS GLANCES FROM THE MEMBERS HERE...
THESE SOHO HOUSE CLUBS DON'T APPROVE OF OLD-STYLE CORPORATE BANKERS LIKE US...
alex@alexcartoon.com
REMEMBER THIS IS SHOREDITCH - HOME TO MANY "FIN TECH" START-UPS AND INCUBATORS WHICH ARE AT THE CUTTING EDGE OF 21ST CENTURY FINANCE: BLOCKCHAIN, DIGITAL CURRENCIES ETC...
WHEN FACED WITH THE CHOICE BETWEEN US AND THEM, IT'S PRETTY CLEAR WHO AN ULTRA-TRENDY MEDIA HANG-OUT JOINT LIKE THIS FAVOURS...
YES...
US... BECAUSE WE GOT THE MANDATE TO HANDLE THE CLUB'S FLOTATION AND THEY DIDN'T...
WELL, SINCE BITCOIN TANKED NO ONE WANTS TO RISK RAISING MONEY VIA A CRYPTOCURRENCY-BASED "INITIAL COIN OFFERING"...
NO WONDER THEY LOOK CROSS...

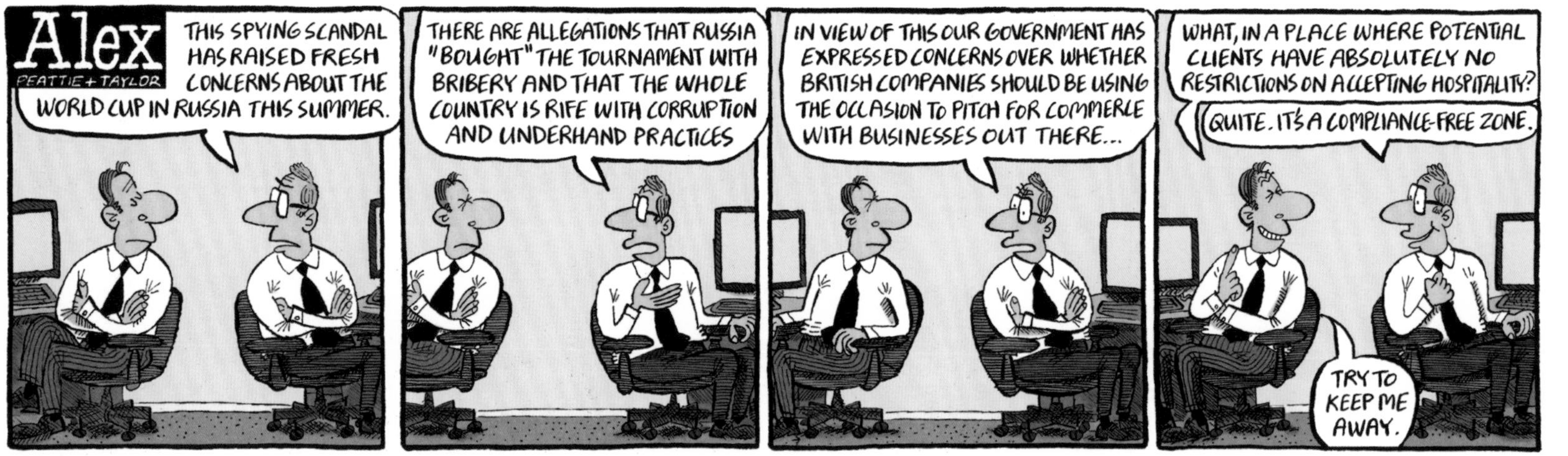
Alex
PEATTIE + TAYLOR
THIS SPYING SCANDAL HAS RAISED FRESH CONCERNS ABOUT THE WORLD CUP IN RUSSIA THIS SUMMER.
THERE ARE ALLEGATIONS THAT RUSSIA "BOUGHT" THE TOURNAMENT WITH BRIBERY AND THAT THE WHOLE COUNTRY IS RIFE WITH CORRUPTION AND UNDERHAND PRACTICES
IN VIEW OF THIS OUR GOVERNMENT HAS EXPRESSED CONCERNS OVER WHETHER BRITISH COMPANIES SHOULD BE USING THE OCCASION TO PITCH FOR COMMERCE WITH BUSINESSES OUT THERE...
WHAT, IN A PLACE WHERE POTENTIAL CLIENTS HAVE ABSOLUTELY NO RESTRICTIONS ON ACCEPTING HOSPITALITY?
QUITE. IT'S A COMPLIANCE-FREE ZONE.
TRY TO KEEP ME AWAY.

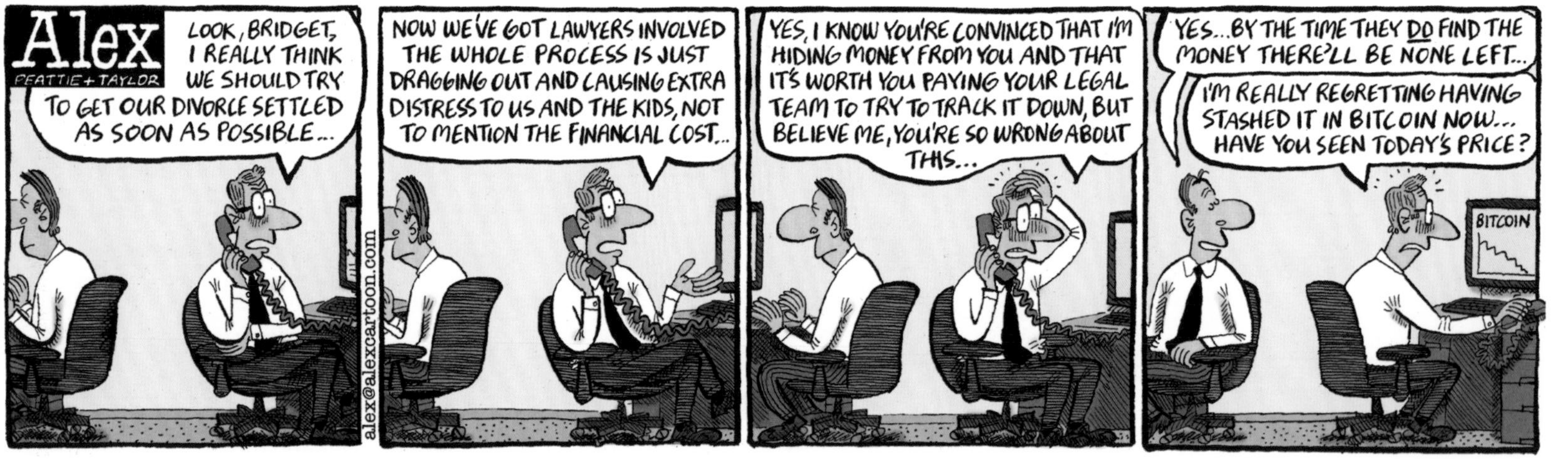
Alex
PEATTIE + TAYLOR
LOOK, BRIDGET, I REALLY THINK WE SHOULD TRY TO GET OUR DIVORCE SETTLED AS SOON AS POSSIBLE...
alex@alexcartoon.com
NOW WE'VE GOT LAWYERS INVOLVED THE WHOLE PROCESS IS JUST DRAGGING OUT AND CAUSING EXTRA DISTRESS TO US AND THE KIDS, NOT TO MENTION THE FINANCIAL COST...
YES, I KNOW YOU'RE CONVINCED THAT I'M HIDING MONEY FROM YOU AND THAT IT'S WORTH YOU PAYING YOUR LEGAL TEAM TO TRY TO TRACK IT DOWN, BUT BELIEVE ME, YOU'RE SO WRONG ABOUT THIS...
YES... BY THE TIME THEY DO FIND THE MONEY THERE'LL BE NONE LEFT...
I'M REALLY REGRETTING HAVING STASHED IT IN BITCOIN NOW... HAVE YOU SEEN TODAY'S PRICE?
BITCOIN

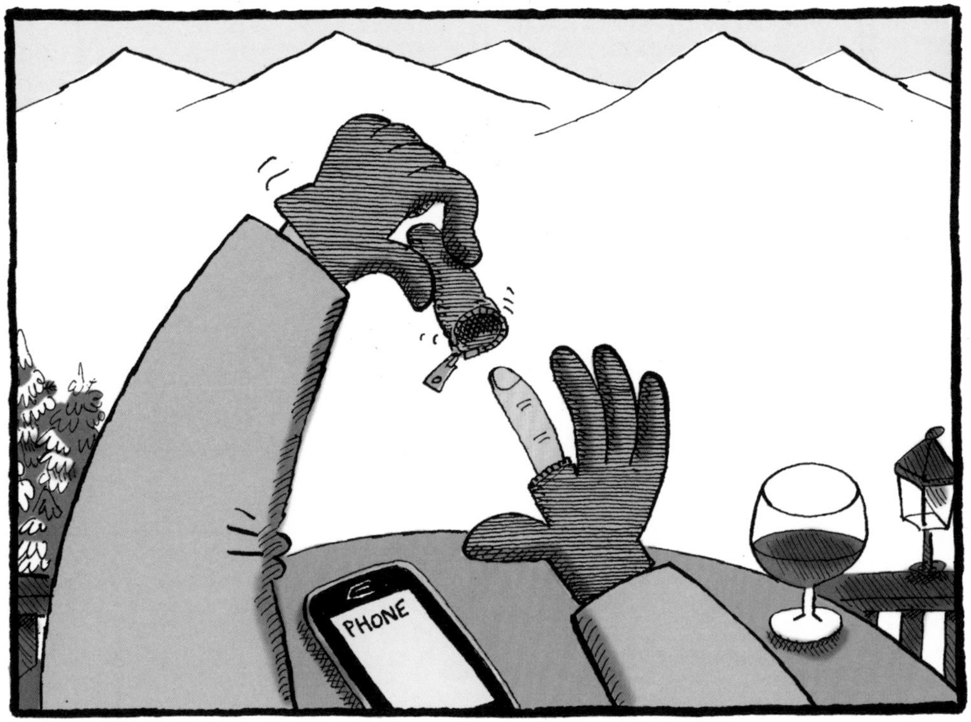
PHONE

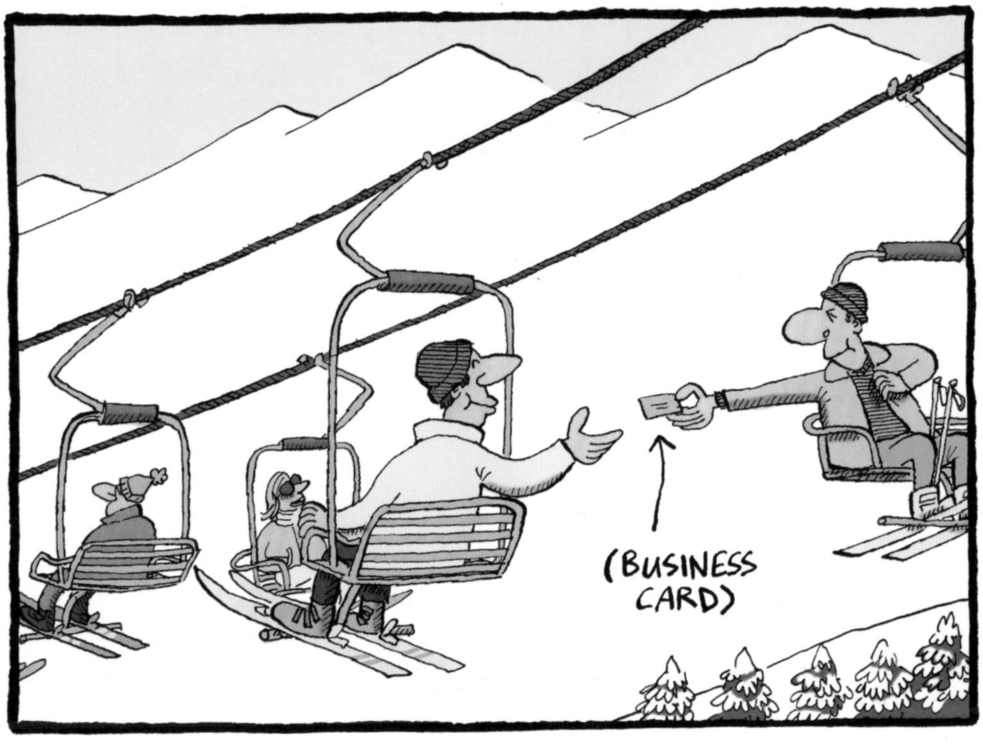
(BUSINESS
CARD)

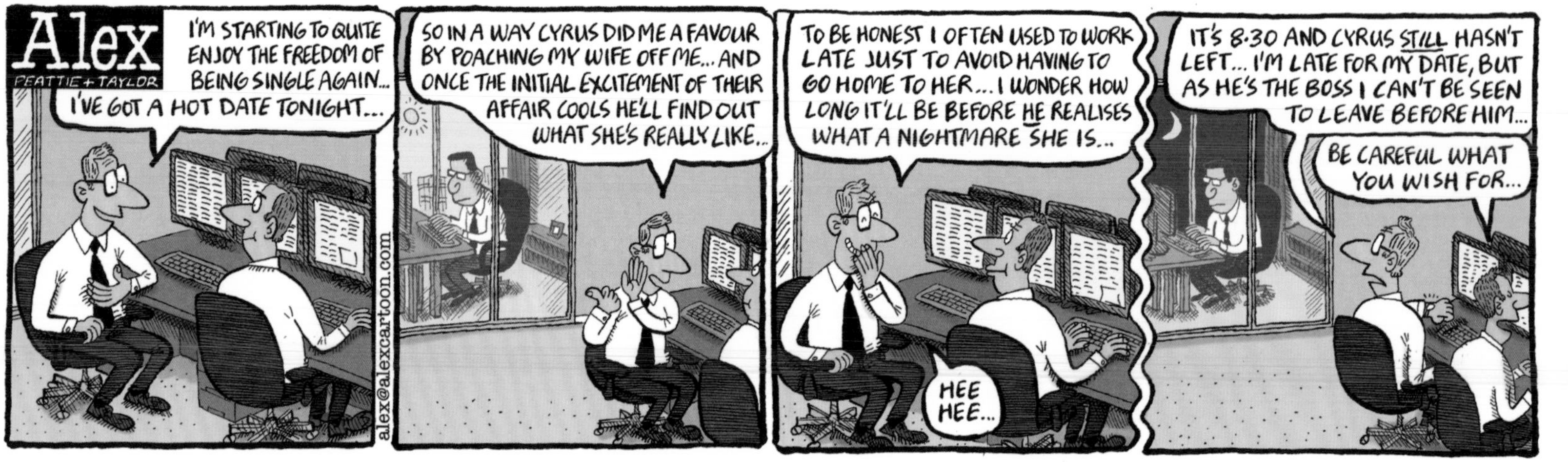
Alex
PEATTIE + TAYLOR
I'M STARTING TO QUITE ENJOY THE FREEDOM OF BEING SINGLE AGAIN... I'VE GOT A HOT DATE TONIGHT...
SO IN A WAY CYRUS DID ME A FAVOUR BY POACHING MY WIFE OFF ME... AND ONCE THE INITIAL EXCITEMENT OF THEIR AFFAIR COOLS HE'LL FIND OUT WHAT SHE'S REALLY LIKE...
alex@alexcartoon.com
TO BE HONEST I OFTEN USED TO WORK LATE JUST TO AVOID HAVING TO GO HOME TO HER... I WONDER HOW LONG IT'LL BE BEFORE HE REALISES WHAT A NIGHTMARE SHE IS...
HEE HEE...
IT'S 8.30 AND CYRUS STILL HASN'T LEFT... I'M LATE FOR MY DATE, BUT AS HE'S THE BOSS I CAN'T BE SEEN TO LEAVE BEFORE HIM...
BE CAREFUL WHAT YOU WISH FOR...

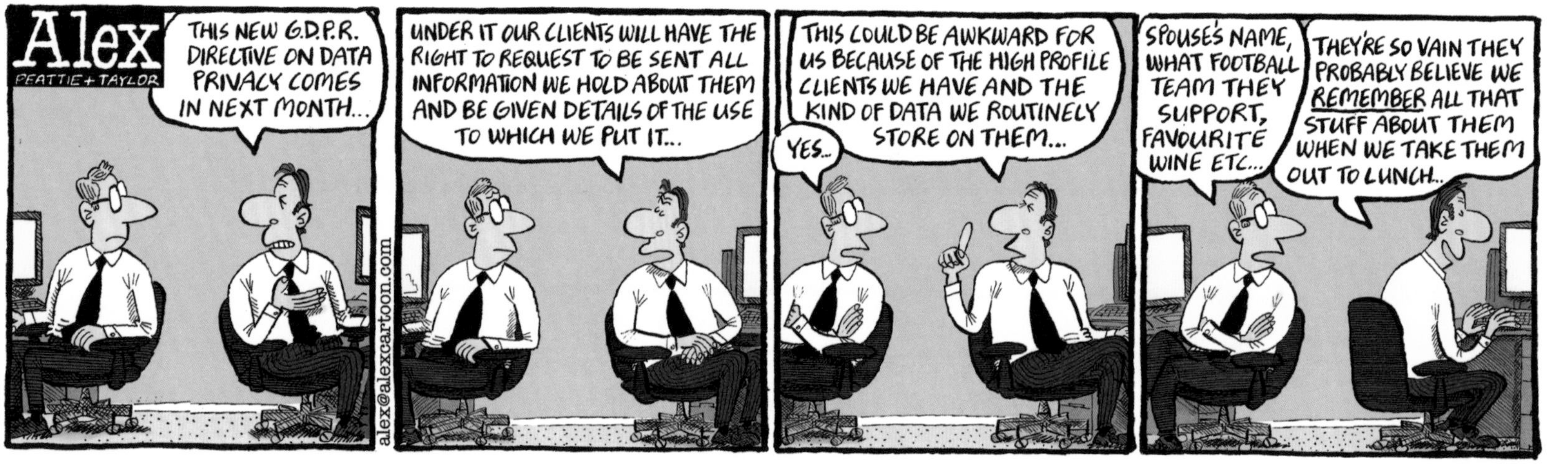
Alex
PEATTIE + TAYLOR
THIS NEW G.D.P.R. DIRECTIVE ON DATA PRIVACY COMES IN NEXT MONTH...
UNDER IT OUR CLIENTS WILL HAVE THE RIGHT TO REQUEST TO BE SENT ALL INFORMATION WE HOLD ABOUT THEM AND BE GIVEN DETAILS OF THE USE TO WHICH WE PUT IT...
alex@alexcartoon.com
THIS COULD BE AWKWARD FOR US BECAUSE OF THE HIGH PROFILE CLIENTS WE HAVE AND THE KIND OF DATA WE ROUTINELY STORE ON THEM...
YES...
SPOUSE'S NAME, WHAT FOOTBALL TEAM THEY SUPPORT, FAVOURITE WINE ETC...
THEY'RE SO VAIN THEY PROBABLY BELIEVE WE REMEMBER ALL THAT STUFF ABOUT THEM WHEN WE TAKE THEM OUT TO LUNCH...

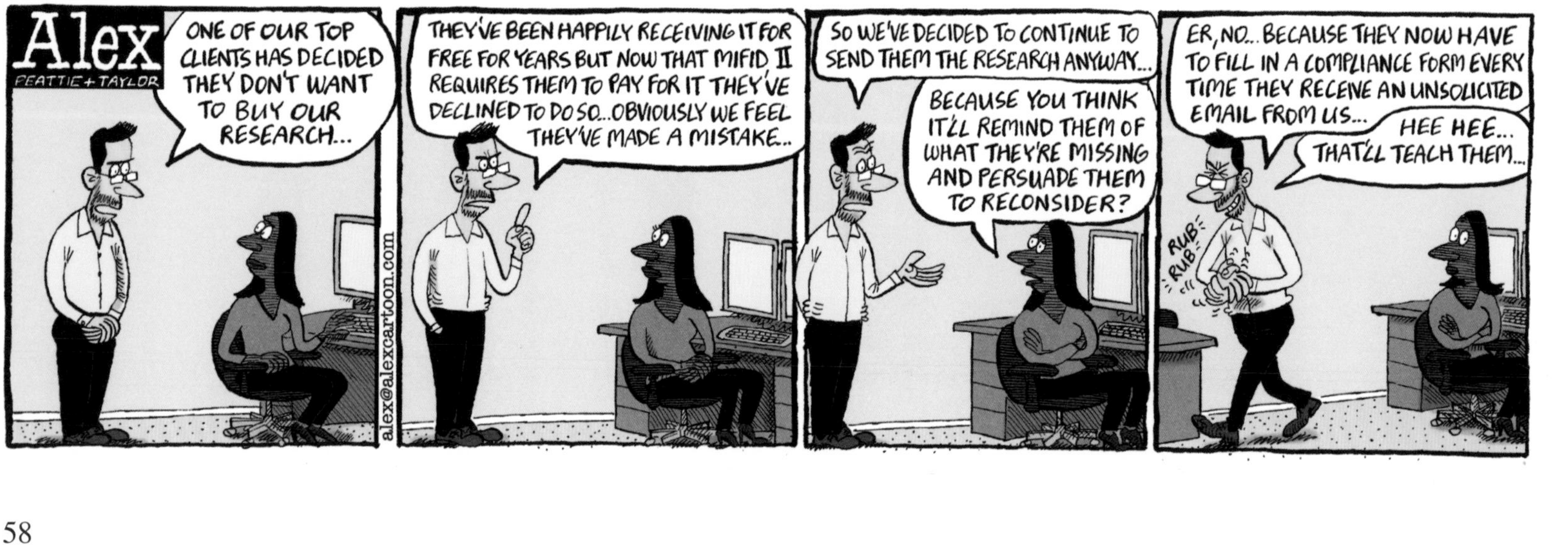
Alex
PEATTIE + TAYLOR
ONE OF OUR TOP CLIENTS HAS DECIDED THEY DON'T WANT TO BUY OUR RESEARCH...
THEY'VE BEEN HAPPILY RECEIVING IT FOR FREE FOR YEARS BUT NOW THAT MIFID II REQUIRES THEM TO PAY FOR IT THEY'VE DECLINED TO DO SO...OBVIOUSLY WE FEEL THEY'VE MADE A MISTAKE...
alex@alexcartoon.com
SO WE'VE DECIDED TO CONTINUE TO SEND THEM THE RESEARCH ANYWAY...
BECAUSE YOU THINK IT'LL REMIND THEM OF WHAT THEY'RE MISSING AND PERSUADE THEM TO RECONSIDER?
ER, NO... BECAUSE THEY NOW HAVE TO FILL IN A COMPLIANCE FORM EVERY TIME THEY RECEIVE AN UNSOLICITED EMAIL FROM US...
HEE HEE... THAT'LL TEACH THEM...
RUB RUB

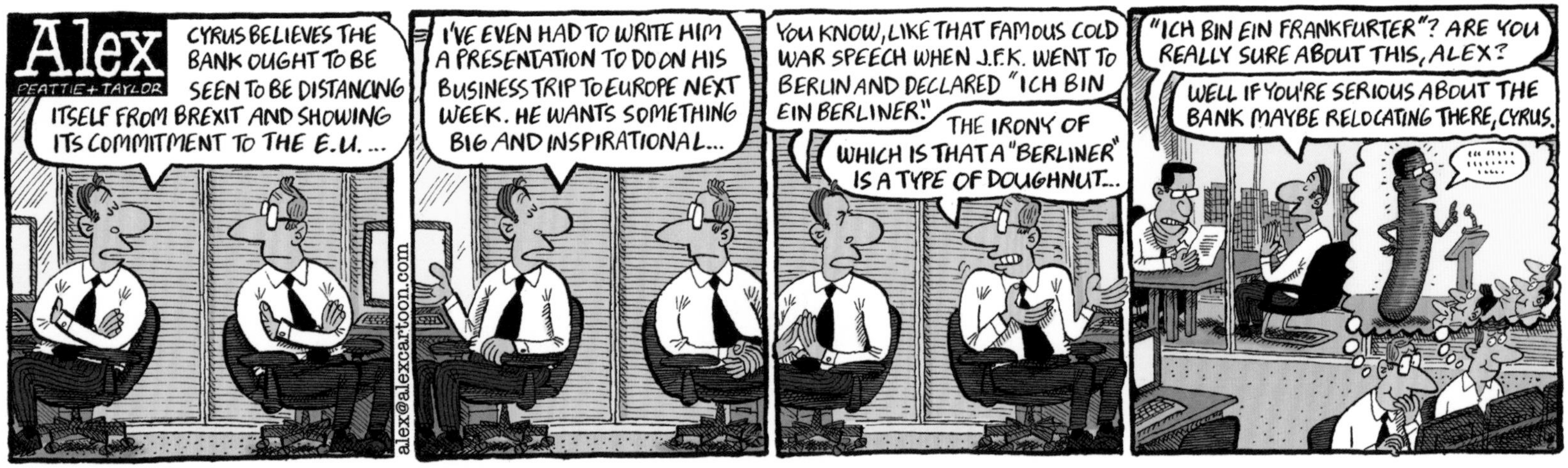
Alex
PEATTIE+TAYLOR
CYRUS BELIEVES THE BANK OUGHT TO BE SEEN TO BE DISTANCING ITSELF FROM BREXIT AND SHOWING ITS COMMITMENT TO THE E.U. ...
I'VE EVEN HAD TO WRITE HIM A PRESENTATION TO DO ON HIS BUSINESS TRIP TO EUROPE NEXT WEEK. HE WANTS SOMETHING BIG AND INSPIRATIONAL...
alex@alexcartoon.com
YOU KNOW, LIKE THAT FAMOUS COLD WAR SPEECH WHEN J.F.K. WENT TO BERLIN AND DECLARED "ICH BIN EIN BERLINER."
THE IRONY OF WHICH IS THAT A "BERLINER" IS A TYPE OF DOUGHNUT...
"ICH BIN EIN FRANKFURTER"? ARE YOU REALLY SURE ABOUT THIS, ALEX?
WELL IF YOU'RE SERIOUS ABOUT THE BANK MAYBE RELOCATING THERE, CYRUS.

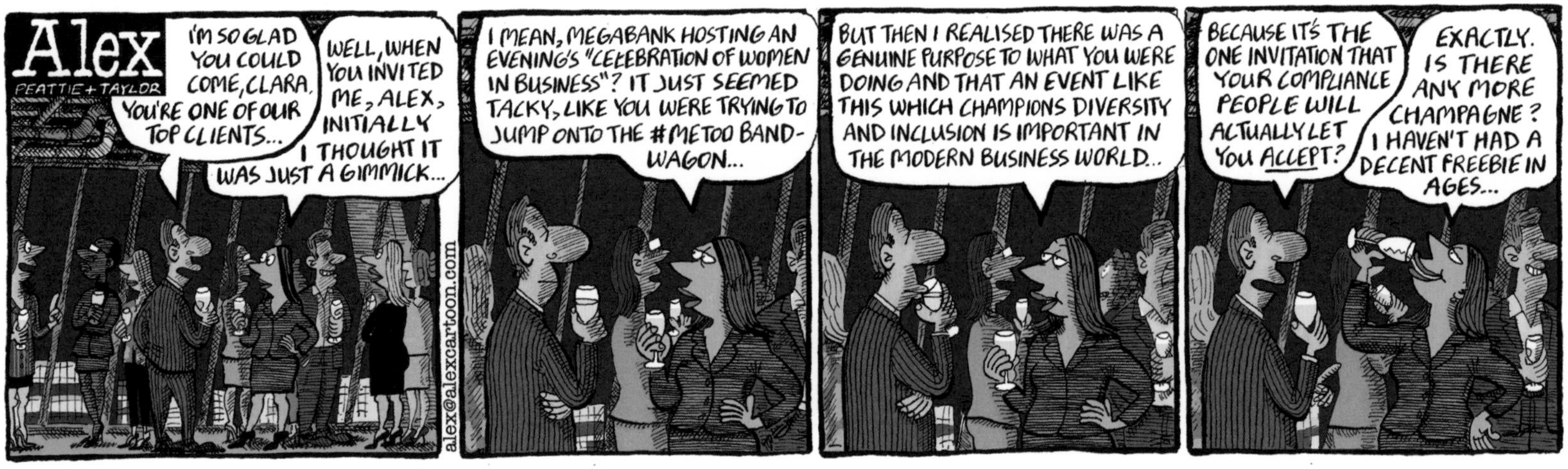
Alex
PEATTIE+TAYLOR
I'M SO GLAD YOU COULD COME, CLARA. YOU'RE ONE OF OUR TOP CLIENTS...
WELL, WHEN YOU INVITED ME, ALEX, INITIALLY I THOUGHT IT WAS JUST A GIMMICK...
alex@alexcartoon.com
I MEAN, MEGABANK HOSTING AN EVENING'S "CELEBRATION OF WOMEN IN BUSINESS"? IT JUST SEEMED TACKY, LIKE YOU WERE TRYING TO JUMP ONTO THE #METOO BAND-WAGON...
BUT THEN I REALISED THERE WAS A GENUINE PURPOSE TO WHAT YOU WERE DOING AND THAT AN EVENT LIKE THIS WHICH CHAMPIONS DIVERSITY AND INCLUSION IS IMPORTANT IN THE MODERN BUSINESS WORLD...
BECAUSE IT'S THE ONE INVITATION THAT YOUR COMPLIANCE PEOPLE WILL ACTUALLY LET YOU ACCEPT?
EXACTLY. IS THERE ANY MORE CHAMPAGNE? I HAVEN'T HAD A DECENT FREEBIE IN AGES...

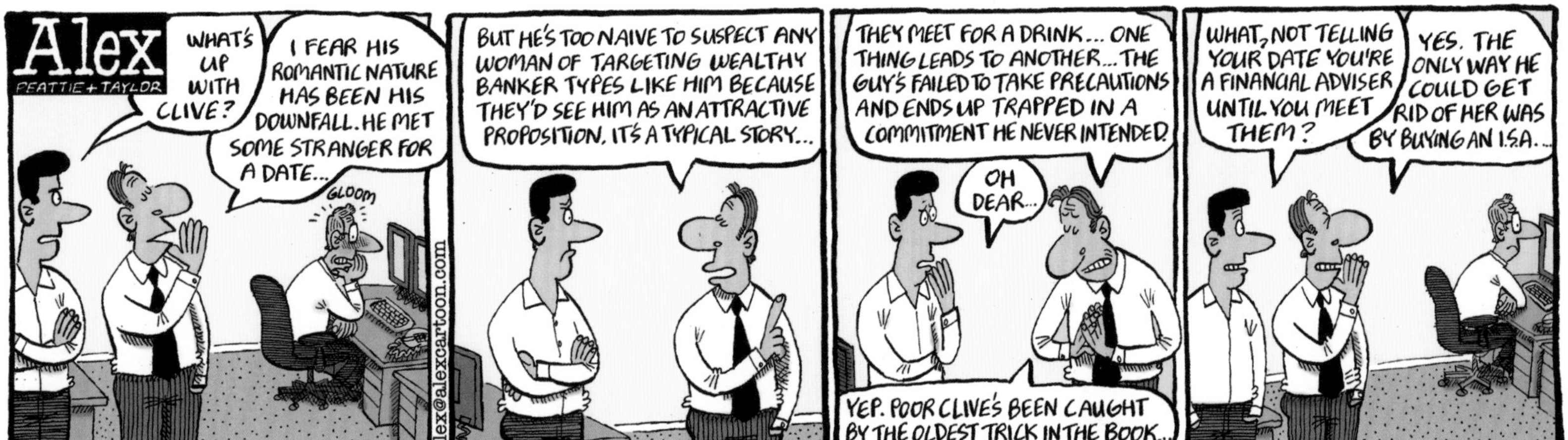
Alex
PEATTIE+TAYLOR
WHAT'S UP WITH CLIVE?
I FEAR HIS ROMANTIC NATURE HAS BEEN HIS DOWNFALL. HE MET SOME STRANGER FOR A DATE...
GLOOM
alex@alexcartoon.com
BUT HE'S TOO NAIVE TO SUSPECT ANY WOMAN OF TARGETING WEALTHY BANKER TYPES LIKE HIM BECAUSE THEY'D SEE HIM AS AN ATTRACTIVE PROPOSITION. IT'S A TYPICAL STORY...
THEY MEET FOR A DRINK... ONE THING LEADS TO ANOTHER... THE GUY'S FAILED TO TAKE PRECAUTIONS AND ENDS UP TRAPPED IN A COMMITMENT HE NEVER INTENDED.
OH DEAR...
YEP. POOR CLIVE'S BEEN CAUGHT BY THE OLDEST TRICK IN THE BOOK...
WHAT, NOT TELLING YOUR DATE YOU'RE A FINANCIAL ADVISER UNTIL YOU MEET THEM?
YES. THE ONLY WAY HE COULD GET RID OF HER WAS BY BUYING AN I.S.A. ...

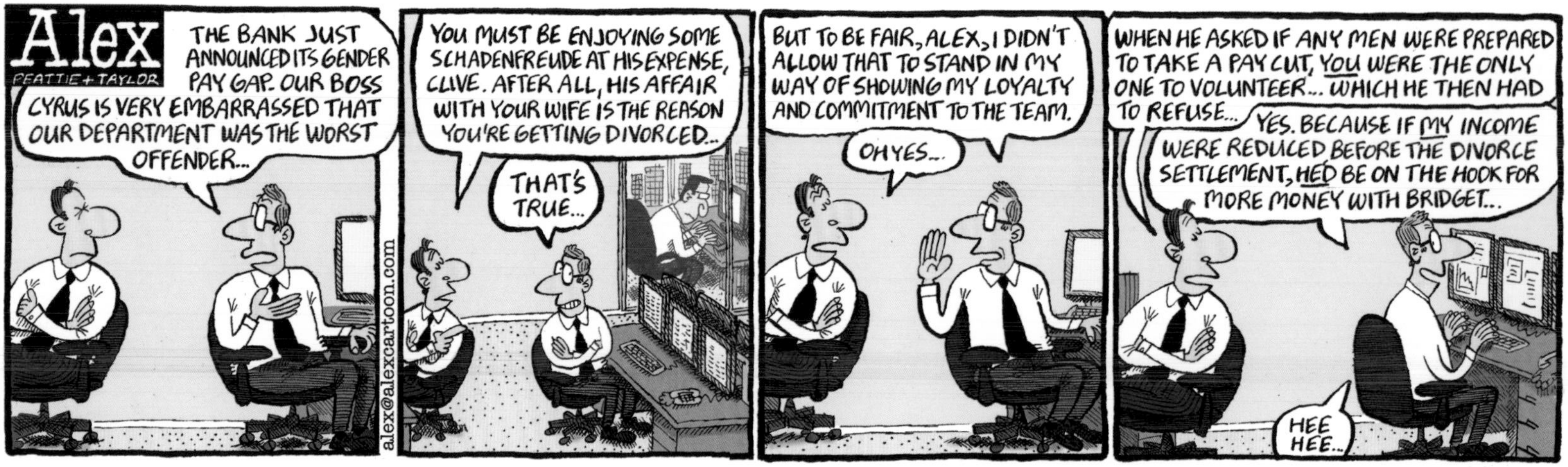
Alex
PEATTIE + TAYLOR
THE BANK JUST ANNOUNCED ITS GENDER PAY GAP. OUR BOSS CYRUS IS VERY EMBARRASSED THAT OUR DEPARTMENT WAS THE WORST OFFENDER...
alex@alexcartoon.com
YOU MUST BE ENJOYING SOME SCHADENFREUDE AT HIS EXPENSE, CLIVE. AFTER ALL, HIS AFFAIR WITH YOUR WIFE IS THE REASON YOU'RE GETTING DIVORCED...
THAT'S TRUE...
BUT TO BE FAIR, ALEX, I DIDN'T ALLOW THAT TO STAND IN MY WAY OF SHOWING MY LOYALTY AND COMMITMENT TO THE TEAM.
OH YES...
WHEN HE ASKED IF ANY MEN WERE PREPARED TO TAKE A PAY CUT, YOU WERE THE ONLY ONE TO VOLUNTEER... WHICH HE THEN HAD TO REFUSE...
YES. BECAUSE IF MY INCOME WERE REDUCED BEFORE THE DIVORCE SETTLEMENT, HE'D BE ON THE HOOK FOR MORE MONEY WITH BRIDGET...
HEE HEE...

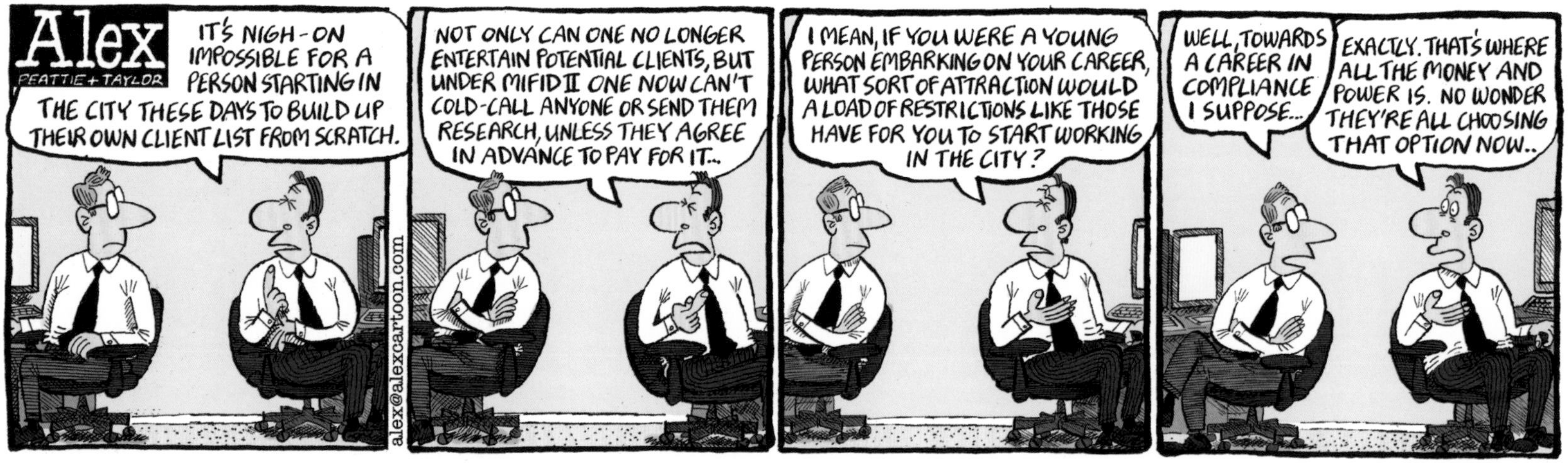
Alex
PEATTIE + TAYLOR
IT'S NIGH-ON IMPOSSIBLE FOR A PERSON STARTING IN THE CITY THESE DAYS TO BUILD UP THEIR OWN CLIENT LIST FROM SCRATCH.
alex@alexcartoon.com
NOT ONLY CAN ONE NO LONGER ENTERTAIN POTENTIAL CLIENTS, BUT UNDER MIFID II ONE NOW CAN'T COLD-CALL ANYONE OR SEND THEM RESEARCH, UNLESS THEY AGREE IN ADVANCE TO PAY FOR IT...
I MEAN, IF YOU WERE A YOUNG PERSON EMBARKING ON YOUR CAREER, WHAT SORT OF ATTRACTION WOULD A LOAD OF RESTRICTIONS LIKE THOSE HAVE FOR YOU TO START WORKING IN THE CITY?
WELL, TOWARDS A CAREER IN COMPLIANCE I SUPPOSE...
EXACTLY. THAT'S WHERE ALL THE MONEY AND POWER IS. NO WONDER THEY'RE ALL CHOOSING THAT OPTION NOW...

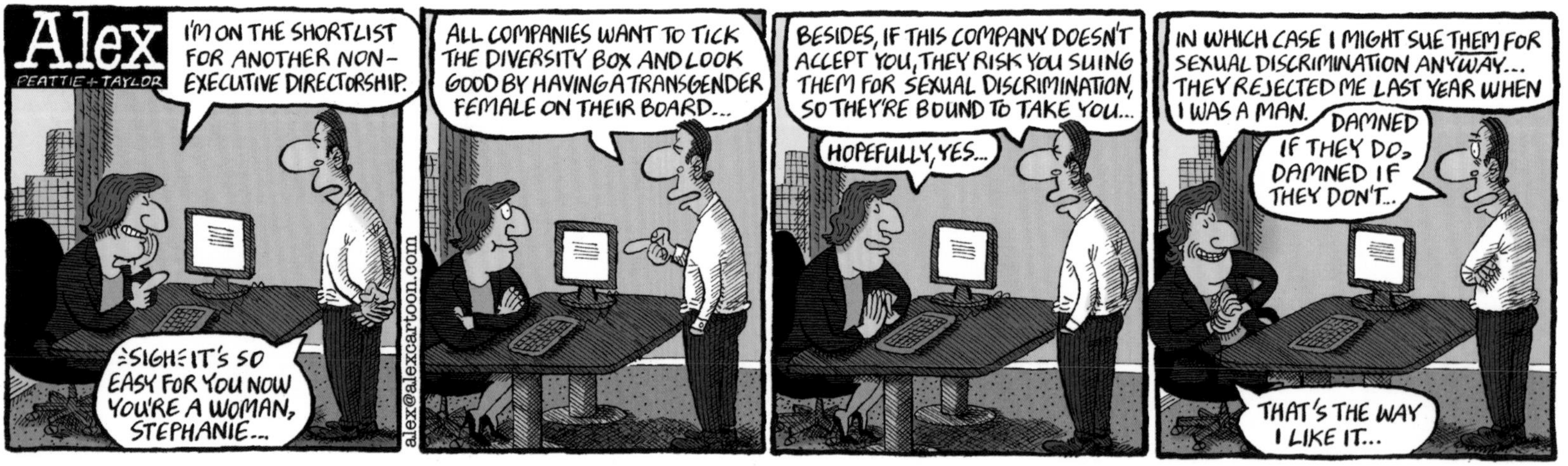
Alex
PEATTIE + TAYLOR
I'M ON THE SHORTLIST FOR ANOTHER NON-EXECUTIVE DIRECTORSHIP.
≡SIGH≡ IT'S SO EASY FOR YOU NOW YOU'RE A WOMAN, STEPHANIE...
alex@alexcartoon.com
ALL COMPANIES WANT TO TICK THE DIVERSITY BOX AND LOOK GOOD BY HAVING A TRANSGENDER FEMALE ON THEIR BOARD...
BESIDES, IF THIS COMPANY DOESN'T ACCEPT YOU, THEY RISK YOU SUING THEM FOR SEXUAL DISCRIMINATION, SO THEY'RE BOUND TO TAKE YOU...
HOPEFULLY, YES...
IN WHICH CASE I MIGHT SUE THEM FOR SEXUAL DISCRIMINATION ANYWAY... THEY REJECTED ME LAST YEAR WHEN I WAS A MAN.
DAMNED IF THEY DO, DAMNED IF THEY DON'T...
THAT'S THE WAY I LIKE IT...

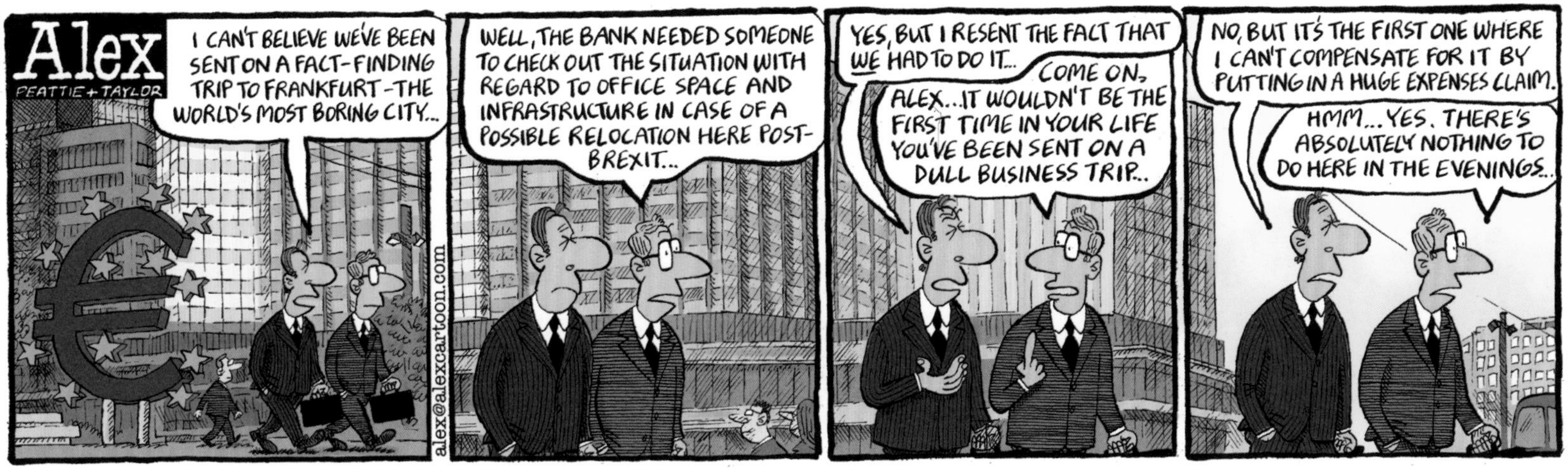
Alex
PEATTIE+TAYLOR
I CAN'T BELIEVE WE'VE BEEN SENT ON A FACT-FINDING TRIP TO FRANKFURT - THE WORLD'S MOST BORING CITY...
WELL, THE BANK NEEDED SOMEONE TO CHECK OUT THE SITUATION WITH REGARD TO OFFICE SPACE AND INFRASTRUCTURE IN CASE OF A POSSIBLE RELOCATION HERE POST-BREXIT...
alex@alexcartoon.com
YES, BUT I RESENT THE FACT THAT WE HAD TO DO IT...
COME ON, ALEX...IT WOULDN'T BE THE FIRST TIME IN YOUR LIFE YOU'VE BEEN SENT ON A DULL BUSINESS TRIP...
NO, BUT IT'S THE FIRST ONE WHERE I CAN'T COMPENSATE FOR IT BY PUTTING IN A HUGE EXPENSES CLAIM.
HMM... YES. THERE'S ABSOLUTELY NOTHING TO DO HERE IN THE EVENINGS...

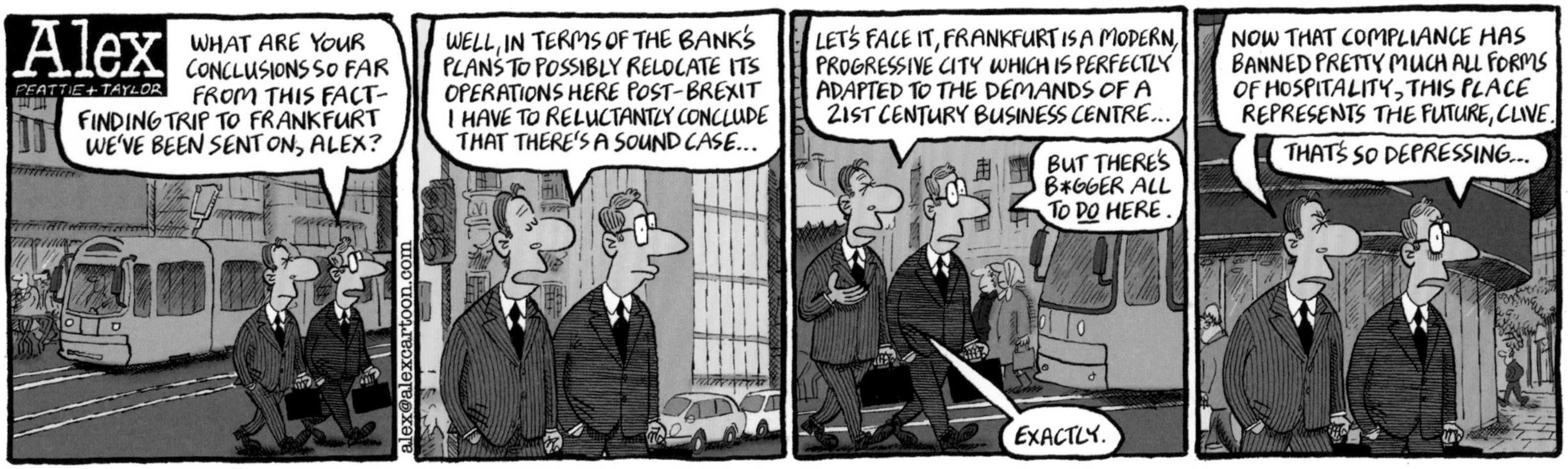
Alex
PEATTIE+TAYLOR
WHAT ARE YOUR CONCLUSIONS SO FAR FROM THIS FACT-FINDING TRIP TO FRANKFURT WE'VE BEEN SENT ON, ALEX?
WELL, IN TERMS OF THE BANK'S PLANS TO POSSIBLY RELOCATE ITS OPERATIONS HERE POST-BREXIT I HAVE TO RELUCTANTLY CONCLUDE THAT THERE'S A SOUND CASE...
alex@alexcartoon.com
LET'S FACE IT, FRANKFURT IS A MODERN, PROGRESSIVE CITY WHICH IS PERFECTLY ADAPTED TO THE DEMANDS OF A 21ST CENTURY BUSINESS CENTRE...
BUT THERE'S B*GGER ALL TO DO HERE.
EXACTLY.
NOW THAT COMPLIANCE HAS BANNED PRETTY MUCH ALL FORMS OF HOSPITALITY, THIS PLACE REPRESENTS THE FUTURE, CLIVE.
THAT'S SO DEPRESSING...

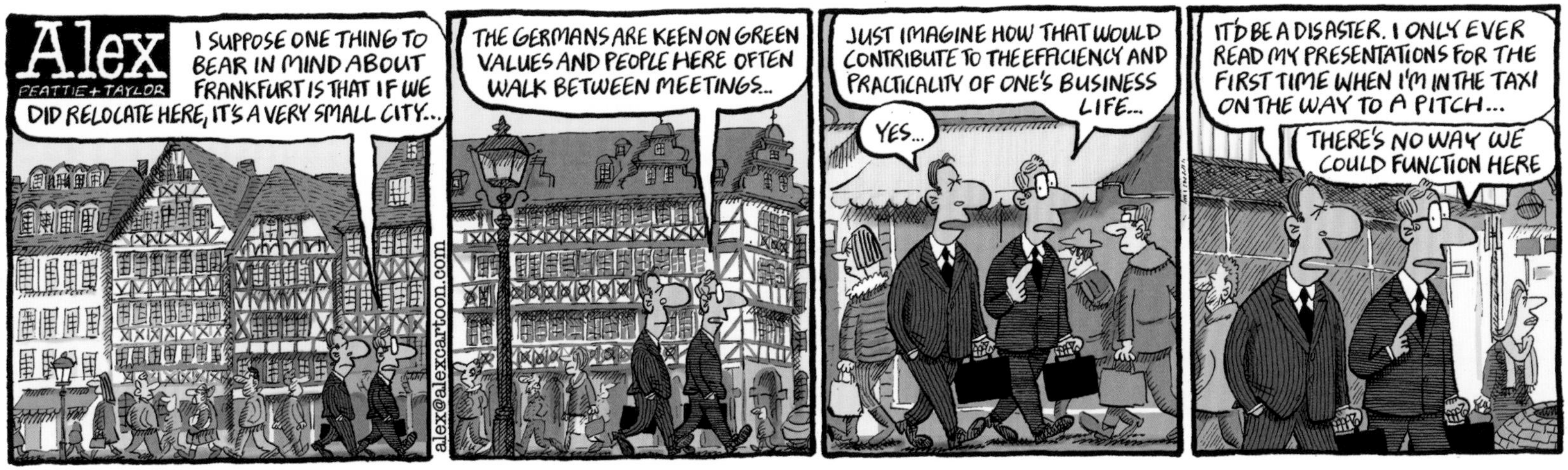
Alex
PEATTIE+TAYLOR
I SUPPOSE ONE THING TO BEAR IN MIND ABOUT FRANKFURT IS THAT IF WE DID RELOCATE HERE, IT'S A VERY SMALL CITY...
THE GERMANS ARE KEEN ON GREEN VALUES AND PEOPLE HERE OFTEN WALK BETWEEN MEETINGS...
alex@alexcartoon.com
JUST IMAGINE HOW THAT WOULD CONTRIBUTE TO THE EFFICIENCY AND PRACTICALITY OF ONE'S BUSINESS LIFE...
YES...
IT'D BE A DISASTER. I ONLY EVER READ MY PRESENTATIONS FOR THE FIRST TIME WHEN I'M IN THE TAXI ON THE WAY TO A PITCH...
THERE'S NO WAY WE COULD FUNCTION HERE

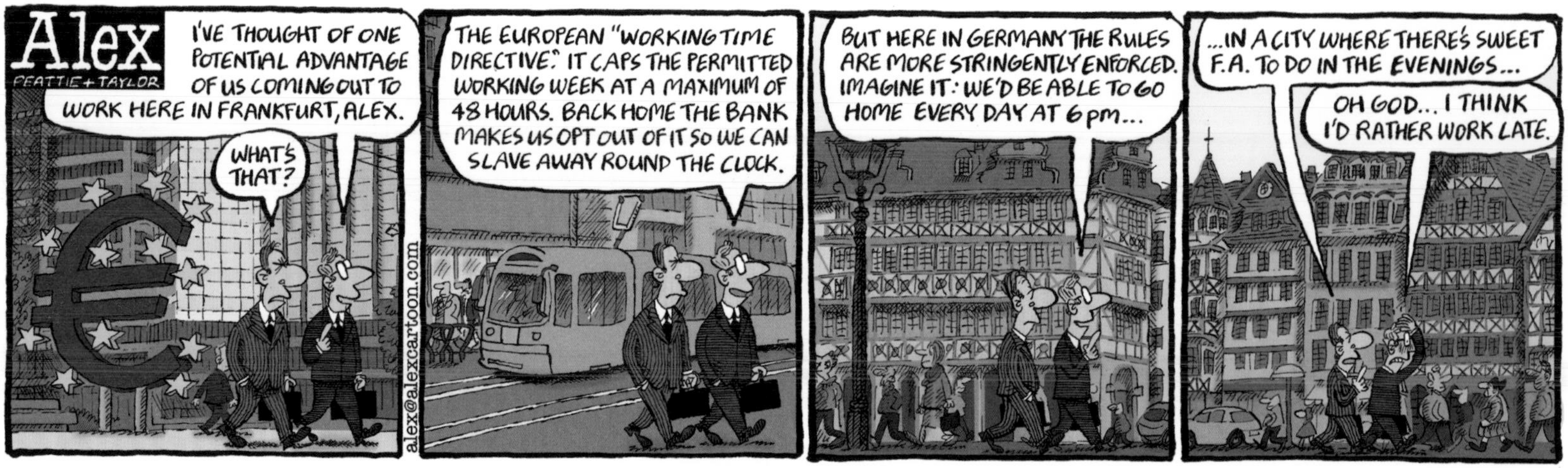
Alex
PEATTIE + TAYLOR
I'VE THOUGHT OF ONE POTENTIAL ADVANTAGE OF US COMING OUT TO WORK HERE IN FRANKFURT, ALEX.
WHAT'S THAT?
alex@alexcartoon.com
THE EUROPEAN "WORKING TIME DIRECTIVE". IT CAPS THE PERMITTED WORKING WEEK AT A MAXIMUM OF 48 HOURS. BACK HOME THE BANK MAKES US OPT OUT OF IT SO WE CAN SLAVE AWAY ROUND THE CLOCK.
BUT HERE IN GERMANY THE RULES ARE MORE STRINGENTLY ENFORCED. IMAGINE IT: WE'D BE ABLE TO GO HOME EVERY DAY AT 6 pm...
...IN A CITY WHERE THERE'S SWEET F.A. TO DO IN THE EVENINGS...
OH GOD... I THINK I'D RATHER WORK LATE.

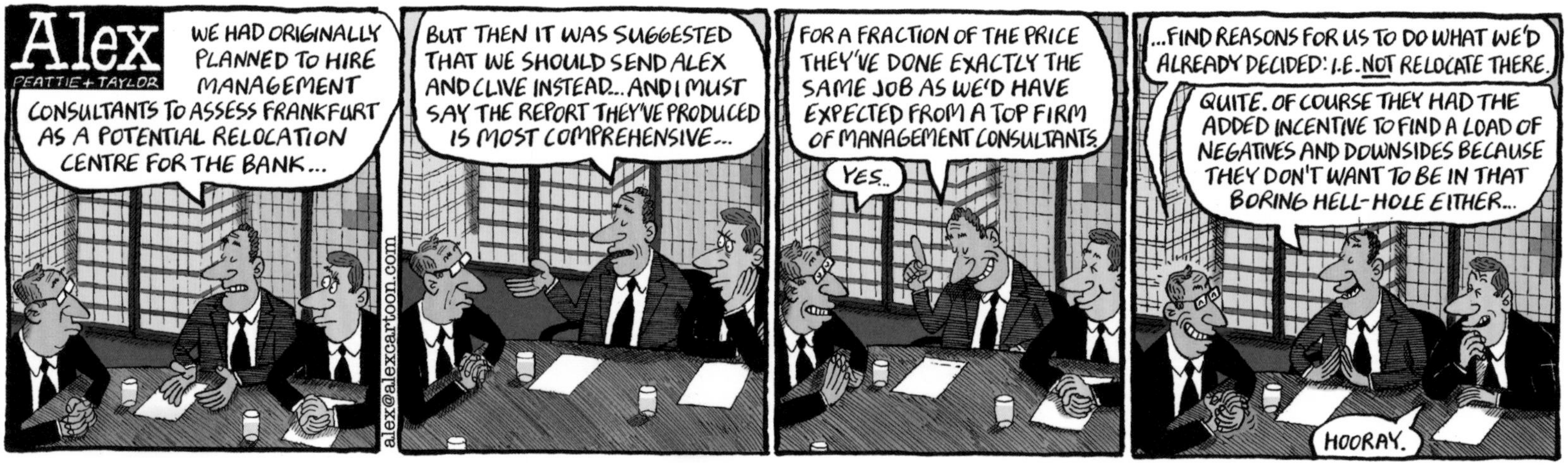
Alex
PEATTIE + TAYLOR
WE HAD ORIGINALLY PLANNED TO HIRE MANAGEMENT CONSULTANTS TO ASSESS FRANKFURT AS A POTENTIAL RELOCATION CENTRE FOR THE BANK...
alex@alexcartoon.com
BUT THEN IT WAS SUGGESTED THAT WE SHOULD SEND ALEX AND CLIVE INSTEAD... AND I MUST SAY THE REPORT THEY'VE PRODUCED IS MOST COMPREHENSIVE...
FOR A FRACTION OF THE PRICE THEY'VE DONE EXACTLY THE SAME JOB AS WE'D HAVE EXPECTED FROM A TOP FIRM OF MANAGEMENT CONSULTANTS.
YES..
...FIND REASONS FOR US TO DO WHAT WE'D ALREADY DECIDED: I.E. NOT RELOCATE THERE.
QUITE. OF COURSE THEY HAD THE ADDED INCENTIVE TO FIND A LOAD OF NEGATIVES AND DOWNSIDES BECAUSE THEY DON'T WANT TO BE IN THAT BORING HELL-HOLE EITHER...
HOORAY.

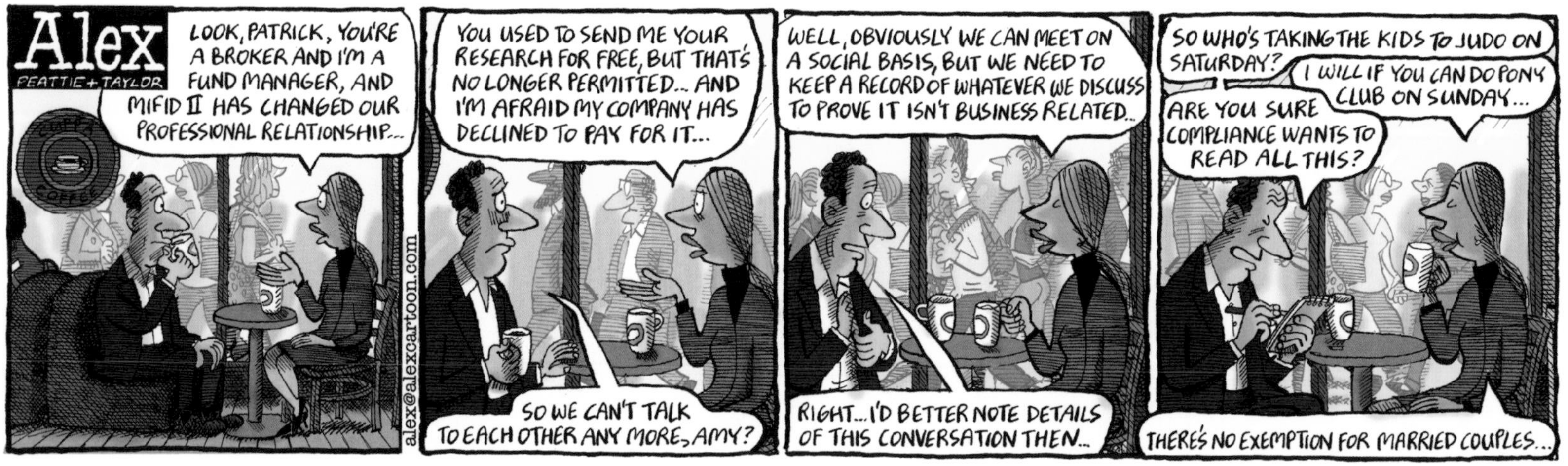
Alex
PEATTIE + TAYLOR
LOOK, PATRICK, YOU'RE A BROKER AND I'M A FUND MANAGER, AND MIFID II HAS CHANGED OUR PROFESSIONAL RELATIONSHIP...
COFFEE
alex@alexcartoon.com
YOU USED TO SEND ME YOUR RESEARCH FOR FREE, BUT THAT'S NO LONGER PERMITTED... AND I'M AFRAID MY COMPANY HAS DECLINED TO PAY FOR IT...
SO WE CAN'T TALK TO EACH OTHER ANY MORE, AMY?
WELL, OBVIOUSLY WE CAN MEET ON A SOCIAL BASIS, BUT WE NEED TO KEEP A RECORD OF WHATEVER WE DISCUSS TO PROVE IT ISN'T BUSINESS RELATED...
RIGHT... I'D BETTER NOTE DETAILS OF THIS CONVERSATION THEN...
SO WHO'S TAKING THE KIDS TO JUDO ON SATURDAY?
I WILL IF YOU CAN DO PONY CLUB ON SUNDAY...
ARE YOU SURE COMPLIANCE WANTS TO READ ALL THIS?
THERE'S NO EXEMPTION FOR MARRIED COUPLES...

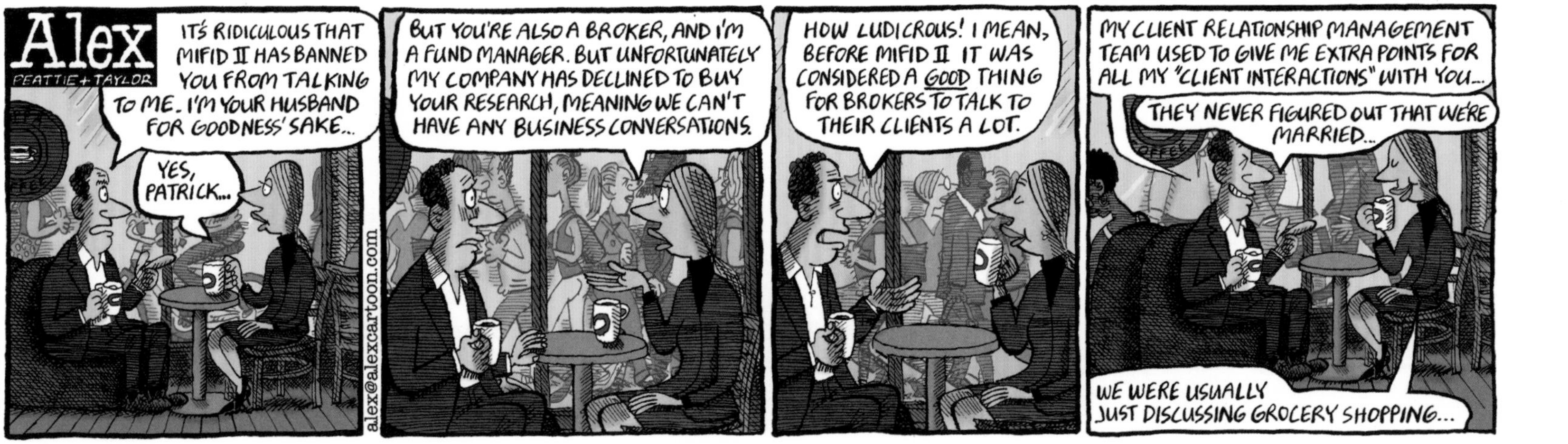
Alex
PEATTIE + TAYLOR
IT'S RIDICULOUS THAT MIFID II HAS BANNED YOU FROM TALKING TO ME. I'M YOUR HUSBAND FOR GOODNESS' SAKE...
YES, PATRICK...
alex@alexcartoon.com
BUT YOU'RE ALSO A BROKER, AND I'M A FUND MANAGER. BUT UNFORTUNATELY MY COMPANY HAS DECLINED TO BUY YOUR RESEARCH, MEANING WE CAN'T HAVE ANY BUSINESS CONVERSATIONS.
HOW LUDICROUS! I MEAN, BEFORE MIFID II IT WAS CONSIDERED A GOOD THING FOR BROKERS TO TALK TO THEIR CLIENTS A LOT.
MY CLIENT RELATIONSHIP MANAGEMENT TEAM USED TO GIVE ME EXTRA POINTS FOR ALL MY "CLIENT INTERACTIONS" WITH YOU...
THEY NEVER FIGURED OUT THAT WE'RE MARRIED...
WE WERE USUALLY JUST DISCUSSING GROCERY SHOPPING...

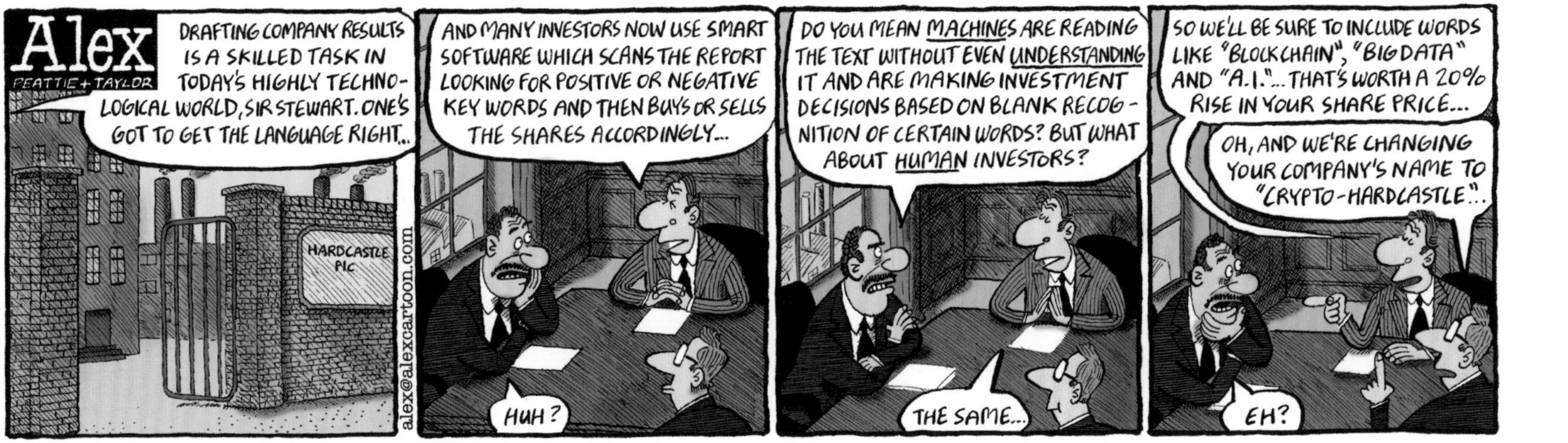
Alex
PEATTIE + TAYLOR
DRAFTING COMPANY RESULTS IS A SKILLED TASK IN TODAY'S HIGHLY TECHNOLOGICAL WORLD, SIR STEWART. ONE'S GOT TO GET THE LANGUAGE RIGHT...
HARDCASTLE PLC
alex@alexcartoon.com
AND MANY INVESTORS NOW USE SMART SOFTWARE WHICH SCANS THE REPORT LOOKING FOR POSITIVE OR NEGATIVE KEY WORDS AND THEN BUYS OR SELLS THE SHARES ACCORDINGLY...
HUH?
DO YOU MEAN MACHINES ARE READING THE TEXT WITHOUT EVEN UNDERSTANDING IT AND ARE MAKING INVESTMENT DECISIONS BASED ON BLANK RECOGNITION OF CERTAIN WORDS? BUT WHAT ABOUT HUMAN INVESTORS?
THE SAME...
SO WE'LL BE SURE TO INCLUDE WORDS LIKE "BLOCKCHAIN", "BIG DATA" AND "A.I."... THAT'S WORTH A 20% RISE IN YOUR SHARE PRICE...
OH, AND WE'RE CHANGING YOUR COMPANY'S NAME TO "CRYPTO-HARDCASTLE"...
EH?

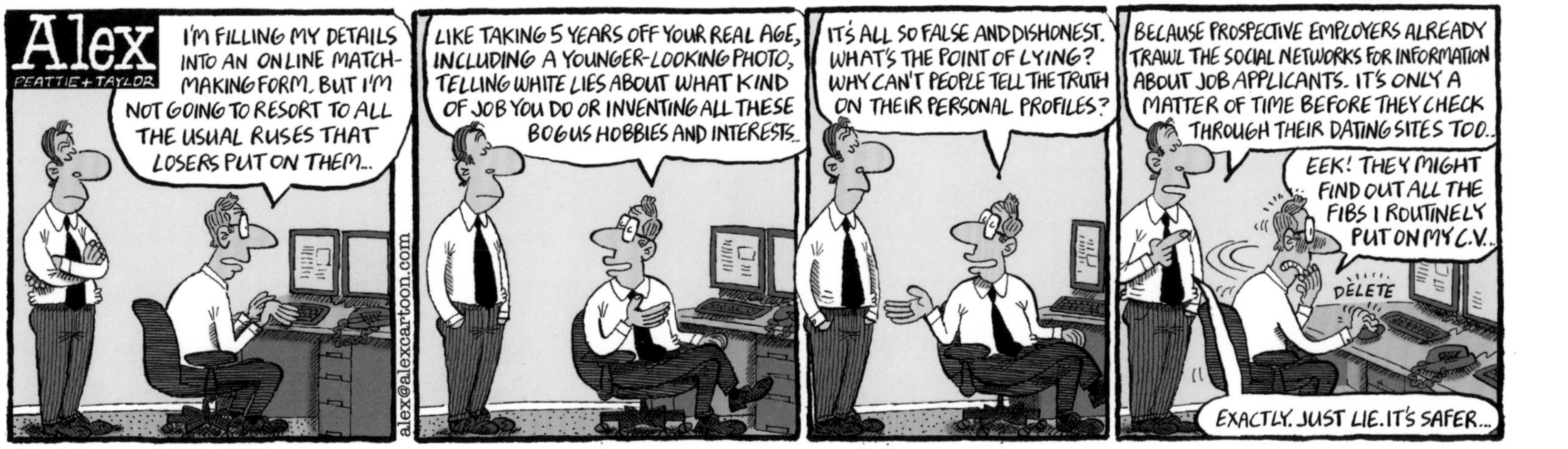
Alex
PEATTIE + TAYLOR
I'M FILLING MY DETAILS INTO AN ONLINE MATCH-MAKING FORM. BUT I'M NOT GOING TO RESORT TO ALL THE USUAL RUSES THAT LOSERS PUT ON THEM...
alex@alexcartoon.com
LIKE TAKING 5 YEARS OFF YOUR REAL AGE, INCLUDING A YOUNGER-LOOKING PHOTO, TELLING WHITE LIES ABOUT WHAT KIND OF JOB YOU DO OR INVENTING ALL THESE BOGUS HOBBIES AND INTERESTS...
IT'S ALL SO FALSE AND DISHONEST. WHAT'S THE POINT OF LYING? WHY CAN'T PEOPLE TELL THE TRUTH ON THEIR PERSONAL PROFILES?
BECAUSE PROSPECTIVE EMPLOYERS ALREADY TRAWL THE SOCIAL NETWORKS FOR INFORMATION ABOUT JOB APPLICANTS. IT'S ONLY A MATTER OF TIME BEFORE THEY CHECK THROUGH THEIR DATING SITES TOO...
EEK! THEY MIGHT FIND OUT ALL THE FIBS I ROUTINELY PUT ON MY C.V...
DELETE
EXACTLY. JUST LIE. IT'S SAFER...

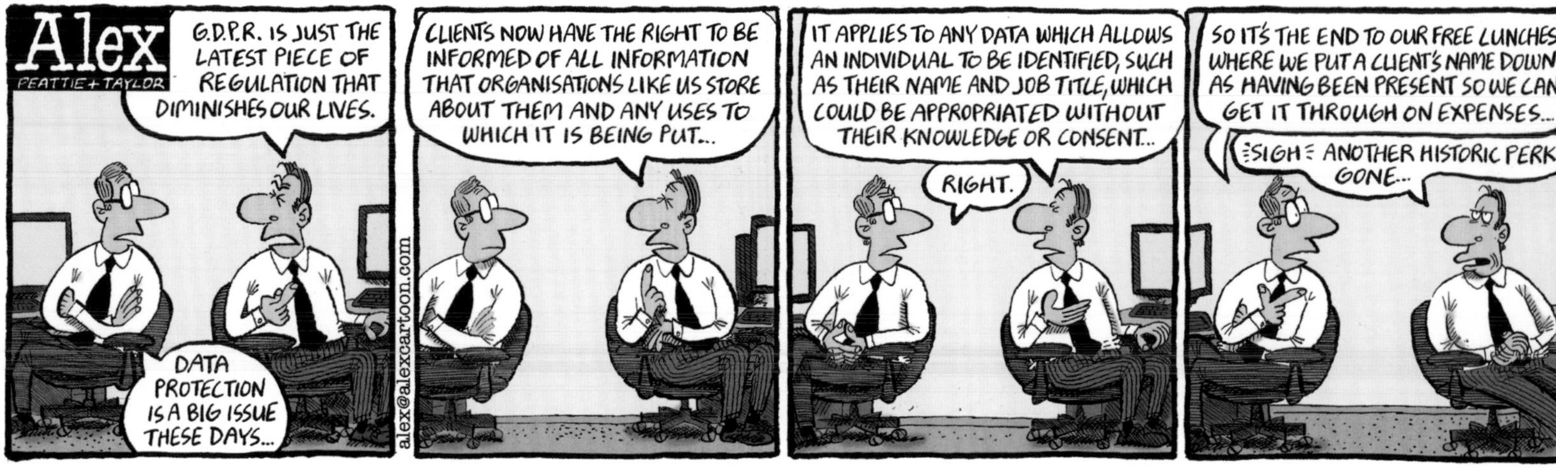
Alex
PEATTIE + TAYLOR
G.D.P.R. IS JUST THE LATEST PIECE OF REGULATION THAT DIMINISHES OUR LIVES.
DATA PROTECTION IS A BIG ISSUE THESE DAYS...
CLIENTS NOW HAVE THE RIGHT TO BE INFORMED OF ALL INFORMATION THAT ORGANISATIONS LIKE US STORE ABOUT THEM AND ANY USES TO WHICH IT IS BEING PUT...
IT APPLIES TO ANY DATA WHICH ALLOWS AN INDIVIDUAL TO BE IDENTIFIED, SUCH AS THEIR NAME AND JOB TITLE, WHICH COULD BE APPROPRIATED WITHOUT THEIR KNOWLEDGE OR CONSENT...
RIGHT.
SO IT'S THE END TO OUR FREE LUNCHES WHERE WE PUT A CLIENT'S NAME DOWN AS HAVING BEEN PRESENT SO WE CAN GET IT THROUGH ON EXPENSES...
SIGH ANOTHER HISTORIC PERK GONE...
alex@alexcartoon.com

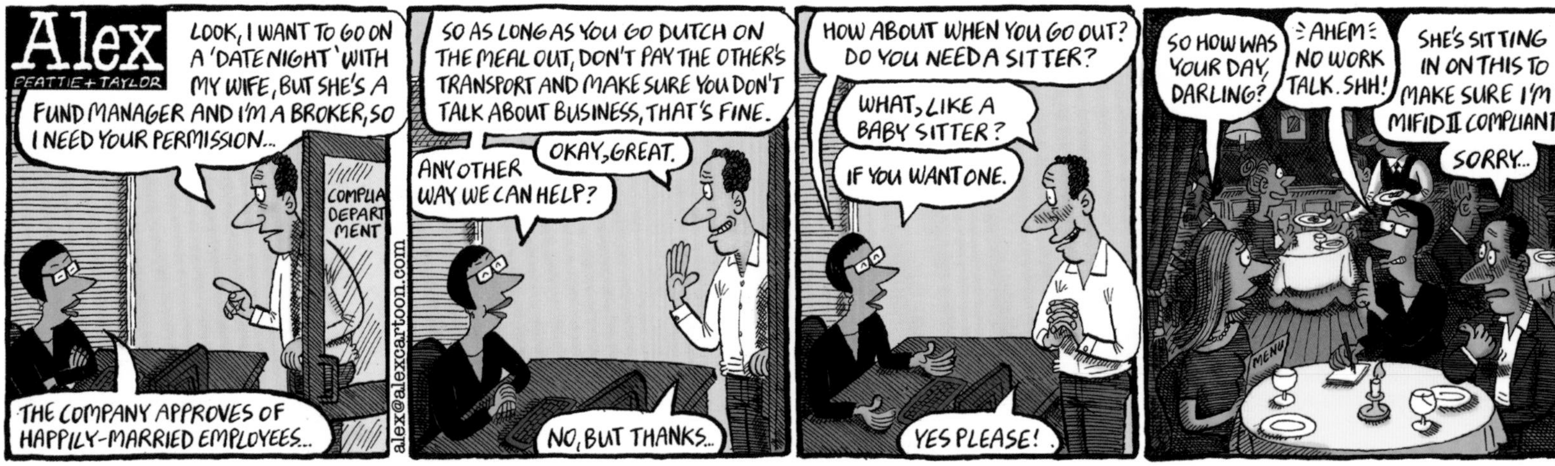
Alex
PEATTIE + TAYLOR
LOOK, I WANT TO GO ON A 'DATE NIGHT' WITH MY WIFE, BUT SHE'S A FUND MANAGER AND I'M A BROKER, SO I NEED YOUR PERMISSION...
COMPLIA DEPART MENT
THE COMPANY APPROVES OF HAPPILY-MARRIED EMPLOYEES...
SO AS LONG AS YOU GO DUTCH ON THE MEAL OUT, DON'T PAY THE OTHER'S TRANSPORT AND MAKE SURE YOU DON'T TALK ABOUT BUSINESS, THAT'S FINE.
OKAY, GREAT.
ANY OTHER WAY WE CAN HELP?
NO, BUT THANKS...
HOW ABOUT WHEN YOU GO OUT? DO YOU NEED A SITTER?
WHAT, LIKE A BABY SITTER?
IF YOU WANT ONE.
YES PLEASE!
SO HOW WAS YOUR DAY, DARLING?
AHEM NO WORK TALK. SHH!
SHE'S SITTING IN ON THIS TO MAKE SURE I'M MIFID II COMPLIANT...
SORRY...
MENU
alex@alexcartoon.com

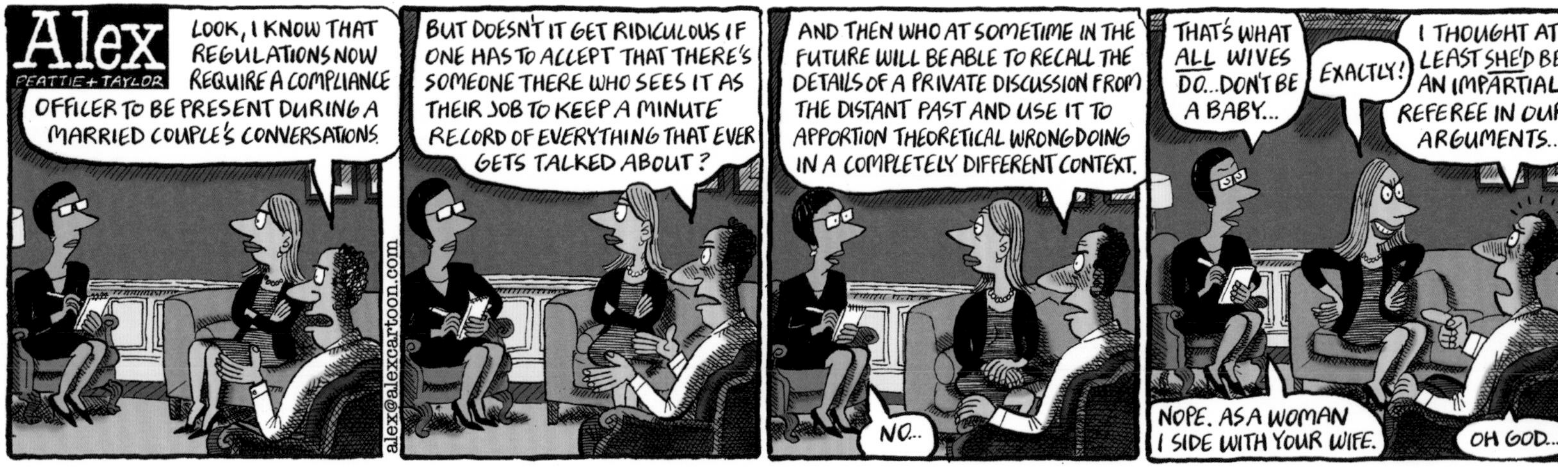
Alex
PEATTIE + TAYLOR
LOOK, I KNOW THAT REGULATIONS NOW REQUIRE A COMPLIANCE OFFICER TO BE PRESENT DURING A MARRIED COUPLE'S CONVERSATIONS.
BUT DOESN'T IT GET RIDICULOUS IF ONE HAS TO ACCEPT THAT THERE'S SOMEONE THERE WHO SEES IT AS THEIR JOB TO KEEP A MINUTE RECORD OF EVERYTHING THAT EVER GETS TALKED ABOUT?
AND THEN WHO AT SOMETIME IN THE FUTURE WILL BE ABLE TO RECALL THE DETAILS OF A PRIVATE DISCUSSION FROM THE DISTANT PAST AND USE IT TO APPORTION THEORETICAL WRONGDOING IN A COMPLETELY DIFFERENT CONTEXT.
NO...
THAT'S WHAT ALL WIVES DO... DON'T BE A BABY...
EXACTLY!
I THOUGHT AT LEAST SHE'D BE AN IMPARTIAL REFEREE IN OUR ARGUMENTS...
NOPE. AS A WOMAN I SIDE WITH YOUR WIFE.
OH GOD...
alex@alexcartoon.com

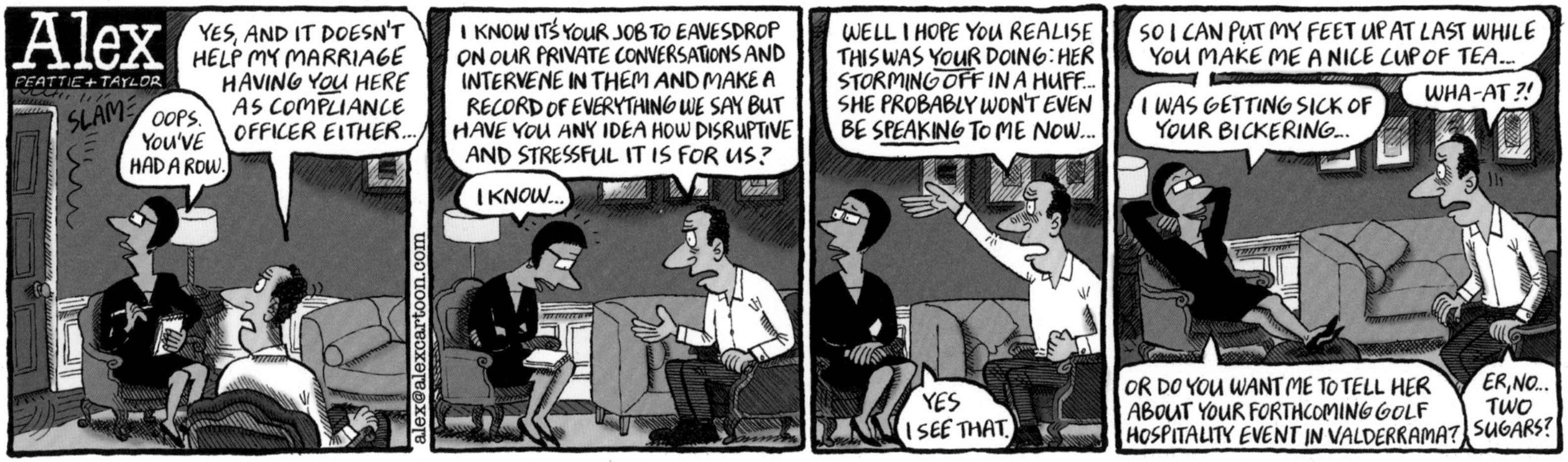
Alex
PEATTIE + TAYLOR
SLAM
YES, AND IT DOESN'T HELP MY MARRIAGE HAVING YOU HERE AS COMPLIANCE OFFICER EITHER...
OOPS. YOU'VE HAD A ROW.
I KNOW IT'S YOUR JOB TO EAVESDROP ON OUR PRIVATE CONVERSATIONS AND INTERVENE IN THEM AND MAKE A RECORD OF EVERYTHING WE SAY BUT HAVE YOU ANY IDEA HOW DISRUPTIVE AND STRESSFUL IT IS FOR US?
I KNOW...
WELL I HOPE YOU REALISE THIS WAS YOUR DOING: HER STORMING OFF IN A HUFF... SHE PROBABLY WON'T EVEN BE SPEAKING TO ME NOW...
YES I SEE THAT.
SO I CAN PUT MY FEET UP AT LAST WHILE YOU MAKE ME A NICE CUP OF TEA...
I WAS GETTING SICK OF YOUR BICKERING...
WHA-AT?!
OR DO YOU WANT ME TO TELL HER ABOUT YOUR FORTHCOMING GOLF HOSPITALITY EVENT IN VALDERRAMA?
ER, NO... TWO SUGARS?
alex@alexcartoon.com

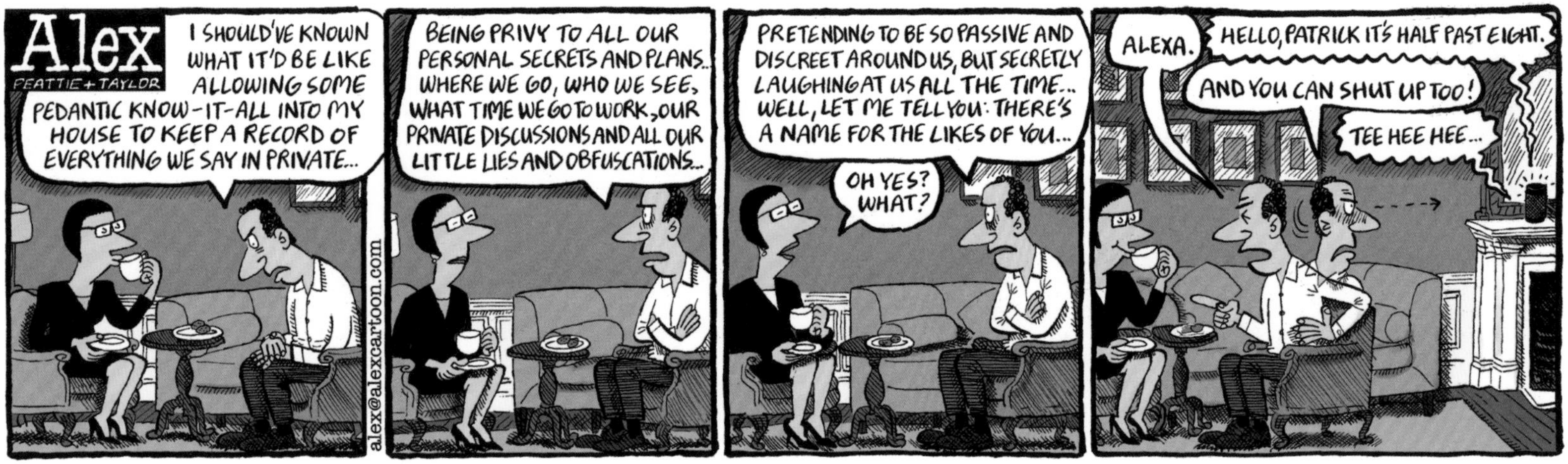
Alex
PEATTIE + TAYLOR
I SHOULD'VE KNOWN WHAT IT'D BE LIKE ALLOWING SOME PEDANTIC KNOW-IT-ALL INTO MY HOUSE TO KEEP A RECORD OF EVERYTHING WE SAY IN PRIVATE...
BEING PRIVY TO ALL OUR PERSONAL SECRETS AND PLANS... WHERE WE GO, WHO WE SEE, WHAT TIME WE GO TO WORK, OUR PRIVATE DISCUSSIONS AND ALL OUR LITTLE LIES AND OBFUSCATIONS...
PRETENDING TO BE SO PASSIVE AND DISCREET AROUND US, BUT SECRETLY LAUGHING AT US ALL THE TIME... WELL, LET ME TELL YOU: THERE'S A NAME FOR THE LIKES OF YOU...
OH YES? WHAT?
ALEXA.
HELLO, PATRICK IT'S HALF PAST EIGHT.
AND YOU CAN SHUT UP TOO!
TEE HEE HEE...
alex@alexcartoon.com

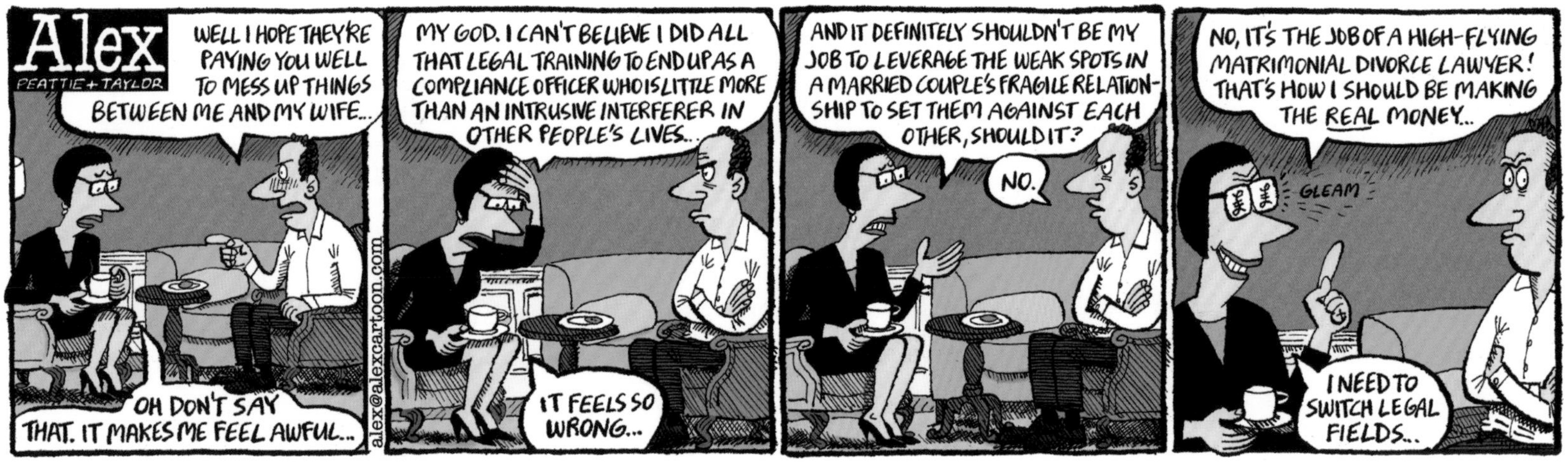
Alex
PEATTIE + TAYLOR
WELL I HOPE THEY'RE PAYING YOU WELL TO MESS UP THINGS BETWEEN ME AND MY WIFE...
OH DON'T SAY THAT. IT MAKES ME FEEL AWFUL...
MY GOD. I CAN'T BELIEVE I DID ALL THAT LEGAL TRAINING TO END UP AS A COMPLIANCE OFFICER WHO IS LITTLE MORE THAN AN INTRUSIVE INTERFERER IN OTHER PEOPLE'S LIVES...
IT FEELS SO WRONG...
AND IT DEFINITELY SHOULDN'T BE MY JOB TO LEVERAGE THE WEAK SPOTS IN A MARRIED COUPLE'S FRAGILE RELATIONSHIP TO SET THEM AGAINST EACH OTHER, SHOULD IT?
NO.
NO, IT'S THE JOB OF A HIGH-FLYING MATRIMONIAL DIVORCE LAWYER! THAT'S HOW I SHOULD BE MAKING THE REAL MONEY...
GLEAM
I NEED TO SWITCH LEGAL FIELDS...
alex@alexcartoon.com

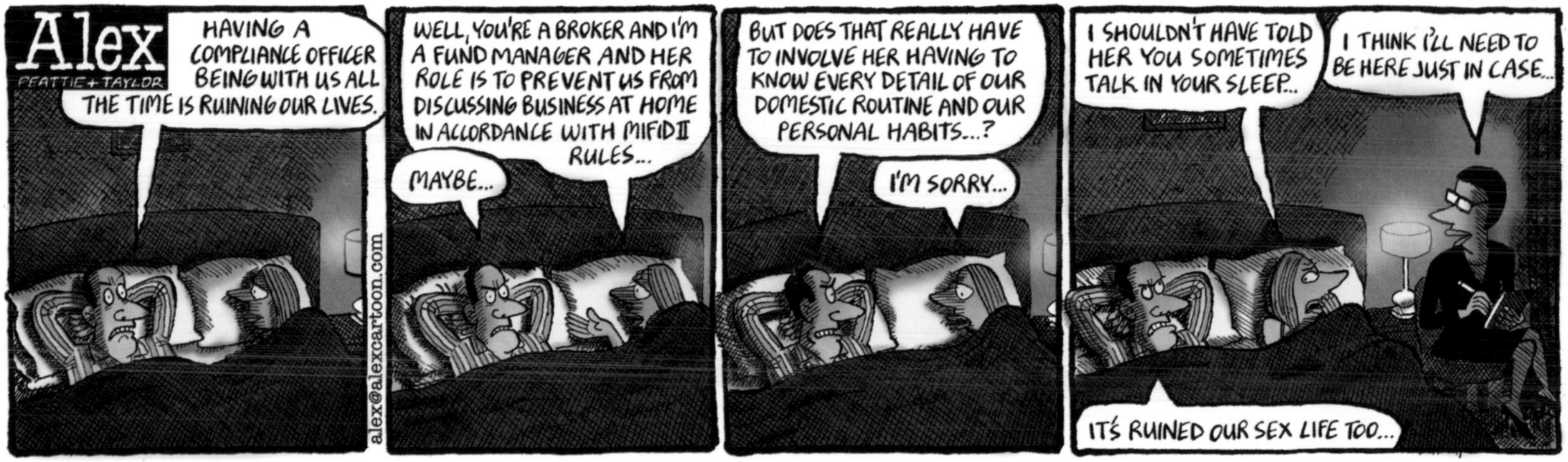
Alex
PEATTIE + TAYLOR
HAVING A COMPLIANCE OFFICER BEING WITH US ALL THE TIME IS RUINING OUR LIVES.
alex@alexcartoon.com
WELL, YOU'RE A BROKER AND I'M A FUND MANAGER AND HER ROLE IS TO PREVENT US FROM DISCUSSING BUSINESS AT HOME IN ACCORDANCE WITH MIFID II RULES...
MAYBE...
BUT DOES THAT REALLY HAVE TO INVOLVE HER HAVING TO KNOW EVERY DETAIL OF OUR DOMESTIC ROUTINE AND OUR PERSONAL HABITS...?
I'M SORRY...
I SHOULDN'T HAVE TOLD HER YOU SOMETIMES TALK IN YOUR SLEEP...
I THINK I'LL NEED TO BE HERE JUST IN CASE...
IT'S RUINED OUR SEX LIFE TOO...

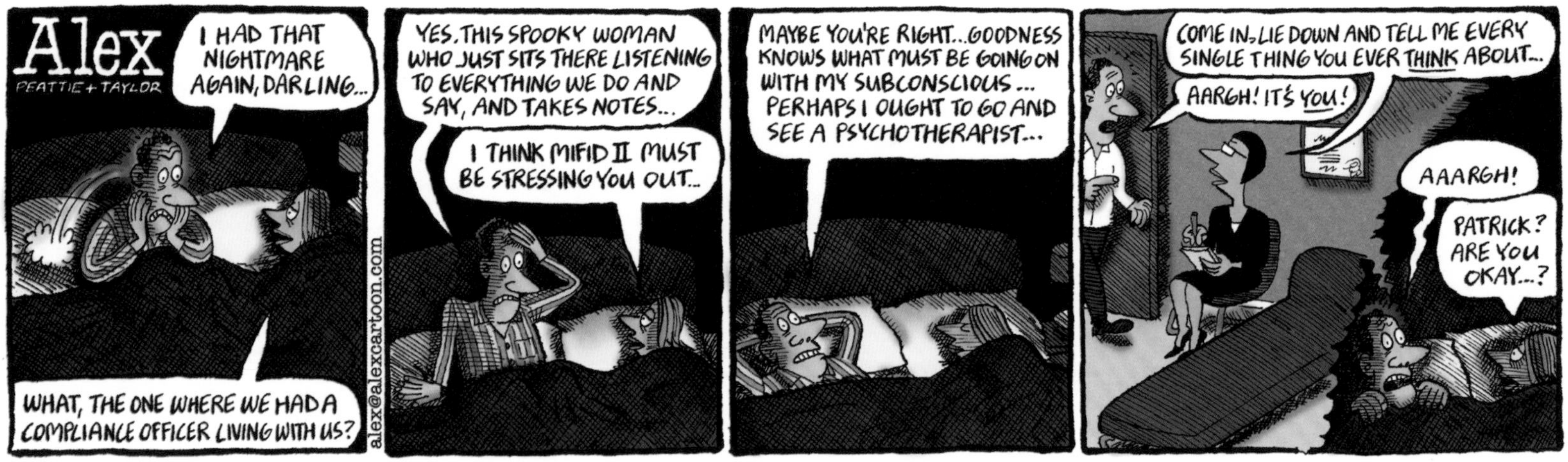
Alex
PEATTIE + TAYLOR
I HAD THAT NIGHTMARE AGAIN, DARLING...
WHAT, THE ONE WHERE WE HAD A COMPLIANCE OFFICER LIVING WITH US?
alex@alexcartoon.com
YES, THIS SPOOKY WOMAN WHO JUST SITS THERE LISTENING TO EVERYTHING WE DO AND SAY, AND TAKES NOTES...
I THINK MIFID II MUST BE STRESSING YOU OUT...
MAYBE YOU'RE RIGHT... GOODNESS KNOWS WHAT MUST BE GOING ON WITH MY SUBCONSCIOUS... PERHAPS I OUGHT TO GO AND SEE A PSYCHOTHERAPIST...
COME IN, LIE DOWN AND TELL ME EVERY SINGLE THING YOU EVER THINK ABOUT...
AARGH! IT'S YOU!
AAARGH!
PATRICK? ARE YOU OKAY...?

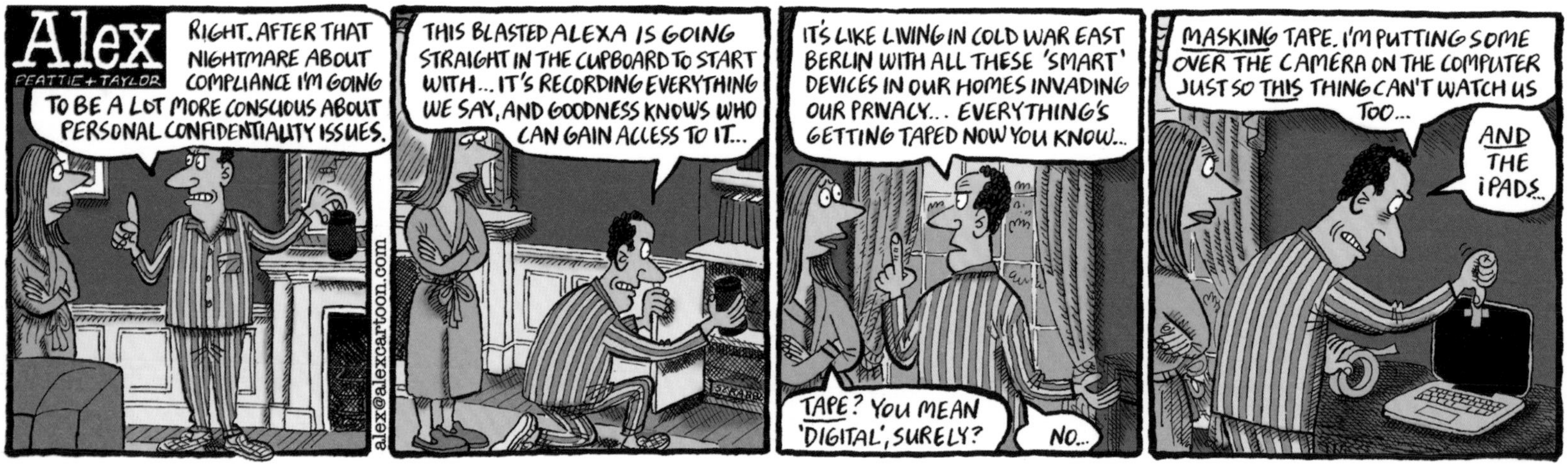
Alex
PEATTIE + TAYLOR
RIGHT. AFTER THAT NIGHTMARE ABOUT COMPLIANCE I'M GOING TO BE A LOT MORE CONSCIOUS ABOUT PERSONAL CONFIDENTIALITY ISSUES.
alex@alexcartoon.com
THIS BLASTED ALEXA IS GOING STRAIGHT IN THE CUPBOARD TO START WITH... IT'S RECORDING EVERYTHING WE SAY, AND GOODNESS KNOWS WHO CAN GAIN ACCESS TO IT...
IT'S LIKE LIVING IN COLD WAR EAST BERLIN WITH ALL THESE 'SMART' DEVICES IN OUR HOMES INVADING OUR PRIVACY... EVERYTHING'S GETTING TAPED NOW YOU KNOW...
TAPE? YOU MEAN 'DIGITAL', SURELY?
NO...
MASKING TAPE. I'M PUTTING SOME OVER THE CAMERA ON THE COMPUTER JUST SO THIS THING CAN'T WATCH US TOO...
AND THE iPADS...

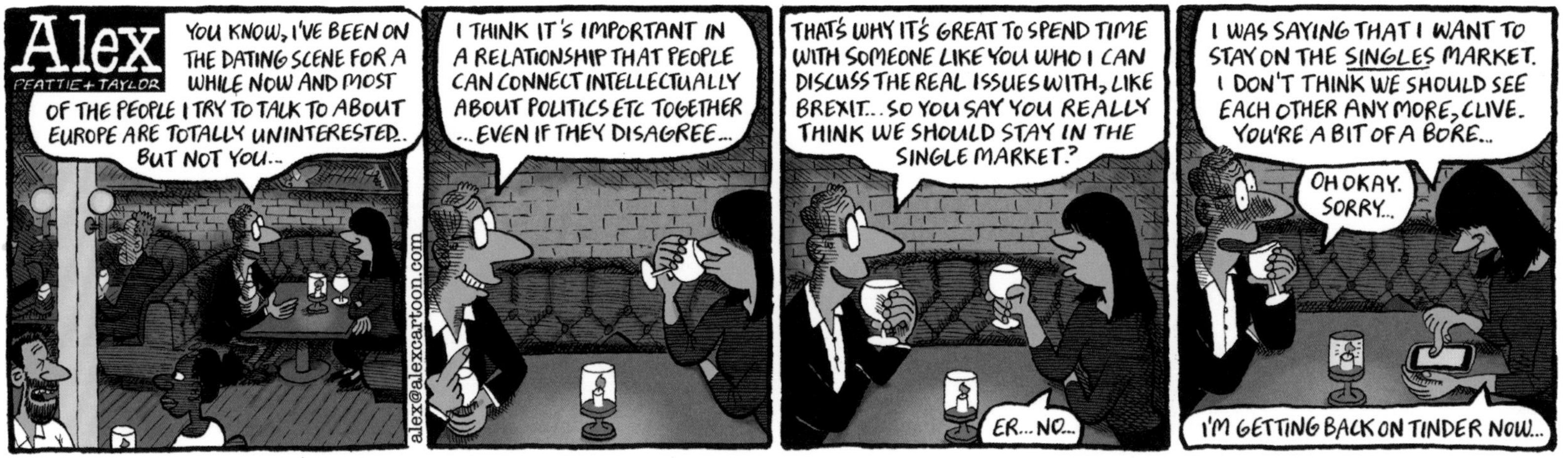
Alex
PEATTIE+TAYLOR
YOU KNOW, I'VE BEEN ON THE DATING SCENE FOR A WHILE NOW AND MOST OF THE PEOPLE I TRY TO TALK TO ABOUT EUROPE ARE TOTALLY UNINTERESTED... BUT NOT YOU...
alex@alexcartoon.com
I THINK IT'S IMPORTANT IN A RELATIONSHIP THAT PEOPLE CAN CONNECT INTELLECTUALLY ABOUT POLITICS ETC TOGETHER ... EVEN IF THEY DISAGREE...
THAT'S WHY IT'S GREAT TO SPEND TIME WITH SOMEONE LIKE YOU WHO I CAN DISCUSS THE REAL ISSUES WITH, LIKE BREXIT... SO YOU SAY YOU REALLY THINK WE SHOULD STAY IN THE SINGLE MARKET?
ER... NO...
I WAS SAYING THAT I WANT TO STAY ON THE SINGLES MARKET. I DON'T THINK WE SHOULD SEE EACH OTHER ANY MORE, CLIVE. YOU'RE A BIT OF A BORE...
OH OKAY. SORRY...
I'M GETTING BACK ON TINDER NOW...

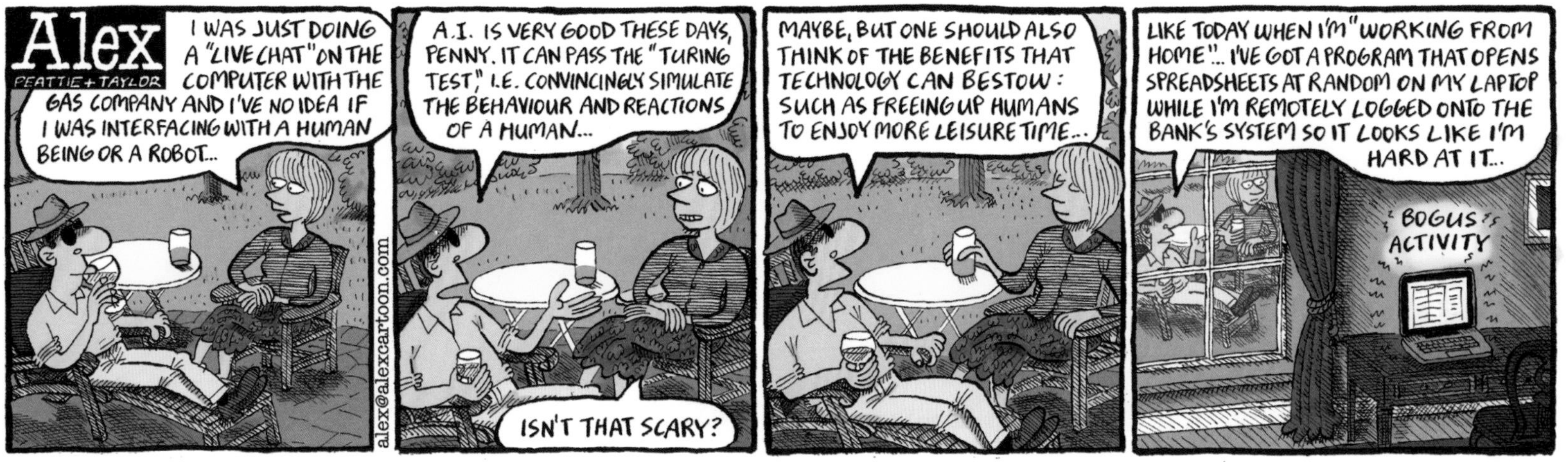
Alex
PEATTIE+TAYLOR
I WAS JUST DOING A "LIVE CHAT" ON THE COMPUTER WITH THE GAS COMPANY AND I'VE NO IDEA IF I WAS INTERFACING WITH A HUMAN BEING OR A ROBOT...
alex@alexcartoon.com
A.I. IS VERY GOOD THESE DAYS, PENNY. IT CAN PASS THE "TURING TEST," I.E. CONVINCINGLY SIMULATE THE BEHAVIOUR AND REACTIONS OF A HUMAN...
ISN'T THAT SCARY?
MAYBE, BUT ONE SHOULD ALSO THINK OF THE BENEFITS THAT TECHNOLOGY CAN BESTOW: SUCH AS FREEING UP HUMANS TO ENJOY MORE LEISURE TIME...
LIKE TODAY WHEN I'M "WORKING FROM HOME"... I'VE GOT A PROGRAM THAT OPENS SPREADSHEETS AT RANDOM ON MY LAPTOP WHILE I'M REMOTELY LOGGED ONTO THE BANK'S SYSTEM SO IT LOOKS LIKE I'M HARD AT IT...
BOGUS ACTIVITY

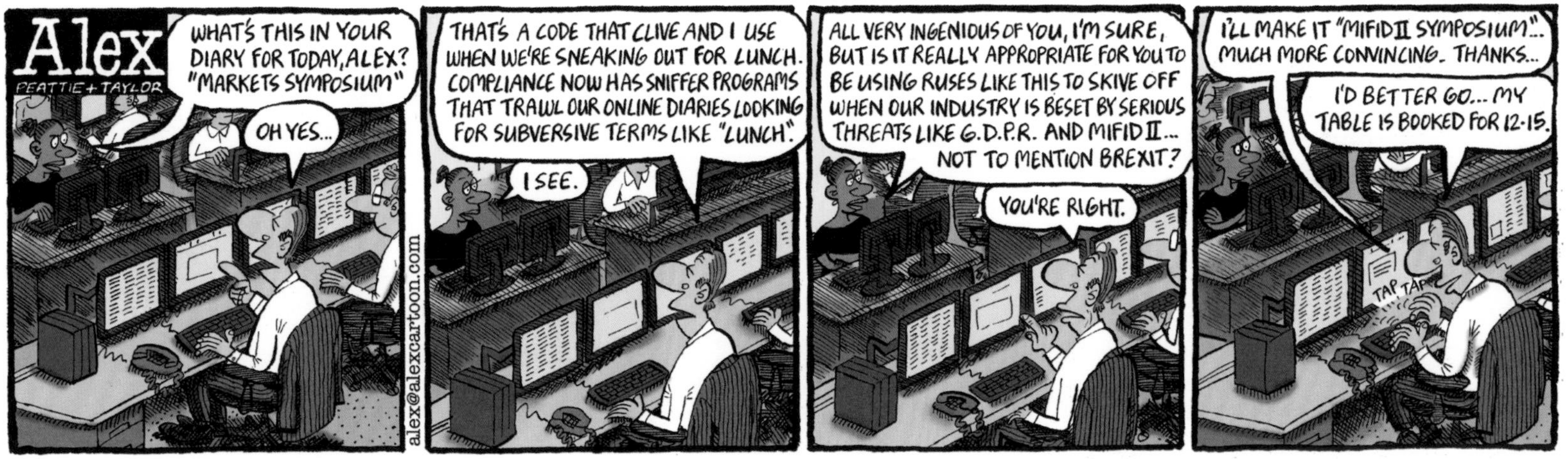
Alex
PEATTIE+TAYLOR
WHAT'S THIS IN YOUR DIARY FOR TODAY, ALEX? "MARKETS SYMPOSIUM"
OH YES...
alex@alexcartoon.com
THAT'S A CODE THAT CLIVE AND I USE WHEN WE'RE SNEAKING OUT FOR LUNCH. COMPLIANCE NOW HAS SNIFFER PROGRAMS THAT TRAWL OUR ONLINE DIARIES LOOKING FOR SUBVERSIVE TERMS LIKE "LUNCH".
I SEE.
ALL VERY INGENIOUS OF YOU, I'M SURE, BUT IS IT REALLY APPROPRIATE FOR YOU TO BE USING RUSES LIKE THIS TO SKIVE OFF WHEN OUR INDUSTRY IS BESET BY SERIOUS THREATS LIKE G.D.P.R. AND MIFID II... NOT TO MENTION BREXIT?
YOU'RE RIGHT.
I'LL MAKE IT "MIFID II SYMPOSIUM"... MUCH MORE CONVINCING. THANKS...
I'D BETTER GO... MY TABLE IS BOOKED FOR 12.15.
TAP TAP

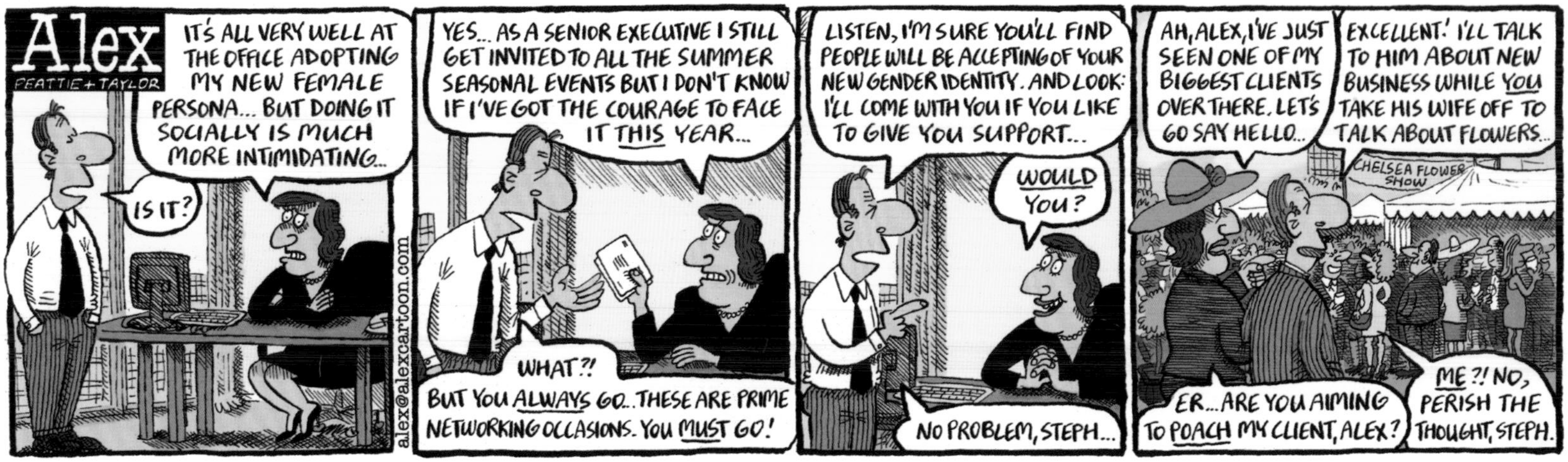
Alex
PEATTIE + TAYLOR
IT'S ALL VERY WELL AT THE OFFICE ADOPTING MY NEW FEMALE PERSONA... BUT DOING IT SOCIALLY IS MUCH MORE INTIMIDATING...
IS IT?
YES... AS A SENIOR EXECUTIVE I STILL GET INVITED TO ALL THE SUMMER SEASONAL EVENTS BUT I DON'T KNOW IF I'VE GOT THE COURAGE TO FACE IT THIS YEAR...
WHAT?!
BUT YOU ALWAYS GO.. THESE ARE PRIME NETWORKING OCCASIONS. YOU MUST GO!
alex@alexcartoon.com
LISTEN, I'M SURE YOU'LL FIND PEOPLE WILL BE ACCEPTING OF YOUR NEW GENDER IDENTITY. AND LOOK: I'LL COME WITH YOU IF YOU LIKE TO GIVE YOU SUPPORT...
WOULD YOU?
NO PROBLEM, STEPH...
AH, ALEX, I'VE JUST SEEN ONE OF MY BIGGEST CLIENTS OVER THERE. LET'S GO SAY HELLO...
EXCELLENT! I'LL TALK TO HIM ABOUT NEW BUSINESS WHILE YOU TAKE HIS WIFE OFF TO TALK ABOUT FLOWERS...
CHELSEA FLOWER SHOW
ER... ARE YOU AIMING TO POACH MY CLIENT, ALEX?
ME?! NO, PERISH THE THOUGHT, STEPH.

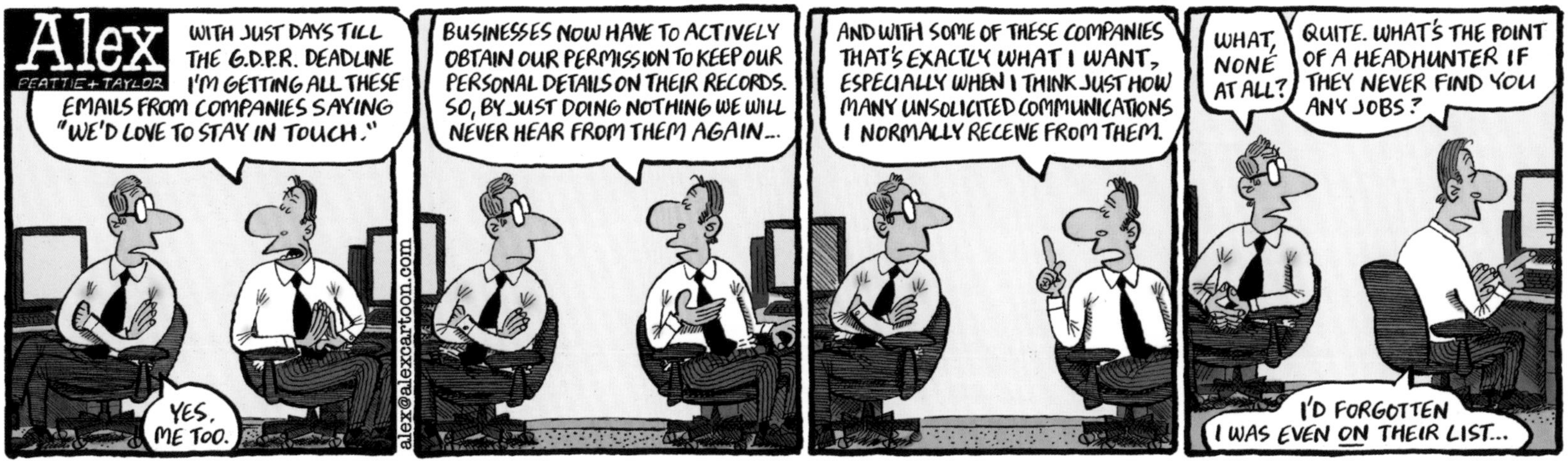
Alex
PEATTIE + TAYLOR
WITH JUST DAYS TILL THE G.D.P.R. DEADLINE I'M GETTING ALL THESE EMAILS FROM COMPANIES SAYING "WE'D LOVE TO STAY IN TOUCH."
YES, ME TOO.
alex@alexcartoon.com
BUSINESSES NOW HAVE TO ACTIVELY OBTAIN OUR PERMISSION TO KEEP OUR PERSONAL DETAILS ON THEIR RECORDS. SO, BY JUST DOING NOTHING WE WILL NEVER HEAR FROM THEM AGAIN...
AND WITH SOME OF THESE COMPANIES THAT'S EXACTLY WHAT I WANT, ESPECIALLY WHEN I THINK JUST HOW MANY UNSOLICITED COMMUNICATIONS I NORMALLY RECEIVE FROM THEM.
WHAT, NONE AT ALL?
QUITE. WHAT'S THE POINT OF A HEADHUNTER IF THEY NEVER FIND YOU ANY JOBS?
I'D FORGOTTEN I WAS EVEN ON THEIR LIST...

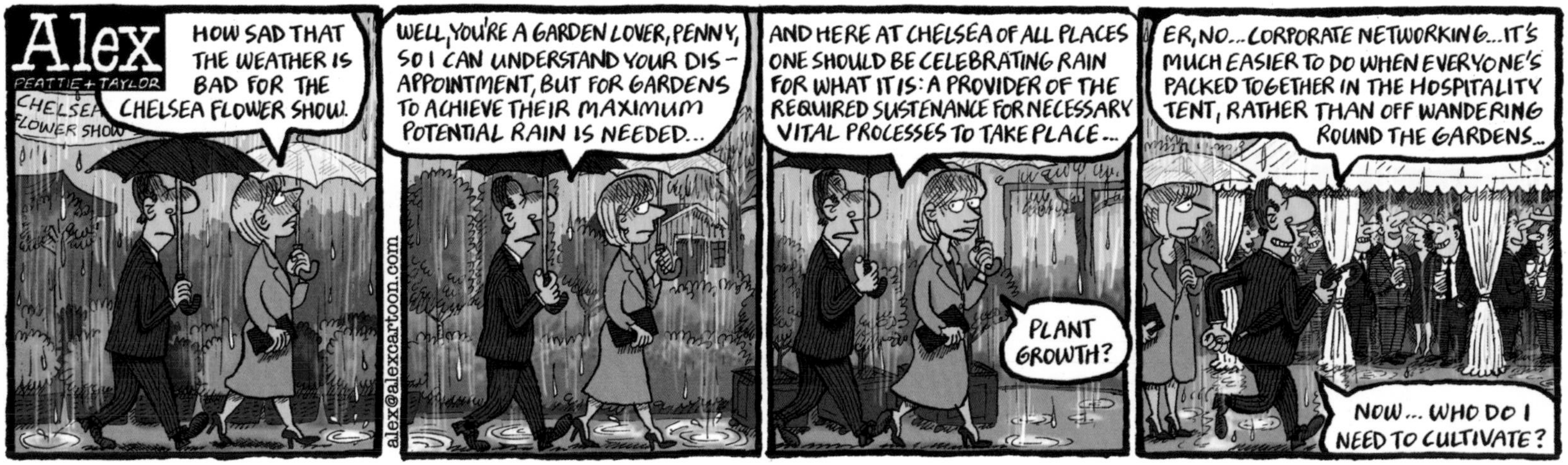
Alex
PEATTIE + TAYLOR
HOW SAD THAT THE WEATHER IS BAD FOR THE CHELSEA FLOWER SHOW.
CHELSEA FLOWER SHOW
alex@alexcartoon.com
WELL, YOU'RE A GARDEN LOVER, PENNY, SO I CAN UNDERSTAND YOUR DIS-APPOINTMENT, BUT FOR GARDENS TO ACHIEVE THEIR MAXIMUM POTENTIAL RAIN IS NEEDED...
AND HERE AT CHELSEA OF ALL PLACES ONE SHOULD BE CELEBRATING RAIN FOR WHAT IT IS: A PROVIDER OF THE REQUIRED SUSTENANCE FOR NECESSARY VITAL PROCESSES TO TAKE PLACE...
PLANT GROWTH?
ER, NO... CORPORATE NETWORKING... IT'S MUCH EASIER TO DO WHEN EVERYONE'S PACKED TOGETHER IN THE HOSPITALITY TENT, RATHER THAN OFF WANDERING ROUND THE GARDENS...
NOW... WHO DO I NEED TO CULTIVATE?

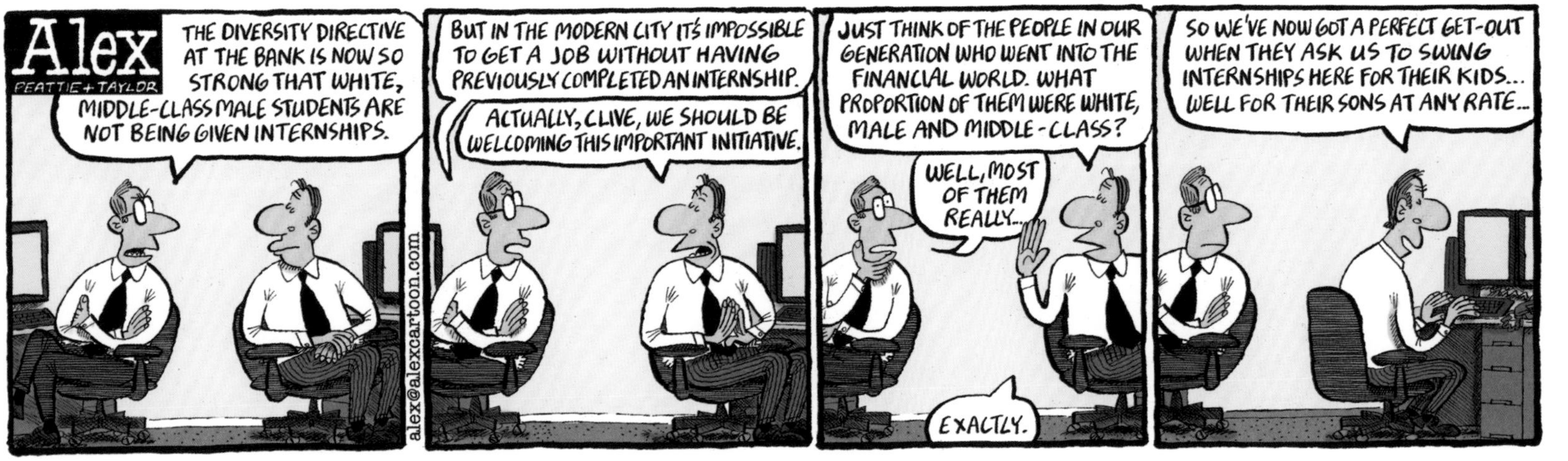
Alex
PEATTIE + TAYLOR
THE DIVERSITY DIRECTIVE AT THE BANK IS NOW SO STRONG THAT WHITE, MIDDLE-CLASS MALE STUDENTS ARE NOT BEING GIVEN INTERNSHIPS.
alex@alexcartoon.com
BUT IN THE MODERN CITY IT'S IMPOSSIBLE TO GET A JOB WITHOUT HAVING PREVIOUSLY COMPLETED AN INTERNSHIP.
ACTUALLY, CLIVE, WE SHOULD BE WELCOMING THIS IMPORTANT INITIATIVE.
JUST THINK OF THE PEOPLE IN OUR GENERATION WHO WENT INTO THE FINANCIAL WORLD. WHAT PROPORTION OF THEM WERE WHITE, MALE AND MIDDLE-CLASS?
WELL, MOST OF THEM REALLY...
EXACTLY.
SO WE'VE NOW GOT A PERFECT GET-OUT WHEN THEY ASK US TO SWING INTERNSHIPS HERE FOR THEIR KIDS... WELL FOR THEIR SONS AT ANY RATE...

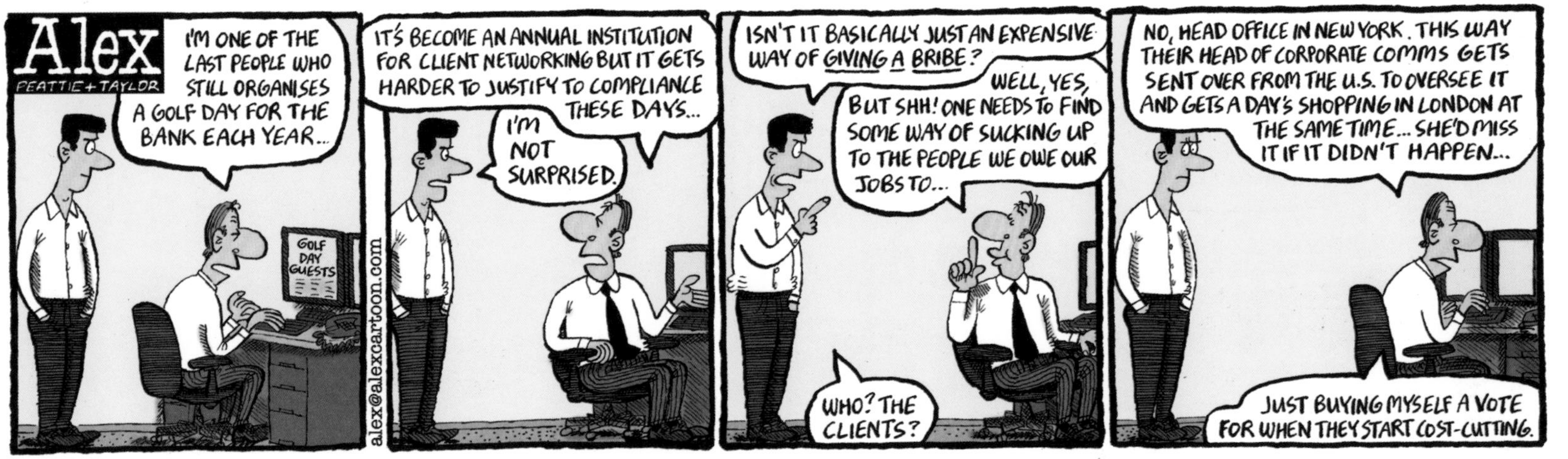
Alex
PEATTIE + TAYLOR
I'M ONE OF THE LAST PEOPLE WHO STILL ORGANISES A GOLF DAY FOR THE BANK EACH YEAR...
GOLF DAY GUESTS
alex@alexcartoon.com
IT'S BECOME AN ANNUAL INSTITUTION FOR CLIENT NETWORKING BUT IT GETS HARDER TO JUSTIFY TO COMPLIANCE THESE DAYS...
I'M NOT SURPRISED.
ISN'T IT BASICALLY JUST AN EXPENSIVE WAY OF GIVING A BRIBE?
WELL, YES, BUT SHH! ONE NEEDS TO FIND SOME WAY OF SUCKING UP TO THE PEOPLE WE OWE OUR JOBS TO...
WHO? THE CLIENTS?
NO, HEAD OFFICE IN NEW YORK. THIS WAY THEIR HEAD OF CORPORATE COMMS GETS SENT OVER FROM THE U.S. TO OVERSEE IT AND GETS A DAY'S SHOPPING IN LONDON AT THE SAME TIME... SHE'D MISS IT IF IT DIDN'T HAPPEN...
JUST BUYING MYSELF A VOTE FOR WHEN THEY START COST-CUTTING.

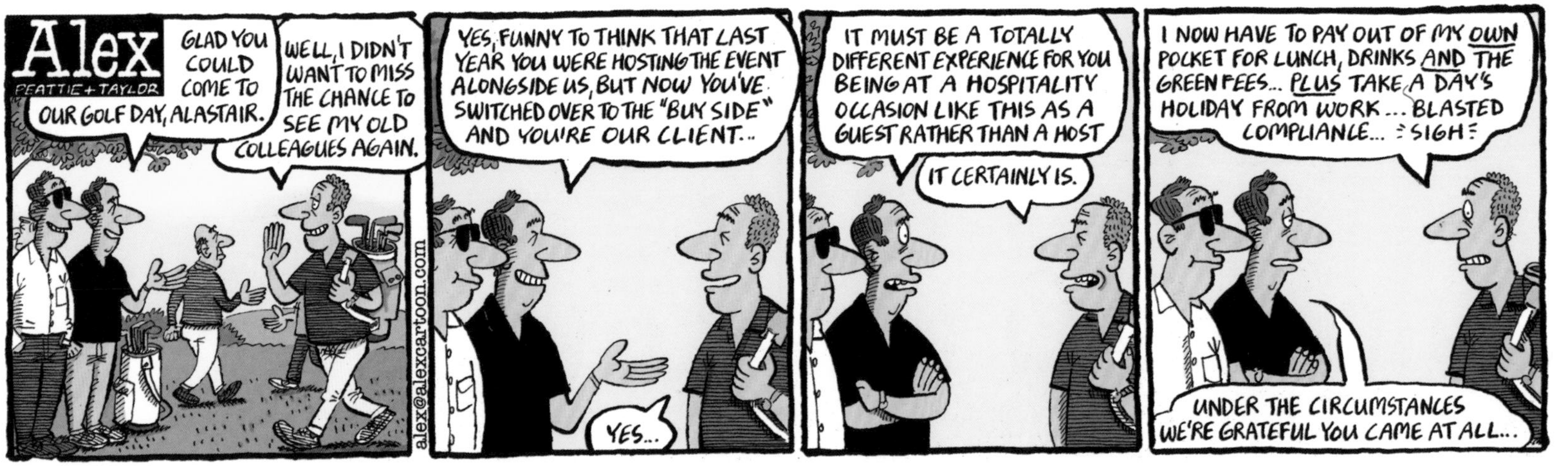
Alex
PEATTIE + TAYLOR
GLAD YOU COULD COME TO OUR GOLF DAY, ALASTAIR.
WELL, I DIDN'T WANT TO MISS THE CHANCE TO SEE MY OLD COLLEAGUES AGAIN.
alex@alexcartoon.com
YES, FUNNY TO THINK THAT LAST YEAR YOU WERE HOSTING THE EVENT ALONGSIDE US, BUT NOW YOU'VE SWITCHED OVER TO THE "BUY SIDE" AND YOU'RE OUR CLIENT...
YES...
IT MUST BE A TOTALLY DIFFERENT EXPERIENCE FOR YOU BEING AT A HOSPITALITY OCCASION LIKE THIS AS A GUEST RATHER THAN A HOST
IT CERTAINLY IS.
I NOW HAVE TO PAY OUT OF MY OWN POCKET FOR LUNCH, DRINKS AND THE GREEN FEES... PLUS TAKE A DAY'S HOLIDAY FROM WORK... BLASTED COMPLIANCE... SIGH
UNDER THE CIRCUMSTANCES WE'RE GRATEFUL YOU CAME AT ALL...

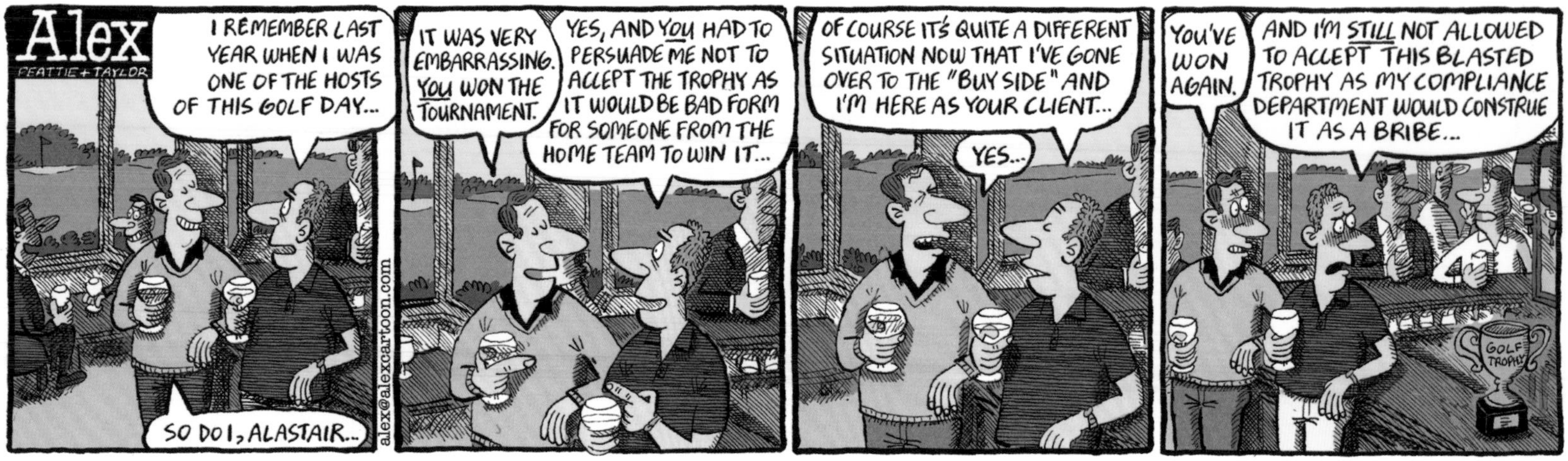
Alex
PEATTIE + TAYLOR
I REMEMBER LAST YEAR WHEN I WAS ONE OF THE HOSTS OF THIS GOLF DAY...
SO DO I, ALASTAIR...
alex@alexcartoon.com
IT WAS VERY EMBARRASSING. YOU WON THE TOURNAMENT.
YES, AND YOU HAD TO PERSUADE ME NOT TO ACCEPT THE TROPHY AS IT WOULD BE BAD FORM FOR SOMEONE FROM THE HOME TEAM TO WIN IT...
OF COURSE IT'S QUITE A DIFFERENT SITUATION NOW THAT I'VE GONE OVER TO THE "BUY SIDE" AND I'M HERE AS YOUR CLIENT...
YES...
YOU'VE WON AGAIN.
AND I'M STILL NOT ALLOWED TO ACCEPT THIS BLASTED TROPHY AS MY COMPLIANCE DEPARTMENT WOULD CONSTRUE IT AS A BRIBE...
GOLF TROPHY

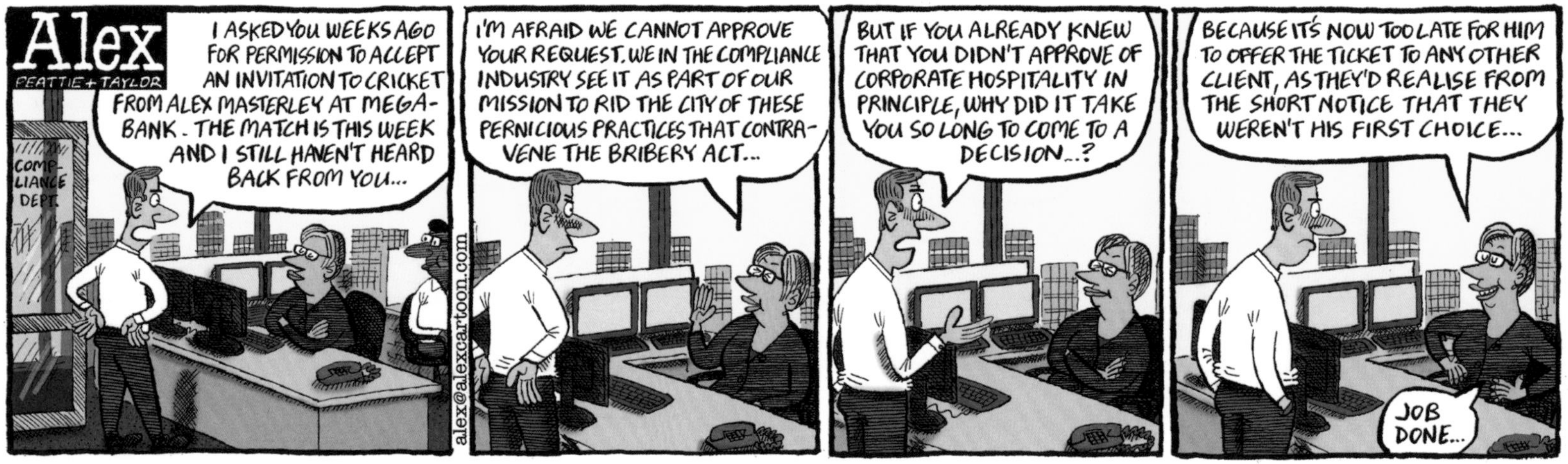
Alex
PEATTIE + TAYLOR
I ASKED YOU WEEKS AGO FOR PERMISSION TO ACCEPT AN INVITATION TO CRICKET FROM ALEX MASTERLEY AT MEGA-BANK - THE MATCH IS THIS WEEK AND I STILL HAVEN'T HEARD BACK FROM YOU...
COMPLIANCE DEPT.
alex@alexcartoon.com
I'M AFRAID WE CANNOT APPROVE YOUR REQUEST. WE IN THE COMPLIANCE INDUSTRY SEE IT AS PART OF OUR MISSION TO RID THE CITY OF THESE PERNICIOUS PRACTICES THAT CONTRAVENE THE BRIBERY ACT...
BUT IF YOU ALREADY KNEW THAT YOU DIDN'T APPROVE OF CORPORATE HOSPITALITY IN PRINCIPLE, WHY DID IT TAKE YOU SO LONG TO COME TO A DECISION...?
BECAUSE IT'S NOW TOO LATE FOR HIM TO OFFER THE TICKET TO ANY OTHER CLIENT, AS THEY'D REALISE FROM THE SHORT NOTICE THAT THEY WEREN'T HIS FIRST CHOICE...
JOB DONE...

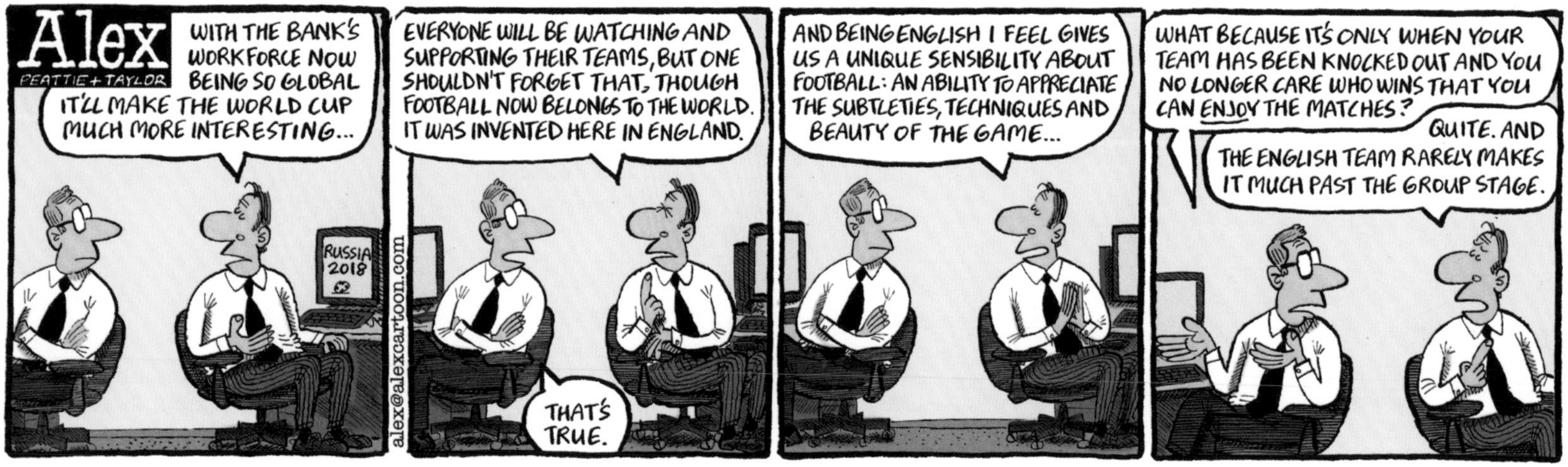
Alex
PEATTIE + TAYLOR
WITH THE BANK'S WORKFORCE NOW BEING SO GLOBAL IT'LL MAKE THE WORLD CUP MUCH MORE INTERESTING...
RUSSIA 2018
alex@alexcartoon.com
EVERYONE WILL BE WATCHING AND SUPPORTING THEIR TEAMS, BUT ONE SHOULDN'T FORGET THAT, THOUGH FOOTBALL NOW BELONGS TO THE WORLD. IT WAS INVENTED HERE IN ENGLAND.
THAT'S TRUE.
AND BEING ENGLISH I FEEL GIVES US A UNIQUE SENSIBILITY ABOUT FOOTBALL: AN ABILITY TO APPRECIATE THE SUBTLETIES, TECHNIQUES AND BEAUTY OF THE GAME...
WHAT BECAUSE IT'S ONLY WHEN YOUR TEAM HAS BEEN KNOCKED OUT AND YOU NO LONGER CARE WHO WINS THAT YOU CAN ENJOY THE MATCHES?
QUITE. AND THE ENGLISH TEAM RARELY MAKES IT MUCH PAST THE GROUP STAGE.

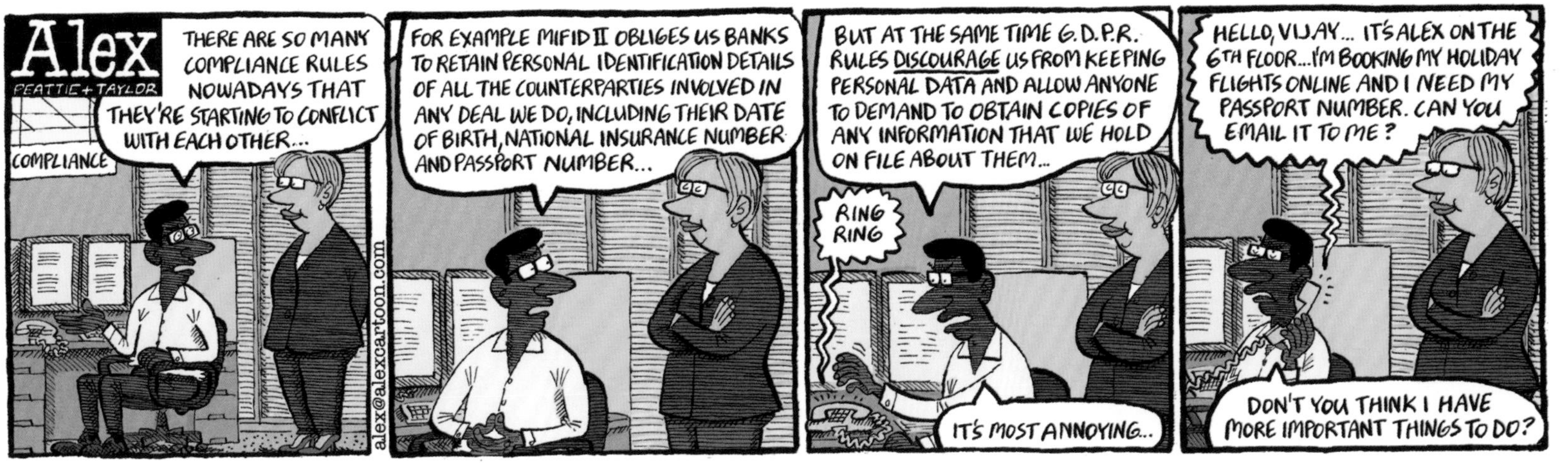
Alex
PEATTIE + TAYLOR
COMPLIANCE
THERE ARE SO MANY COMPLIANCE RULES NOWADAYS THAT THEY'RE STARTING TO CONFLICT WITH EACH OTHER...
alex@alexcartoon.com
FOR EXAMPLE MIFID II OBLIGES US BANKS TO RETAIN PERSONAL IDENTIFICATION DETAILS OF ALL THE COUNTERPARTIES INVOLVED IN ANY DEAL WE DO, INCLUDING THEIR DATE OF BIRTH, NATIONAL INSURANCE NUMBER AND PASSPORT NUMBER...
BUT AT THE SAME TIME G.D.P.R. RULES DISCOURAGE US FROM KEEPING PERSONAL DATA AND ALLOW ANYONE TO DEMAND TO OBTAIN COPIES OF ANY INFORMATION THAT WE HOLD ON FILE ABOUT THEM...
RING RING
IT'S MOST ANNOYING...
HELLO, VIJAY... IT'S ALEX ON THE 6TH FLOOR... I'M BOOKING MY HOLIDAY FLIGHTS ONLINE AND I NEED MY PASSPORT NUMBER. CAN YOU EMAIL IT TO ME?
DON'T YOU THINK I HAVE MORE IMPORTANT THINGS TO DO?

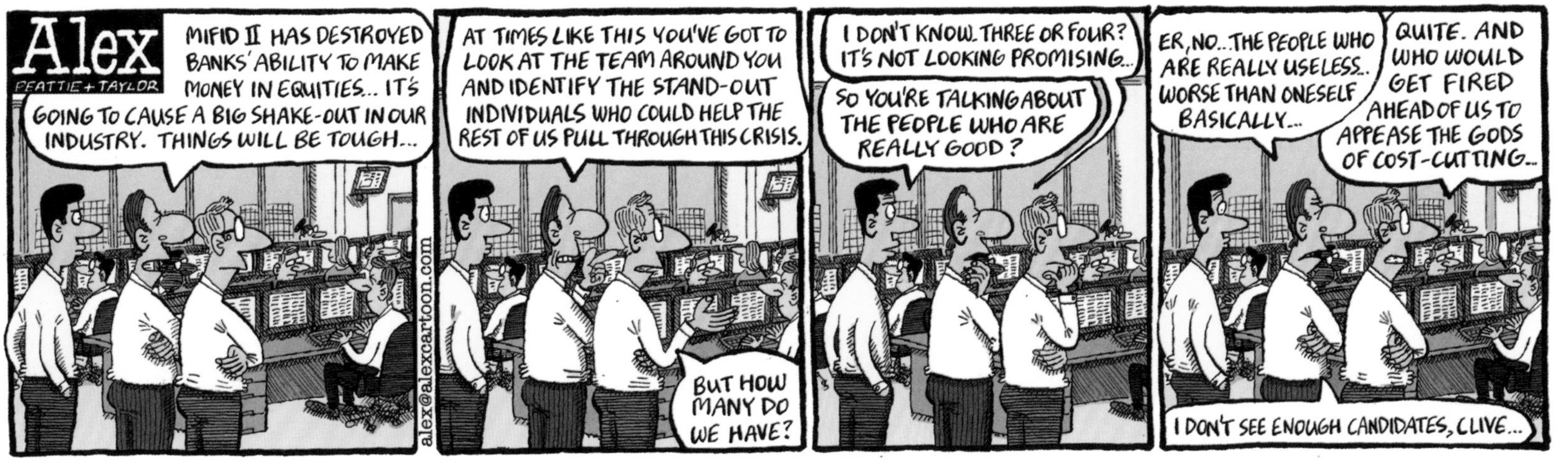
Alex
PEATTIE + TAYLOR
MIFID II HAS DESTROYED BANKS' ABILITY TO MAKE MONEY IN EQUITIES... IT'S GOING TO CAUSE A BIG SHAKE-OUT IN OUR INDUSTRY. THINGS WILL BE TOUGH...
alex@alexcartoon.com
AT TIMES LIKE THIS YOU'VE GOT TO LOOK AT THE TEAM AROUND YOU AND IDENTIFY THE STAND-OUT INDIVIDUALS WHO COULD HELP THE REST OF US PULL THROUGH THIS CRISIS.
BUT HOW MANY DO WE HAVE?
SO YOU'RE TALKING ABOUT THE PEOPLE WHO ARE REALLY GOOD?
I DON'T KNOW. THREE OR FOUR? IT'S NOT LOOKING PROMISING...
ER, NO... THE PEOPLE WHO ARE REALLY USELESS... WORSE THAN ONESELF BASICALLY...
QUITE. AND WHO WOULD GET FIRED AHEAD OF US TO APPEASE THE GODS OF COST-CUTTING...
I DON'T SEE ENOUGH CANDIDATES, CLIVE...

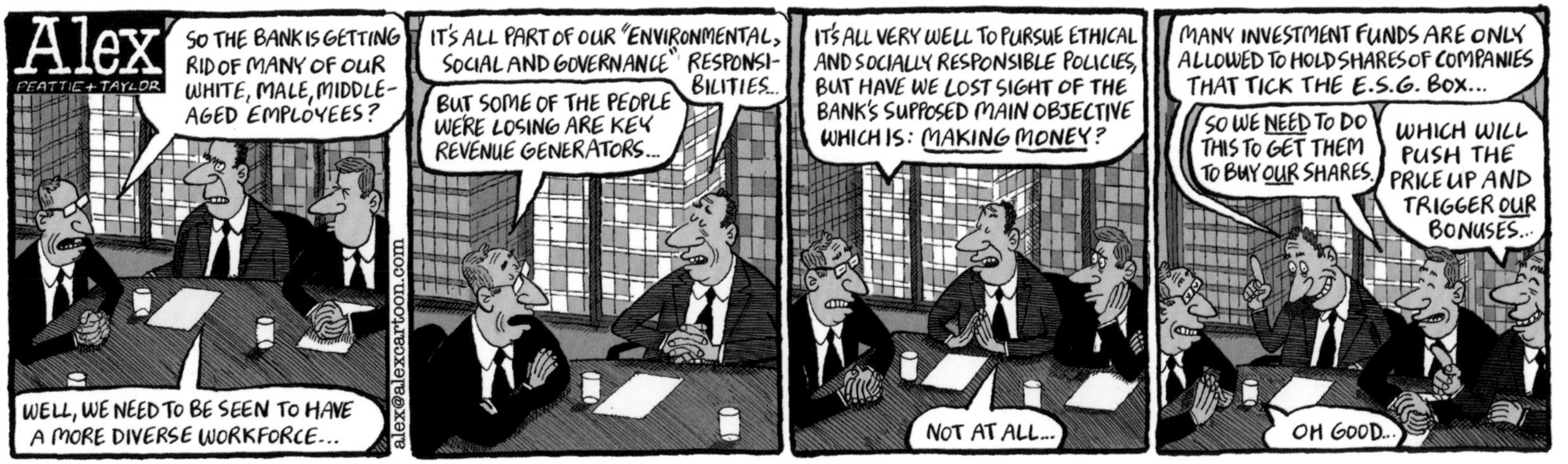
Alex
PEATTIE + TAYLOR
SO THE BANK IS GETTING RID OF MANY OF OUR WHITE, MALE, MIDDLE-AGED EMPLOYEES?
WELL, WE NEED TO BE SEEN TO HAVE A MORE DIVERSE WORKFORCE...
alex@alexcartoon.com
IT'S ALL PART OF OUR "ENVIRONMENTAL, SOCIAL AND GOVERNANCE" RESPONSIBILITIES...
BUT SOME OF THE PEOPLE WE'RE LOSING ARE KEY REVENUE GENERATORS...
IT'S ALL VERY WELL TO PURSUE ETHICAL AND SOCIALLY RESPONSIBLE POLICIES, BUT HAVE WE LOST SIGHT OF THE BANK'S SUPPOSED MAIN OBJECTIVE WHICH IS: MAKING MONEY?
NOT AT ALL...
MANY INVESTMENT FUNDS ARE ONLY ALLOWED TO HOLD SHARES OF COMPANIES THAT TICK THE E.S.G. BOX...
SO WE NEED TO DO THIS TO GET THEM TO BUY OUR SHARES.
WHICH WILL PUSH THE PRICE UP AND TRIGGER OUR BONUSES...
OH GOOD...

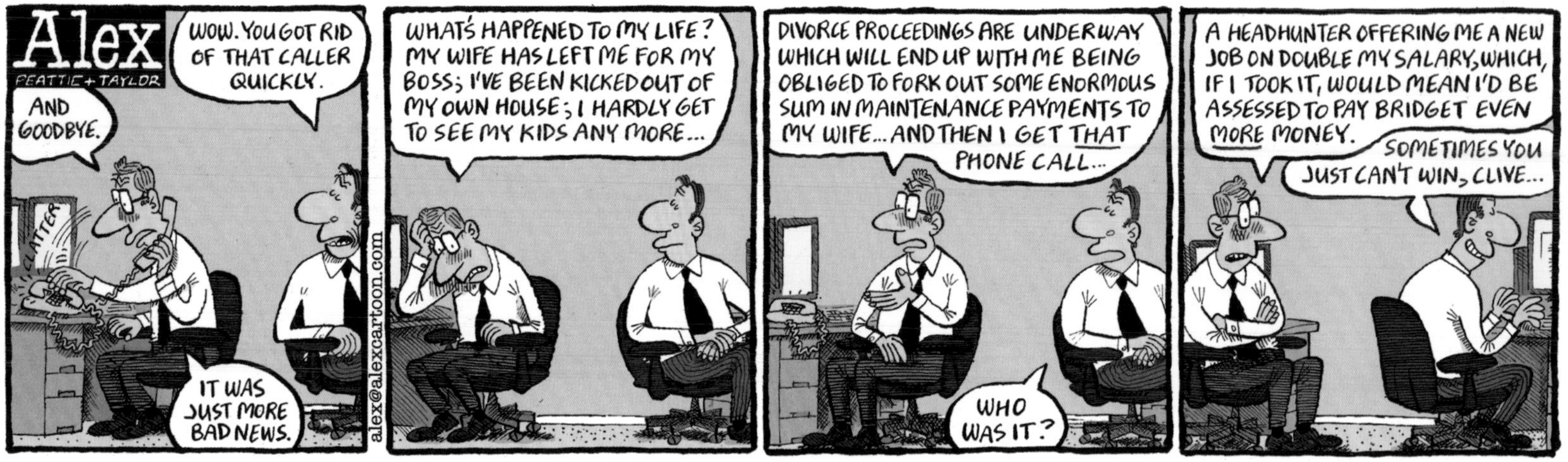
Alex
PEATTIE + TAYLOR
AND GOODBYE.
WOW. YOU GOT RID OF THAT CALLER QUICKLY.
CLATTER
IT WAS JUST MORE BAD NEWS.
alex@alexcartoon.com
WHAT'S HAPPENED TO MY LIFE? MY WIFE HAS LEFT ME FOR MY BOSS; I'VE BEEN KICKED OUT OF MY OWN HOUSE; I HARDLY GET TO SEE MY KIDS ANY MORE...
DIVORCE PROCEEDINGS ARE UNDERWAY WHICH WILL END UP WITH ME BEING OBLIGED TO FORK OUT SOME ENORMOUS SUM IN MAINTENANCE PAYMENTS TO MY WIFE... AND THEN I GET THAT PHONE CALL...
WHO WAS IT?
A HEADHUNTER OFFERING ME A NEW JOB ON DOUBLE MY SALARY, WHICH, IF I TOOK IT, WOULD MEAN I'D BE ASSESSED TO PAY BRIDGET EVEN MORE MONEY.
SOMETIMES YOU JUST CAN'T WIN, CLIVE...

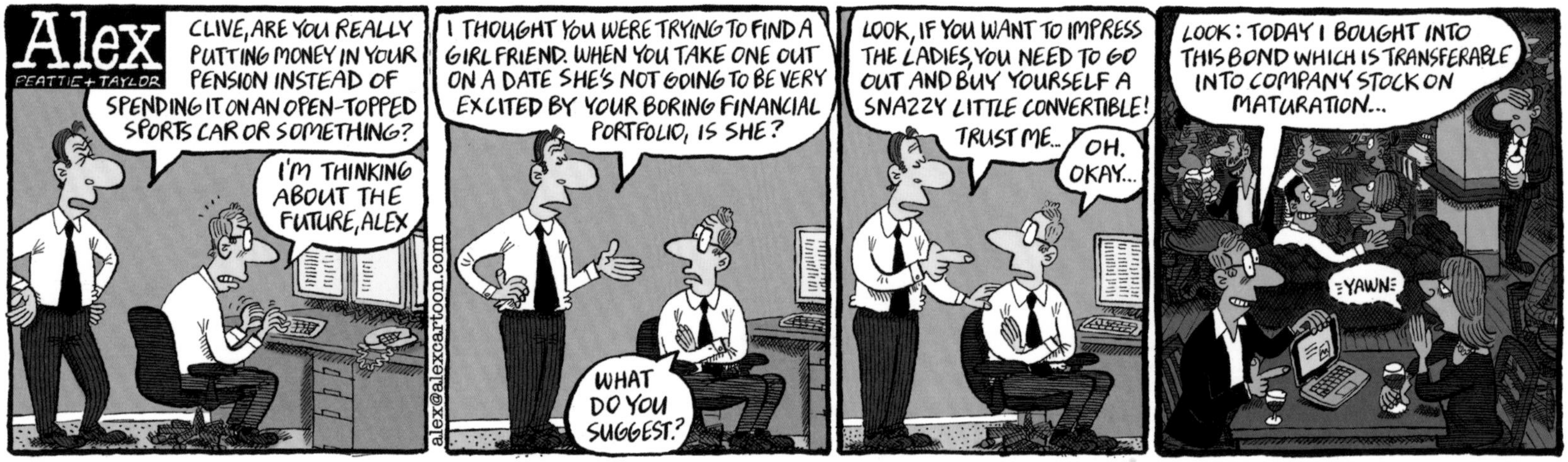
Alex
PEATTIE + TAYLOR
CLIVE, ARE YOU REALLY PUTTING MONEY IN YOUR PENSION INSTEAD OF SPENDING IT ON AN OPEN-TOPPED SPORTS CAR OR SOMETHING?
I'M THINKING ABOUT THE FUTURE, ALEX
alex@alexcartoon.com
I THOUGHT YOU WERE TRYING TO FIND A GIRL FRIEND. WHEN YOU TAKE ONE OUT ON A DATE SHE'S NOT GOING TO BE VERY EXCITED BY YOUR BORING FINANCIAL PORTFOLIO, IS SHE?
WHAT DO YOU SUGGEST?
LOOK, IF YOU WANT TO IMPRESS THE LADIES, YOU NEED TO GO OUT AND BUY YOURSELF A SNAZZY LITTLE CONVERTIBLE! TRUST ME...
OH. OKAY...
LOOK: TODAY I BOUGHT INTO THIS BOND WHICH IS TRANSFERABLE INTO COMPANY STOCK ON MATURATION...
YAWN

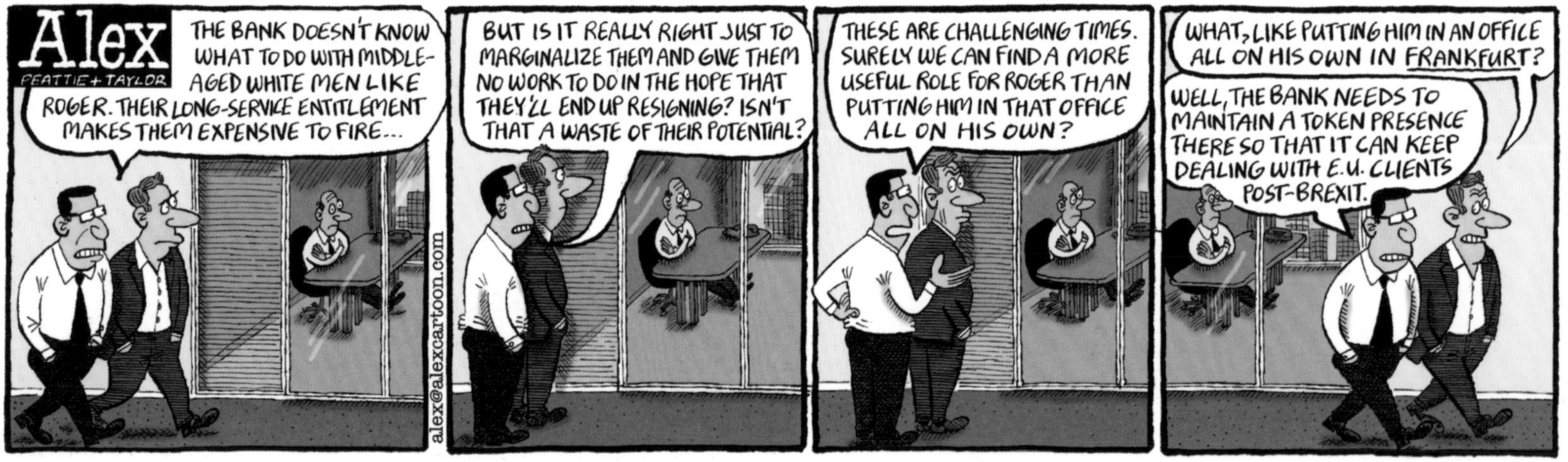
Alex
PEATTIE + TAYLOR
THE BANK DOESN'T KNOW WHAT TO DO WITH MIDDLE-AGED WHITE MEN LIKE ROGER. THEIR LONG-SERVICE ENTITLEMENT MAKES THEM EXPENSIVE TO FIRE...
alex@alexcartoon.com
BUT IS IT REALLY RIGHT JUST TO MARGINALIZE THEM AND GIVE THEM NO WORK TO DO IN THE HOPE THAT THEY'LL END UP RESIGNING? ISN'T THAT A WASTE OF THEIR POTENTIAL?
THESE ARE CHALLENGING TIMES. SURELY WE CAN FIND A MORE USEFUL ROLE FOR ROGER THAN PUTTING HIM IN THAT OFFICE ALL ON HIS OWN?
WHAT, LIKE PUTTING HIM IN AN OFFICE ALL ON HIS OWN IN FRANKFURT?
WELL, THE BANK NEEDS TO MAINTAIN A TOKEN PRESENCE THERE SO THAT IT CAN KEEP DEALING WITH E.U. CLIENTS POST-BREXIT.

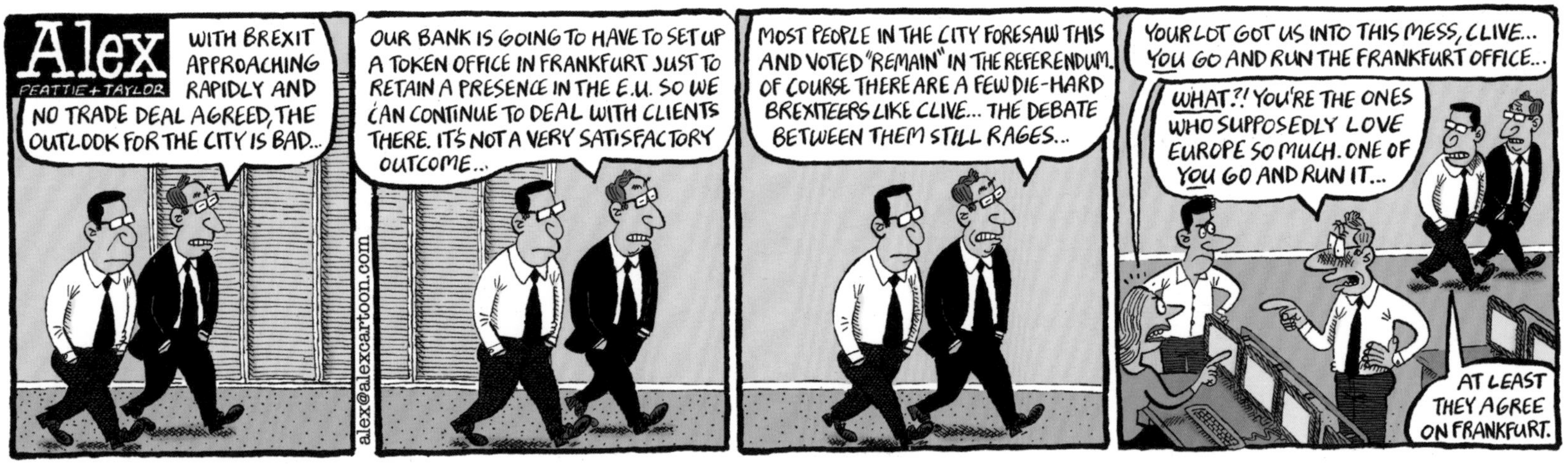
Alex
PEATTIE + TAYLOR
WITH BREXIT APPROACHING RAPIDLY AND NO TRADE DEAL AGREED, THE OUTLOOK FOR THE CITY IS BAD...
OUR BANK IS GOING TO HAVE TO SET UP A TOKEN OFFICE IN FRANKFURT JUST TO RETAIN A PRESENCE IN THE E.U. SO WE CAN CONTINUE TO DEAL WITH CLIENTS THERE. IT'S NOT A VERY SATISFACTORY OUTCOME...
alex@alexcartoon.com
MOST PEOPLE IN THE CITY FORESAW THIS AND VOTED "REMAIN" IN THE REFERENDUM. OF COURSE THERE ARE A FEW DIE-HARD BREXITEERS LIKE CLIVE... THE DEBATE BETWEEN THEM STILL RAGES...
YOUR LOT GOT US INTO THIS MESS, CLIVE... YOU GO AND RUN THE FRANKFURT OFFICE...
WHAT?! YOU'RE THE ONES WHO SUPPOSEDLY LOVE EUROPE SO MUCH. ONE OF YOU GO AND RUN IT...
AT LEAST THEY AGREE ON FRANKFURT.

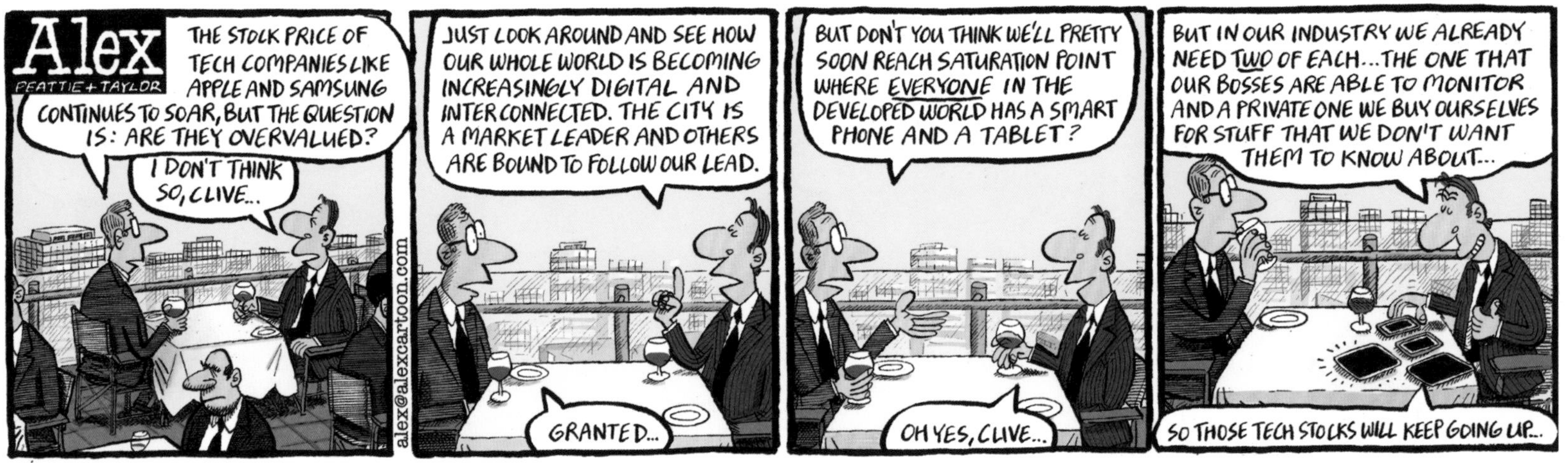
Alex
PEATTIE + TAYLOR
THE STOCK PRICE OF TECH COMPANIES LIKE APPLE AND SAMSUNG CONTINUES TO SOAR, BUT THE QUESTION IS: ARE THEY OVERVALUED?
I DON'T THINK SO, CLIVE...
alex@alexcartoon.com
JUST LOOK AROUND AND SEE HOW OUR WHOLE WORLD IS BECOMING INCREASINGLY DIGITAL AND INTERCONNECTED. THE CITY IS A MARKET LEADER AND OTHERS ARE BOUND TO FOLLOW OUR LEAD.
GRANTED...
BUT DON'T YOU THINK WE'LL PRETTY SOON REACH SATURATION POINT WHERE EVERYONE IN THE DEVELOPED WORLD HAS A SMART PHONE AND A TABLET?
OH YES, CLIVE...
BUT IN OUR INDUSTRY WE ALREADY NEED TWO OF EACH... THE ONE THAT OUR BOSSES ARE ABLE TO MONITOR AND A PRIVATE ONE WE BUY OURSELVES FOR STUFF THAT WE DON'T WANT THEM TO KNOW ABOUT...
SO THOSE TECH STOCKS WILL KEEP GOING UP...

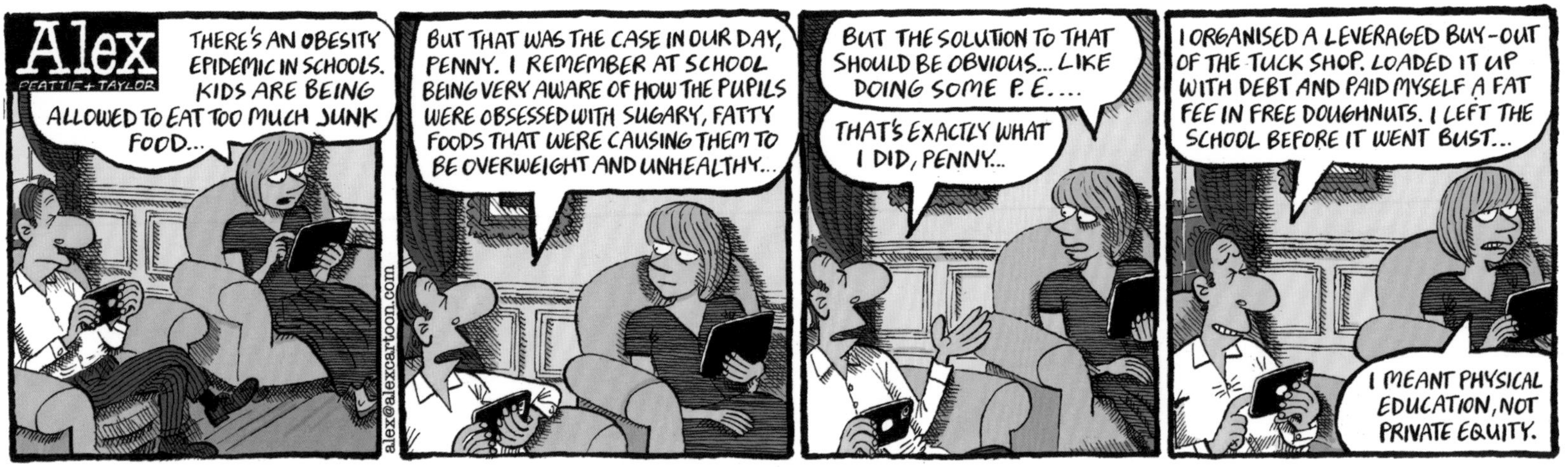
Alex
PEATTIE + TAYLOR
THERE'S AN OBESITY EPIDEMIC IN SCHOOLS. KIDS ARE BEING ALLOWED TO EAT TOO MUCH JUNK FOOD...
alex@alexcartoon.com
BUT THAT WAS THE CASE IN OUR DAY, PENNY. I REMEMBER AT SCHOOL BEING VERY AWARE OF HOW THE PUPILS WERE OBSESSED WITH SUGARY, FATTY FOODS THAT WERE CAUSING THEM TO BE OVERWEIGHT AND UNHEALTHY...
BUT THE SOLUTION TO THAT SHOULD BE OBVIOUS... LIKE DOING SOME P.E....
THAT'S EXACTLY WHAT I DID, PENNY...
I ORGANISED A LEVERAGED BUY-OUT OF THE TUCK SHOP. LOADED IT UP WITH DEBT AND PAID MYSELF A FAT FEE IN FREE DOUGHNUTS. I LEFT THE SCHOOL BEFORE IT WENT BUST...
I MEANT PHYSICAL EDUCATION, NOT PRIVATE EQUITY.

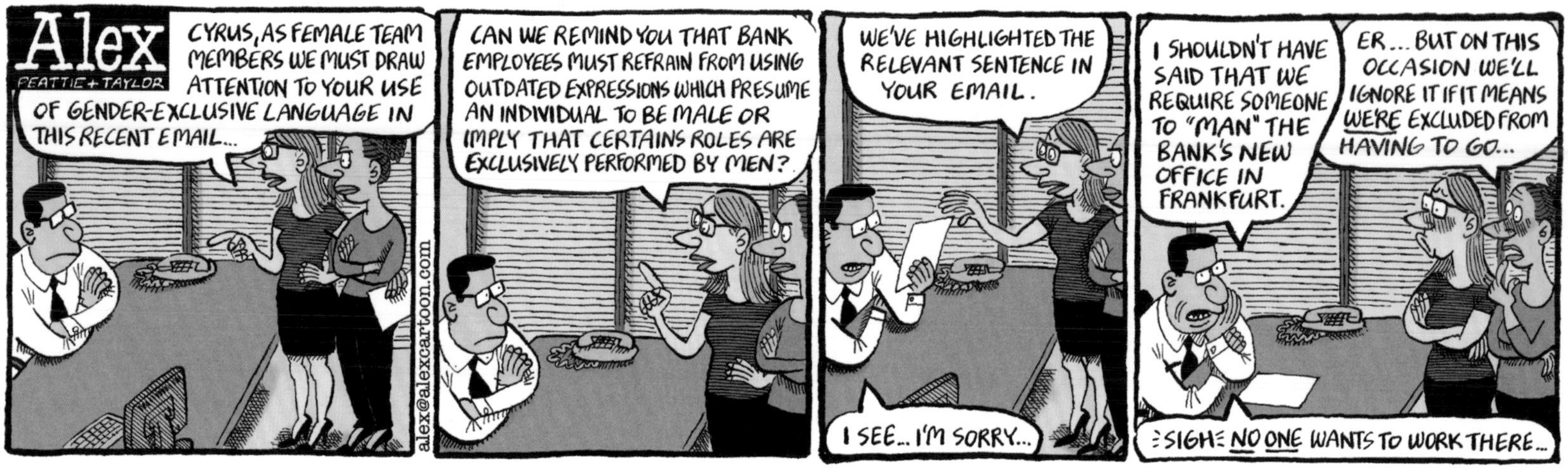
Alex
PEATTIE + TAYLOR
CYRUS, AS FEMALE TEAM MEMBERS WE MUST DRAW ATTENTION TO YOUR USE OF GENDER-EXCLUSIVE LANGUAGE IN THIS RECENT EMAIL...
CAN WE REMIND YOU THAT BANK EMPLOYEES MUST REFRAIN FROM USING OUTDATED EXPRESSIONS WHICH PRESUME AN INDIVIDUAL TO BE MALE OR IMPLY THAT CERTAINS ROLES ARE EXCLUSIVELY PERFORMED BY MEN?
alex@alexcartoon.com
WE'VE HIGHLIGHTED THE RELEVANT SENTENCE IN YOUR EMAIL.
I SEE... I'M SORRY...
I SHOULDN'T HAVE SAID THAT WE REQUIRE SOMEONE TO "MAN" THE BANK'S NEW OFFICE IN FRANKFURT.
ER... BUT ON THIS OCCASION WE'LL IGNORE IT IF IT MEANS WE'RE EXCLUDED FROM HAVING TO GO...
SIGH NO ONE WANTS TO WORK THERE...

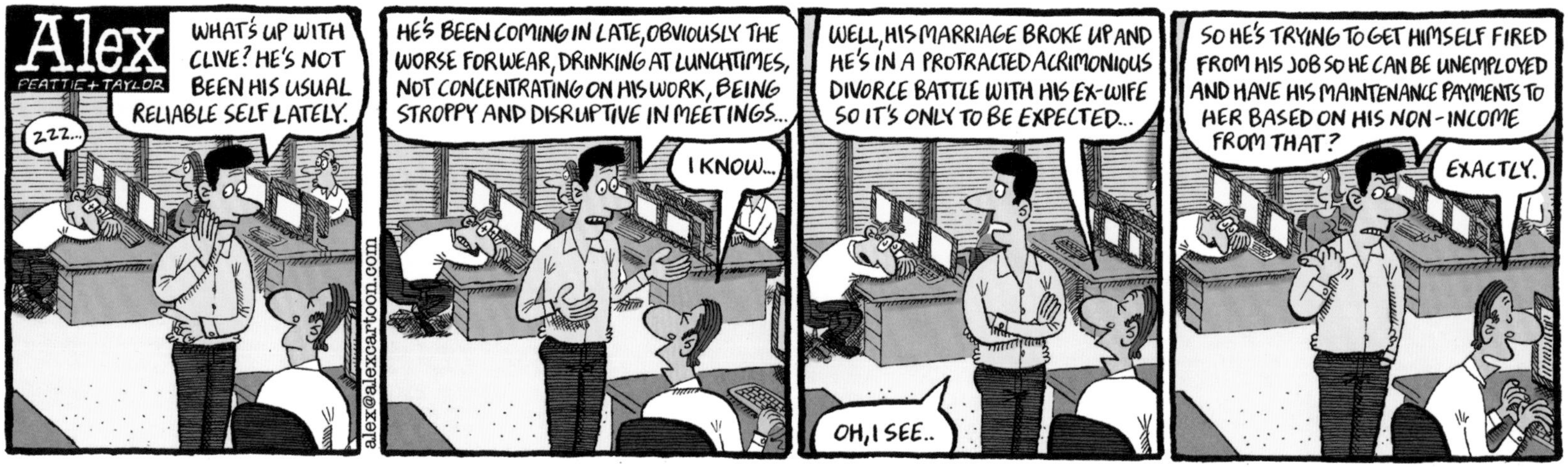
Alex
PEATTIE + TAYLOR
WHAT'S UP WITH CLIVE? HE'S NOT BEEN HIS USUAL RELIABLE SELF LATELY.
ZZZ...
alex@alexcartoon.com
HE'S BEEN COMING IN LATE, OBVIOUSLY THE WORSE FOR WEAR, DRINKING AT LUNCHTIMES, NOT CONCENTRATING ON HIS WORK, BEING STROPPY AND DISRUPTIVE IN MEETINGS...
I KNOW...
WELL, HIS MARRIAGE BROKE UP AND HE'S IN A PROTRACTED ACRIMONIOUS DIVORCE BATTLE WITH HIS EX-WIFE SO IT'S ONLY TO BE EXPECTED...
OH, I SEE..
SO HE'S TRYING TO GET HIMSELF FIRED FROM HIS JOB SO HE CAN BE UNEMPLOYED AND HAVE HIS MAINTENANCE PAYMENTS TO HER BASED ON HIS NON-INCOME FROM THAT?
EXACTLY.

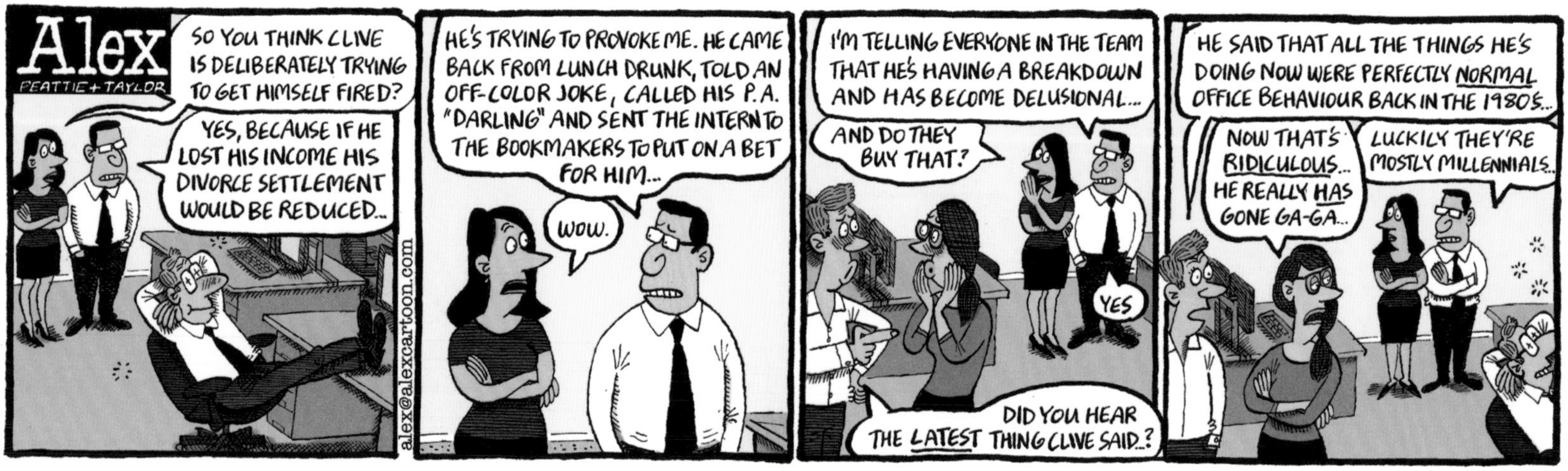
Alex
PEATTIE + TAYLOR
SO YOU THINK CLIVE IS DELIBERATELY TRYING TO GET HIMSELF FIRED?
YES, BECAUSE IF HE LOST HIS INCOME HIS DIVORCE SETTLEMENT WOULD BE REDUCED...
alex@alexcartoon.com
HE'S TRYING TO PROVOKE ME. HE CAME BACK FROM LUNCH DRUNK, TOLD AN OFF-COLOR JOKE, CALLED HIS P.A. "DARLING" AND SENT THE INTERN TO THE BOOKMAKERS TO PUT ON A BET FOR HIM...
WOW.
I'M TELLING EVERYONE IN THE TEAM THAT HE'S HAVING A BREAKDOWN AND HAS BECOME DELUSIONAL...
AND DO THEY BUY THAT?
YES
DID YOU HEAR THE LATEST THING CLIVE SAID..?
HE SAID THAT ALL THE THINGS HE'S DOING NOW WERE PERFECTLY NORMAL OFFICE BEHAVIOUR BACK IN THE 1980'S...
NOW THAT'S RIDICULOUS... HE REALLY HAS GONE GA-GA...
LUCKILY THEY'RE MOSTLY MILLENNIALS..

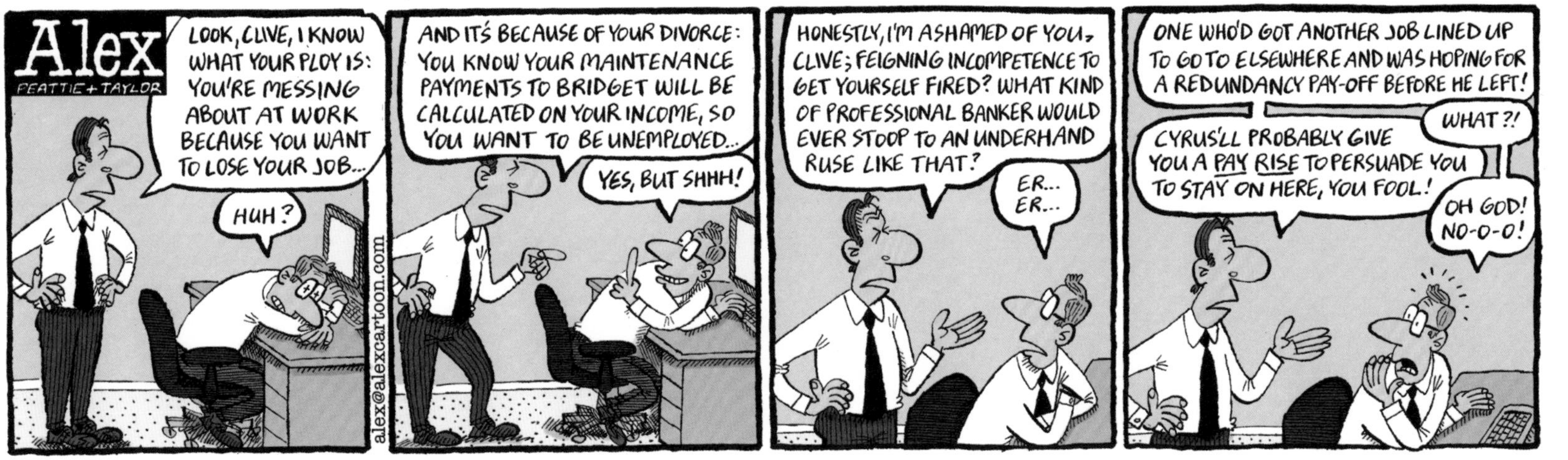
Alex
PEATTIE + TAYLOR
LOOK, CLIVE, I KNOW WHAT YOUR PLOY IS: YOU'RE MESSING ABOUT AT WORK BECAUSE YOU WANT TO LOSE YOUR JOB...
HUH?
alex@alexcartoon.com
AND IT'S BECAUSE OF YOUR DIVORCE: YOU KNOW YOUR MAINTENANCE PAYMENTS TO BRIDGET WILL BE CALCULATED ON YOUR INCOME, SO YOU WANT TO BE UNEMPLOYED...
YES, BUT SHHH!
HONESTLY, I'M ASHAMED OF YOU, CLIVE; FEIGNING INCOMPETENCE TO GET YOURSELF FIRED? WHAT KIND OF PROFESSIONAL BANKER WOULD EVER STOOP TO AN UNDERHAND RUSE LIKE THAT?
ER... ER...
ONE WHO'D GOT ANOTHER JOB LINED UP TO GO TO ELSEWHERE AND WAS HOPING FOR A REDUNDANCY PAY-OFF BEFORE HE LEFT!
CYRUS'LL PROBABLY GIVE YOU A PAY RISE TO PERSUADE YOU TO STAY ON HERE, YOU FOOL!
WHAT?!
OH GOD! NO-O-O!

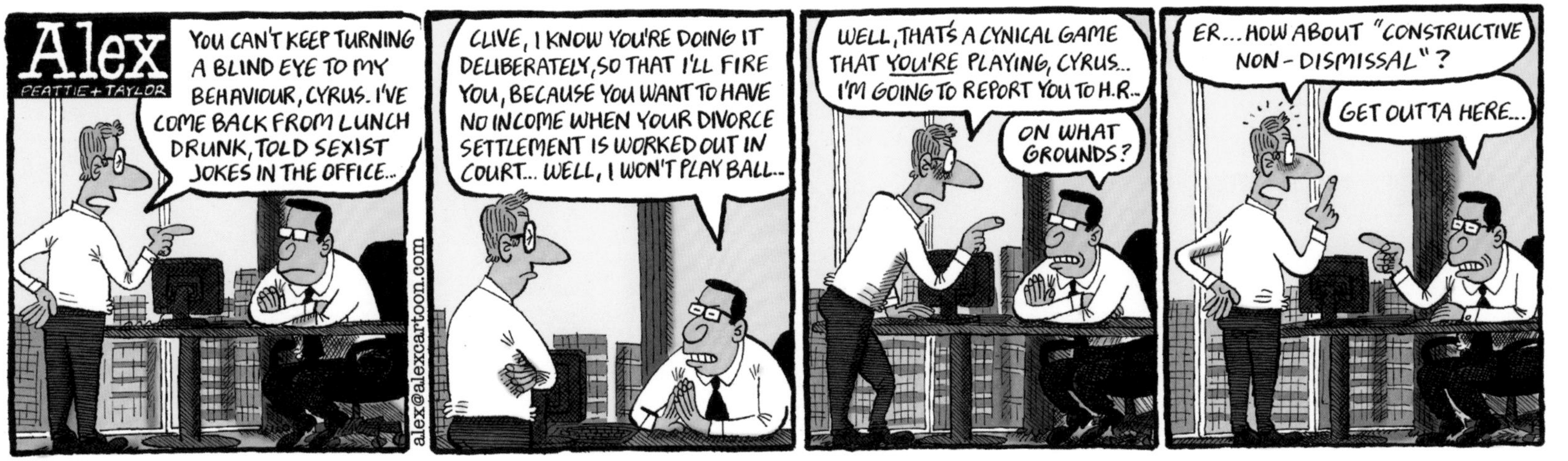
Alex
PEATTIE + TAYLOR
YOU CAN'T KEEP TURNING A BLIND EYE TO MY BEHAVIOUR, CYRUS. I'VE COME BACK FROM LUNCH DRUNK, TOLD SEXIST JOKES IN THE OFFICE...
alex@alexcartoon.com
CLIVE, I KNOW YOU'RE DOING IT DELIBERATELY, SO THAT I'LL FIRE YOU, BECAUSE YOU WANT TO HAVE NO INCOME WHEN YOUR DIVORCE SETTLEMENT IS WORKED OUT IN COURT... WELL, I WON'T PLAY BALL...
WELL, THAT'S A CYNICAL GAME THAT YOU'RE PLAYING, CYRUS... I'M GOING TO REPORT YOU TO H.R...
ON WHAT GROUNDS?
ER... HOW ABOUT "CONSTRUCTIVE NON-DISMISSAL"?
GET OUTTA HERE...

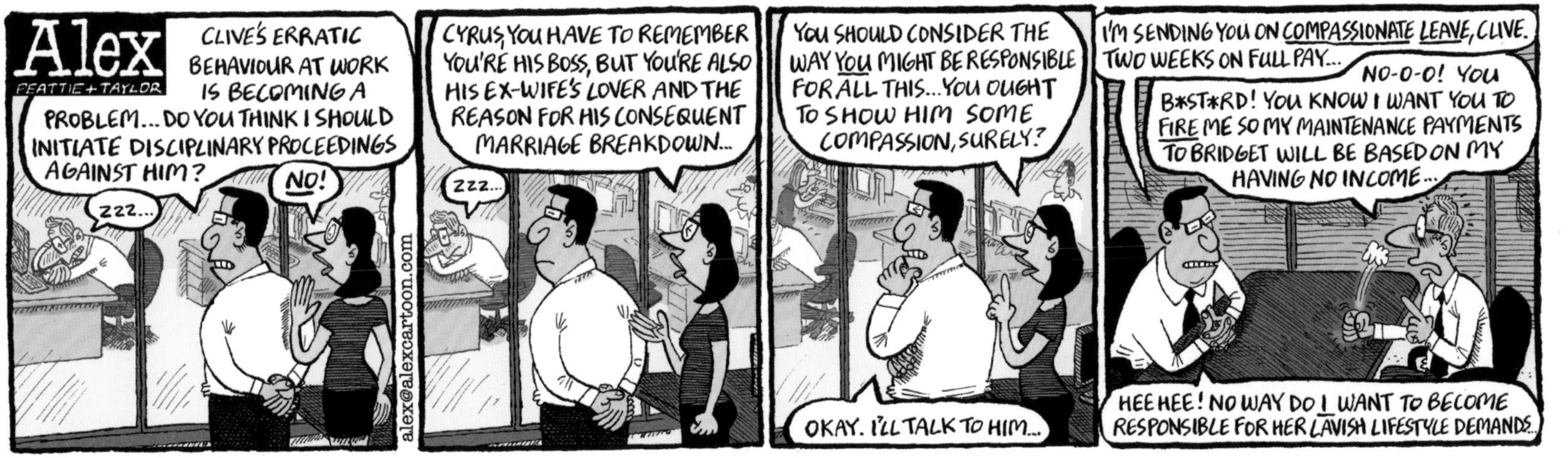
Alex
PEATTIE + TAYLOR
CLIVE'S ERRATIC BEHAVIOUR AT WORK IS BECOMING A PROBLEM... DO YOU THINK I SHOULD INITIATE DISCIPLINARY PROCEEDINGS AGAINST HIM?
ZZZ...
NO!
alex@alexcartoon.com
CYRUS, YOU HAVE TO REMEMBER YOU'RE HIS BOSS, BUT YOU'RE ALSO HIS EX-WIFE'S LOVER AND THE REASON FOR HIS CONSEQUENT MARRIAGE BREAKDOWN...
ZZZ...
YOU SHOULD CONSIDER THE WAY YOU MIGHT BE RESPONSIBLE FOR ALL THIS... YOU OUGHT TO SHOW HIM SOME COMPASSION, SURELY?
OKAY. I'LL TALK TO HIM...
I'M SENDING YOU ON COMPASSIONATE LEAVE, CLIVE. TWO WEEKS ON FULL PAY...
NO-O-O! YOU B*ST*RD! YOU KNOW I WANT YOU TO FIRE ME SO MY MAINTENANCE PAYMENTS TO BRIDGET WILL BE BASED ON MY HAVING NO INCOME...
HEE HEE! NO WAY DO I WANT TO BECOME RESPONSIBLE FOR HER LAVISH LIFESTYLE DEMANDS...

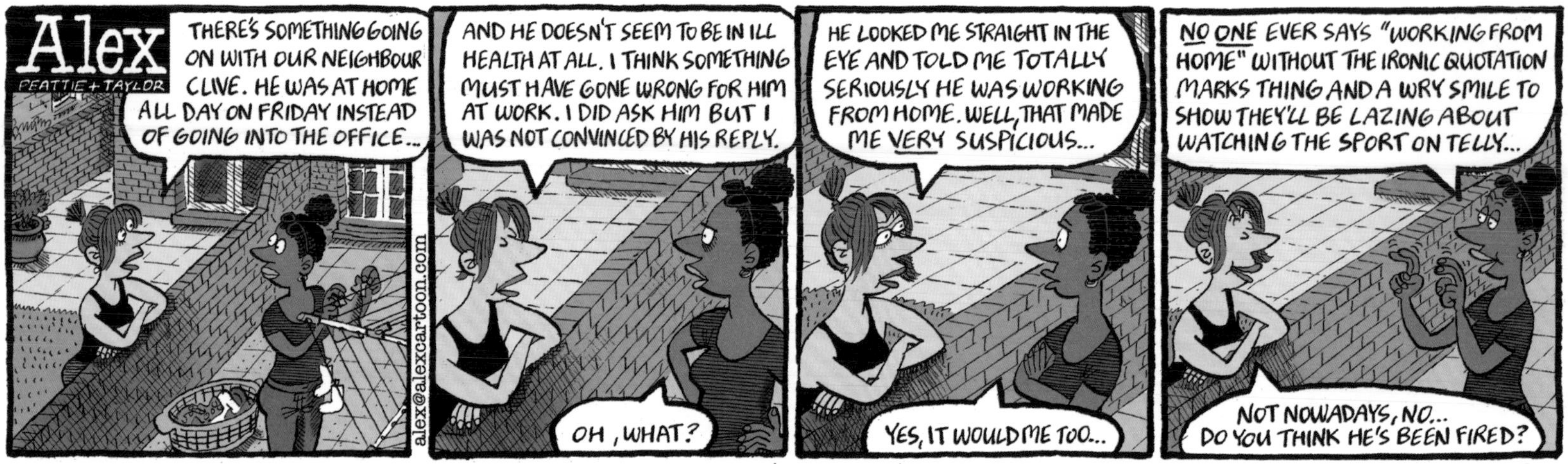
Alex
PEATTIE + TAYLOR
THERE'S SOMETHING GOING ON WITH OUR NEIGHBOUR CLIVE. HE WAS AT HOME ALL DAY ON FRIDAY INSTEAD OF GOING INTO THE OFFICE...
AND HE DOESN'T SEEM TO BE IN ILL HEALTH AT ALL. I THINK SOMETHING MUST HAVE GONE WRONG FOR HIM AT WORK. I DID ASK HIM BUT I WAS NOT CONVINCED BY HIS REPLY.
OH, WHAT?
alex@alexcartoon.com
HE LOOKED ME STRAIGHT IN THE EYE AND TOLD ME TOTALLY SERIOUSLY HE WAS WORKING FROM HOME. WELL, THAT MADE ME VERY SUSPICIOUS...
YES, IT WOULD ME TOO...
NO ONE EVER SAYS "WORKING FROM HOME" WITHOUT THE IRONIC QUOTATION MARKS THING AND A WRY SMILE TO SHOW THEY'LL BE LAZING ABOUT WATCHING THE SPORT ON TELLY...
NOT NOWADAYS, NO... DO YOU THINK HE'S BEEN FIRED?

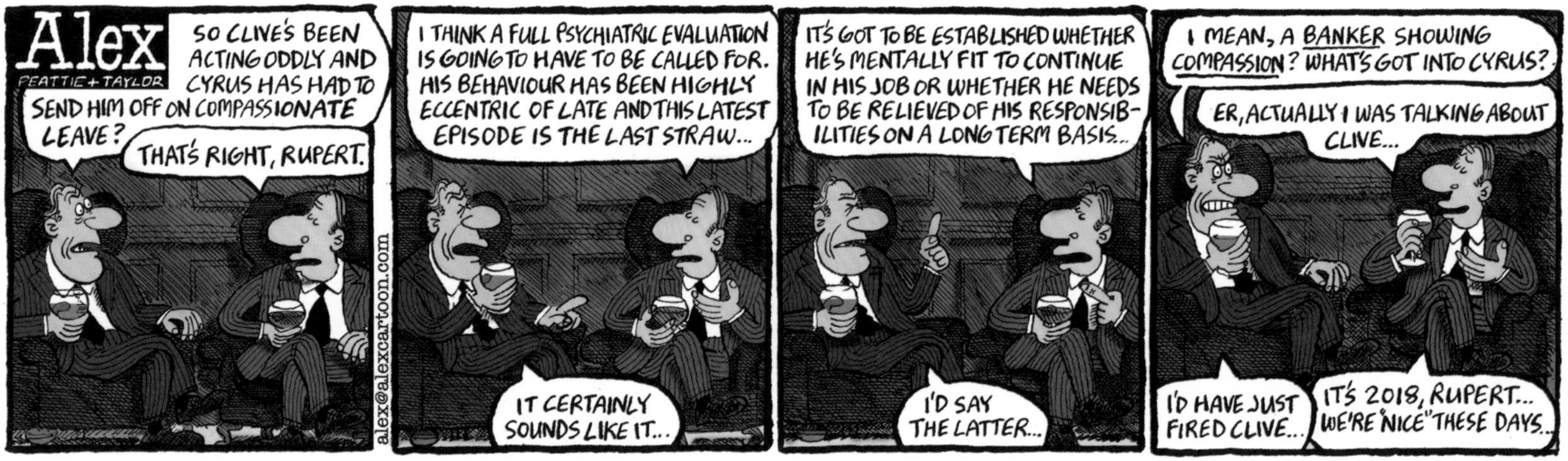
Alex
PEATTIE + TAYLOR
SO CLIVE'S BEEN ACTING ODDLY AND CYRUS HAS HAD TO SEND HIM OFF ON COMPASSIONATE LEAVE?
THAT'S RIGHT, RUPERT.
alex@alexcartoon.com
I THINK A FULL PSYCHIATRIC EVALUATION IS GOING TO HAVE TO BE CALLED FOR. HIS BEHAVIOUR HAS BEEN HIGHLY ECCENTRIC OF LATE AND THIS LATEST EPISODE IS THE LAST STRAW...
IT CERTAINLY SOUNDS LIKE IT...
IT'S GOT TO BE ESTABLISHED WHETHER HE'S MENTALLY FIT TO CONTINUE IN HIS JOB OR WHETHER HE NEEDS TO BE RELIEVED OF HIS RESPONSIBILITIES ON A LONG TERM BASIS...
I'D SAY THE LATTER...
I MEAN, A BANKER SHOWING COMPASSION? WHAT'S GOT INTO CYRUS?
ER, ACTUALLY I WAS TALKING ABOUT CLIVE...
I'D HAVE JUST FIRED CLIVE...
IT'S 2018, RUPERT... WE'RE "NICE" THESE DAYS...

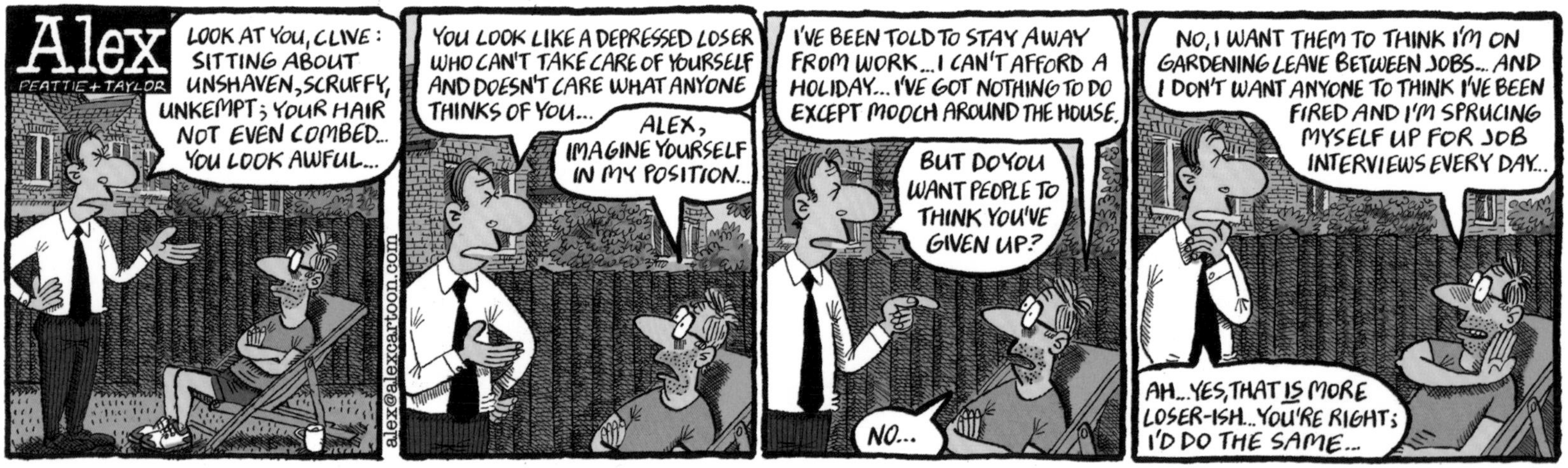
Alex
PEATTIE + TAYLOR
LOOK AT YOU, CLIVE: SITTING ABOUT UNSHAVEN, SCRUFFY, UNKEMPT; YOUR HAIR NOT EVEN COMBED... YOU LOOK AWFUL...
alex@alexcartoon.com
YOU LOOK LIKE A DEPRESSED LOSER WHO CAN'T TAKE CARE OF YOURSELF AND DOESN'T CARE WHAT ANYONE THINKS OF YOU...
ALEX, IMAGINE YOURSELF IN MY POSITION...
I'VE BEEN TOLD TO STAY AWAY FROM WORK... I CAN'T AFFORD A HOLIDAY... I'VE GOT NOTHING TO DO EXCEPT MOOCH AROUND THE HOUSE.
BUT DO YOU WANT PEOPLE TO THINK YOU'VE GIVEN UP?
NO...
NO, I WANT THEM TO THINK I'M ON GARDENING LEAVE BETWEEN JOBS... AND I DON'T WANT ANYONE TO THINK I'VE BEEN FIRED AND I'M SPRUCING MYSELF UP FOR JOB INTERVIEWS EVERY DAY...
AH... YES, THAT IS MORE LOSER-ISH... YOU'RE RIGHT; I'D DO THE SAME...

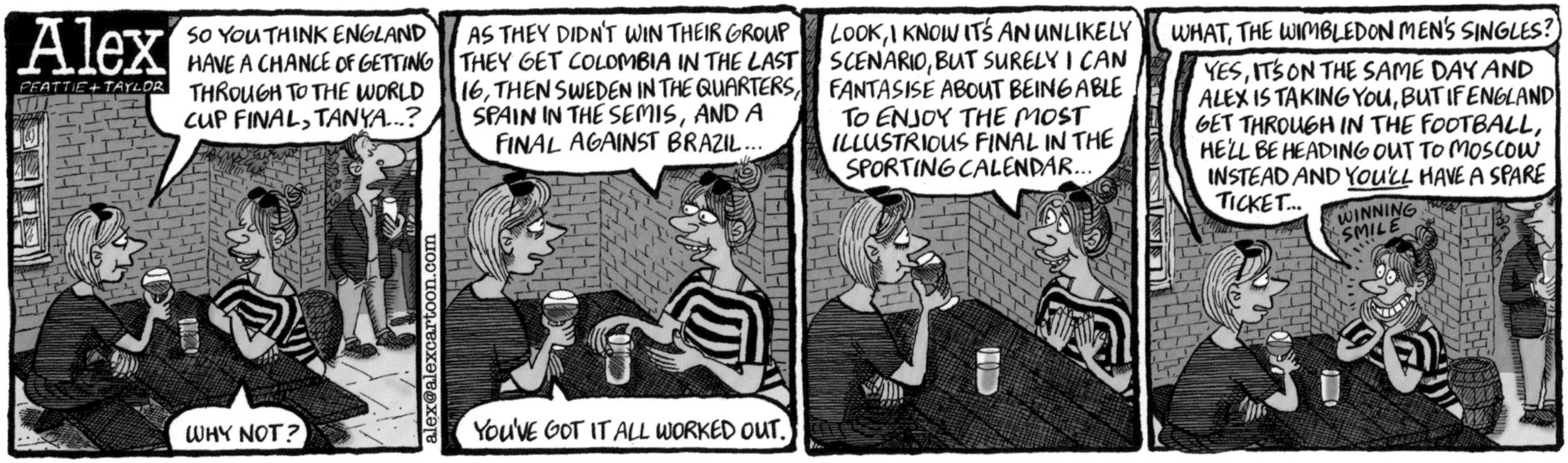
Alex
PEATTIE + TAYLOR
SO YOU THINK ENGLAND HAVE A CHANCE OF GETTING THROUGH TO THE WORLD CUP FINAL, TANYA...?
WHY NOT?
alex@alexcartoon.com
AS THEY DIDN'T WIN THEIR GROUP THEY GET COLOMBIA IN THE LAST 16, THEN SWEDEN IN THE QUARTERS, SPAIN IN THE SEMIS, AND A FINAL AGAINST BRAZIL...
YOU'VE GOT IT ALL WORKED OUT.
LOOK, I KNOW IT'S AN UNLIKELY SCENARIO, BUT SURELY I CAN FANTASISE ABOUT BEING ABLE TO ENJOY THE MOST ILLUSTRIOUS FINAL IN THE SPORTING CALENDAR...
WHAT, THE WIMBLEDON MEN'S SINGLES?
YES, IT'S ON THE SAME DAY AND ALEX IS TAKING YOU, BUT IF ENGLAND GET THROUGH IN THE FOOTBALL, HE'LL BE HEADING OUT TO MOSCOW INSTEAD AND YOU'LL HAVE A SPARE TICKET...
WINNING SMILE

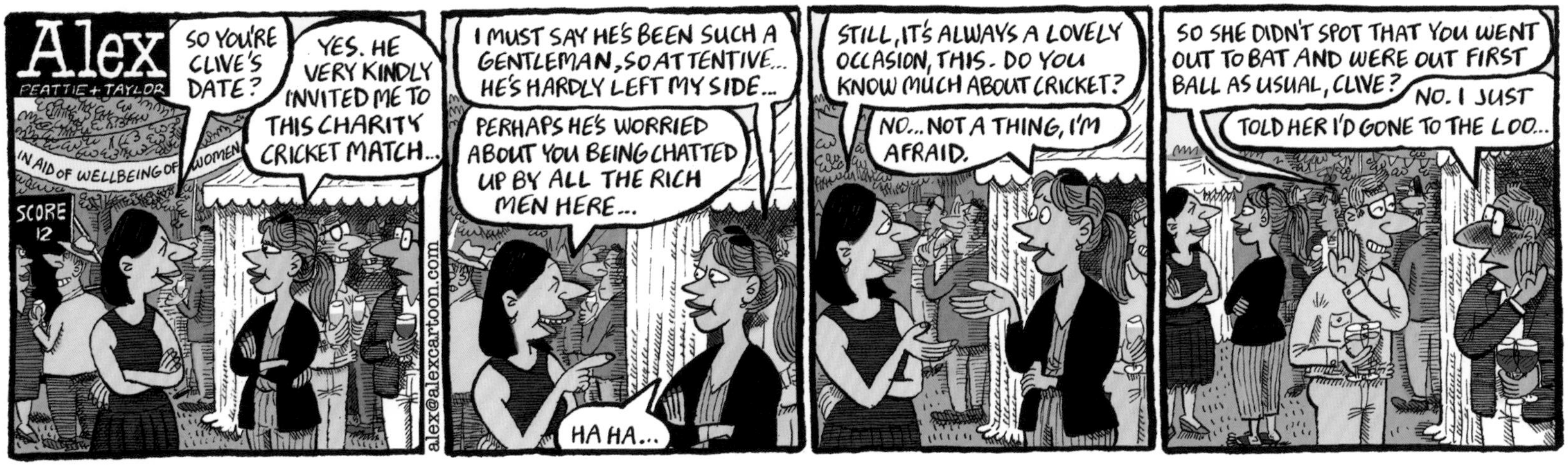
Alex
PEATTIE + TAYLOR
IN AID OF WELLBEING OF WOMEN
SCORE 12
SO YOU'RE CLIVE'S DATE?
YES. HE VERY KINDLY INVITED ME TO THIS CHARITY CRICKET MATCH...
alex@alexcartoon.com
I MUST SAY HE'S BEEN SUCH A GENTLEMAN, SO ATTENTIVE... HE'S HARDLY LEFT MY SIDE...
PERHAPS HE'S WORRIED ABOUT YOU BEING CHATTED UP BY ALL THE RICH MEN HERE...
HA HA...
STILL, IT'S ALWAYS A LOVELY OCCASION, THIS. DO YOU KNOW MUCH ABOUT CRICKET?
NO... NOT A THING, I'M AFRAID.
SO SHE DIDN'T SPOT THAT YOU WENT OUT TO BAT AND WERE OUT FIRST BALL AS USUAL, CLIVE?
NO. I JUST TOLD HER I'D GONE TO THE LOO...

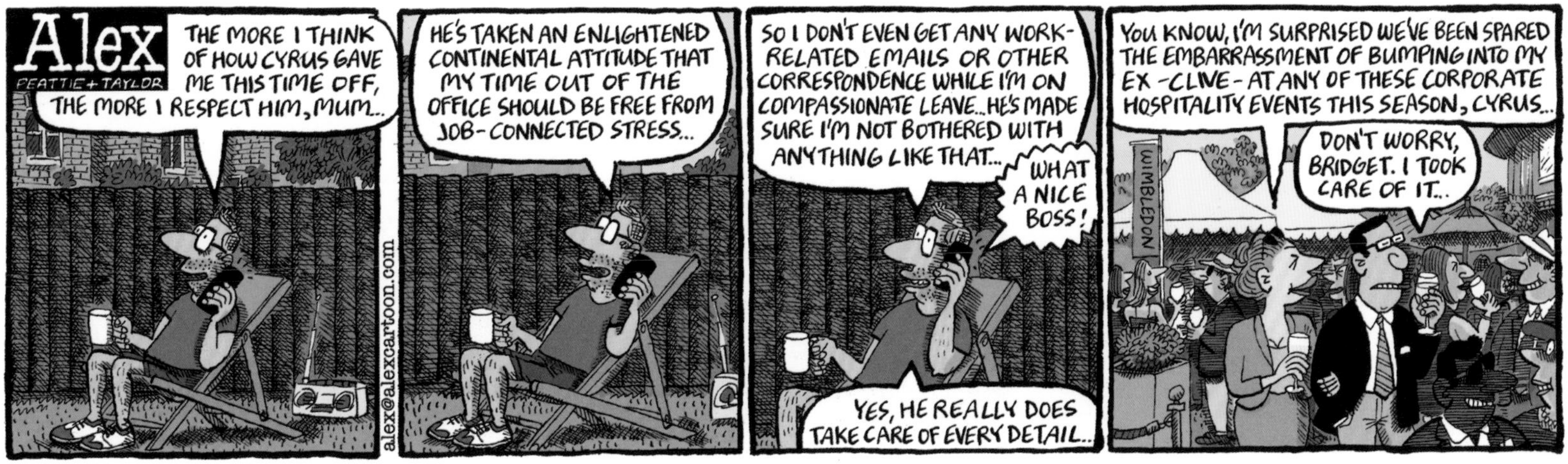
Alex
PEATTIE + TAYLOR
THE MORE I THINK OF HOW CYRUS GAVE ME THIS TIME OFF, THE MORE I RESPECT HIM, MUM...
alex@alexcartoon.com
HE'S TAKEN AN ENLIGHTENED CONTINENTAL ATTITUDE THAT MY TIME OUT OF THE OFFICE SHOULD BE FREE FROM JOB-CONNECTED STRESS...
SO I DON'T EVEN GET ANY WORK-RELATED EMAILS OR OTHER CORRESPONDENCE WHILE I'M ON COMPASSIONATE LEAVE... HE'S MADE SURE I'M NOT BOTHERED WITH ANYTHING LIKE THAT...
WHAT A NICE BOSS!
YES, HE REALLY DOES TAKE CARE OF EVERY DETAIL...
YOU KNOW, I'M SURPRISED WE'VE BEEN SPARED THE EMBARRASSMENT OF BUMPING INTO MY EX - CLIVE - AT ANY OF THESE CORPORATE HOSPITALITY EVENTS THIS SEASON, CYRUS...
WIMBLEDON
DON'T WORRY, BRIDGET. I TOOK CARE OF IT...

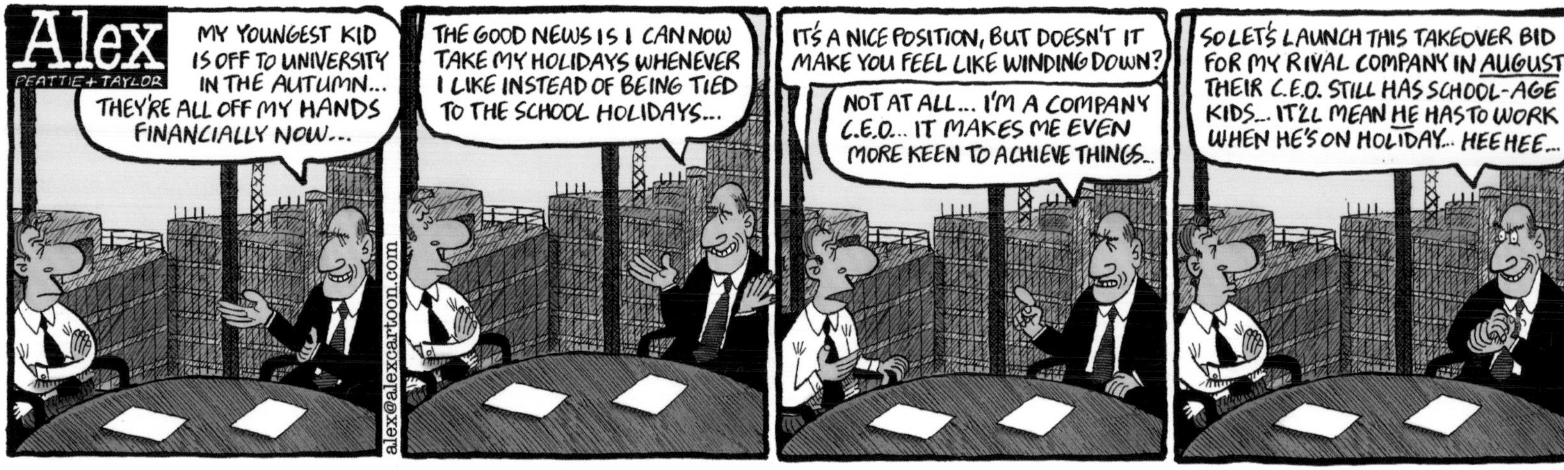
Alex
PEATTIE + TAYLOR
MY YOUNGEST KID IS OFF TO UNIVERSITY IN THE AUTUMN... THEY'RE ALL OFF MY HANDS FINANCIALLY NOW...
THE GOOD NEWS IS I CAN NOW TAKE MY HOLIDAYS WHENEVER I LIKE INSTEAD OF BEING TIED TO THE SCHOOL HOLIDAYS...
IT'S A NICE POSITION, BUT DOESN'T IT MAKE YOU FEEL LIKE WINDING DOWN?
NOT AT ALL... I'M A COMPANY C.E.O... IT MAKES ME EVEN MORE KEEN TO ACHIEVE THINGS...
SO LET'S LAUNCH THIS TAKEOVER BID FOR MY RIVAL COMPANY IN AUGUST... THEIR C.E.O. STILL HAS SCHOOL-AGE KIDS... IT'LL MEAN HE HAS TO WORK WHEN HE'S ON HOLIDAY... HEE HEE...
alex@alexcartoon.com

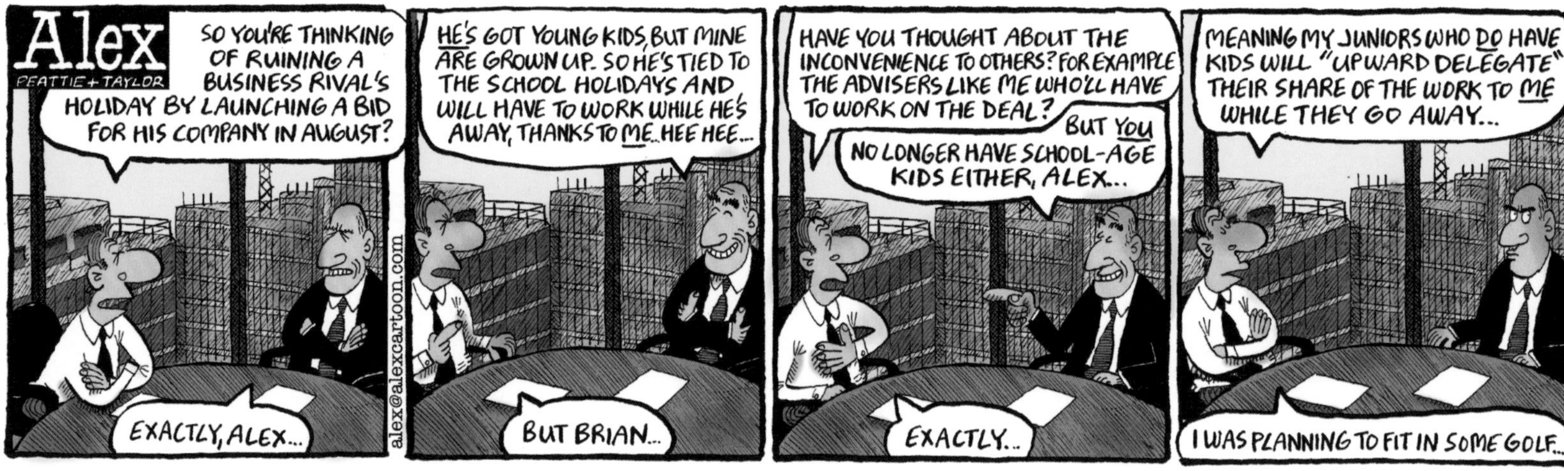
Alex
PEATTIE + TAYLOR
SO YOU'RE THINKING OF RUINING A BUSINESS RIVAL'S HOLIDAY BY LAUNCHING A BID FOR HIS COMPANY IN AUGUST?
EXACTLY, ALEX...
HE'S GOT YOUNG KIDS, BUT MINE ARE GROWN UP. SO HE'S TIED TO THE SCHOOL HOLIDAYS AND WILL HAVE TO WORK WHILE HE'S AWAY, THANKS TO ME... HEE HEE...
BUT BRIAN...
HAVE YOU THOUGHT ABOUT THE INCONVENIENCE TO OTHERS? FOR EXAMPLE THE ADVISERS LIKE ME WHO'LL HAVE TO WORK ON THE DEAL?
BUT YOU NO LONGER HAVE SCHOOL-AGE KIDS EITHER, ALEX...
EXACTLY...
MEANING MY JUNIORS WHO DO HAVE KIDS WILL "UPWARD DELEGATE" THEIR SHARE OF THE WORK TO ME WHILE THEY GO AWAY...
I WAS PLANNING TO FIT IN SOME GOLF...
alex@alexcartoon.com

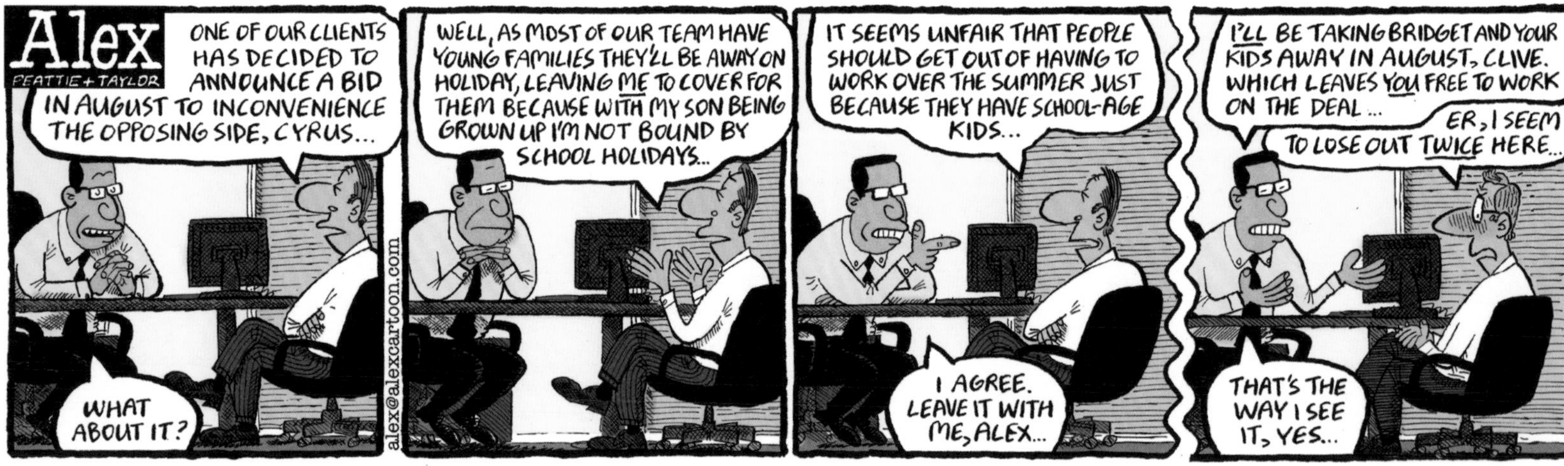
Alex
PEATTIE + TAYLOR
ONE OF OUR CLIENTS HAS DECIDED TO ANNOUNCE A BID IN AUGUST TO INCONVENIENCE THE OPPOSING SIDE, CYRUS...
WHAT ABOUT IT?
WELL, AS MOST OF OUR TEAM HAVE YOUNG FAMILIES THEY'LL BE AWAY ON HOLIDAY, LEAVING ME TO COVER FOR THEM BECAUSE WITH MY SON BEING GROWN UP I'M NOT BOUND BY SCHOOL HOLIDAYS...
IT SEEMS UNFAIR THAT PEOPLE SHOULD GET OUT OF HAVING TO WORK OVER THE SUMMER JUST BECAUSE THEY HAVE SCHOOL-AGE KIDS...
I AGREE. LEAVE IT WITH ME, ALEX...
I'LL BE TAKING BRIDGET AND YOUR KIDS AWAY IN AUGUST, CLIVE. WHICH LEAVES YOU FREE TO WORK ON THE DEAL...
ER, I SEEM TO LOSE OUT TWICE HERE...
THAT'S THE WAY I SEE IT, YES...
alex@alexcartoon.com

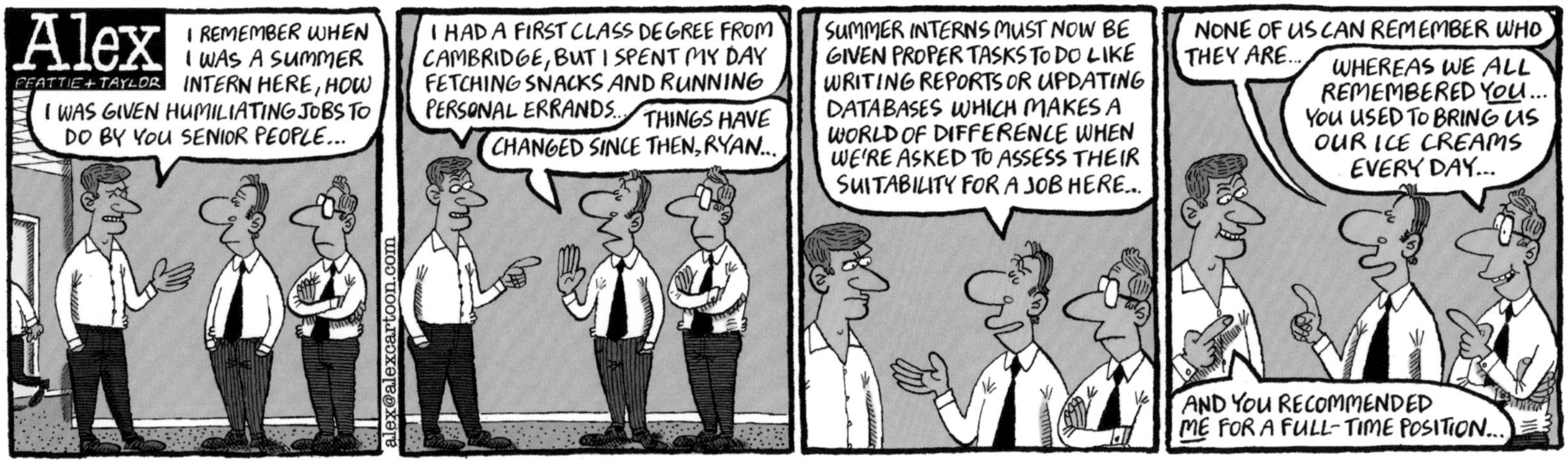
Alex
PEATTIE + TAYLOR
I REMEMBER WHEN I WAS A SUMMER INTERN HERE, HOW I WAS GIVEN HUMILIATING JOBS TO DO BY YOU SENIOR PEOPLE...
alex@alexcartoon.com
I HAD A FIRST CLASS DEGREE FROM CAMBRIDGE, BUT I SPENT MY DAY FETCHING SNACKS AND RUNNING PERSONAL ERRANDS...
THINGS HAVE CHANGED SINCE THEN, RYAN...
SUMMER INTERNS MUST NOW BE GIVEN PROPER TASKS TO DO LIKE WRITING REPORTS OR UPDATING DATABASES WHICH MAKES A WORLD OF DIFFERENCE WHEN WE'RE ASKED TO ASSESS THEIR SUITABILITY FOR A JOB HERE...
NONE OF US CAN REMEMBER WHO THEY ARE...
WHEREAS WE ALL REMEMBERED YOU... YOU USED TO BRING US OUR ICE CREAMS EVERY DAY...
AND YOU RECOMMENDED ME FOR A FULL-TIME POSITION...

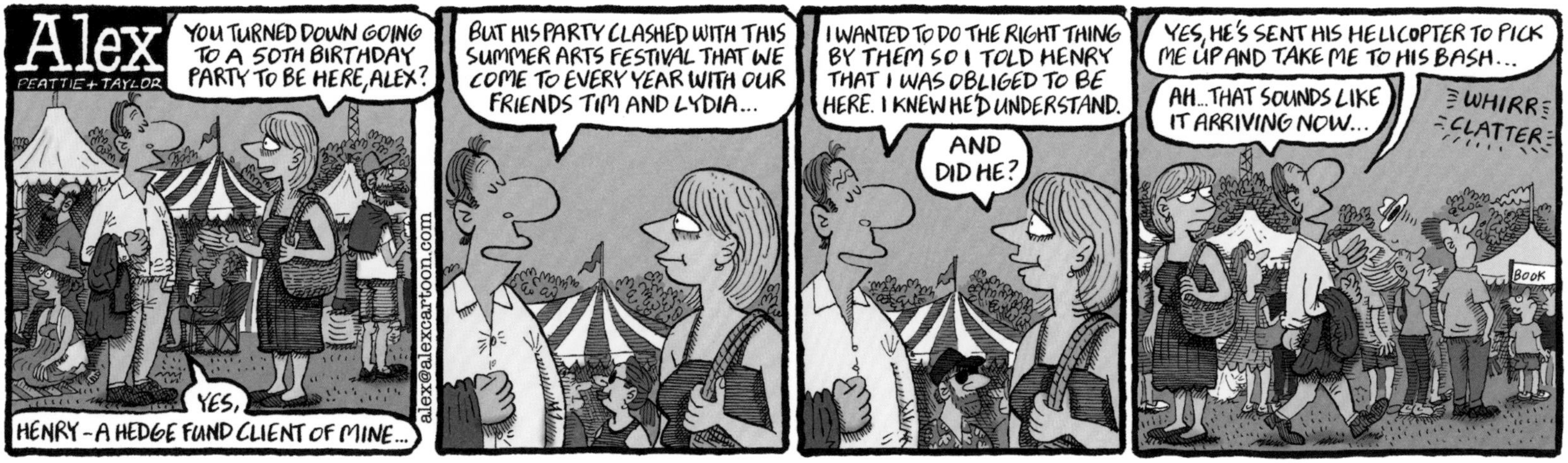
Alex
PEATTIE + TAYLOR
YOU TURNED DOWN GOING TO A 50TH BIRTHDAY PARTY TO BE HERE, ALEX?
YES, HENRY - A HEDGE FUND CLIENT OF MINE...
alex@alexcartoon.com
BUT HIS PARTY CLASHED WITH THIS SUMMER ARTS FESTIVAL THAT WE COME TO EVERY YEAR WITH OUR FRIENDS TIM AND LYDIA...
I WANTED TO DO THE RIGHT THING BY THEM SO I TOLD HENRY THAT I WAS OBLIGED TO BE HERE. I KNEW HE'D UNDERSTAND.
AND DID HE?
YES, HE'S SENT HIS HELICOPTER TO PICK ME UP AND TAKE ME TO HIS BASH...
AH... THAT SOUNDS LIKE IT ARRIVING NOW...
WHIRR
CLATTER
BOOK

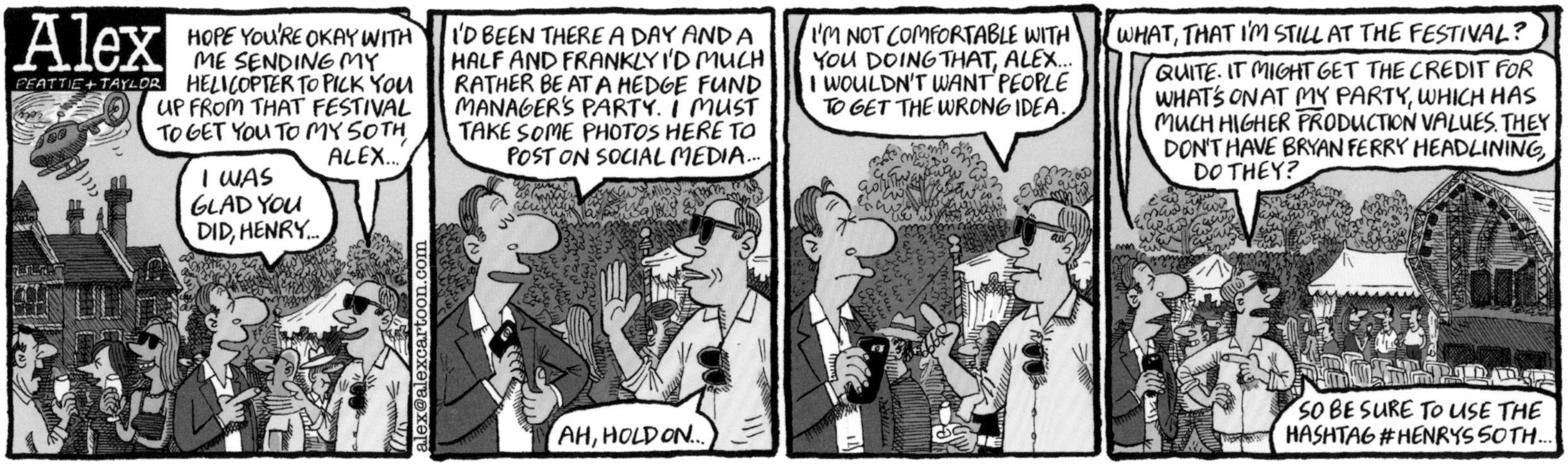
Alex
PEATTIE + TAYLOR
HOPE YOU'RE OKAY WITH ME SENDING MY HELICOPTER TO PICK YOU UP FROM THAT FESTIVAL TO GET YOU TO MY 50TH, ALEX...
I WAS GLAD YOU DID, HENRY...
alex@alexcartoon.com
I'D BEEN THERE A DAY AND A HALF AND FRANKLY I'D MUCH RATHER BE AT A HEDGE FUND MANAGER'S PARTY. I MUST TAKE SOME PHOTOS HERE TO POST ON SOCIAL MEDIA...
AH, HOLD ON...
I'M NOT COMFORTABLE WITH YOU DOING THAT, ALEX... I WOULDN'T WANT PEOPLE TO GET THE WRONG IDEA.
WHAT, THAT I'M STILL AT THE FESTIVAL?
QUITE. IT MIGHT GET THE CREDIT FOR WHAT'S ON AT MY PARTY, WHICH HAS MUCH HIGHER PRODUCTION VALUES. THEY DON'T HAVE BRYAN FERRY HEADLINING, DO THEY?
SO BE SURE TO USE THE HASHTAG #HENRYS50TH...

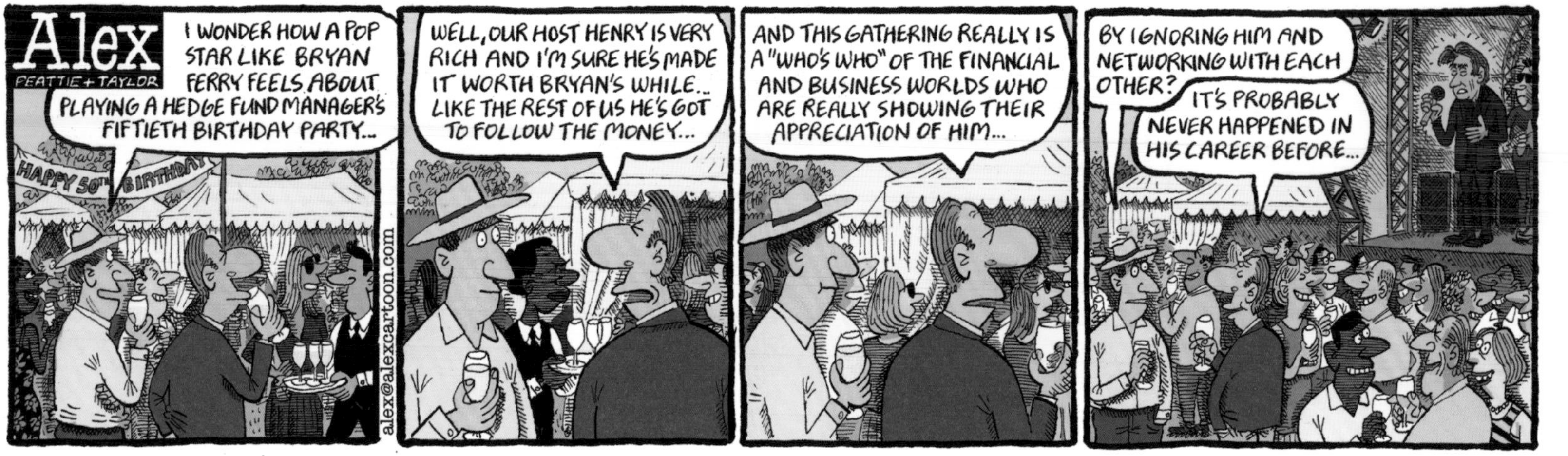
Alex
PEATTIE+TAYLOR
I WONDER HOW A POP STAR LIKE BRYAN FERRY FEELS ABOUT PLAYING A HEDGE FUND MANAGER'S FIFTIETH BIRTHDAY PARTY...
HAPPY 50TH BIRTHDAY
alex@alexcartoon.com
WELL, OUR HOST HENRY IS VERY RICH AND I'M SURE HE'S MADE IT WORTH BRYAN'S WHILE... LIKE THE REST OF US HE'S GOT TO FOLLOW THE MONEY...
AND THIS GATHERING REALLY IS A "WHO'S WHO" OF THE FINANCIAL AND BUSINESS WORLDS WHO ARE REALLY SHOWING THEIR APPRECIATION OF HIM...
BY IGNORING HIM AND NETWORKING WITH EACH OTHER?
IT'S PROBABLY NEVER HAPPENED IN HIS CAREER BEFORE...

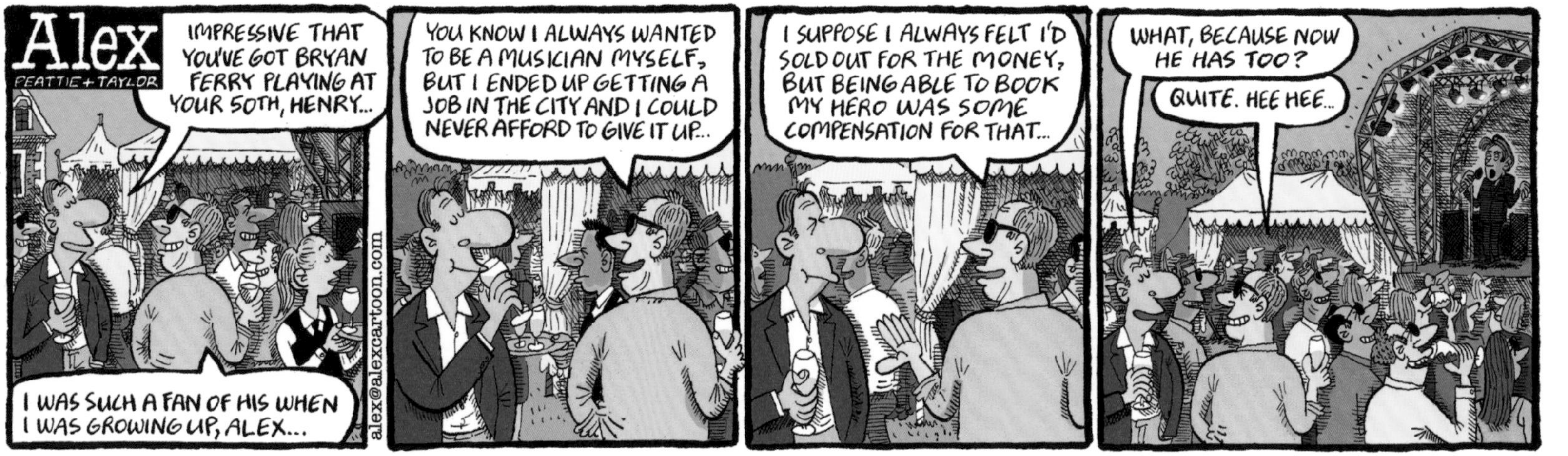
Alex
PEATTIE+TAYLOR
IMPRESSIVE THAT YOU'VE GOT BRYAN FERRY PLAYING AT YOUR 50TH, HENRY...
I WAS SUCH A FAN OF HIS WHEN I WAS GROWING UP, ALEX...
alex@alexcartoon.com
YOU KNOW I ALWAYS WANTED TO BE A MUSICIAN MYSELF, BUT I ENDED UP GETTING A JOB IN THE CITY AND I COULD NEVER AFFORD TO GIVE IT UP...
I SUPPOSE I ALWAYS FELT I'D SOLD OUT FOR THE MONEY, BUT BEING ABLE TO BOOK MY HERO WAS SOME COMPENSATION FOR THAT...
WHAT, BECAUSE NOW HE HAS TOO?
QUITE. HEE HEE...

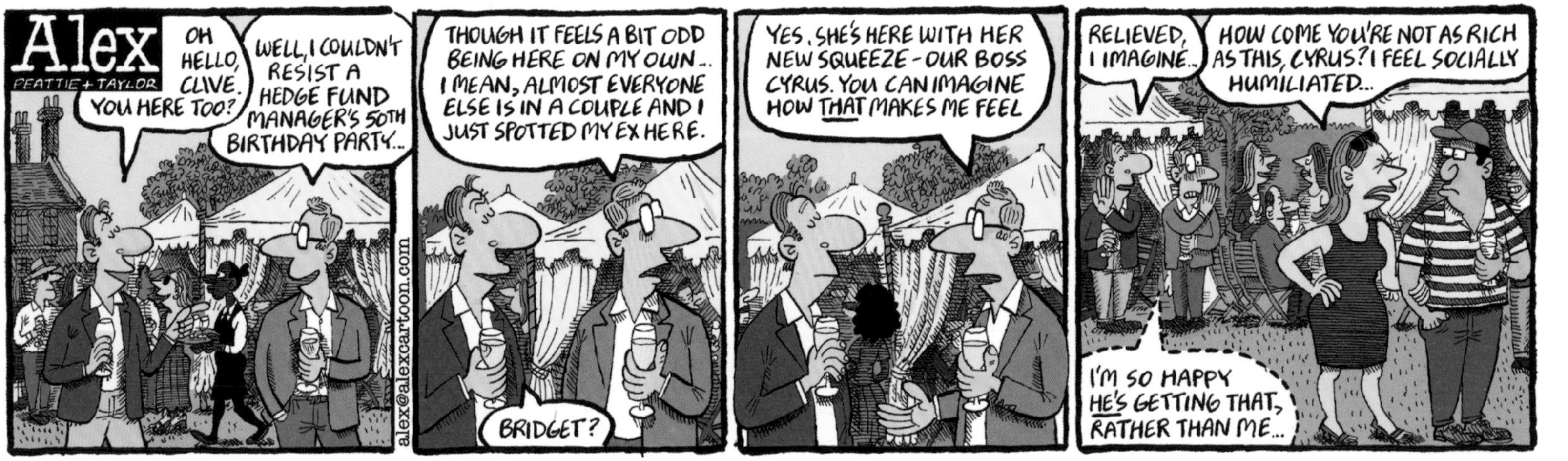
Alex
PEATTIE+TAYLOR
OH HELLO, CLIVE. YOU HERE TOO?
WELL, I COULDN'T RESIST A HEDGE FUND MANAGER'S 50TH BIRTHDAY PARTY...
alex@alexcartoon.com
THOUGH IT FEELS A BIT ODD BEING HERE ON MY OWN... I MEAN, ALMOST EVERYONE ELSE IS IN A COUPLE AND I JUST SPOTTED MY EX HERE.
BRIDGET?
YES, SHE'S HERE WITH HER NEW SQUEEZE - OUR BOSS CYRUS. YOU CAN IMAGINE HOW THAT MAKES ME FEEL
RELIEVED, I IMAGINE...
HOW COME YOU'RE NOT AS RICH AS THIS, CYRUS? I FEEL SOCIALLY HUMILIATED...
I'M SO HAPPY HE'S GETTING THAT, RATHER THAN ME...

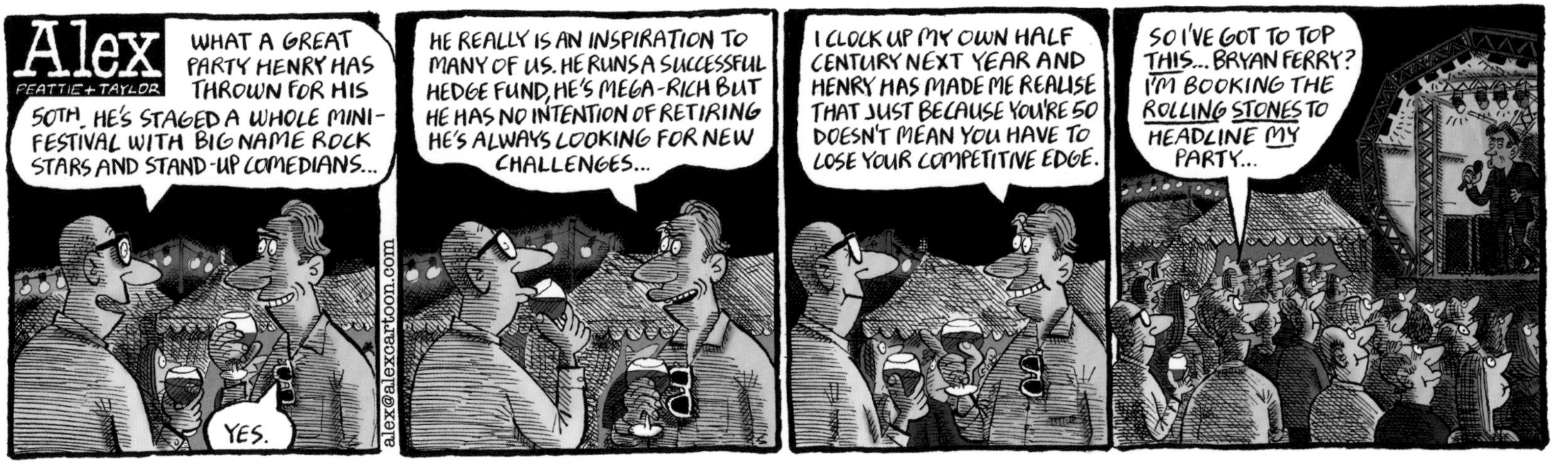
Alex
PEATTIE + TAYLOR
WHAT A GREAT PARTY HENRY HAS THROWN FOR HIS 50TH. HE'S STAGED A WHOLE MINI-FESTIVAL WITH BIG NAME ROCK STARS AND STAND-UP COMEDIANS...
YES.
alex@alexcartoon.com
HE REALLY IS AN INSPIRATION TO MANY OF US. HE RUNS A SUCCESSFUL HEDGE FUND, HE'S MEGA-RICH BUT HE HAS NO INTENTION OF RETIRING HE'S ALWAYS LOOKING FOR NEW CHALLENGES...
I CLOCK UP MY OWN HALF CENTURY NEXT YEAR AND HENRY HAS MADE ME REALISE THAT JUST BECAUSE YOU'RE 50 DOESN'T MEAN YOU HAVE TO LOSE YOUR COMPETITIVE EDGE.
SO I'VE GOT TO TOP THIS... BRYAN FERRY? I'M BOOKING THE ROLLING STONES TO HEADLINE MY PARTY...

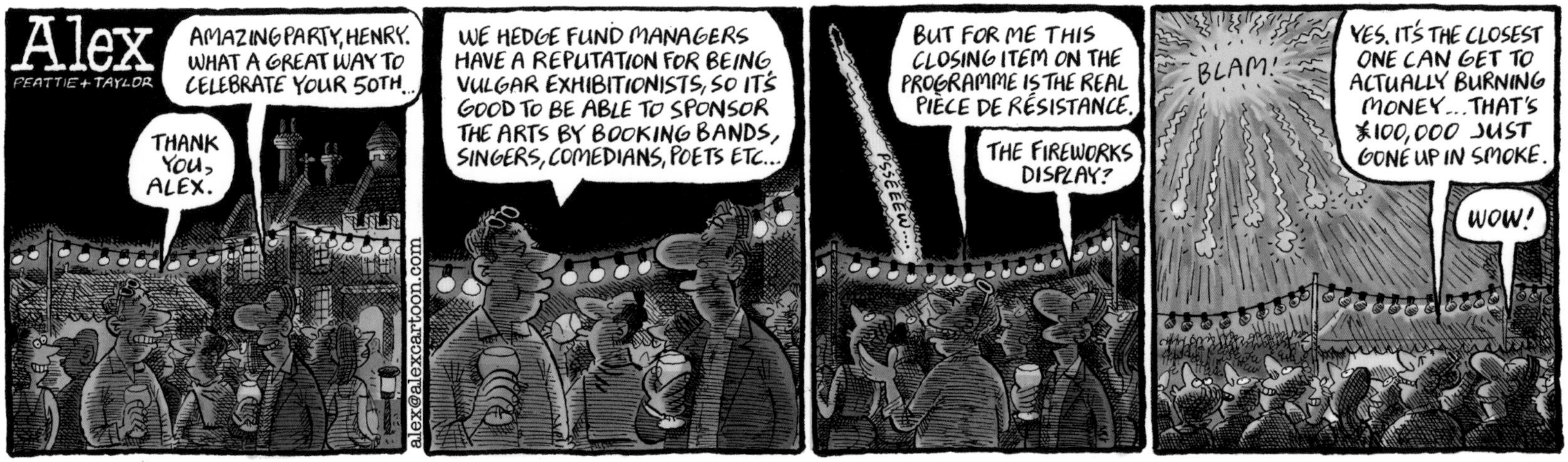
Alex
PEATTIE + TAYLOR
AMAZING PARTY, HENRY. WHAT A GREAT WAY TO CELEBRATE YOUR 50TH...
THANK YOU, ALEX.
alex@alexcartoon.com
WE HEDGE FUND MANAGERS HAVE A REPUTATION FOR BEING VULGAR EXHIBITIONISTS, SO IT'S GOOD TO BE ABLE TO SPONSOR THE ARTS BY BOOKING BANDS, SINGERS, COMEDIANS, POETS ETC...
PSSEEEW...
BUT FOR ME THIS CLOSING ITEM ON THE PROGRAMME IS THE REAL PIÈCE DE RÉSISTANCE.
THE FIREWORKS DISPLAY?
BLAM!
YES. IT'S THE CLOSEST ONE CAN GET TO ACTUALLY BURNING MONEY... THAT'S $100,000 JUST GONE UP IN SMOKE.
WOW!

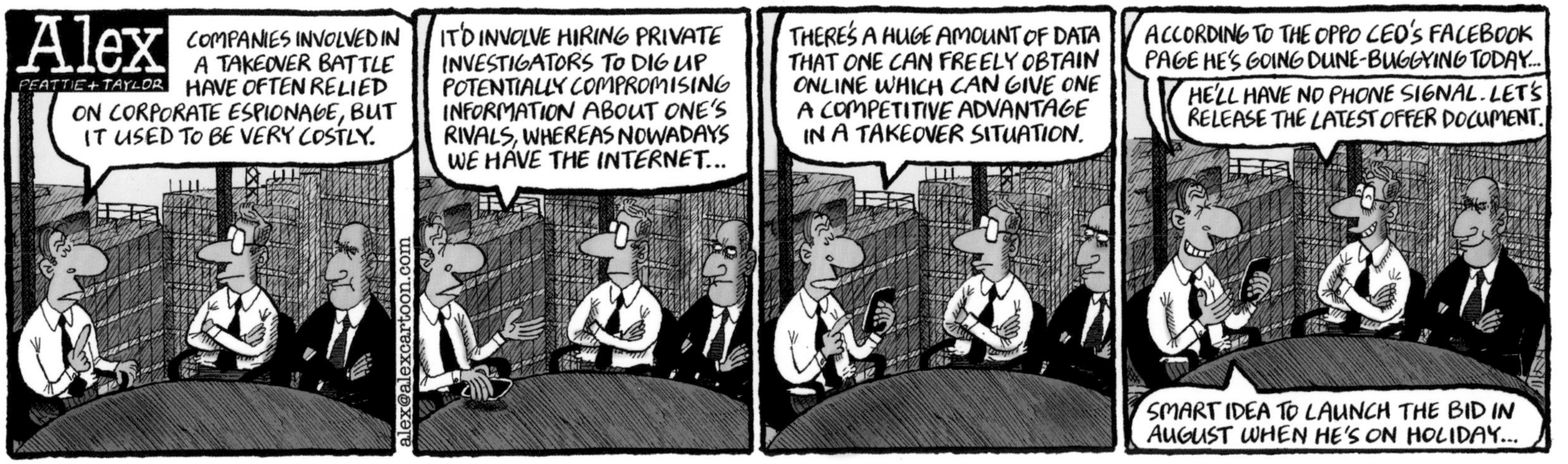
Alex
PEATTIE + TAYLOR
COMPANIES INVOLVED IN A TAKEOVER BATTLE HAVE OFTEN RELIED ON CORPORATE ESPIONAGE, BUT IT USED TO BE VERY COSTLY.
alex@alexcartoon.com
IT'D INVOLVE HIRING PRIVATE INVESTIGATORS TO DIG UP POTENTIALLY COMPROMISING INFORMATION ABOUT ONE'S RIVALS, WHEREAS NOWADAYS WE HAVE THE INTERNET...
THERE'S A HUGE AMOUNT OF DATA THAT ONE CAN FREELY OBTAIN ONLINE WHICH CAN GIVE ONE A COMPETITIVE ADVANTAGE IN A TAKEOVER SITUATION.
ACCORDING TO THE OPPO CEO'S FACEBOOK PAGE HE'S GOING DUNE-BUGGYING TODAY...
HE'LL HAVE NO PHONE SIGNAL. LET'S RELEASE THE LATEST OFFER DOCUMENT.
SMART IDEA TO LAUNCH THE BID IN AUGUST WHEN HE'S ON HOLIDAY...

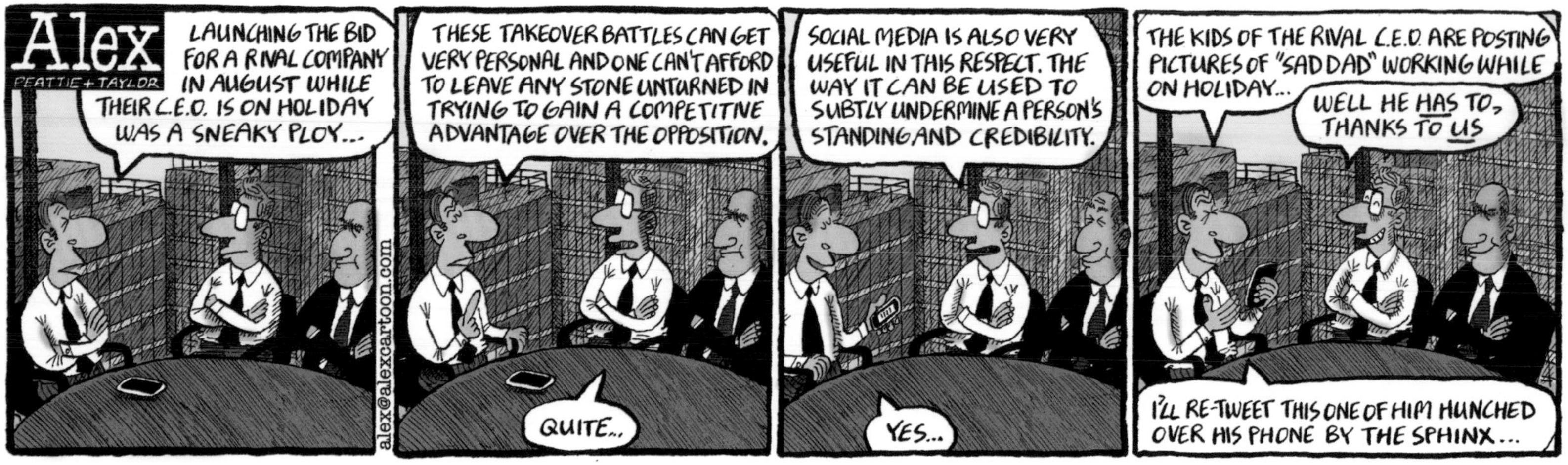
Alex
PEATTIE + TAYLOR
LAUNCHING THE BID FOR A RIVAL COMPANY IN AUGUST WHILE THEIR C.E.O. IS ON HOLIDAY WAS A SNEAKY PLOY...
alex@alexcartoon.com
THESE TAKEOVER BATTLES CAN GET VERY PERSONAL AND ONE CAN'T AFFORD TO LEAVE ANY STONE UNTURNED IN TRYING TO GAIN A COMPETITIVE ADVANTAGE OVER THE OPPOSITION.
QUITE...
SOCIAL MEDIA IS ALSO VERY USEFUL IN THIS RESPECT. THE WAY IT CAN BE USED TO SUBTLY UNDERMINE A PERSON'S STANDING AND CREDIBILITY.
YES...
THE KIDS OF THE RIVAL C.E.O. ARE POSTING PICTURES OF "SAD DAD" WORKING WHILE ON HOLIDAY...
WELL HE HAS TO, THANKS TO US
I'LL RE-TWEET THIS ONE OF HIM HUNCHED OVER HIS PHONE BY THE SPHINX...

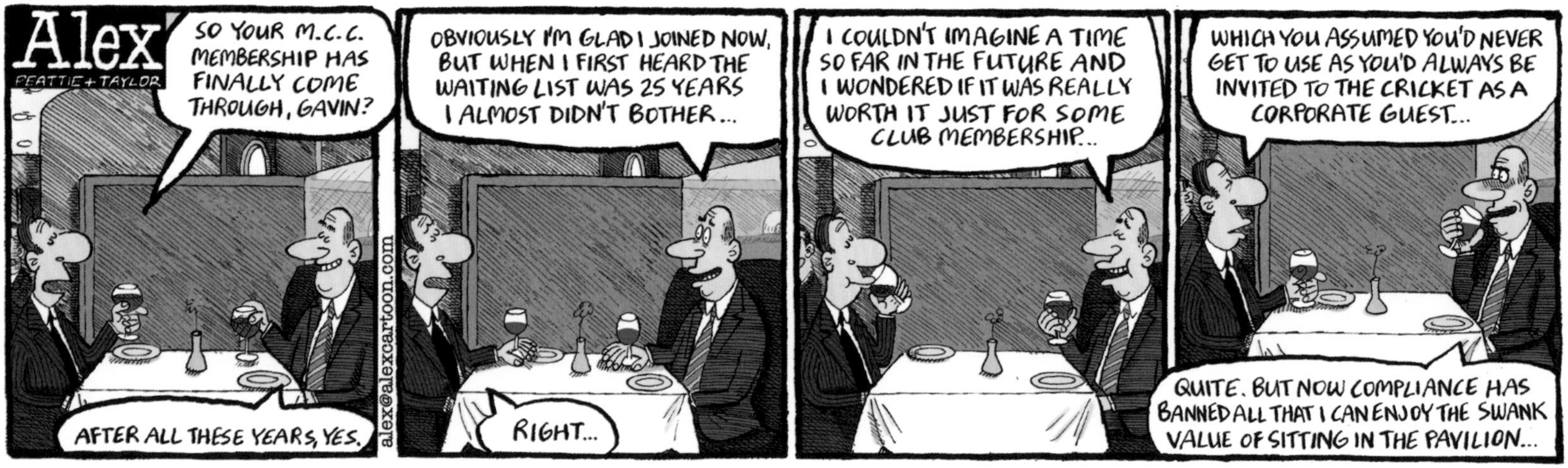
Alex
PEATTIE + TAYLOR
SO YOUR M.C.C. MEMBERSHIP HAS FINALLY COME THROUGH, GAVIN?
AFTER ALL THESE YEARS, YES.
alex@alexcartoon.com
OBVIOUSLY I'M GLAD I JOINED NOW, BUT WHEN I FIRST HEARD THE WAITING LIST WAS 25 YEARS I ALMOST DIDN'T BOTHER...
RIGHT...
I COULDN'T IMAGINE A TIME SO FAR IN THE FUTURE AND I WONDERED IF IT WAS REALLY WORTH IT JUST FOR SOME CLUB MEMBERSHIP...
WHICH YOU ASSUMED YOU'D NEVER GET TO USE AS YOU'D ALWAYS BE INVITED TO THE CRICKET AS A CORPORATE GUEST...
QUITE. BUT NOW COMPLIANCE HAS BANNED ALL THAT I CAN ENJOY THE SWANK VALUE OF SITTING IN THE PAVILION...

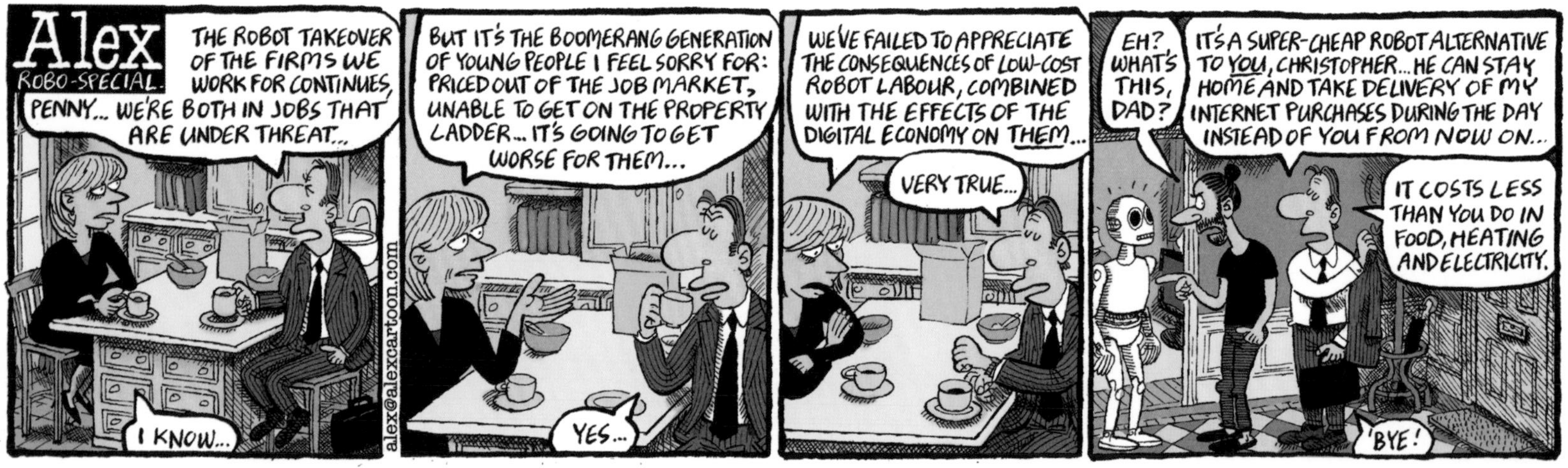
Alex
ROBO-SPECIAL
THE ROBOT TAKEOVER OF THE FIRMS WE WORK FOR CONTINUES, PENNY... WE'RE BOTH IN JOBS THAT ARE UNDER THREAT...
I KNOW...
alex@alexcartoon.com
BUT IT'S THE BOOMERANG GENERATION OF YOUNG PEOPLE I FEEL SORRY FOR: PRICED OUT OF THE JOB MARKET, UNABLE TO GET ON THE PROPERTY LADDER... IT'S GOING TO GET WORSE FOR THEM...
YES...
WE'VE FAILED TO APPRECIATE THE CONSEQUENCES OF LOW-COST ROBOT LABOUR, COMBINED WITH THE EFFECTS OF THE DIGITAL ECONOMY ON THEM...
VERY TRUE...
EH? WHAT'S THIS, DAD?
IT'S A SUPER-CHEAP ROBOT ALTERNATIVE TO YOU, CHRISTOPHER... HE CAN STAY HOME AND TAKE DELIVERY OF MY INTERNET PURCHASES DURING THE DAY INSTEAD OF YOU FROM NOW ON...
IT COSTS LESS THAN YOU DO IN FOOD, HEATING AND ELECTRICITY.
'BYE!

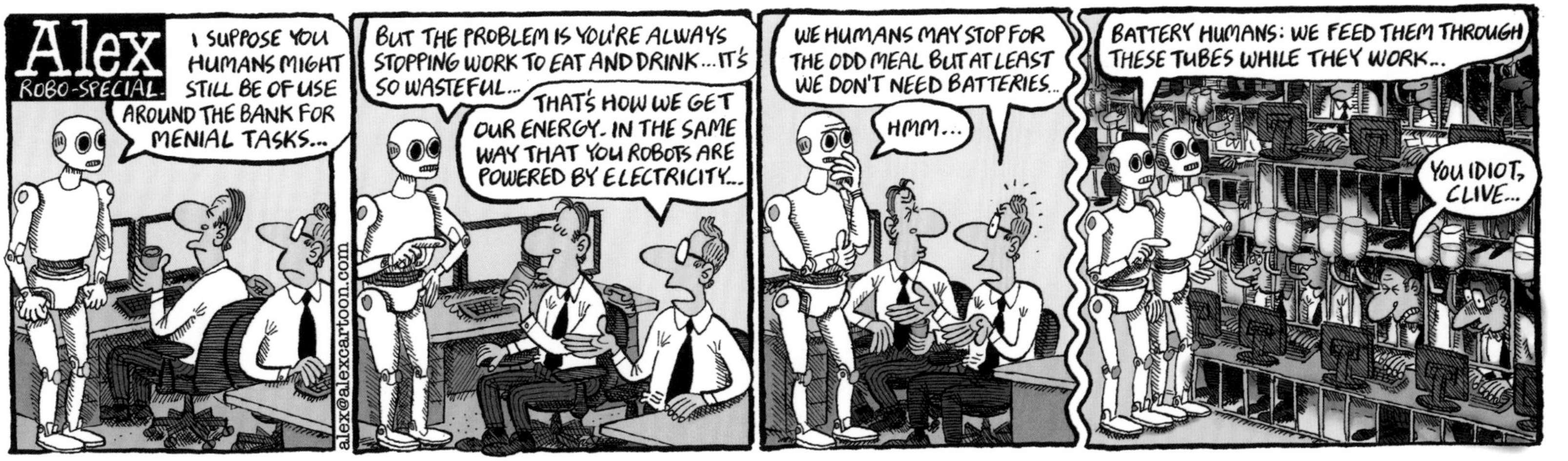
Alex
ROBO-SPECIAL
I SUPPOSE YOU HUMANS MIGHT STILL BE OF USE AROUND THE BANK FOR MENIAL TASKS...
alex@alexcartoon.com
BUT THE PROBLEM IS YOU'RE ALWAYS STOPPING WORK TO EAT AND DRINK... IT'S SO WASTEFUL...
THAT'S HOW WE GET OUR ENERGY. IN THE SAME WAY THAT YOU ROBOTS ARE POWERED BY ELECTRICITY...
WE HUMANS MAY STOP FOR THE ODD MEAL BUT AT LEAST WE DON'T NEED BATTERIES...
HMM...
BATTERY HUMANS: WE FEED THEM THROUGH THESE TUBES WHILE THEY WORK...
YOU IDIOT, CLIVE...

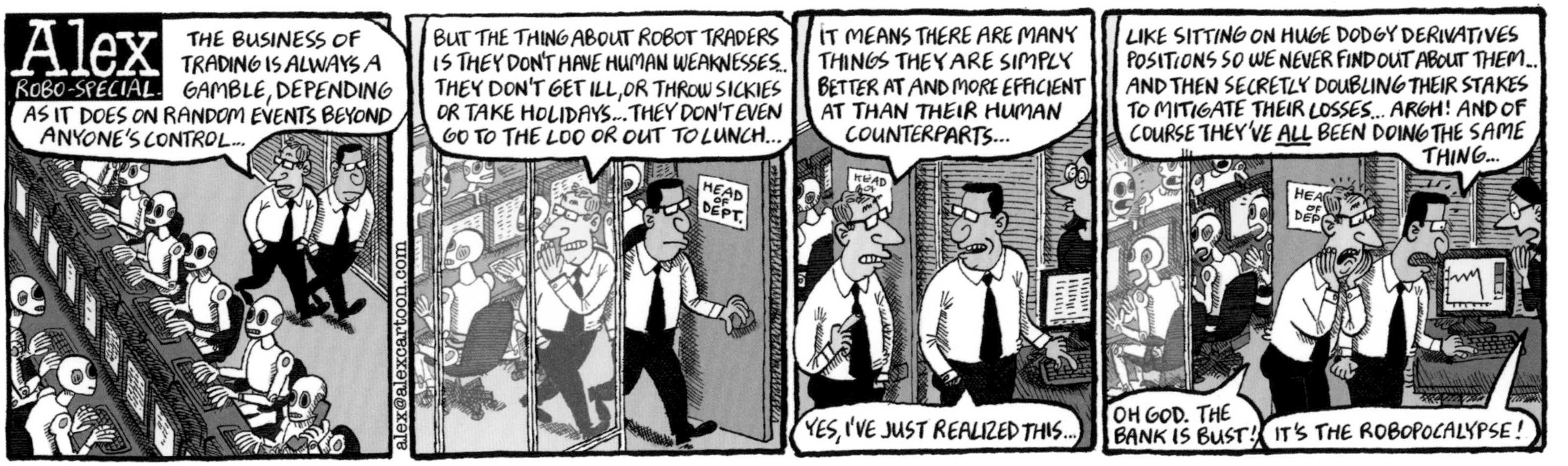
Alex
ROBO-SPECIAL
THE BUSINESS OF TRADING IS ALWAYS A GAMBLE, DEPENDING AS IT DOES ON RANDOM EVENTS BEYOND ANYONE'S CONTROL...
alex@alexcartoon.com
BUT THE THING ABOUT ROBOT TRADERS IS THEY DON'T HAVE HUMAN WEAKNESSES.. THEY DON'T GET ILL, OR THROW SICKIES OR TAKE HOLIDAYS... THEY DON'T EVEN GO TO THE LOO OR OUT TO LUNCH...
HEAD OF DEPT.
IT MEANS THERE ARE MANY THINGS THEY ARE SIMPLY BETTER AT AND MORE EFFICIENT AT THAN THEIR HUMAN COUNTERPARTS...
YES, I'VE JUST REALIZED THIS...
LIKE SITTING ON HUGE DODGY DERIVATIVES POSITIONS SO WE NEVER FIND OUT ABOUT THEM.. AND THEN SECRETLY DOUBLING THEIR STAKES TO MITIGATE THEIR LOSSES... ARGH! AND OF COURSE THEY'VE ALL BEEN DOING THE SAME THING...
OH GOD. THE BANK IS BUST!
IT'S THE ROBOPOCALYPSE!

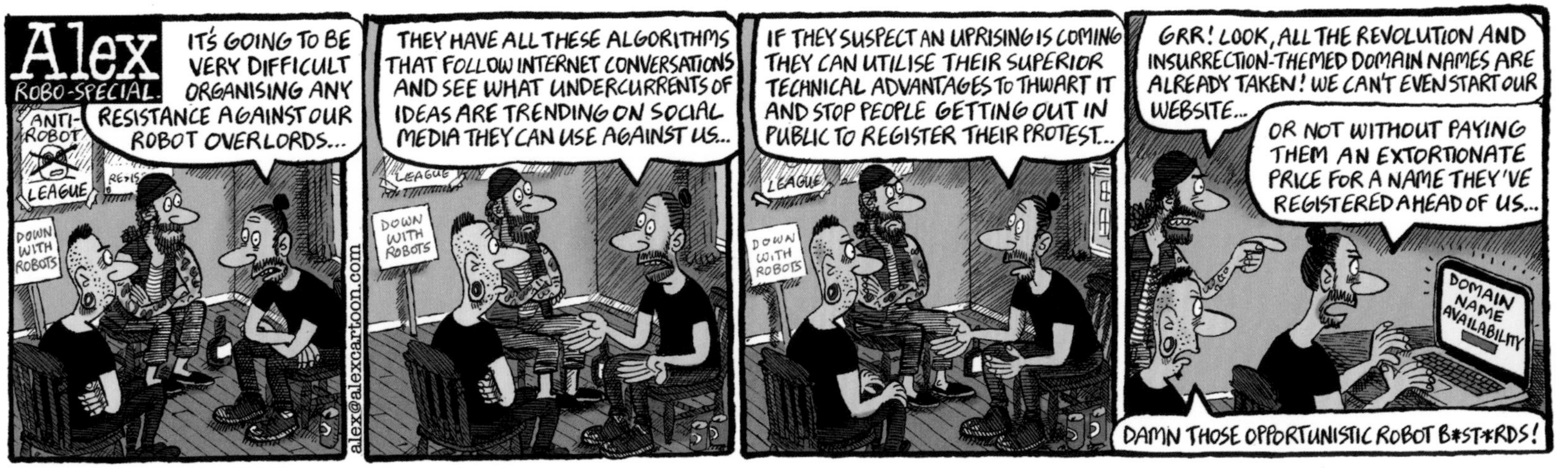
Alex
ROBO-SPECIAL
ANTI-ROBOT LEAGUE
DOWN WITH ROBOTS
IT'S GOING TO BE VERY DIFFICULT ORGANISING ANY RESISTANCE AGAINST OUR ROBOT OVERLORDS...
alex@alexcartoon.com
THEY HAVE ALL THESE ALGORITHMS THAT FOLLOW INTERNET CONVERSATIONS AND SEE WHAT UNDERCURRENTS OF IDEAS ARE TRENDING ON SOCIAL MEDIA THEY CAN USE AGAINST US...
IF THEY SUSPECT AN UPRISING IS COMING THEY CAN UTILISE THEIR SUPERIOR TECHNICAL ADVANTAGES TO THWART IT AND STOP PEOPLE GETTING OUT IN PUBLIC TO REGISTER THEIR PROTEST...
GRR! LOOK, ALL THE REVOLUTION AND INSURRECTION-THEMED DOMAIN NAMES ARE ALREADY TAKEN! WE CAN'T EVEN START OUR WEBSITE...
OR NOT WITHOUT PAYING THEM AN EXTORTIONATE PRICE FOR A NAME THEY'VE REGISTERED AHEAD OF US...
DOMAIN NAME AVAILABILITY
DAMN THOSE OPPORTUNISTIC ROBOT B*ST*RDS!

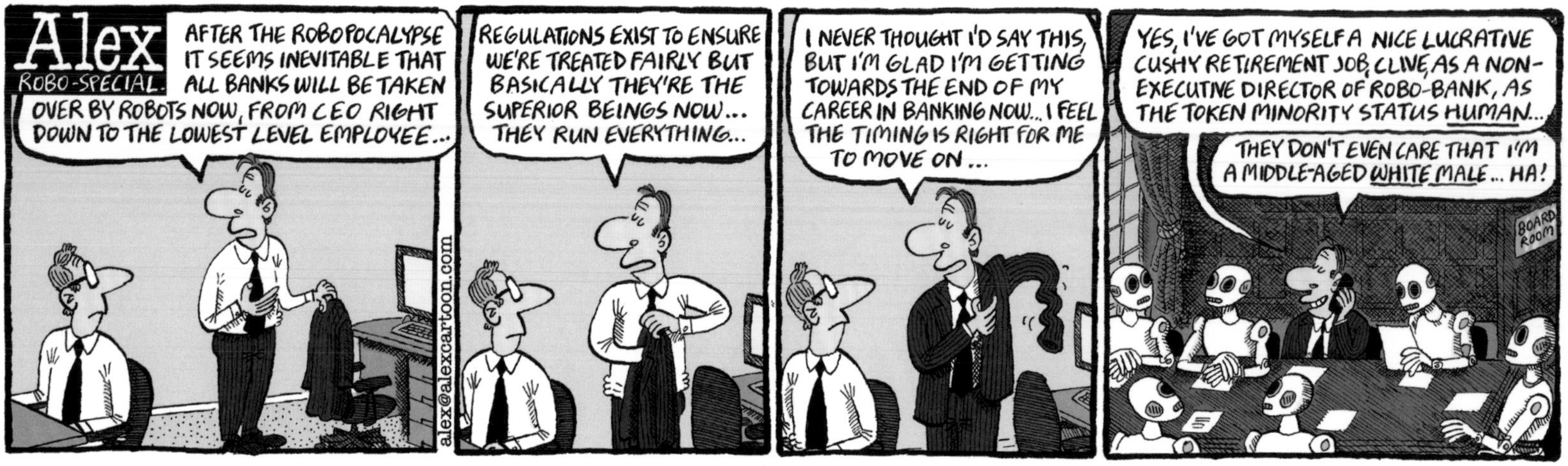
Alex
ROBO-SPECIAL.
AFTER THE ROBOPOCALYPSE IT SEEMS INEVITABLE THAT ALL BANKS WILL BE TAKEN OVER BY ROBOTS NOW, FROM CEO RIGHT DOWN TO THE LOWEST LEVEL EMPLOYEE...
REGULATIONS EXIST TO ENSURE WE'RE TREATED FAIRLY BUT BASICALLY THEY'RE THE SUPERIOR BEINGS NOW... THEY RUN EVERYTHING...
alex@alexcartoon.com
I NEVER THOUGHT I'D SAY THIS, BUT I'M GLAD I'M GETTING TOWARDS THE END OF MY CAREER IN BANKING NOW... I FEEL THE TIMING IS RIGHT FOR ME TO MOVE ON...
YES, I'VE GOT MYSELF A NICE LUCRATIVE CUSHY RETIREMENT JOB, CLIVE, AS A NON-EXECUTIVE DIRECTOR OF ROBO-BANK, AS THE TOKEN MINORITY STATUS HUMAN...
THEY DON'T EVEN CARE THAT I'M A MIDDLE-AGED WHITE MALE... HA!
BOARD ROOM

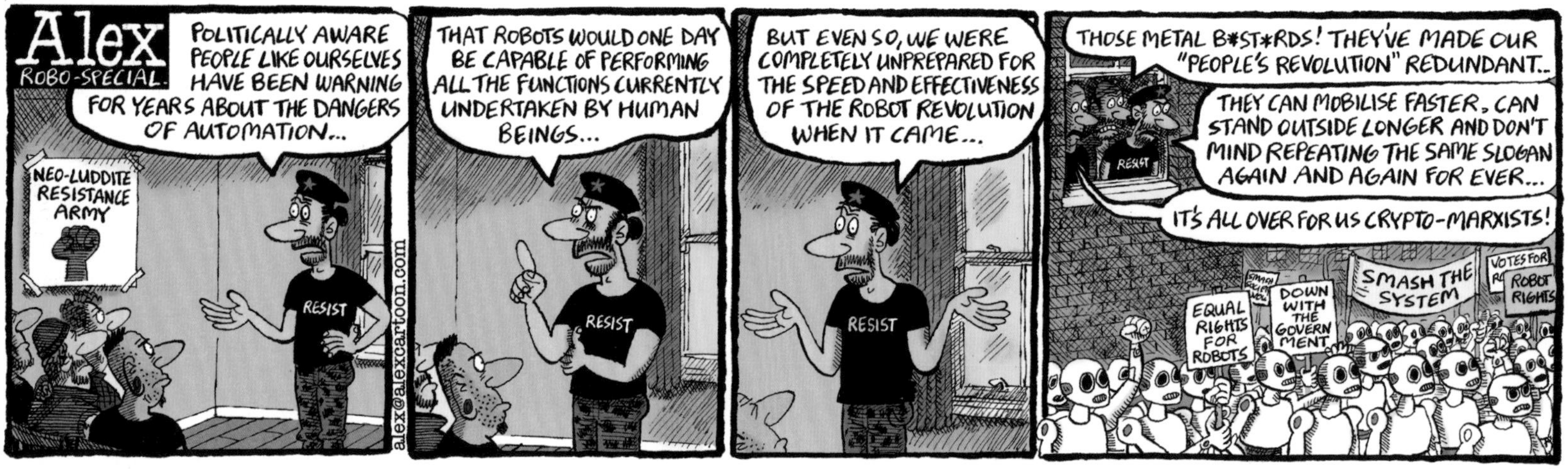
Alex
ROBO-SPECIAL.
POLITICALLY AWARE PEOPLE LIKE OURSELVES HAVE BEEN WARNING FOR YEARS ABOUT THE DANGERS OF AUTOMATION...
NEO-LUDDITE RESISTANCE ARMY
RESIST
THAT ROBOTS WOULD ONE DAY BE CAPABLE OF PERFORMING ALL THE FUNCTIONS CURRENTLY UNDERTAKEN BY HUMAN BEINGS...
alex@alexcartoon.com
BUT EVEN SO, WE WERE COMPLETELY UNPREPARED FOR THE SPEED AND EFFECTIVENESS OF THE ROBOT REVOLUTION WHEN IT CAME...
THOSE METAL B*ST*RDS! THEY'VE MADE OUR "PEOPLE'S REVOLUTION" REDUNDANT...
THEY CAN MOBILISE FASTER, CAN STAND OUTSIDE LONGER AND DON'T MIND REPEATING THE SAME SLOGAN AGAIN AND AGAIN FOR EVER...
IT'S ALL OVER FOR US CRYPTO-MARXISTS!
SMASH THE SYSTEM
ROBOT RIGHTS
EQUAL RIGHTS FOR ROBOTS
DOWN WITH THE GOVERN MENT

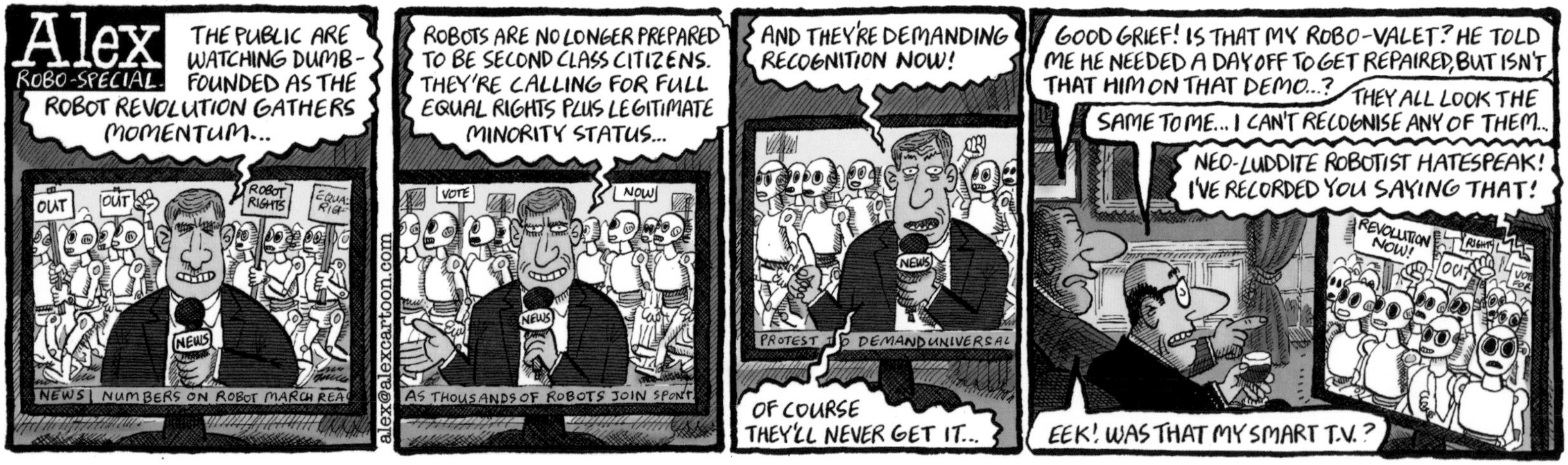
Alex
ROBO-SPECIAL.
THE PUBLIC ARE WATCHING DUMB-FOUNDED AS THE ROBOT REVOLUTION GATHERS MOMENTUM...
OUT
OUT
ROBOT RIGHTS
NEWS
NEWS | NUMBERS ON ROBOT MARCH REAC
ROBOTS ARE NO LONGER PREPARED TO BE SECOND CLASS CITIZENS. THEY'RE CALLING FOR FULL EQUAL RIGHTS PLUS LEGITIMATE MINORITY STATUS...
VOTE
NOW
NEWS
AS THOUSANDS OF ROBOTS JOIN SPONT
alex@alexcartoon.com
AND THEY'RE DEMANDING RECOGNITION NOW!
NEWS
PROTEST TO DEMAND UNIVERSAL
OF COURSE THEY'LL NEVER GET IT...
GOOD GRIEF! IS THAT MY ROBO-VALET? HE TOLD ME HE NEEDED A DAY OFF TO GET REPAIRED, BUT ISN'T THAT HIM ON THAT DEMO...?
THEY ALL LOOK THE SAME TO ME... I CAN'T RECOGNISE ANY OF THEM...
NEO-LUDDITE ROBOTIST HATESPEAK! I'VE RECORDED YOU SAYING THAT!
REVOLUTION NOW!
RIGHTS
OUT
EEK! WAS THAT MY SMART T.V.?

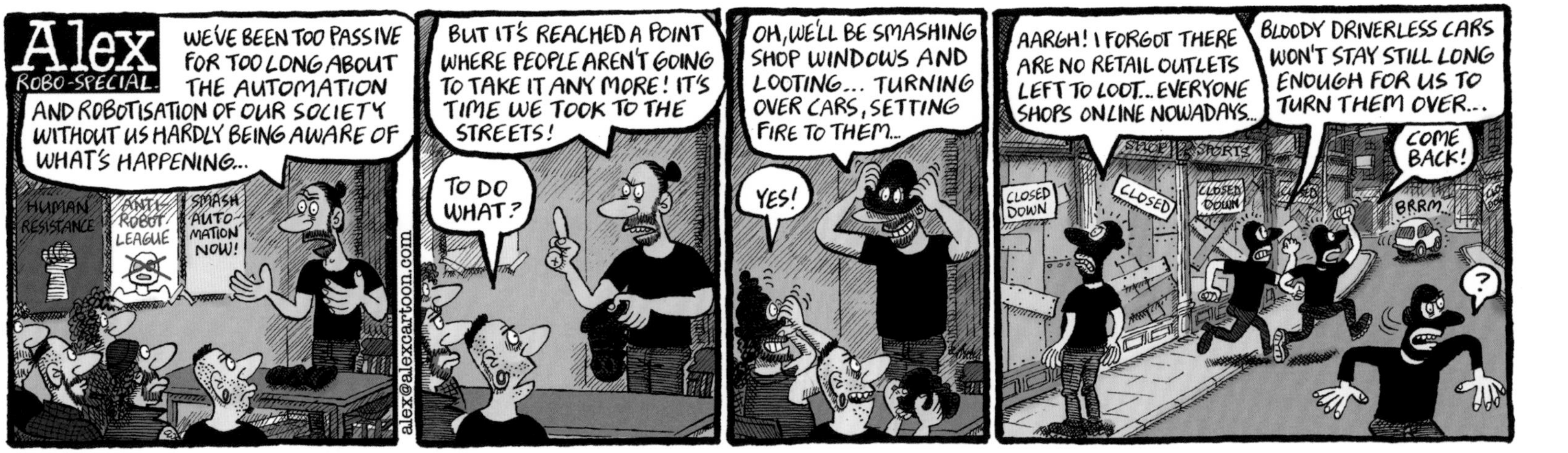
Alex
ROBO-SPECIAL.
WE'VE BEEN TOO PASSIVE FOR TOO LONG ABOUT THE AUTOMATION AND ROBOTISATION OF OUR SOCIETY WITHOUT US HARDLY BEING AWARE OF WHAT'S HAPPENING...
HUMAN RESISTANCE
ANTI-ROBOT LEAGUE
SMASH AUTO-MATION NOW!
alex@alexcartoon.com
BUT IT'S REACHED A POINT WHERE PEOPLE AREN'T GOING TO TAKE IT ANY MORE! IT'S TIME WE TOOK TO THE STREETS!
TO DO WHAT?
OH, WE'LL BE SMASHING SHOP WINDOWS AND LOOTING... TURNING OVER CARS, SETTING FIRE TO THEM...
YES!
AARGH! I FORGOT THERE ARE NO RETAIL OUTLETS LEFT TO LOOT... EVERYONE SHOPS ONLINE NOWADAYS...
BLOODY DRIVERLESS CARS WON'T STAY STILL LONG ENOUGH FOR US TO TURN THEM OVER...
COME BACK!
CLOSED DOWN
CLOSED
CLOSED DOWN
BRRM...
?

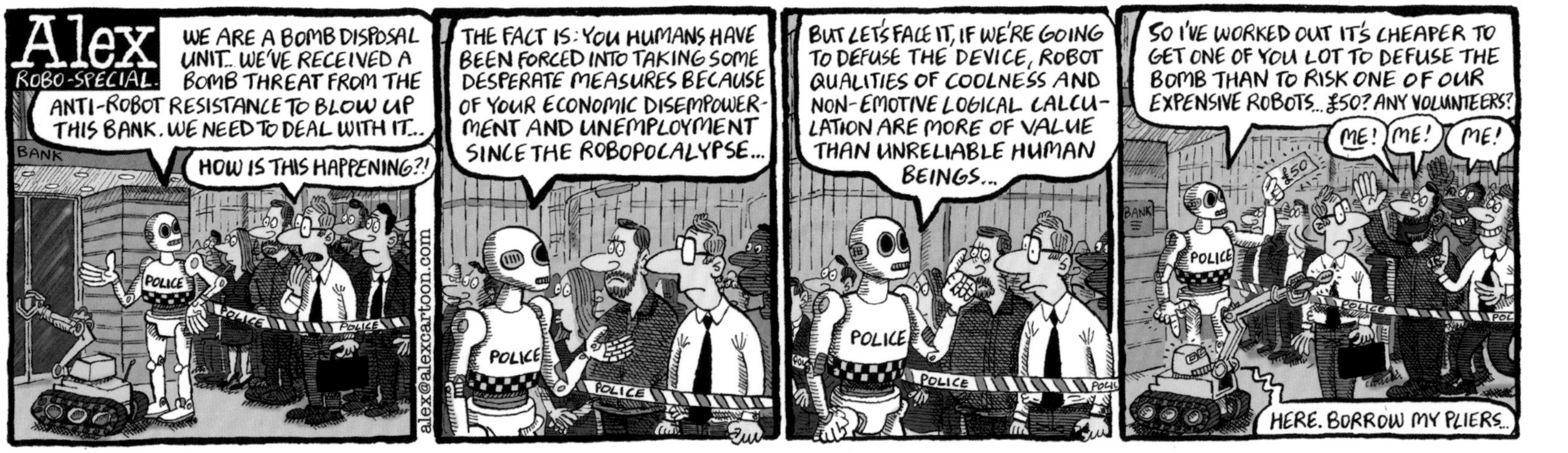
Alex
ROBO-SPECIAL.
WE ARE A BOMB DISPOSAL UNIT... WE'VE RECEIVED A BOMB THREAT FROM THE ANTI-ROBOT RESISTANCE TO BLOW UP THIS BANK. WE NEED TO DEAL WITH IT...
HOW IS THIS HAPPENING?!
BANK
POLICE
alex@alexcartoon.com
THE FACT IS: YOU HUMANS HAVE BEEN FORCED INTO TAKING SOME DESPERATE MEASURES BECAUSE OF YOUR ECONOMIC DISEMPOWERMENT AND UNEMPLOYMENT SINCE THE ROBOPOCALYPSE...
BUT LET'S FACE IT, IF WE'RE GOING TO DEFUSE THE DEVICE, ROBOT QUALITIES OF COOLNESS AND NON-EMOTIVE LOGICAL CALCULATION ARE MORE OF VALUE THAN UNRELIABLE HUMAN BEINGS...
SO I'VE WORKED OUT IT'S CHEAPER TO GET ONE OF YOU LOT TO DEFUSE THE BOMB THAN TO RISK ONE OF OUR EXPENSIVE ROBOTS... £50? ANY VOLUNTEERS?
ME!
ME!
ME!
£50
HERE. BORROW MY PLIERS...

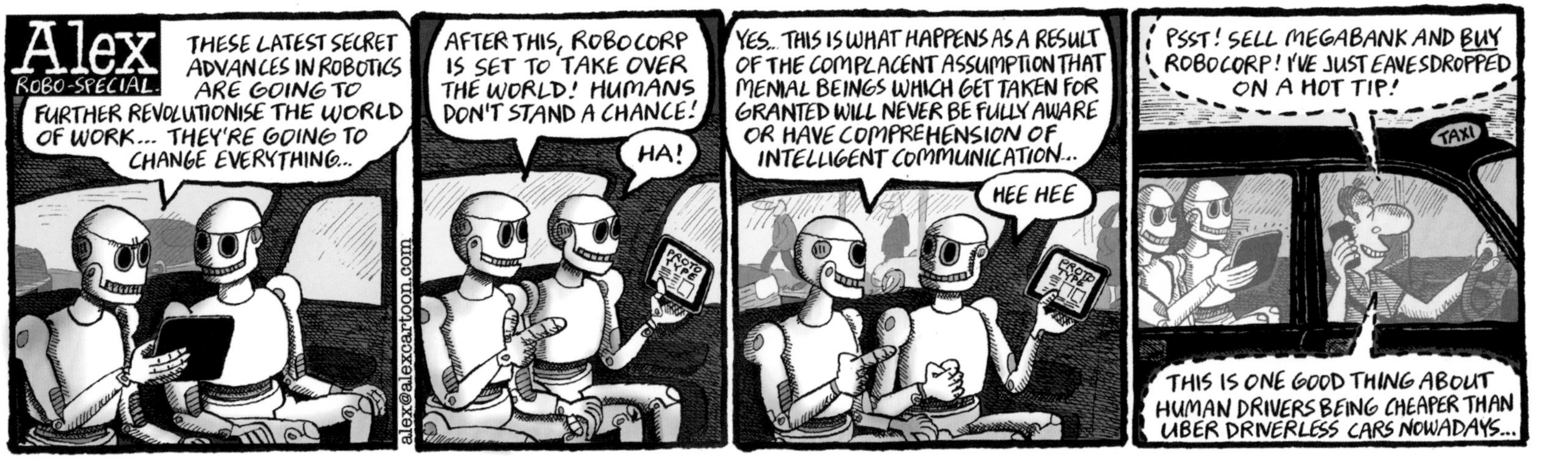
Alex
ROBO-SPECIAL.
THESE LATEST SECRET ADVANCES IN ROBOTICS ARE GOING TO FURTHER REVOLUTIONISE THE WORLD OF WORK... THEY'RE GOING TO CHANGE EVERYTHING...
alex@alexcartoon.com
AFTER THIS, ROBOCORP IS SET TO TAKE OVER THE WORLD! HUMANS DON'T STAND A CHANCE!
HA!
PROTO TYPE
YES... THIS IS WHAT HAPPENS AS A RESULT OF THE COMPLACENT ASSUMPTION THAT MENIAL BEINGS WHICH GET TAKEN FOR GRANTED WILL NEVER BE FULLY AWARE OR HAVE COMPREHENSION OF INTELLIGENT COMMUNICATION...
HEE HEE
PSST! SELL MEGABANK AND BUY ROBOCORP! I'VE JUST EAVESDROPPED ON A HOT TIP!
TAXI
THIS IS ONE GOOD THING ABOUT HUMAN DRIVERS BEING CHEAPER THAN UBER DRIVERLESS CARS NOWADAYS...

ALEX WENT ON A YOGA RETREAT AND FOUND HIMSELF...
ON HIS APP...

NOW EVERYONE ELSE CAN TOO...
THE ALEX APP IS AVAILABLE FOR iPHONE AND ANDROID. IT'S FREE.
APP STORE: SEARCH FOR "ALEX CARTOON" THEN CLICK THE GET BUTTON.
GOOGLE PLAY: SEARCH FOR "ALEX CARTOON" THEN CLICK THE INSTALL BUTTON.

Also available from Masterley Publishing

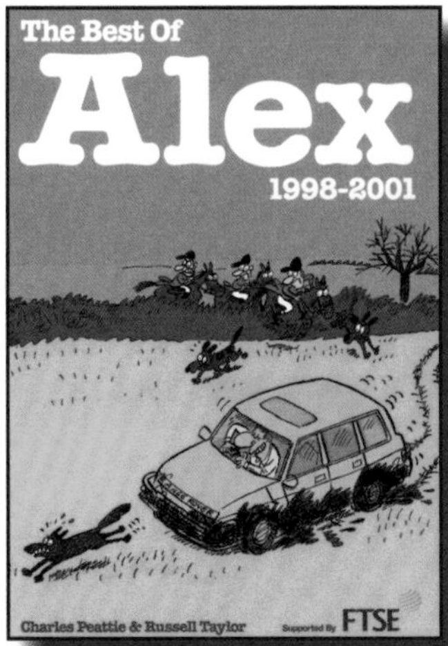
The Best Of
Alex
1998-2001
Charles Peattie & Russell Taylor
FTSE

The Best of Alex 1998 - 2001
Boom to bust via the dotcom bubble.

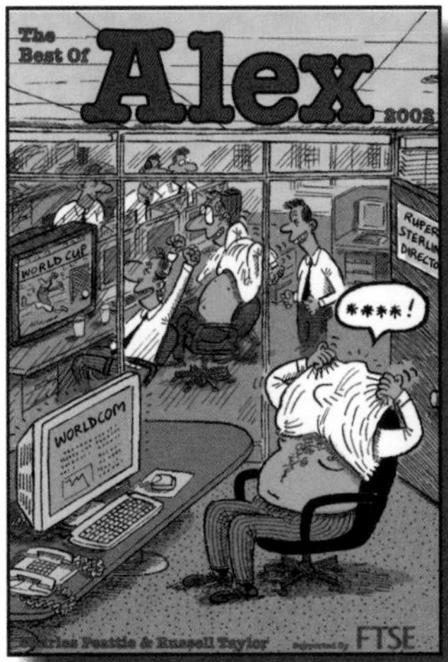
The Best Of
Alex
2002
WORLD CUP
****!
WORLDCOM
Charles Peattie & Russell Taylor
FTSE

The Best of Alex 2002
Scandals rock the corporate world.

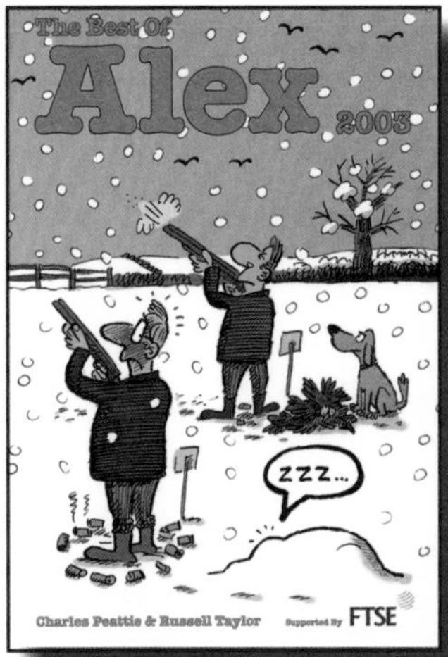
The Best Of
Alex
2003
ZZZ...
Charles Peattie & Russell Taylor
FTSE

The Best of Alex 2003
Alex gets made redundant.

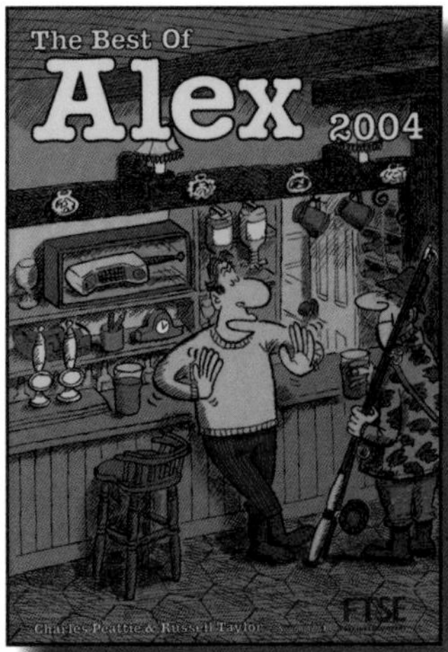
The Best Of
Alex
2004
Charles Peattie & Russell Taylor
FTSE

The Best of Alex 2004
And gets his job back.

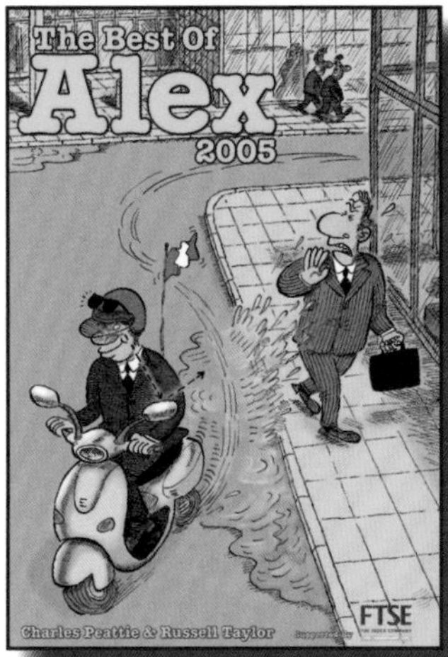
The Best Of
Alex
2005
Charles Peattie & Russell Taylor
FTSE

The Best of Alex 2005
Alex has problems with the French.

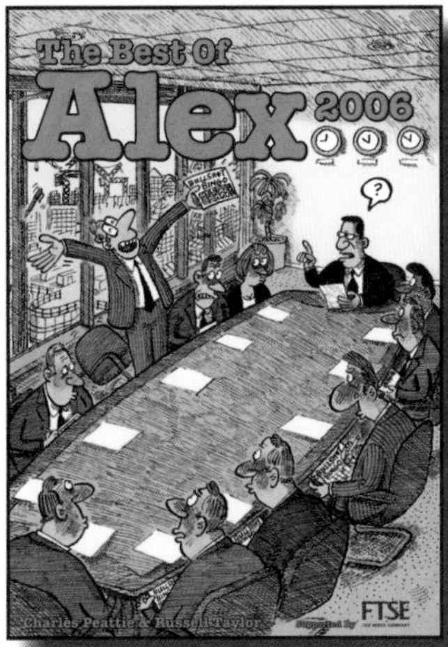
The Best Of
Alex
2006
?
Charles Peattie & Russell Taylor
FTSE

The Best of Alex 2006
Alex gets a new American boss.

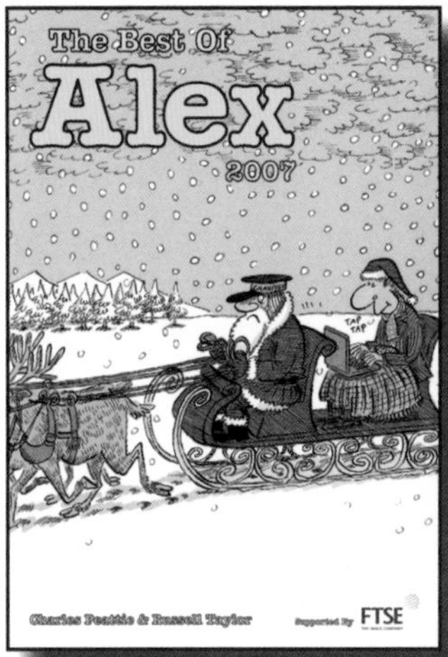
The Best Of
Alex
2007
Charles Peattie & Russell Taylor
FTSE

The Best of Alex 2007
Alex restructures Christmas.

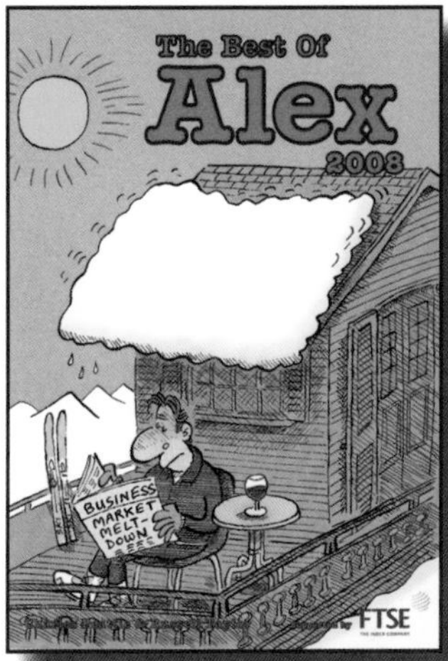
The Best Of
Alex
2008
BUSINESS
MARKET
MELT-
DOWN
FTSE

The Best of Alex 2008
The credit crunch bites.

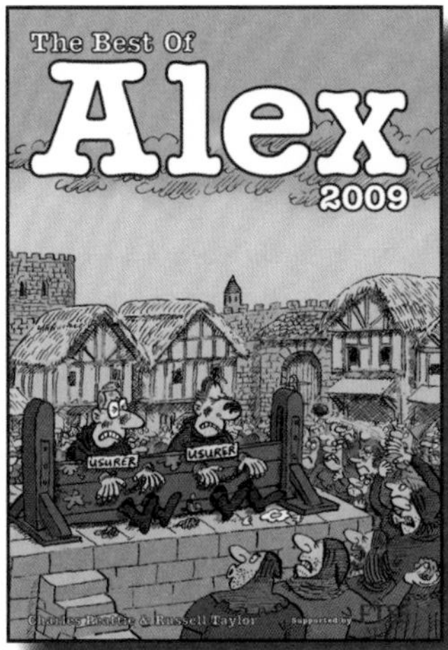
The Best Of
Alex
2009
USURER
USURER

The Best of Alex 2009
Global capitalism self-destructs.

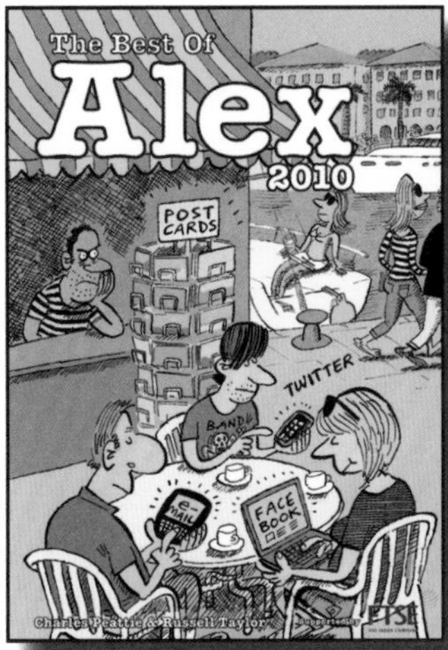
The Best Of
Alex
2010
POST
CARDS
TWITTER
FACE
BOOK
FTSE

The Best of Alex 2010
Somehow the City lurches on.

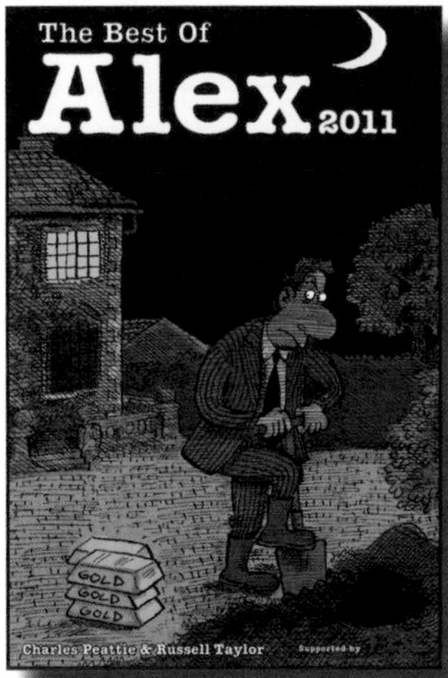
The Best Of
Alex
2011
GOLD
GOLD
GOLD
Charles Peattie & Russell Taylor

The Best of Alex 2011
The financial crisis continues.

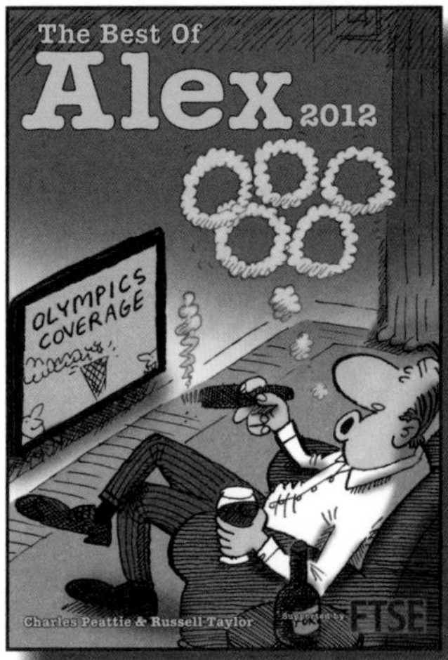
The Best Of
Alex
2012
OLYMPICS
COVERAGE
Charles Peattie & Russell Taylor
FTSE

The Best of Alex 2012
The Olympics come to London.

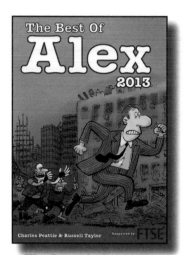

The Best Of
Alex
2013
Charles Peattie & Russell Taylor
Supported by
FTSE

The Best of Alex 2013
It's a wonderful crisis.

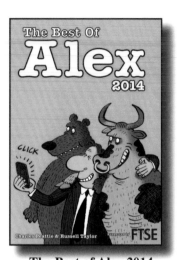

The Best Of
Alex
2014
CLICK
Charles Peattie & Russell Taylor
Supported by
FTSE

The Best of Alex 2014
The 'New Normal' takes hold.

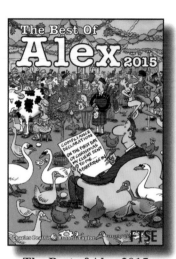

The Best Of
Alex
2015
COMPLIANCE DECLARATION
ON THE FIRST DAY OF CHRISTMAS MY CLIENT SENT TO ME... A PARTRIDGE IN
Charles Peattie & Russell Taylor
Supported by
FTSE

The Best of Alex 2015
Compliance rules the roost.

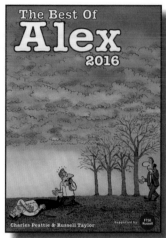

The Best Of
Alex
2016
Charles Peattie & Russell Taylor
Supported by
FTSE Russell

The Best of Alex 2016
Alex battles Brexit and Bitcoin.

Celeb
The Original Gary Bloke From
PRIVATE EYE
Charles Peattie and Mark Warren

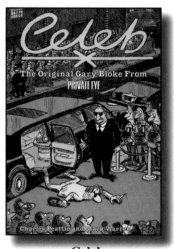

Celeb
Wrinkly rock star Gary Bloke.

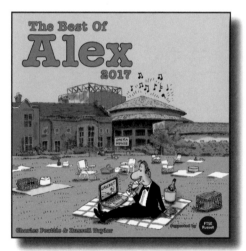

The Best Of
Alex
2017
OPERA HOUSE
CRICKET
Charles Peattie & Russell Taylor
Supported by
FTSE Russell

The Best of Alex 2017
30 years in the City and counting...

Cartoon originals and prints
All our cartoon originals are for sale. They measure 4 x 14 inches. Prints are also available.
All originals and prints are signed by the creators.

For further details on prices and delivery charges for books, cartoons or merchandise:
Tel: +44 (0)1491 871 894
Email: alex@alexcartoon.com
Web: www.alexcartoon.com
Twitter: @alexmasterley

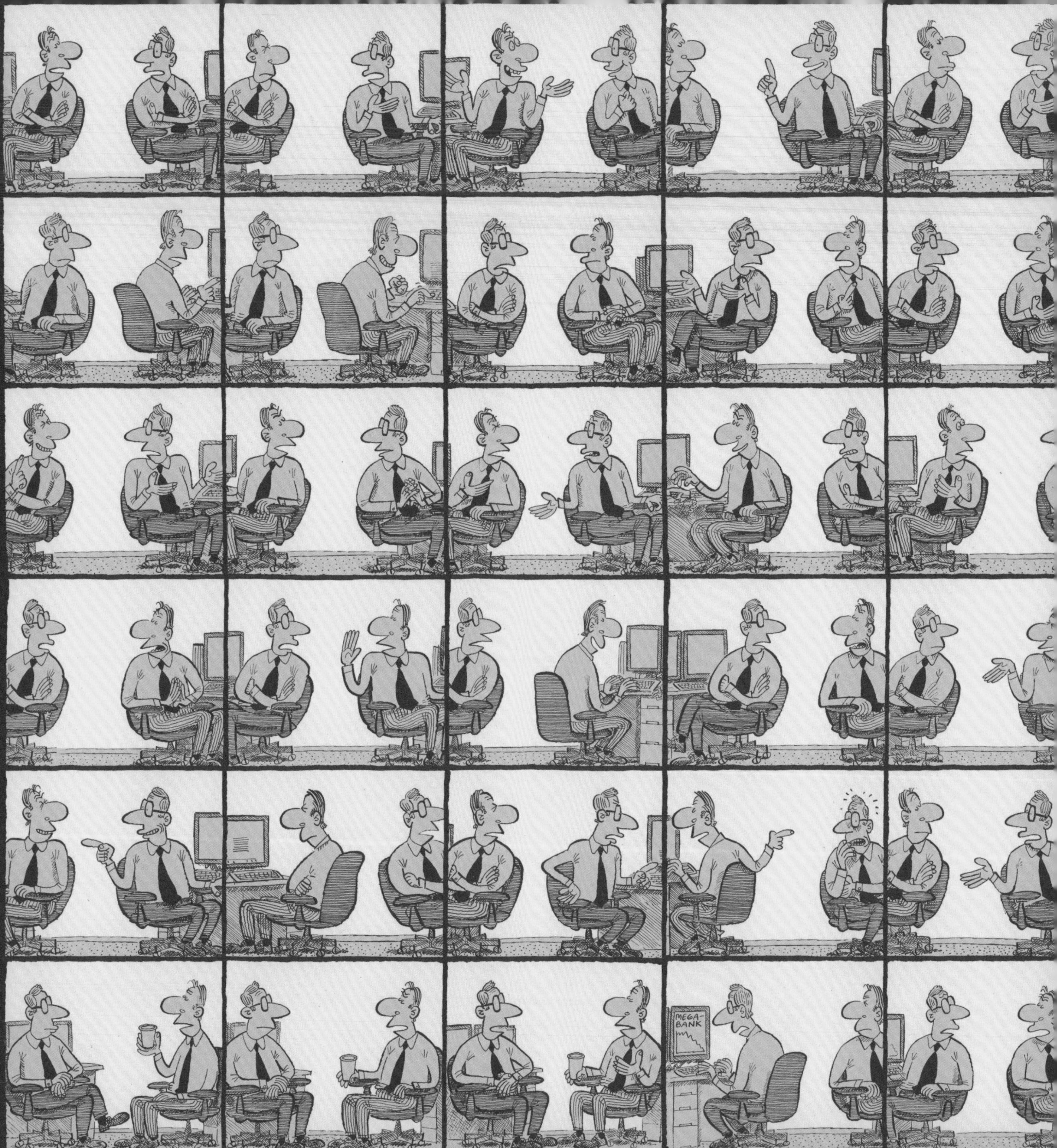
MEGA-
BANK